"I love to read manga!"

"I love to draw manga so much I don't know what to do!"

"I draw, therefore I am!"

"That's all the proof I need to know that I exist!!!"

—*Hiromu Arakawa, 2002*

Born in Hokkaido (northern Japan), Hiromu Arakawa first attracted national attention in 1999 with her award-winning manga Stray Dog. Her series Fullmetal Alchemist debuted in 2001 in Square Enix's monthly manga anthology Shonen Gangan.

FULLMETAL ALCHEMIST
VOL. 3

Story and Art by Hiromu Arakawa

Translation/Akira Watanabe
English Adaptation/Jake Forbes
Touch-up Art & Lettering/Wayne Truman
Design/Amy Martin
Editor/Jason Thompson
Series Consultant/Egan Loo

Editor in Chief, Books/Alvin Lu
Editor in Chief, Magazines/Marc Weidenbaum
VP, Publishing Licensing/Rika Inouye
VP, Sales & Product Marketing/Gonzalo Ferreyra
VP, Creative/Linda Espinosa
Publisher/Hyoe Narita

Printed in the U.S.A.

Published by VIZ Media, LLC
P.O. Box 77010
San Francisco, CA 94107

10 9 8 7 6 5
First printing, August 2005
Fifth printing, July 2008

www.viz.com

store.viz.com

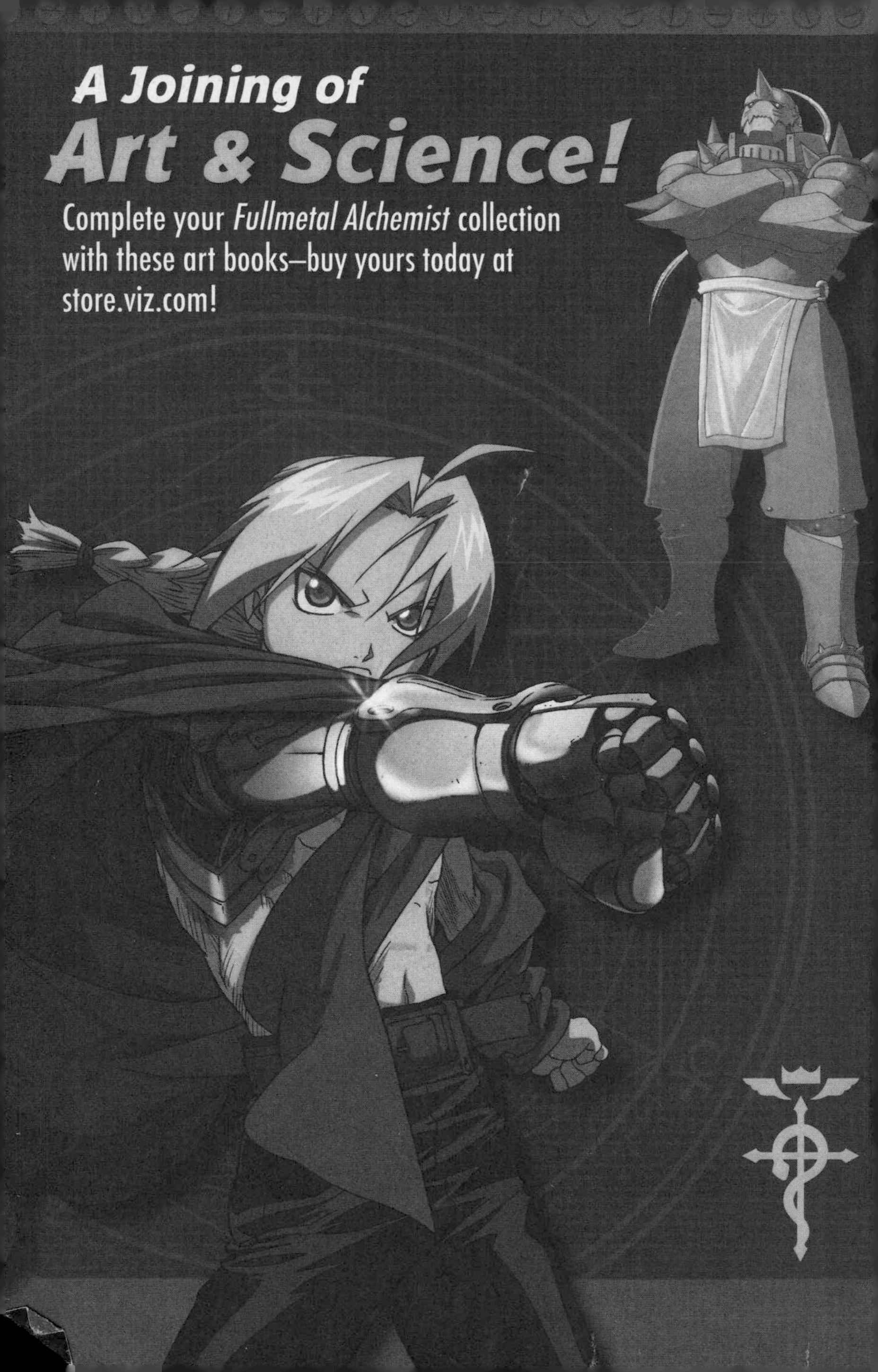
A Joining of
Art & Science!
Complete your Fullmetal Alchemist collection
with these art books—buy yours today at
store.viz.com!

The Art of Fullmetal Alchemist

Contains all the manga artwork from 2001 to 2003!
- Gorgeously painted illustrations
- Color title pages, Japanese tankobon and promotional artwork
- Main character portraits and character designs from the video games

And a special two-page message from series creator Hiromu Arakawa!

Hardcover
$19⁹⁹

The Art of Fullmetal Alchemist: The Anime

Includes art inspired by the popular anime series!
- Initial character designs
- Cel art
- Production notes

Plus, an interview with Yoshiyuki Ito, character designer for the anime!

Hardcover
$19⁹⁹

FULLMETAL ALCHEMIST

ART OF

www.viz.com
store.viz.com

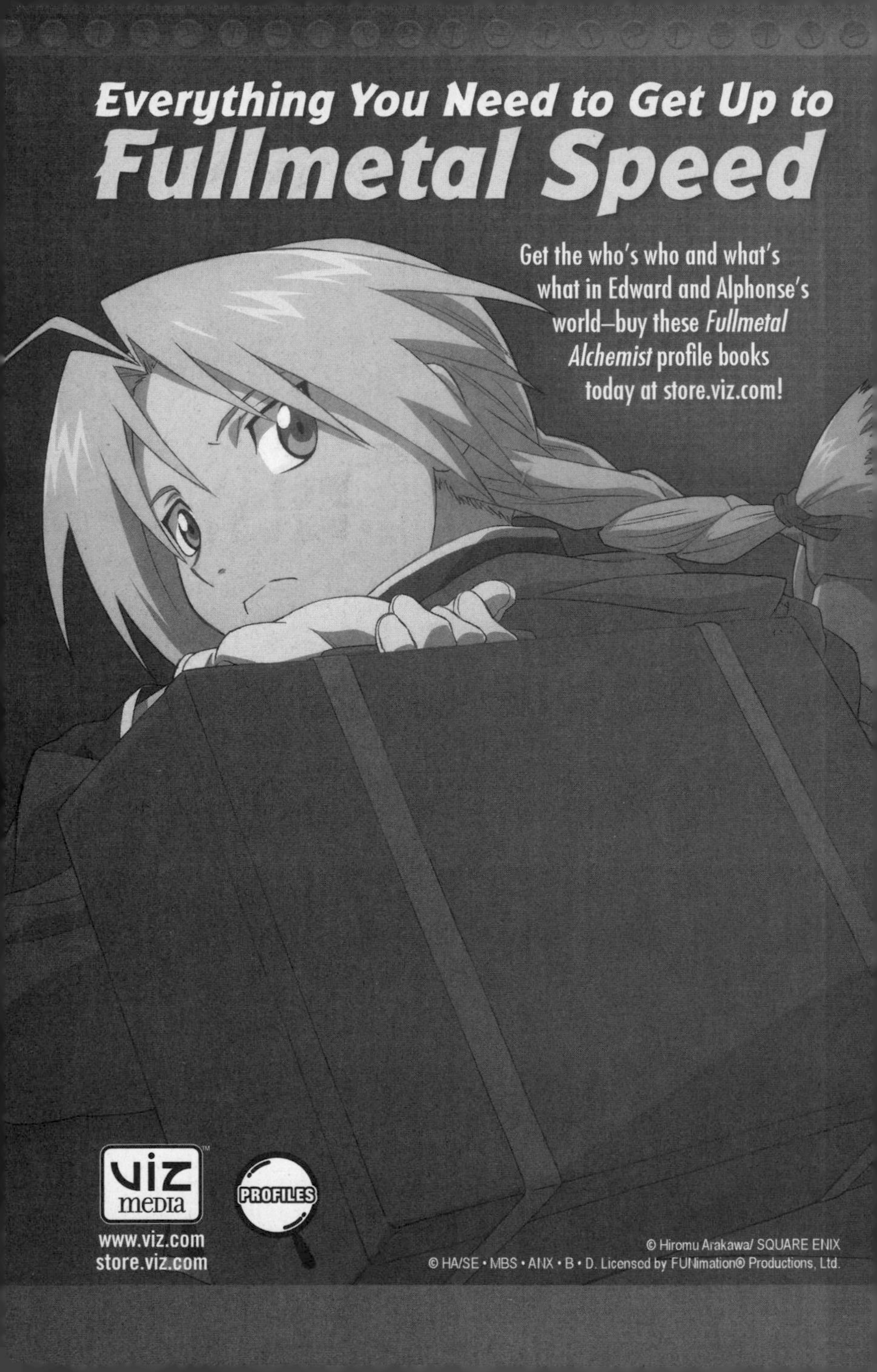
Everything You Need to Get Up to
Fullmetal Speed
Get the who's who and what's what in Edward and Alphonse's world–buy these *Fullmetal Alchemist* profile books today at store.viz.com!
viz media
PROFILES
www.viz.com
store.viz.com
© Hiromu Arakawa/ SQUARE ENIX
© HA/SE • MBS • ANX • B • D. Licensed by FUNimation® Productions, Ltd.

Fullmetal Alchemist Profiles

Get the background story and world history of the manga, plus:

- Character bios
- New, original artwork
- Interview with creator Hiromu Arakawa
- Bonus manga episode only available in this book

Fullmetal Alchemist Anime Profiles

Stay on top of your favorite episodes and characters with:

- Actual cel artwork from the TV series
- Summaries of all 51 TV episodes
- Definitive cast biographies
- Exclusive poster for your wall

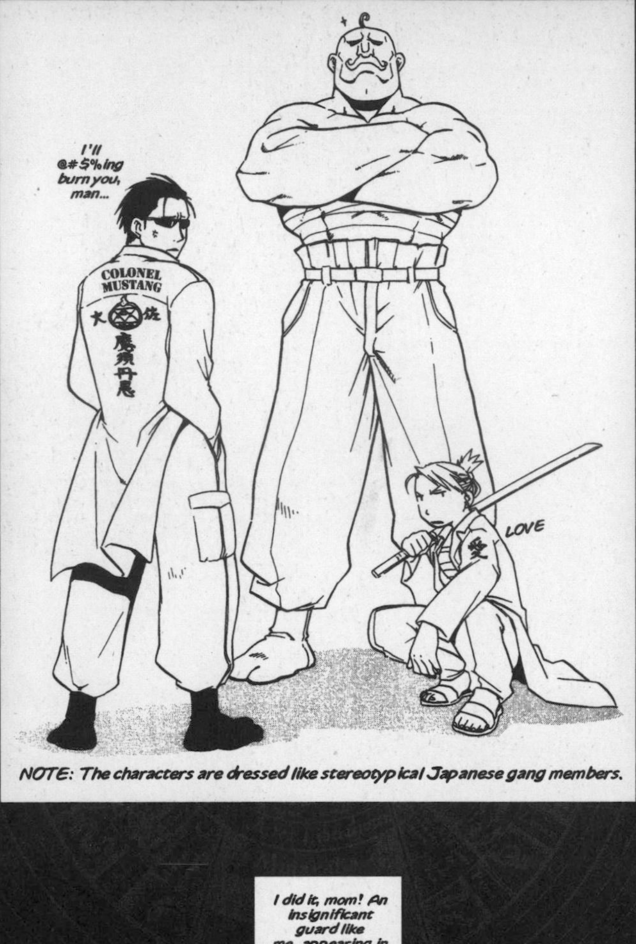
I'll @#$%ing burn you, man...
COLONEL MUSTANG
大佐
魔須丹愚
LOVE
愛
NOTE: The characters are dressed like stereotypical Japanese gang members.

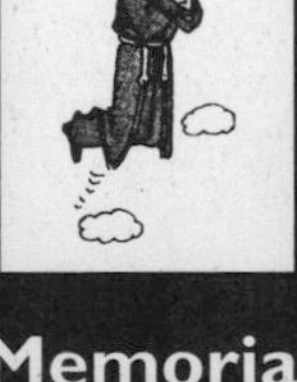
I did it, mom! An insignificant guard like me...appearing in a bonus in the graphic novel...!

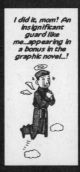

In Memoriam

FULLMETAL ALCHEMIST PREVIEW

MAYBE I SHOULD KILL YOU AFTER ALL, HM?
THOSE WHO REACH TOO FAR FOR THE TRUTH WILL ONLY END UP WITH TEARS...
♪
THAT CRAZY ARSONIST, KIMBLEY.
JUST ACCEPT IT.
YOU'LL FEEL BETTER THAT WAY.
EVERYTHING HAPPENS ACCORDING TO THE WILL OF GOD!

FULLMETAL ALCHEMIST VOL. 4
COMING IN NOVEMBER 2005!

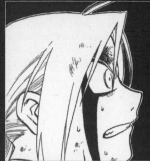

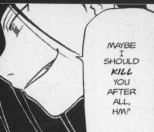

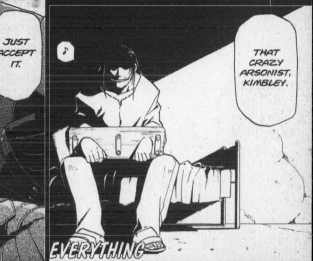

I Made Pinako's Hairstyle like This Just So I Could Do This Joke (Seriously!)

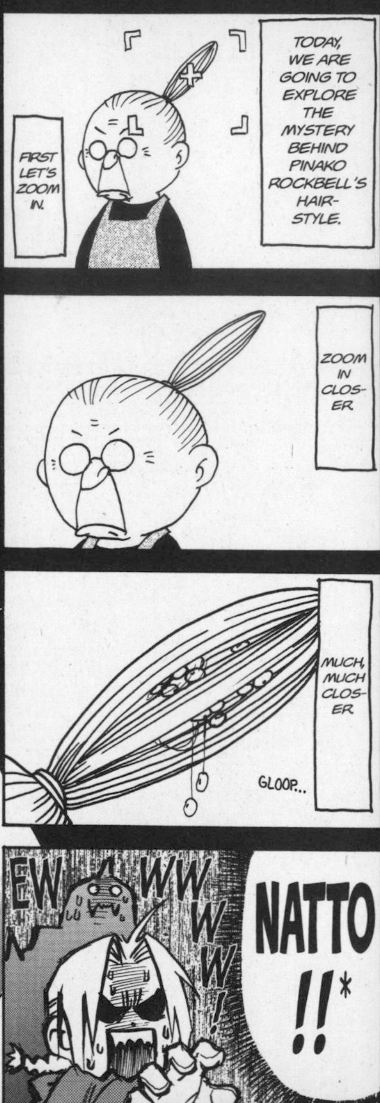
TODAY, WE ARE GOING TO EXPLORE THE MYSTERY BEHIND PINAKO ROCKBELL'S HAIR-STYLE.
FIRST LET'S ZOOM IN.
ZOOM IN CLOS-ER
MUCH, MUCH CLOS-ER
GLOOP...
NATTO!!*
EWWWWWW!

*NATTO = FERMENTED SOYBEANS

FULLMETAL ALCHEMIST 3

SPECIAL THANKS TO...

KEISUI TAKAEDA-SAN
SANKICHI HINODEYA-CHAN
JUN MORIYASU-SAN
MASANORI-SAN
JUNSHI BABA-SAN
YOICHI KAMITONO-CHAN
NANKAKUREMAN-SAN
NORIKO GUNJO-SAN
HASHIDA-KUN

YUICHI SHIMOMURA-SHI (MANAGER)

AND YOU!!

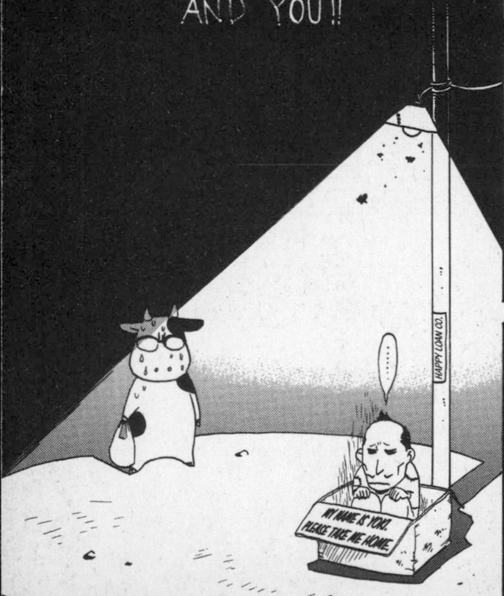
HAPPY LOAN CO.
MY NAME IS YOKO. PLEASE TAKE ME HOME.

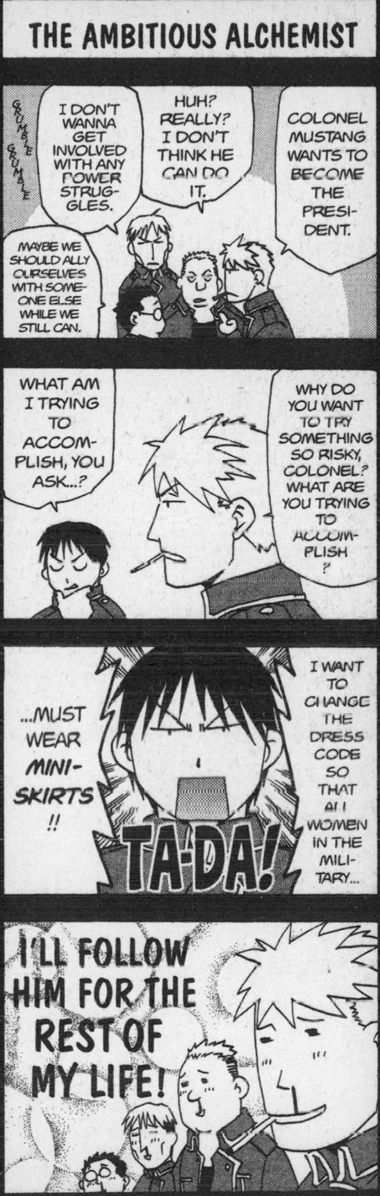
THE AMBITIOUS ALCHEMIST
COLONEL MUSTANG WANTS TO BECOME THE PRESIDENT.
HUH? REALLY? I DON'T THINK HE CAN DO IT.
I DON'T WANNA GET INVOLVED WITH ANY POWER STRUGGLES.
GRUMBLE GRUMBLE
MAYBE WE SHOULD ALLY OURSELVES WITH SOMEONE ELSE WHILE WE STILL CAN.
WHY DO YOU WANT TO TRY SOMETHING SO RISKY, COLONEL? WHAT ARE YOU TRYING TO ACCOMPLISH?
WHAT AM I TRYING TO ACCOMPLISH, YOU ASK...?
I WANT TO CHANGE THE DRESS CODE SO THAT ALL WOMEN IN THE MILITARY...
TA-DA!
...MUST WEAR MINI-SKIRTS!!
I'LL FOLLOW HIM FOR THE REST OF MY LIFE!
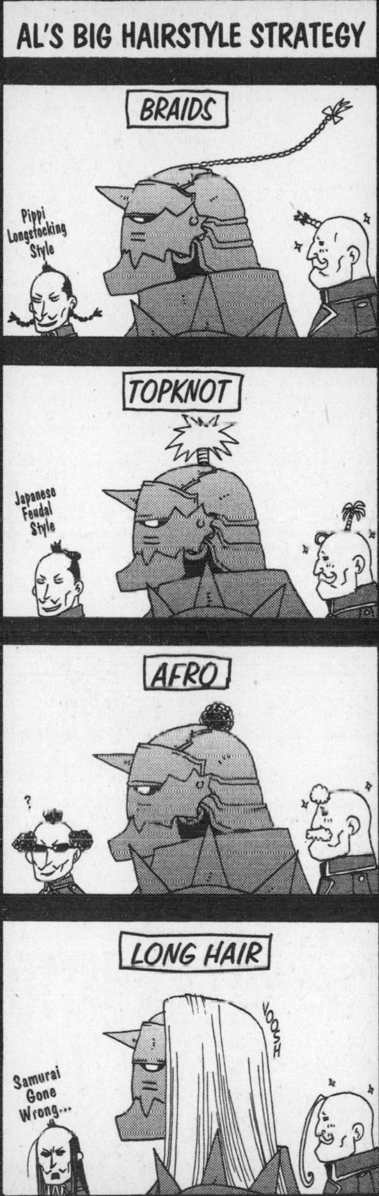
AL'S BIG HAIRSTYLE STRATEGY
BRAIDS
Pippi Longstocking Style
TOPKNOT
Japanese Feudal Style
AFRO
?
LONG HAIR
VOOSH
Samurai Gone Wrong...

EXTRA

The heroine of Fullmetal Alchemist.

PINAKO ROCKBELL

SHAKE, DEN.

anti-fan-service

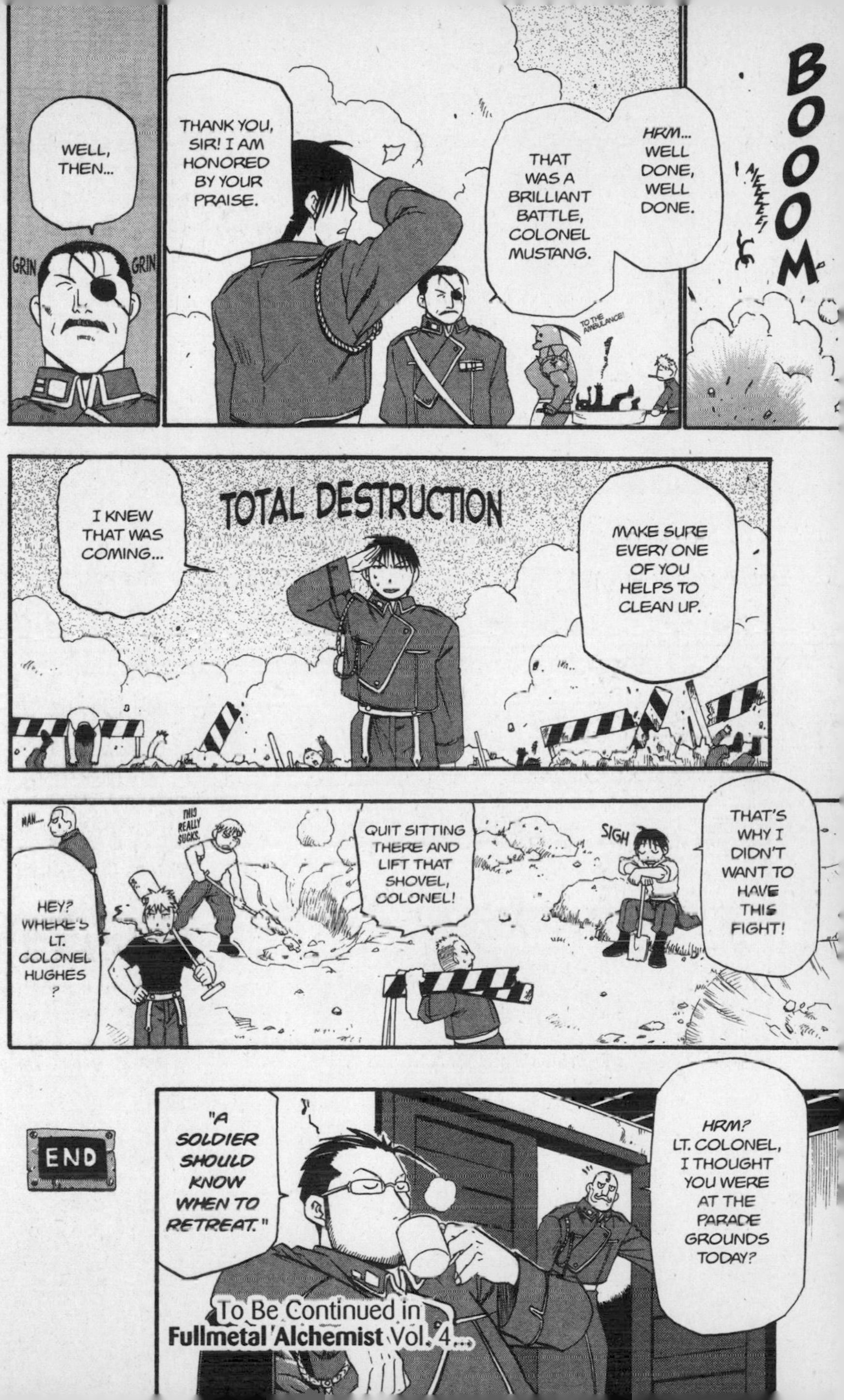
BOOOOM
AIEEEEE!
HRM... WELL DONE, WELL DONE.
THAT WAS A BRILLIANT BATTLE, COLONEL MUSTANG.
TO THE AMBULANCE!
THANK YOU, SIR! I AM HONORED BY YOUR PRAISE.
WELL, THEN...
GRIN GRIN
TOTAL DESTRUCTION
MAKE SURE EVERY ONE OF YOU HELPS TO CLEAN UP.
I KNEW THAT WAS COMING...
THAT'S WHY I DIDN'T WANT TO HAVE THIS FIGHT!
SIGH
QUIT SITTING THERE AND LIFT THAT SHOVEL, COLONEL!
THIS REALLY SUCKS.
MAN...
HEY? WHERE'S LT. COLONEL HUGHES?
HRM? LT. COLONEL, I THOUGHT YOU WERE AT THE PARADE GROUNDS TODAY?
"A SOLDIER SHOULD KNOW WHEN TO RETREAT."
END
To Be Continued in Fullmetal Alchemist Vol. 4...

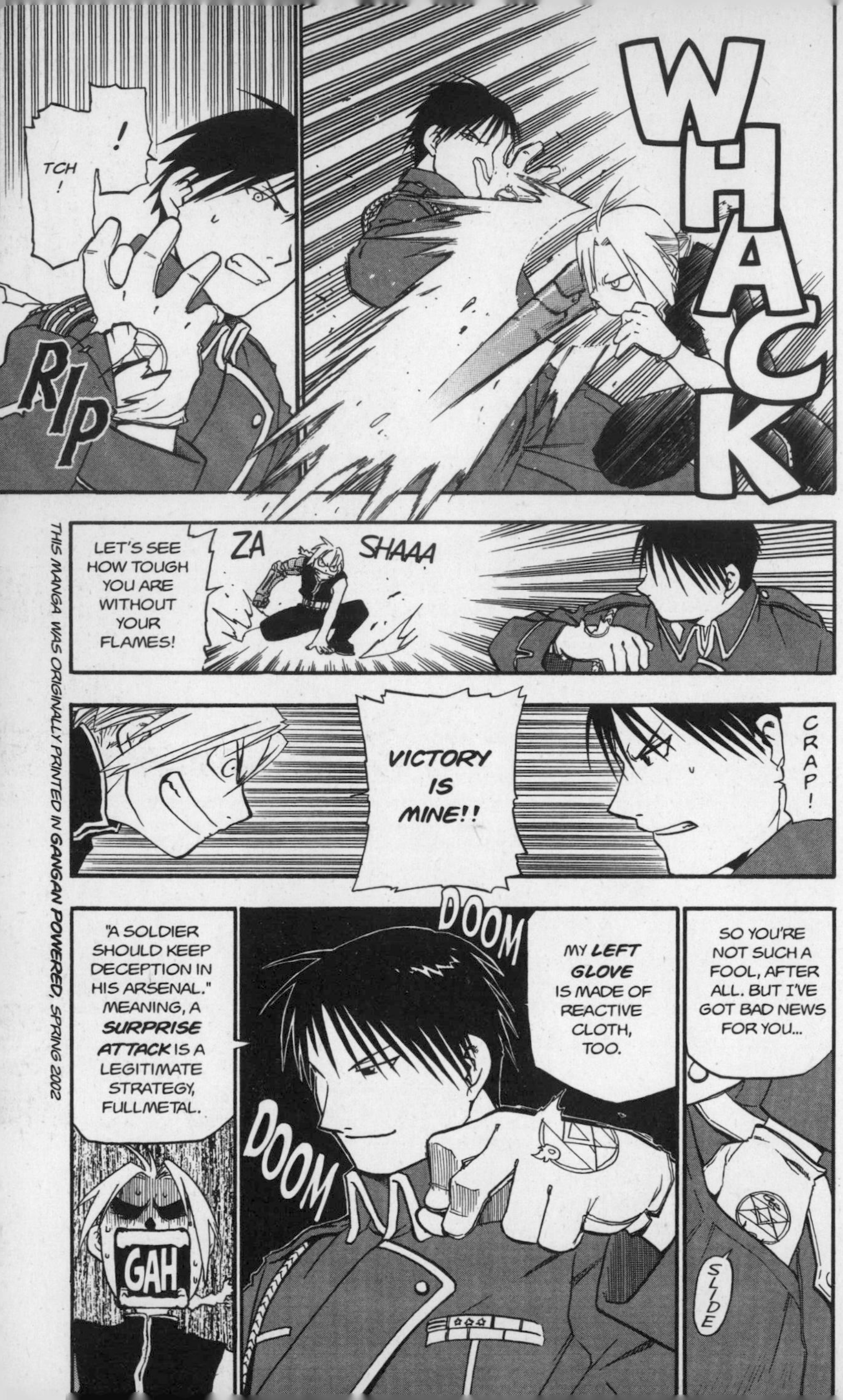
WHACK
!
TCH!
RIP
ZA
SHAAA
LET'S SEE HOW TOUGH YOU ARE WITHOUT YOUR FLAMES!
CRAP!
VICTORY IS MINE!!
SO YOU'RE NOT SUCH A FOOL, AFTER ALL. BUT I'VE GOT BAD NEWS FOR YOU...
SLIDE
MY LEFT GLOVE IS MADE OF REACTIVE CLOTH, TOO.
DOOM
DOOM
"A SOLDIER SHOULD KEEP DECEPTION IN HIS ARSENAL." MEANING, A SURPRISE ATTACK IS A LEGITIMATE STRATEGY, FULLMETAL.
GAH

THIS MANGA WAS ORIGINALLY PRINTED IN GANGAN POWERED, SPRING 2002

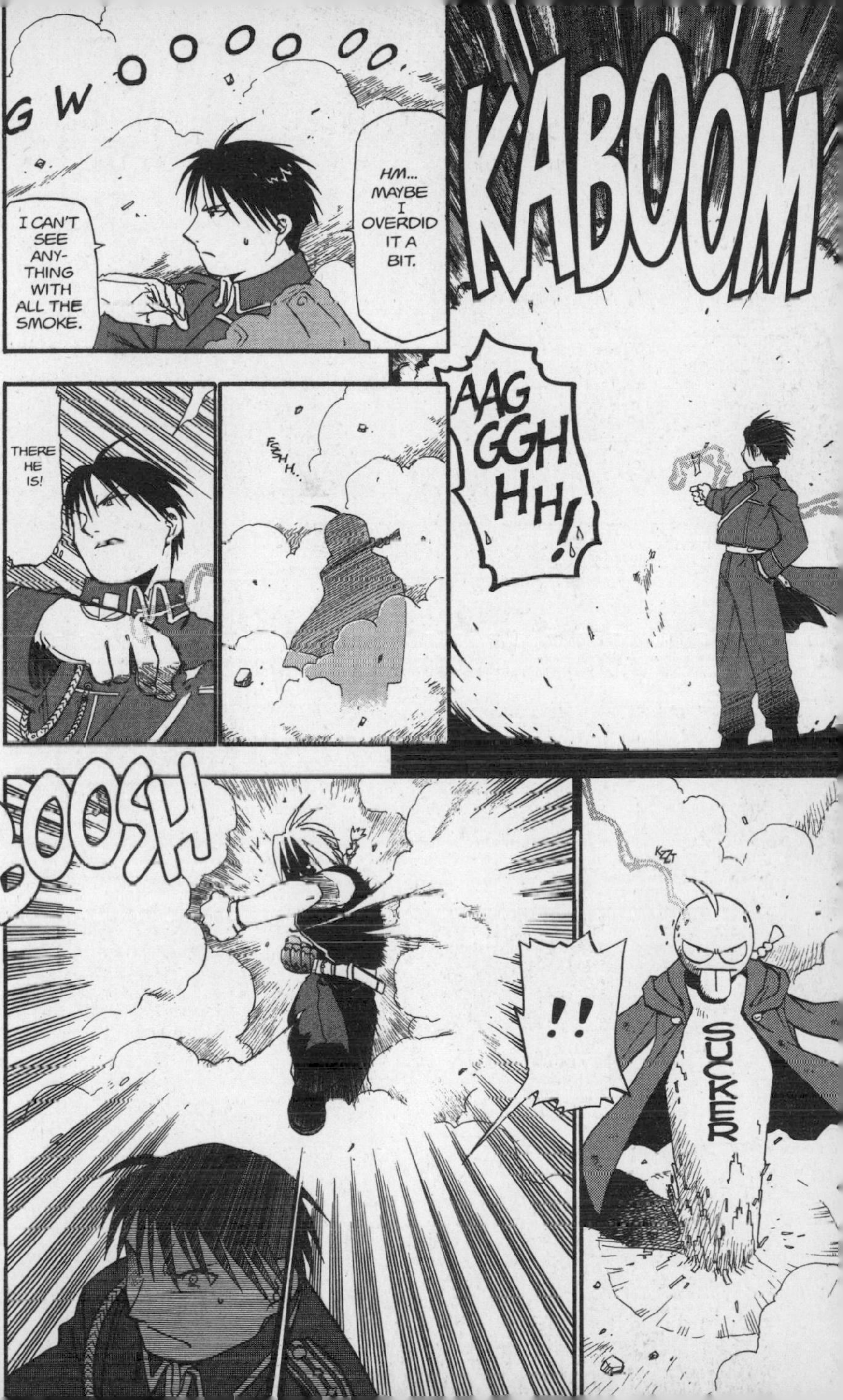
KABOOM
AAGGGHHH!
GWOOOOOO...
HM... MAYBE I OVERDID IT A BIT.
I CAN'T SEE ANYTHING WITH ALL THE SMOKE.
FSSHH...
THERE HE IS!
KZZT
!!
SUCKER
BOOSH

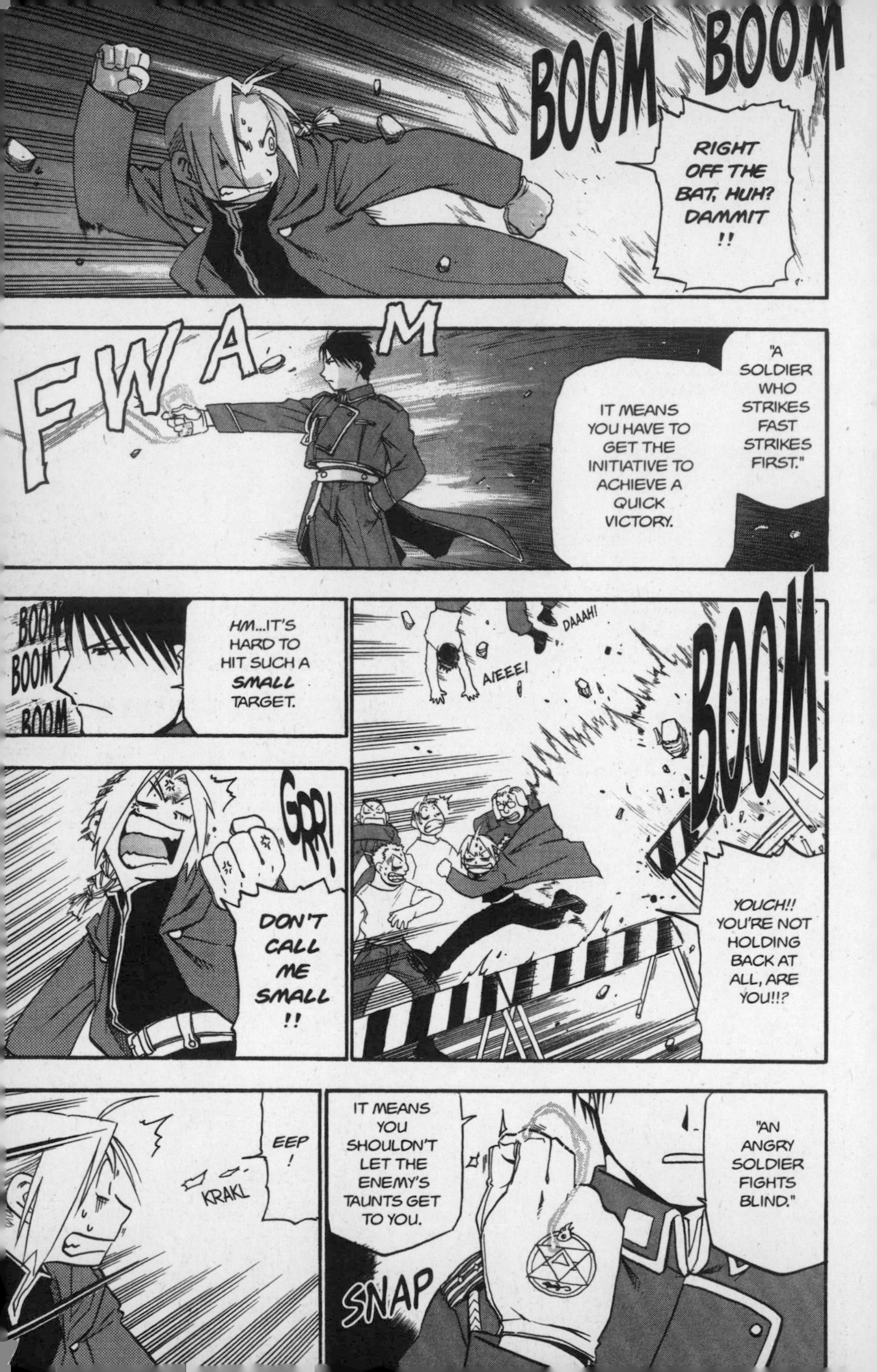
BOOM BOOM
RIGHT OFF THE BAT, HUH? DAMMIT!!
"A SOLDIER WHO STRIKES FAST STRIKES FIRST."
IT MEANS YOU HAVE TO GET THE INITIATIVE TO ACHIEVE A QUICK VICTORY.
FWAM
BOOM
DAAAH!
AIEEE!
YOUCH!! YOU'RE NOT HOLDING BACK AT ALL, ARE YOU!!?
BOOM BOOM BOOM
HM...IT'S HARD TO HIT SUCH A SMALL TARGET.
GRR!
DON'T CALL ME SMALL!!
"AN ANGRY SOLDIER FIGHTS BLIND."
IT MEANS YOU SHOULDN'T LET THE ENEMY'S TAUNTS GET TO YOU.
SNAP
EEP!
KRAKL

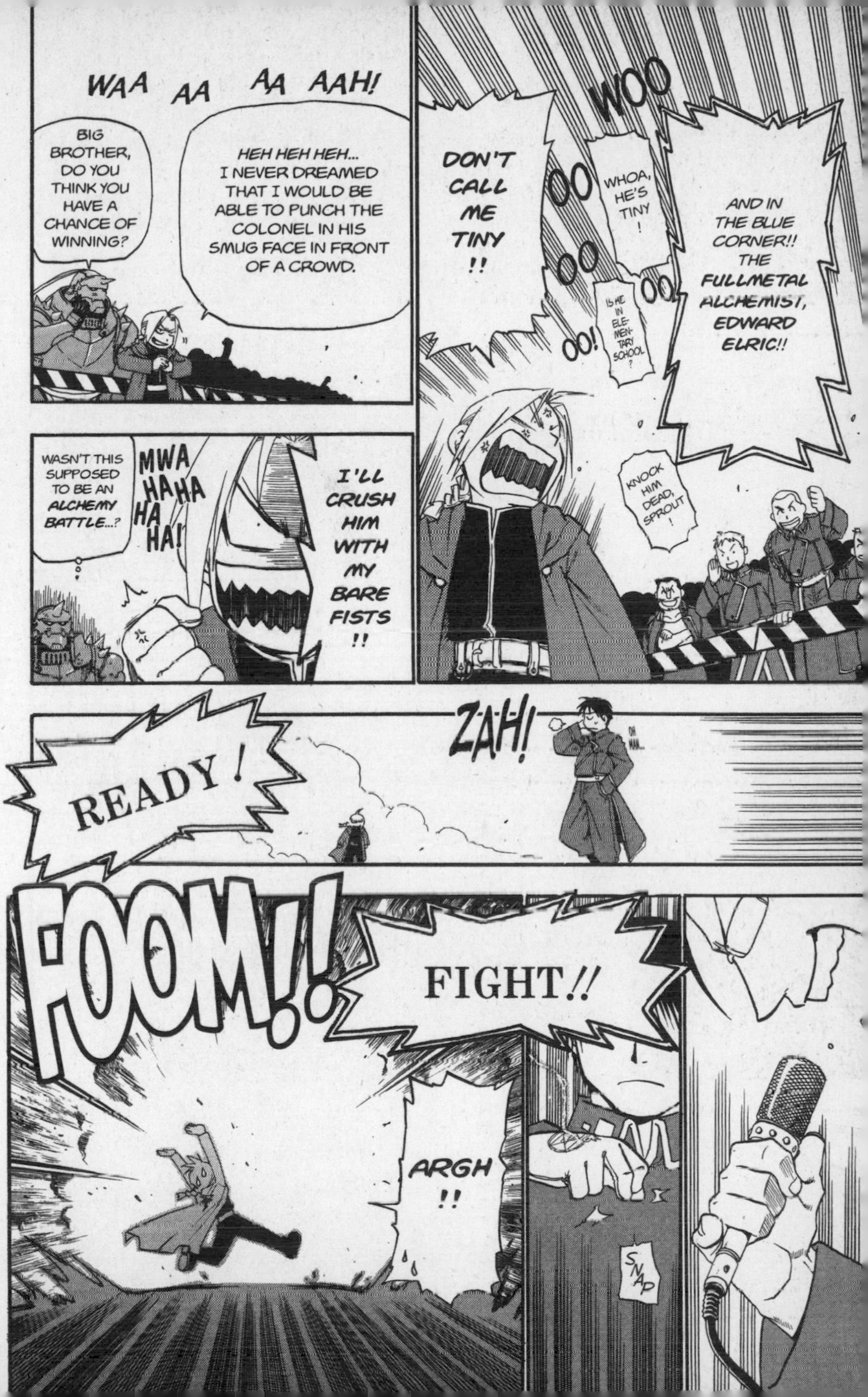
WOO
OO OO OO OO!
AND IN THE BLUE CORNER!! THE FULLMETAL ALCHEMIST, EDWARD ELRIC!!
WHOA, HE'S TINY!
IS HE IN ELE-MEN-TARY SCHOOL?
DON'T CALL ME TINY!!
KNOCK HIM DEAD, SPROUT!
WAA AA AA AAH!
HEH HEH HEH... I NEVER DREAMED THAT I WOULD BE ABLE TO PUNCH THE COLONEL IN HIS SMUG FACE IN FRONT OF A CROWD.
BIG BROTHER, DO YOU THINK YOU HAVE A CHANCE OF WINNING?
I'LL CRUSH HIM WITH MY BARE FISTS!!
MWA HA HA HA HA!
WASN'T THIS SUPPOSED TO BE AN *ALCHEMY BATTLE*...?
OH MAN...
ZAH!
READY!
FIGHT!!
SNAP
FOOM!!
ARGH!!

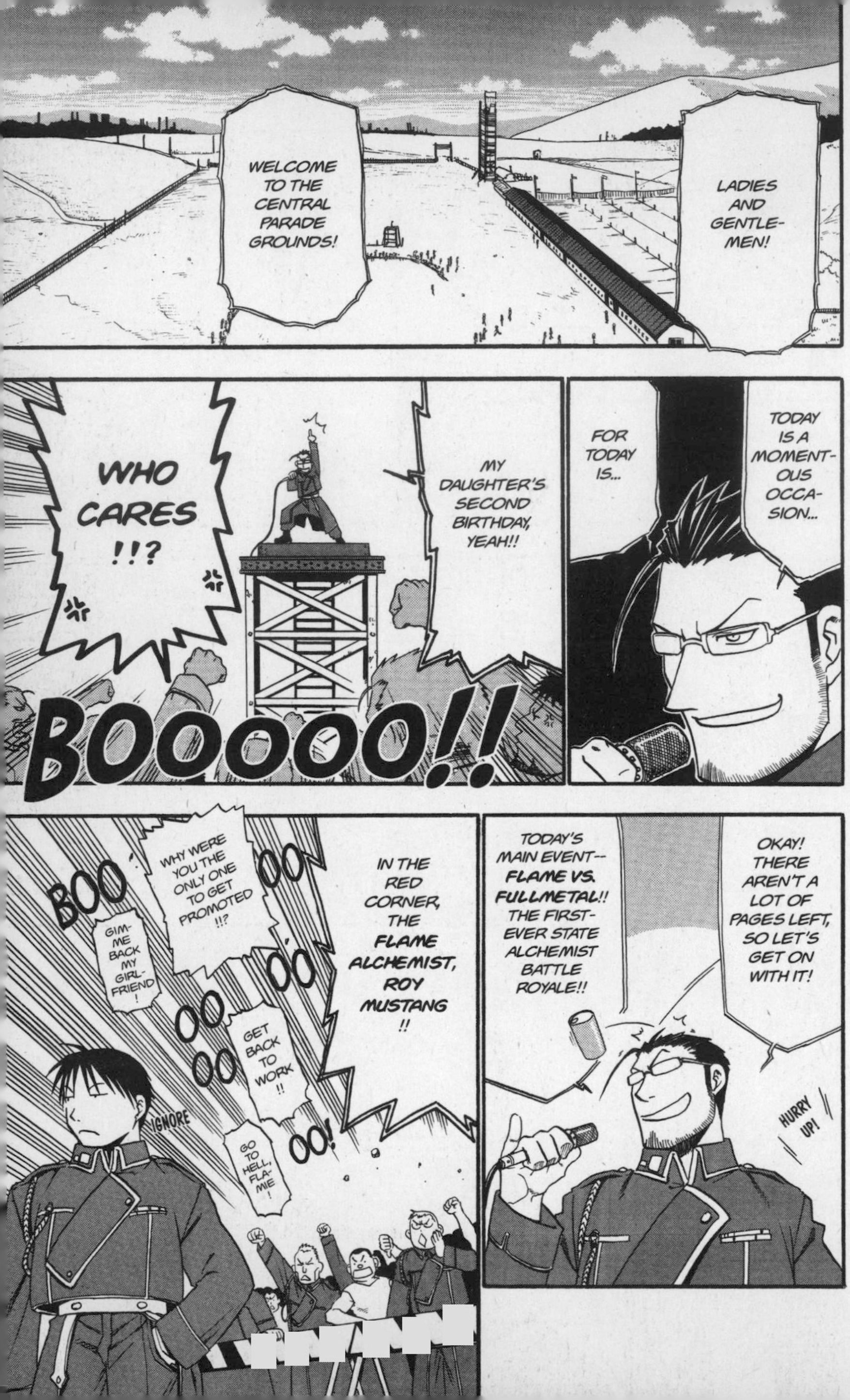
LADIES AND GENTLEMEN!
WELCOME TO THE CENTRAL PARADE GROUNDS!
TODAY IS A MOMENTOUS OCCASION...
FOR TODAY IS...
MY DAUGHTER'S SECOND BIRTHDAY, YEAH!!
WHO CARES!!?
BOOOOO!!
OKAY! THERE AREN'T A LOT OF PAGES LEFT, SO LET'S GET ON WITH IT!
TODAY'S MAIN EVENT-- **FLAME VS. FULLMETAL!!** THE FIRST-EVER STATE ALCHEMIST BATTLE ROYALE!!
HURRY UP!
IN THE RED CORNER, THE **FLAME ALCHEMIST, ROY MUSTANG**!!
WHY WERE YOU THE ONLY ONE TO GET PROMOTED!!?
BOO
OO
OO
OO
OO
OO!
GIMME BACK MY GIRLFRIEND!
GET BACK TO WORK!!
IGNORE
GO TO HELL, FLAMIE!

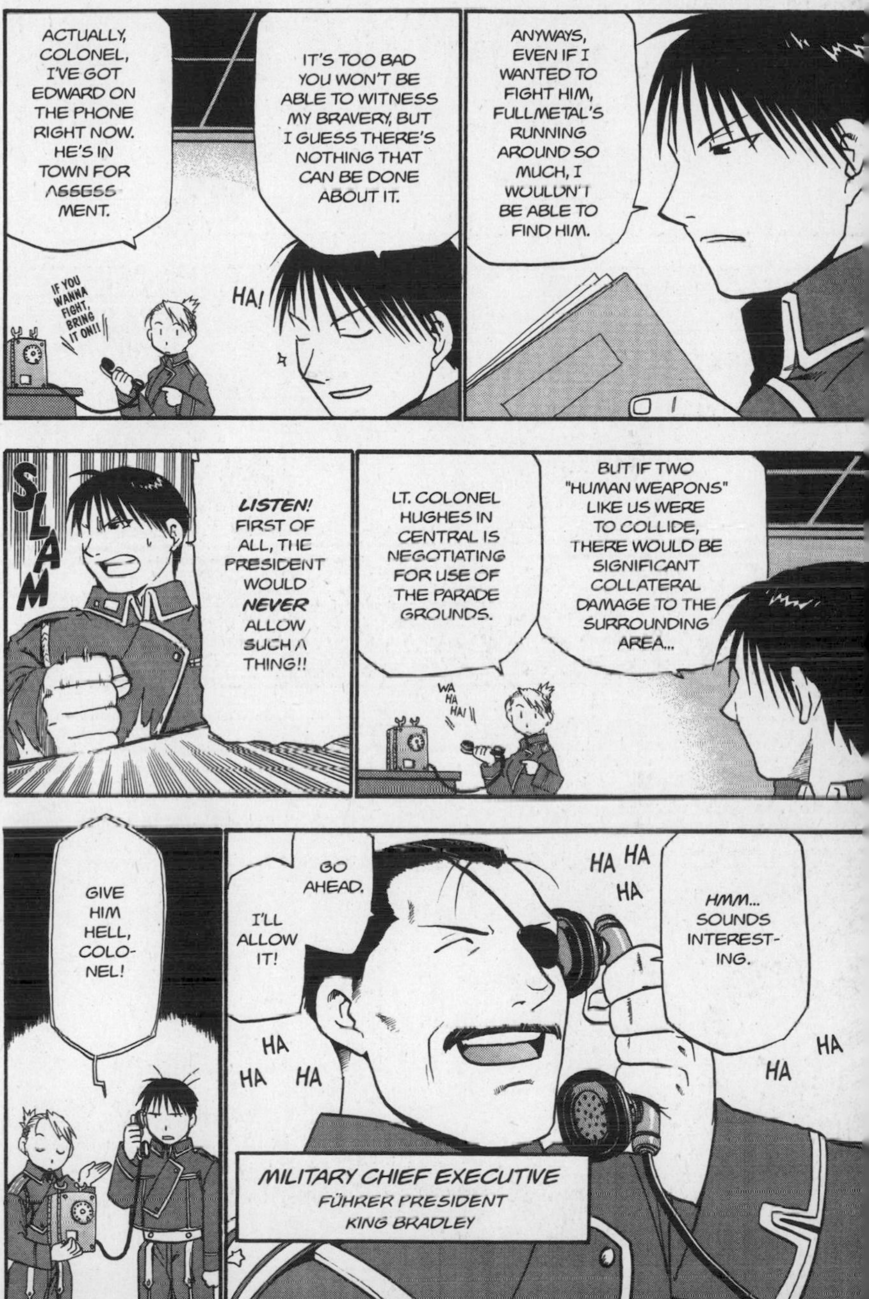
ANYWAYS, EVEN IF I WANTED TO FIGHT HIM, FULLMETAL'S RUNNING AROUND SO MUCH, I WOULDN'T BE ABLE TO FIND HIM.
IT'S TOO BAD YOU WON'T BE ABLE TO WITNESS MY BRAVERY, BUT I GUESS THERE'S NOTHING THAT CAN BE DONE ABOUT IT.
HA!
ACTUALLY, COLONEL, I'VE GOT EDWARD ON THE PHONE RIGHT NOW. HE'S IN TOWN FOR ASSESS-MENT.
IF YOU WANNA FIGHT, BRING IT ON!!
BUT IF TWO "HUMAN WEAPONS" LIKE US WERE TO COLLIDE, THERE WOULD BE SIGNIFICANT COLLATERAL DAMAGE TO THE SURROUNDING AREA...
LT. COLONEL HUGHES IN CENTRAL IS NEGOTIATING FOR USE OF THE PARADE GROUNDS.
WA HA HA!
LISTEN! FIRST OF ALL, THE PRESIDENT WOULD *NEVER* ALLOW SUCH A THING!!
SLAM
HMM... SOUNDS INTEREST-ING.
HA HA HA
GO AHEAD.
I'LL ALLOW IT!
HA HA HA
HA HA
MILITARY CHIEF EXECUTIVE
FÜHRER PRESIDENT
KING BRADLEY
GIVE HIM HELL, COLO-NEL!

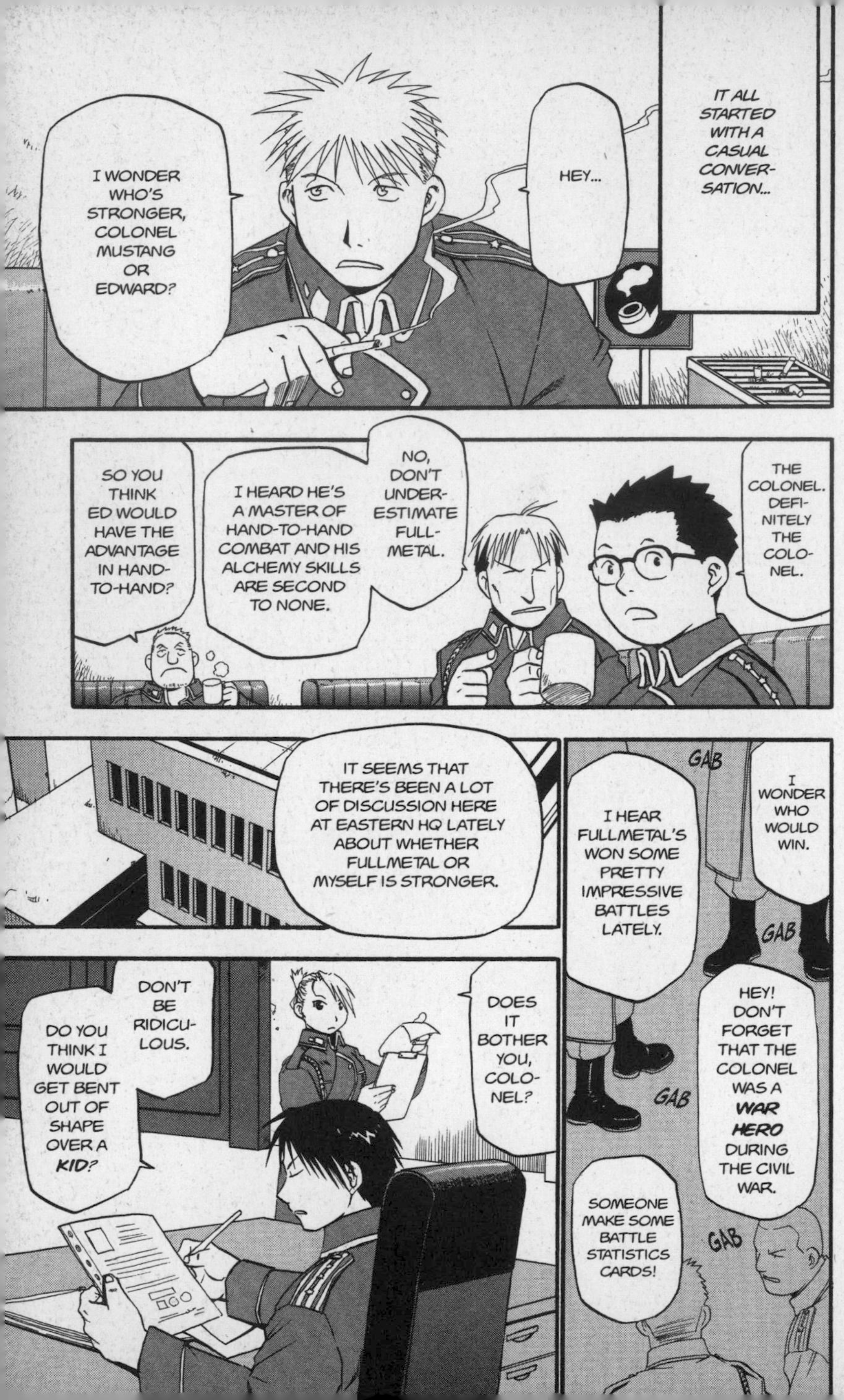
IT ALL STARTED WITH A CASUAL CONVERSATION...
HEY...
I WONDER WHO'S STRONGER, COLONEL MUSTANG OR EDWARD?
THE COLONEL. DEFINITELY THE COLONEL.
NO, DON'T UNDERESTIMATE FULLMETAL.
I HEARD HE'S A MASTER OF HAND-TO-HAND COMBAT AND HIS ALCHEMY SKILLS ARE SECOND TO NONE.
SO YOU THINK ED WOULD HAVE THE ADVANTAGE IN HAND-TO-HAND?
GAB
I WONDER WHO WOULD WIN.
I HEAR FULLMETAL'S WON SOME PRETTY IMPRESSIVE BATTLES LATELY.
GAB
HEY! DON'T FORGET THAT THE COLONEL WAS A **WAR HERO** DURING THE CIVIL WAR.
GAB
GAB
SOMEONE MAKE SOME BATTLE STATISTICS CARDS!
IT SEEMS THAT THERE'S BEEN A LOT OF DISCUSSION HERE AT EASTERN HQ LATELY ABOUT WHETHER FULLMETAL OR MYSELF IS STRONGER.
DOES IT BOTHER YOU, COLONEL?
DON'T BE RIDICULOUS.
DO YOU THINK I WOULD GET BENT OUT OF SHAPE OVER A ***KID***?

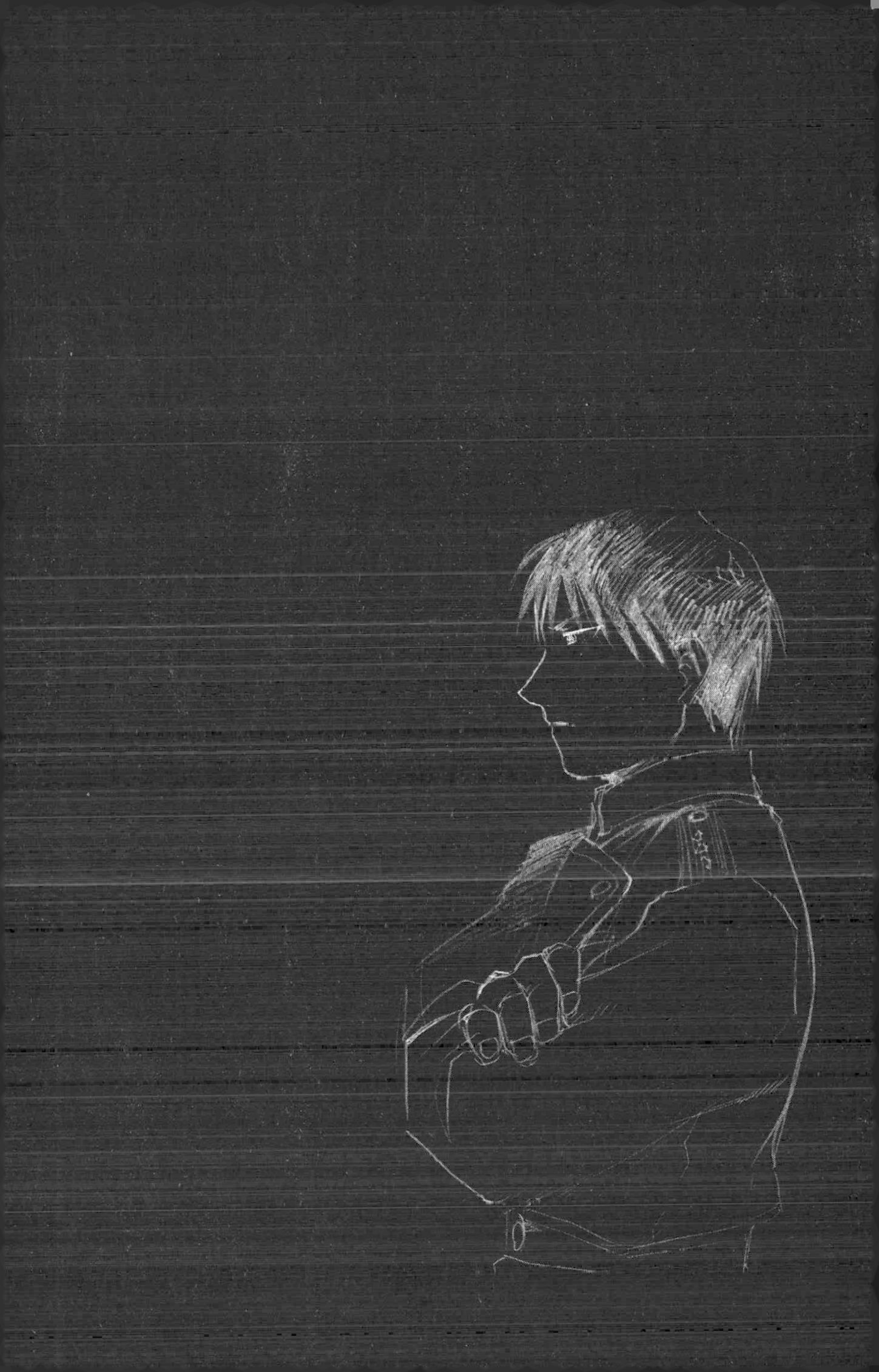

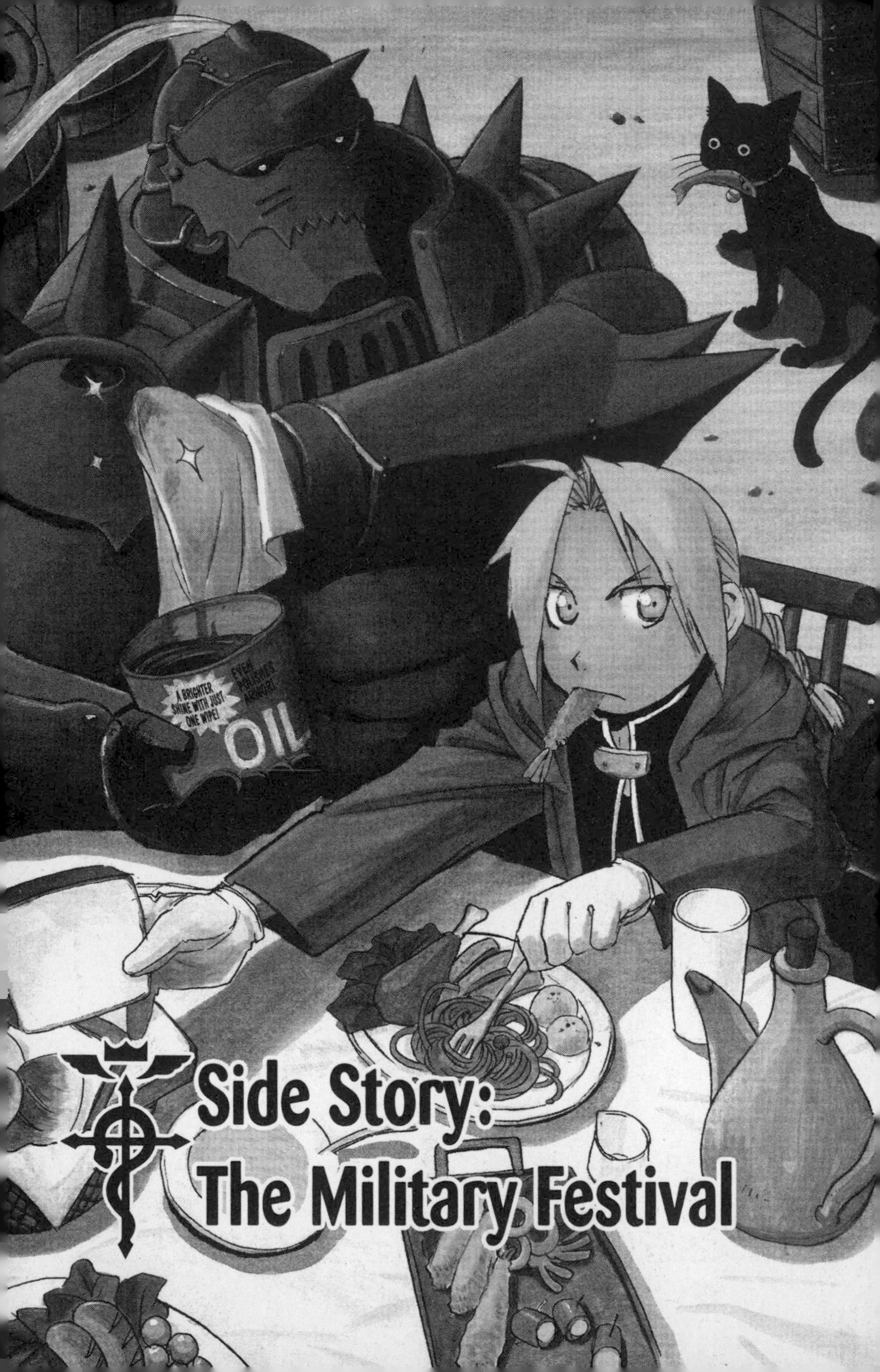
A BRIGHTER SHINE WITH JUST ONE WIPE!
OIL
Side Story:
The Military Festival

鋼の錬金術師

FULLMETAL ALCHEMIST

3

荒川弘

HIROMU ARAKAWA

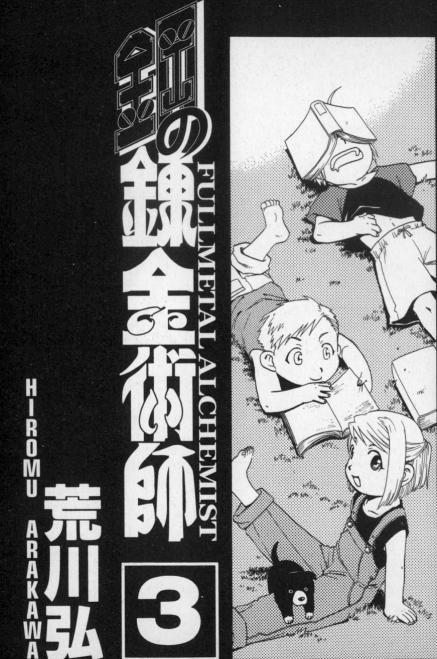

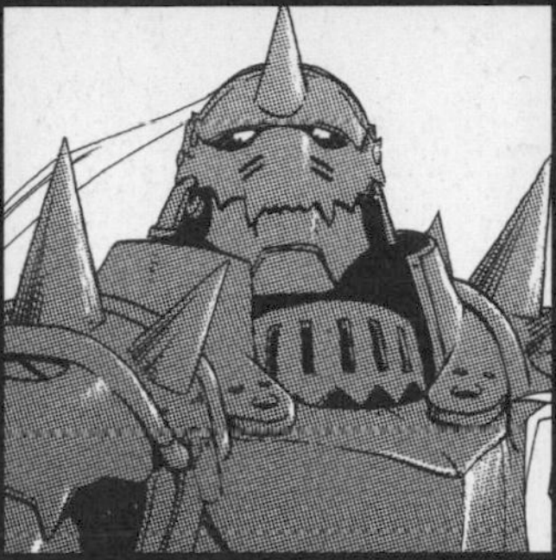

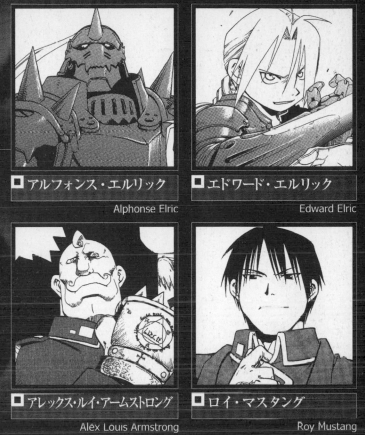

アルフォンス・エルリック

Alphonse Elric

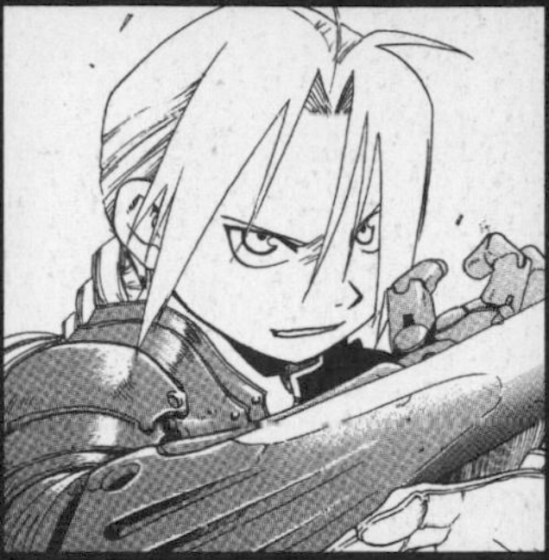

エドワード・エルリック

Edward Elric

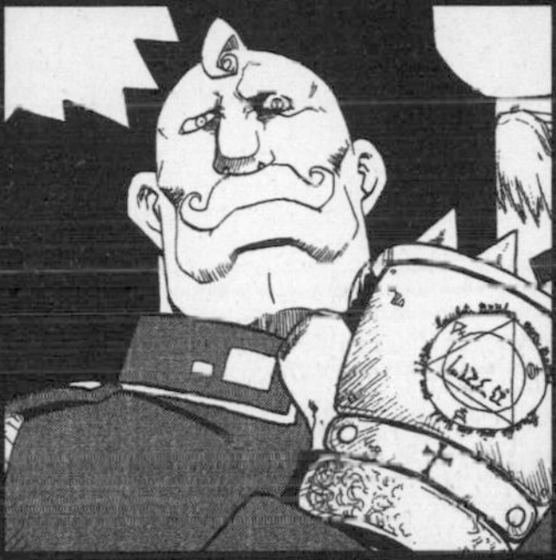

アレックス・ルイ・アームストロング

Alex Louis Armstrong

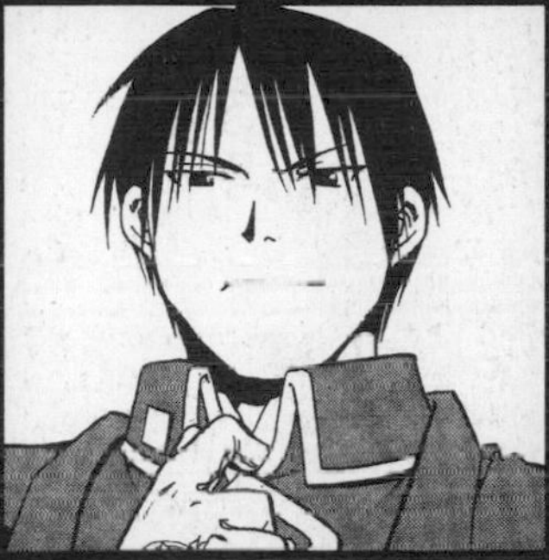

ロイ・マスタング

Roy Mustang

Using a forbidden alchemical ritual, the Elric brothers attempted to bring their dead mother back to life. But the ritual went wrong, consuming Edward Elric's leg and Alphonse Elric's entire body. At the cost of his arm, Edward was able to graft his brother's soul into a suit of armor. Equipped with mechanical "auto-mail" to replace his missing limbs, Edward becomes a state alchemist, serving the military on deadly missions. Now, the two brothers roam the world in search of a way to regain what they have lost...

During a near-fatal encounter with an assassin named Scar, Edward's auto-mail arm is destroyed and Alphonse is incapacitated. Escorted by Major Armstrong, the damaged Elric brothers return to their hometown for repairs...

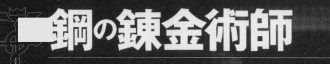

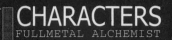

鋼の錬金術師

FULLMETAL ALCHEMIST

CHARACTERS

FULLMETAL ALCHEMIST

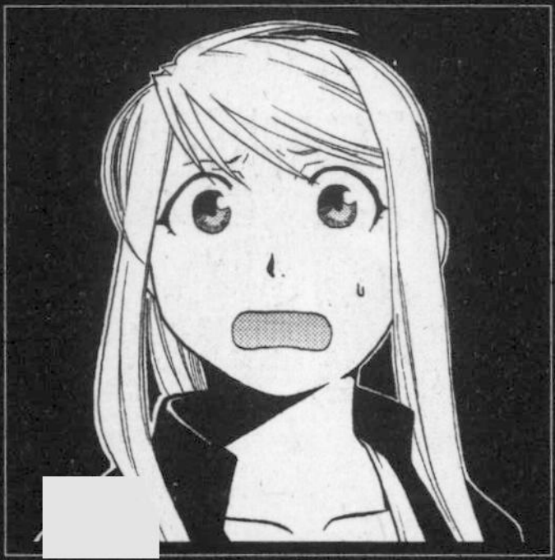

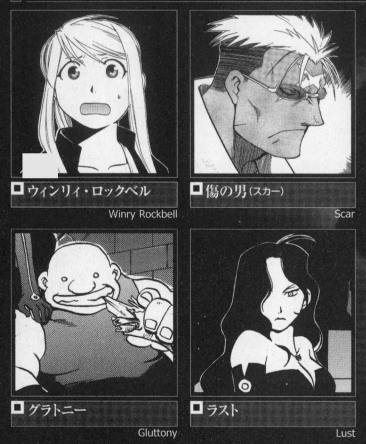

□ ウィンリィ・ロックベル

Winry Rockbell

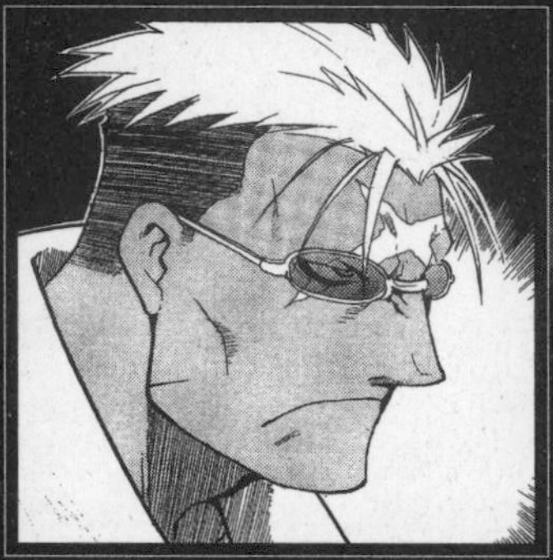

□ 傷の男（スカー）

Scar

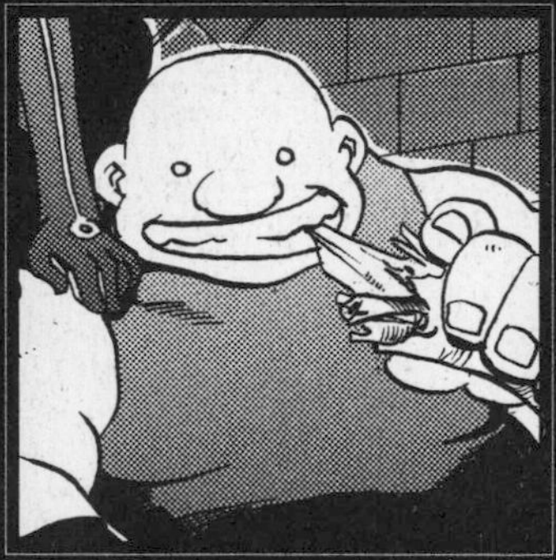

□ グラトニー

Gluttony

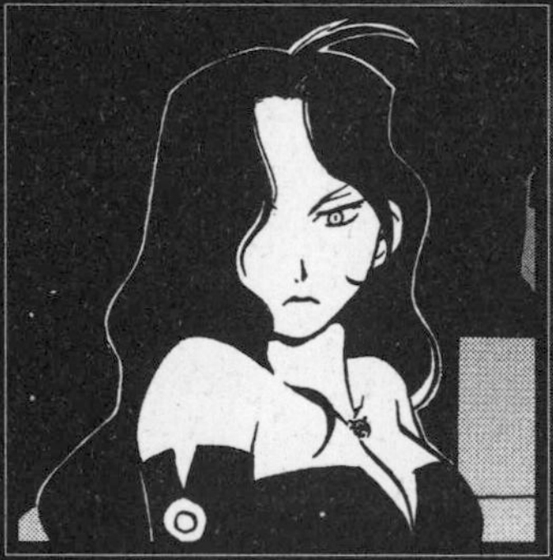

□ ラスト

Lust

OUTLINE

FULLMETAL ALCHEMIST

CONTENTS

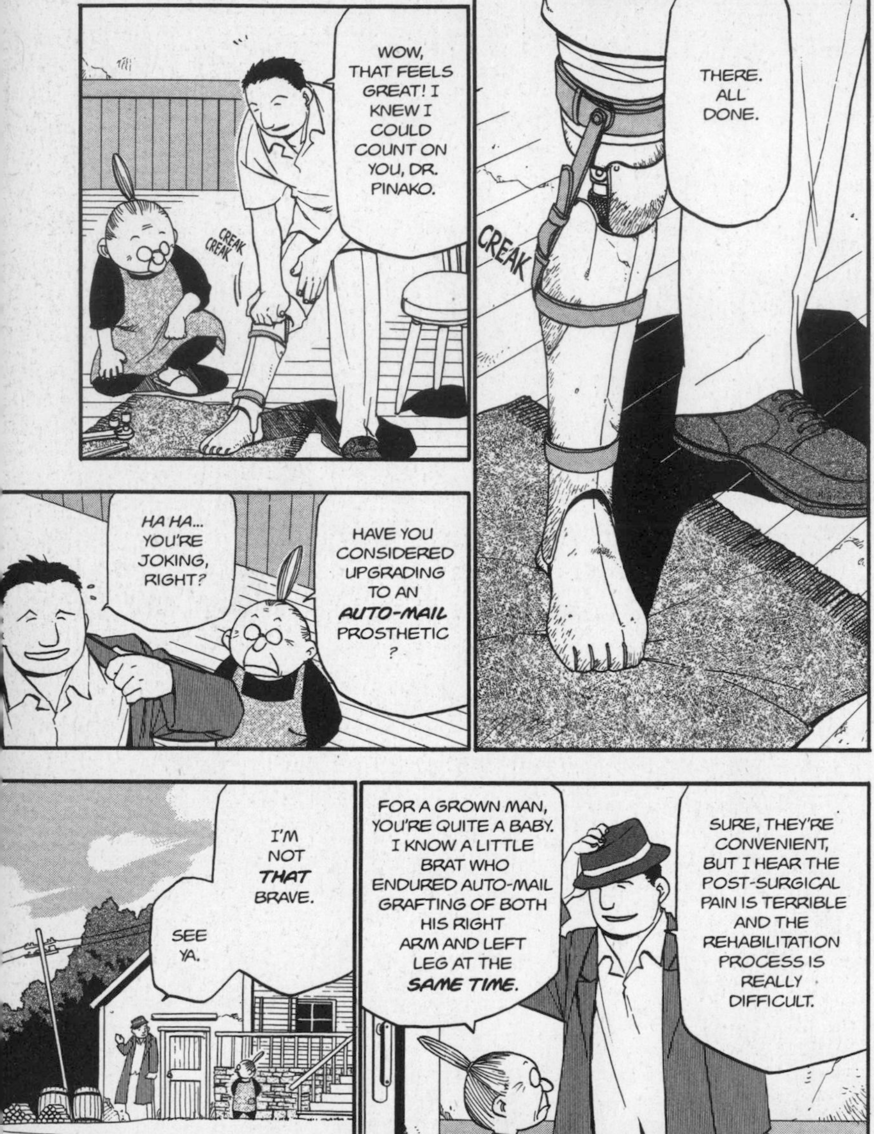
THERE. ALL DONE.
CREAK
WOW, THAT FEELS GREAT! I KNEW I COULD COUNT ON YOU, DR. PINAKO.
CREAK CREAK
HAVE YOU CONSIDERED UPGRADING TO AN AUTO-MAIL PROSTHETIC?
HA HA... YOU'RE JOKING, RIGHT?
SURE, THEY'RE CONVENIENT, BUT I HEAR THE POST-SURGICAL PAIN IS TERRIBLE AND THE REHABILITATION PROCESS IS REALLY DIFFICULT.
FOR A GROWN MAN, YOU'RE QUITE A BABY. I KNOW A LITTLE BRAT WHO ENDURED AUTO-MAIL GRAFTING OF BOTH HIS RIGHT ARM AND LEFT LEG AT THE SAME TIME.
I'M NOT THAT BRAVE.
SEE YA.

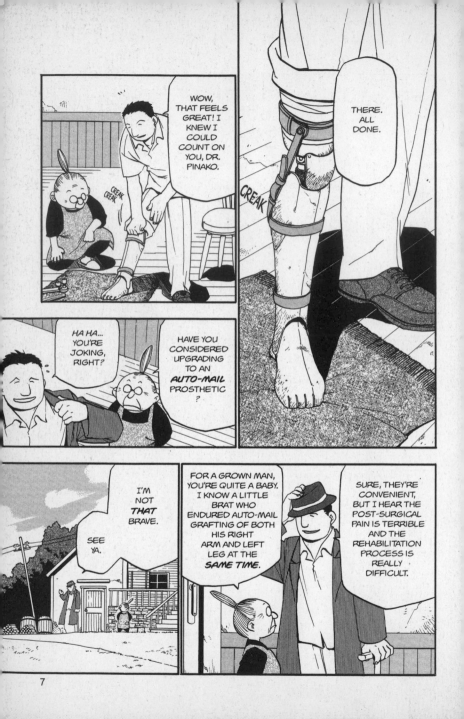

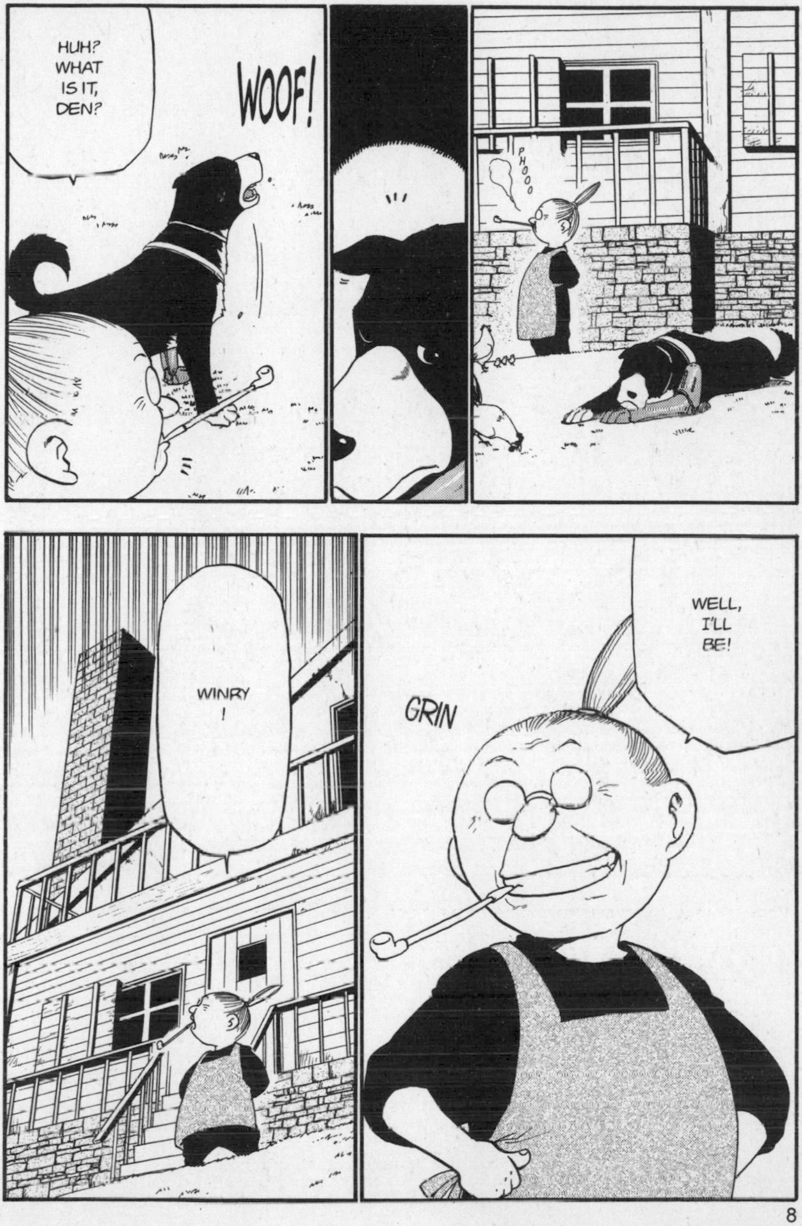
PHOOO
HUH? WHAT IS IT, DEN?
WOOF!
WELL, I'LL BE!
GRIN
WINRY!

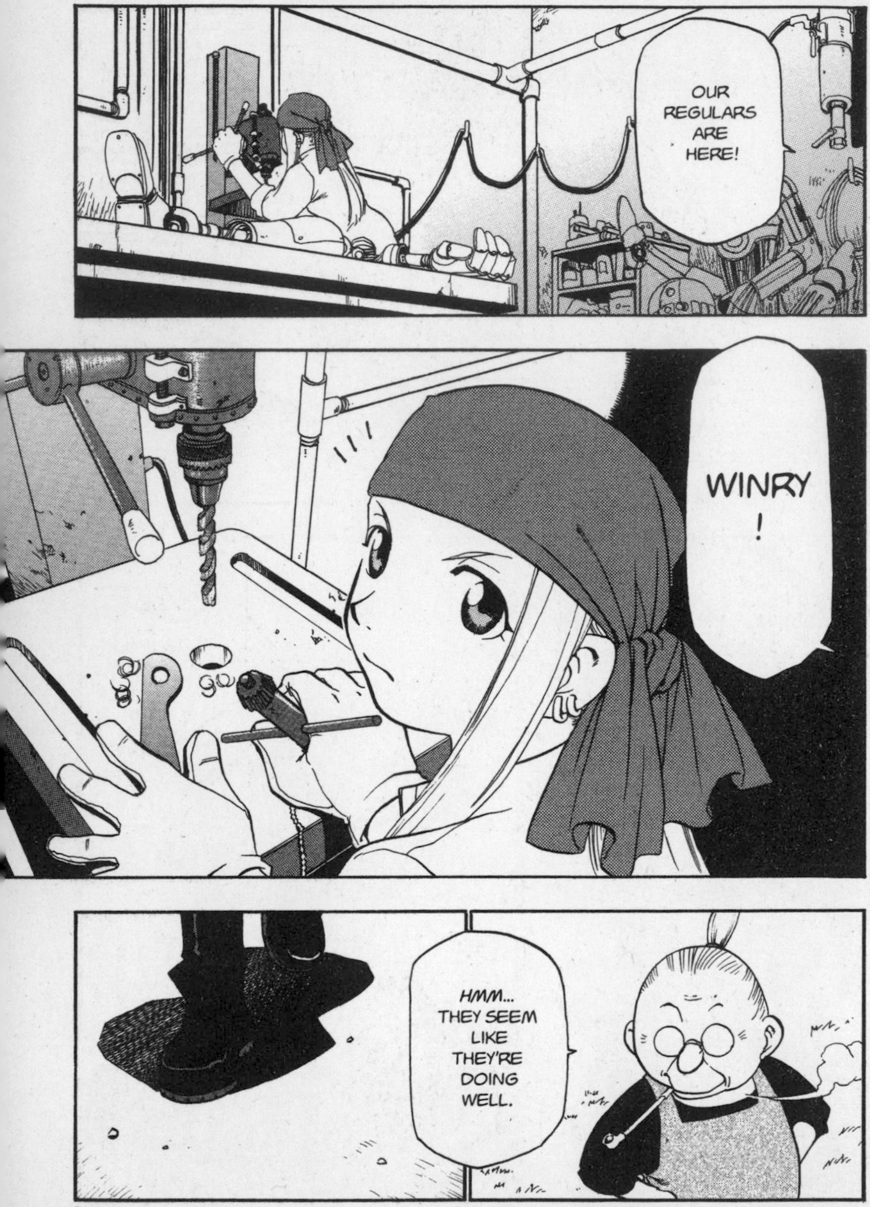
OUR REGULARS ARE HERE!
WINRY !
HMM... THEY SEEM LIKE THEY'RE DOING WELL.

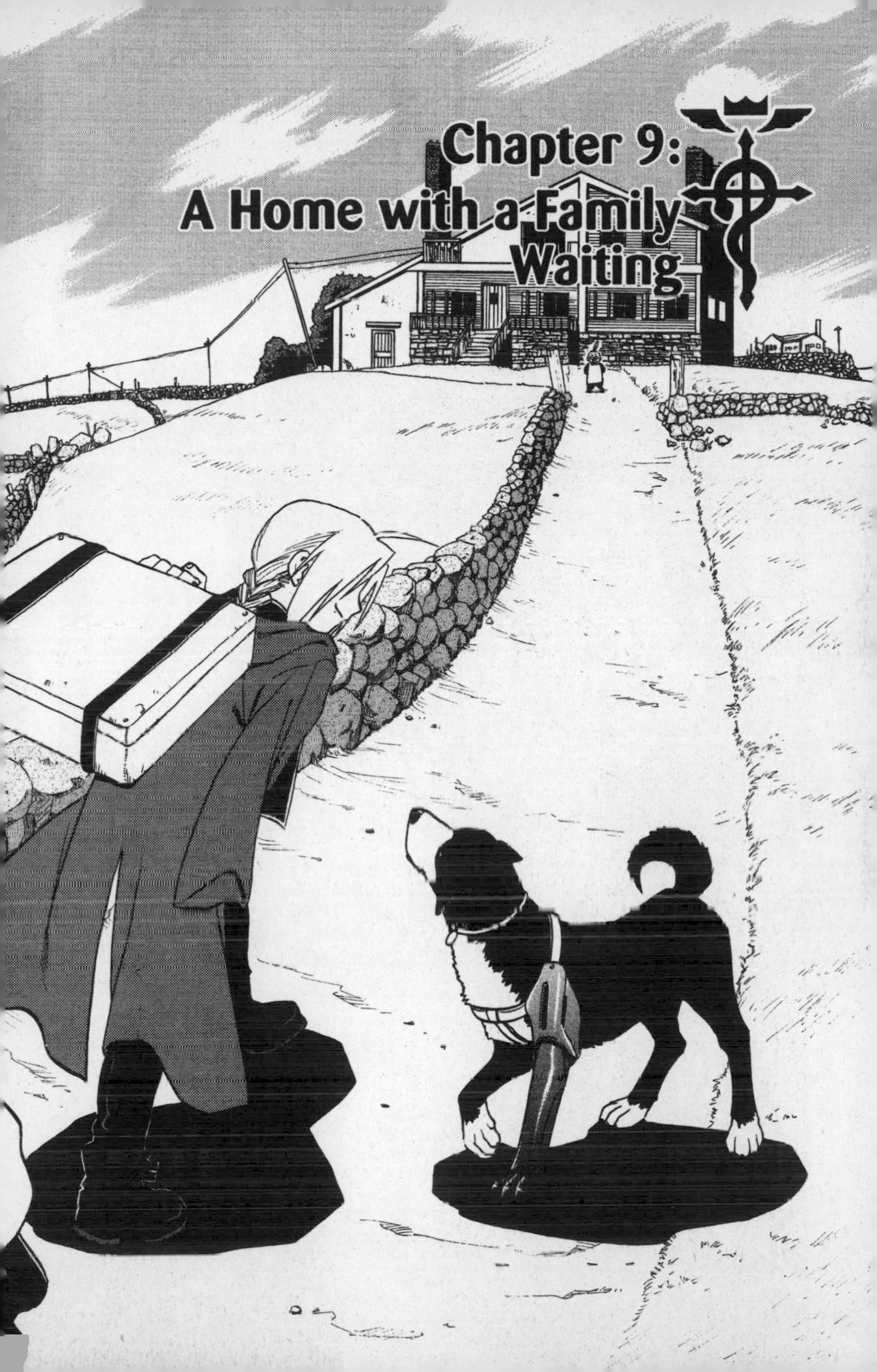
Chapter 9:
A Home with a Family Waiting

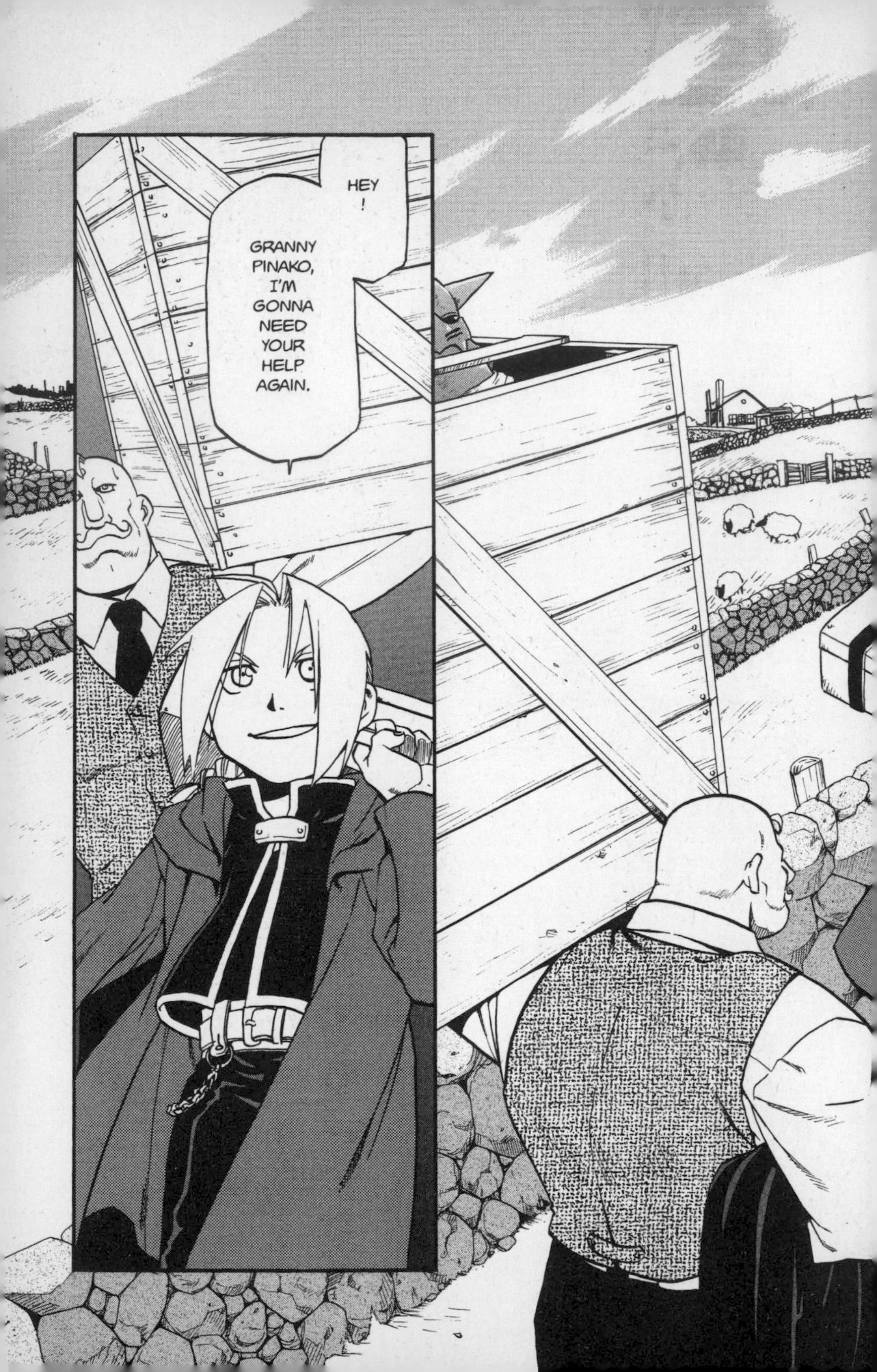
HEY!
GRANNY PINAKO, I'M GONNA NEED YOUR HELP AGAIN.

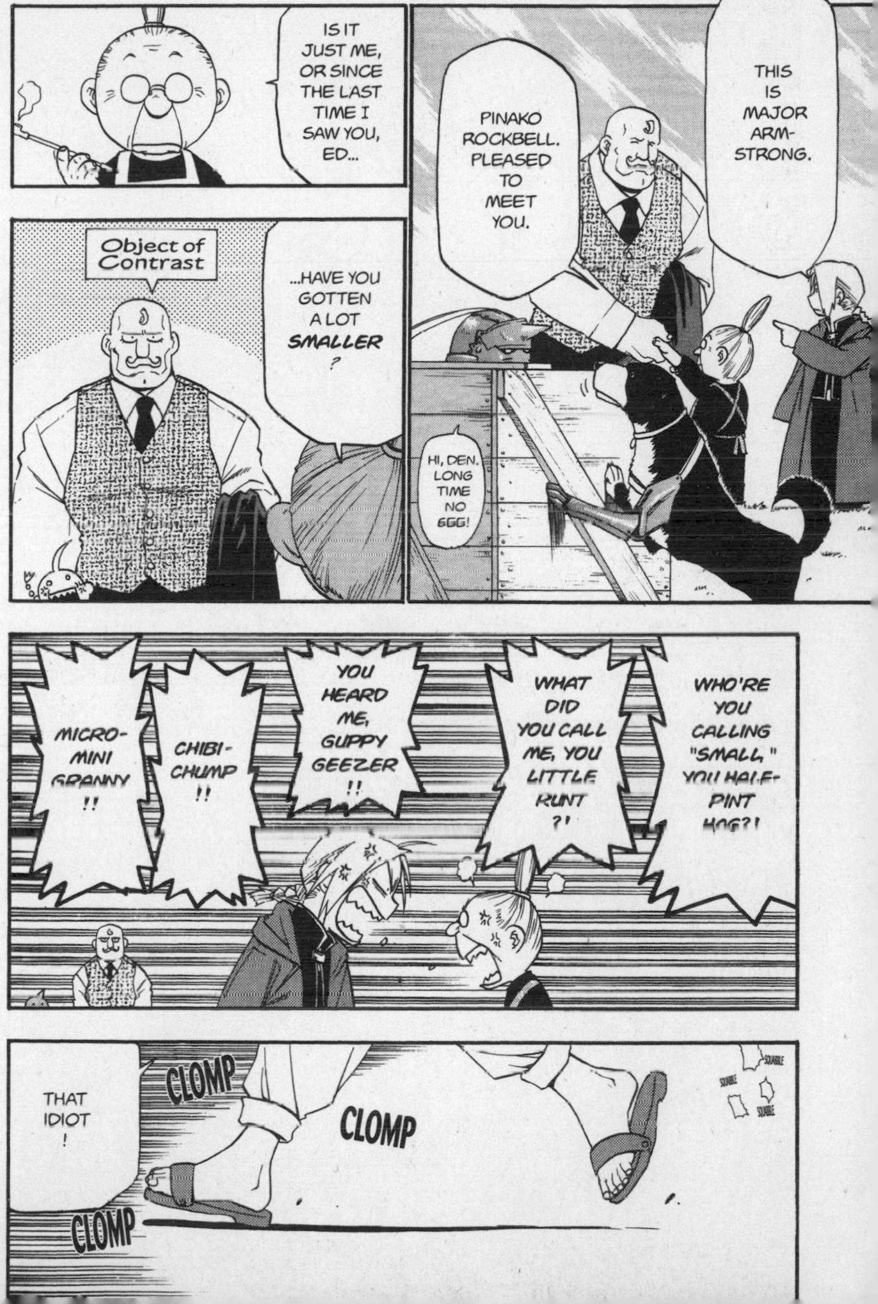
THIS IS MAJOR ARM-STRONG.
PINAKO ROCKBELL. PLEASED TO MEET YOU.
HI, DEN. LONG TIME NO SEE!
IS IT JUST ME, OR SINCE THE LAST TIME I SAW YOU, ED...
Object of Contrast
...HAVE YOU GOTTEN A LOT SMALLER?
WHO'RE YOU CALLING "SMALL," YOU HALF-PINT HAG?!
WHAT DID YOU CALL ME, YOU LITTLE RUNT?!
YOU HEARD ME, GUPPY GEEZER!!
CHIBI-CHUMP!!
MICRO-MINI GRANNY!!
SQUABBLE
SQUABBLE
SQUABBLE
CLOMP
CLOMP
CLOMP
THAT IDIOT!

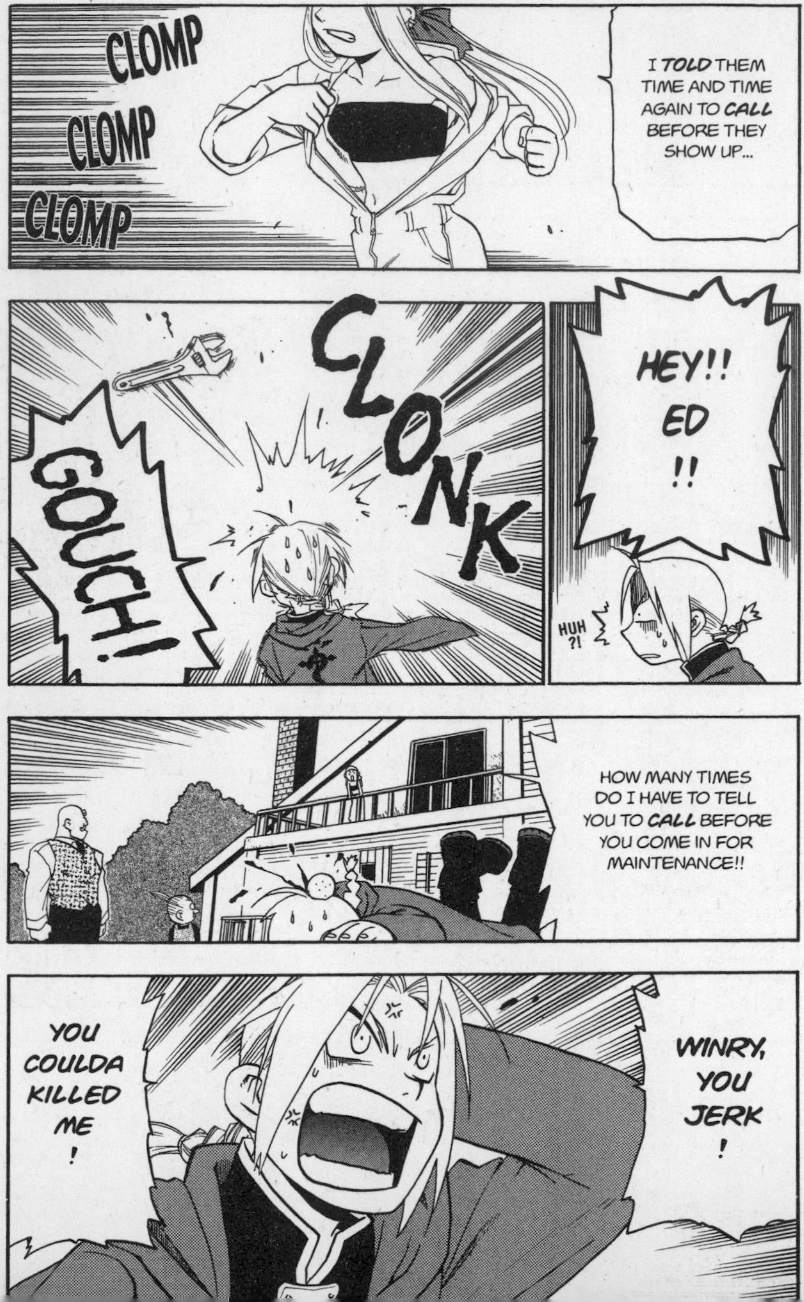
I TOLD THEM TIME AND TIME AGAIN TO CALL BEFORE THEY SHOW UP...
CLOMP
CLOMP
CLOMP
HEY!! ED !!
HUH ?!
CLONK
GOUCH!
HOW MANY TIMES DO I HAVE TO TELL YOU TO CALL BEFORE YOU COME IN FOR MAINTENANCE!!
WINRY, YOU JERK !
YOU COULDA KILLED ME !

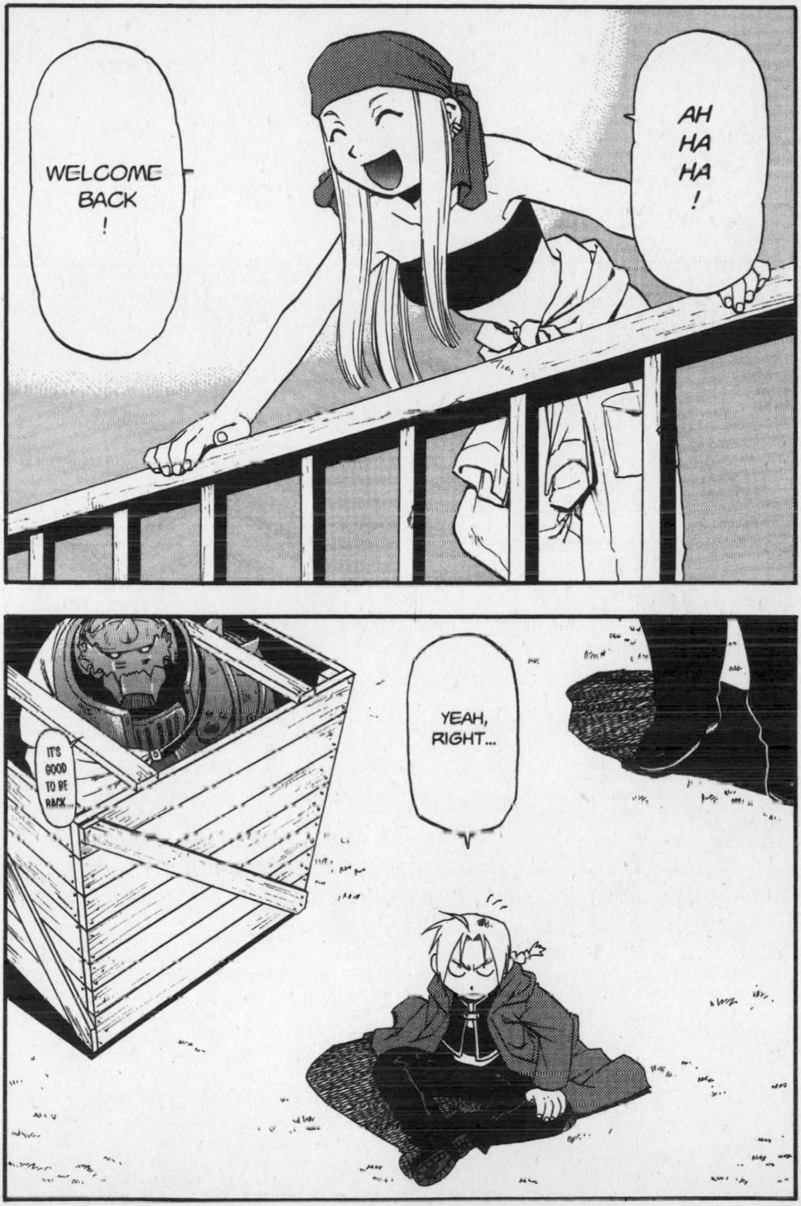
AH HA HA!
WELCOME BACK!
YEAH, RIGHT...
IT'S GOOD TO BE BACK...

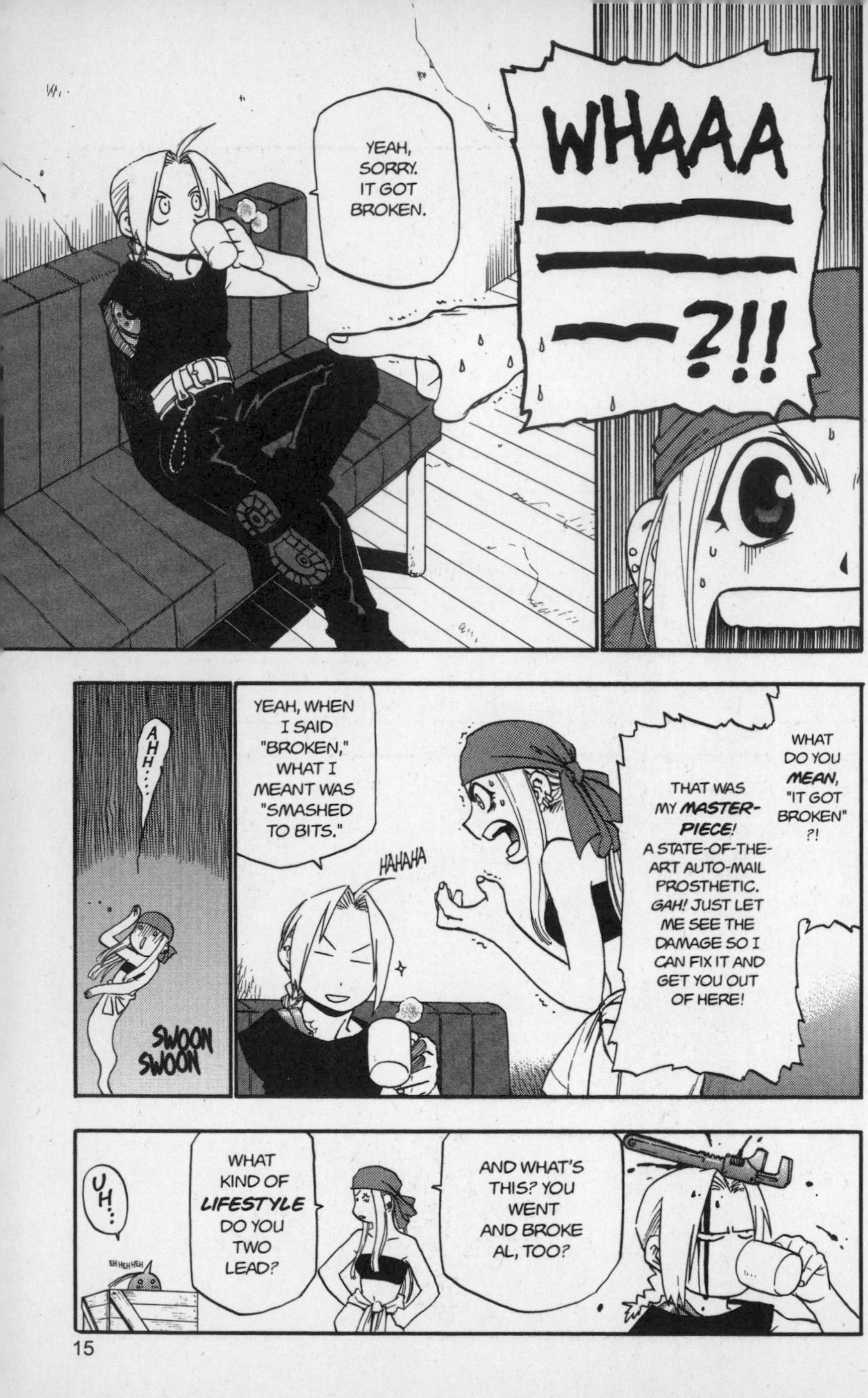
WHAAAA———?!!
YEAH, SORRY. IT GOT BROKEN.
WHAT DO YOU *MEAN*, "IT GOT BROKEN" ?!
THAT WAS MY ***MASTERPIECE***! A STATE-OF-THE-ART AUTO-MAIL PROSTHETIC. *GAH!* JUST LET ME SEE THE DAMAGE SO I CAN FIX IT AND GET YOU OUT OF HERE!
YEAH, WHEN I SAID "BROKEN," WHAT I MEANT WAS "SMASHED TO BITS."
HAHAHA
AHH...
SWOON SWOON
AND WHAT'S THIS? YOU WENT AND BROKE AL, TOO?
WHAT KIND OF ***LIFESTYLE*** DO YOU TWO LEAD?
EH HEH HEH
UH...

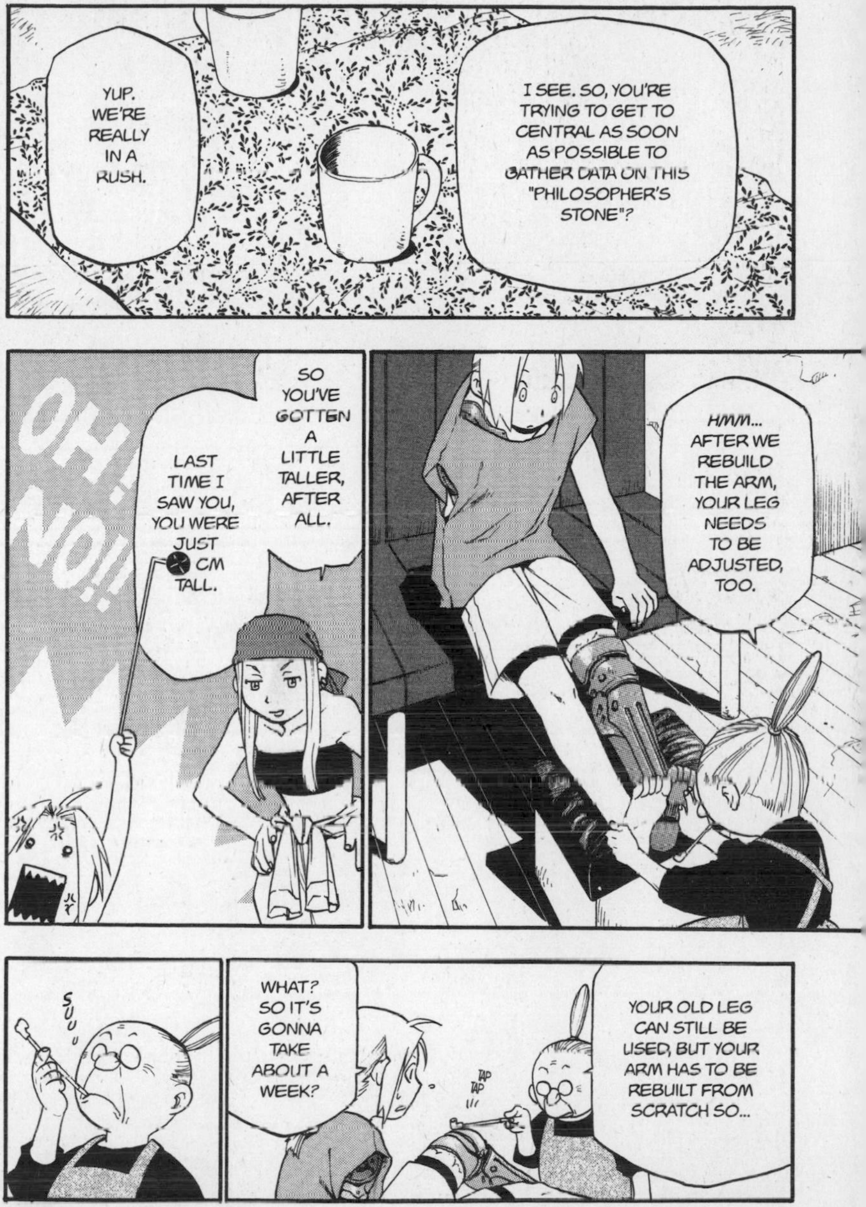
I SEE. SO, YOU'RE TRYING TO GET TO CENTRAL AS SOON AS POSSIBLE TO GATHER DATA ON THIS "PHILOSOPHER'S STONE"?
YUP. WE'RE REALLY IN A RUSH.
HMM... AFTER WE REBUILD THE ARM, YOUR LEG NEEDS TO BE ADJUSTED, TOO.
SO YOU'VE GOTTEN A LITTLE TALLER, AFTER ALL.
LAST TIME I SAW YOU, YOU WERE JUST CM TALL.
OH!! NO!!
YOUR OLD LEG CAN STILL BE USED, BUT YOUR ARM HAS TO BE REBUILT FROM SCRATCH SO...
TAP TAP
WHAT? SO IT'S GONNA TAKE ABOUT A WEEK?
SUUU

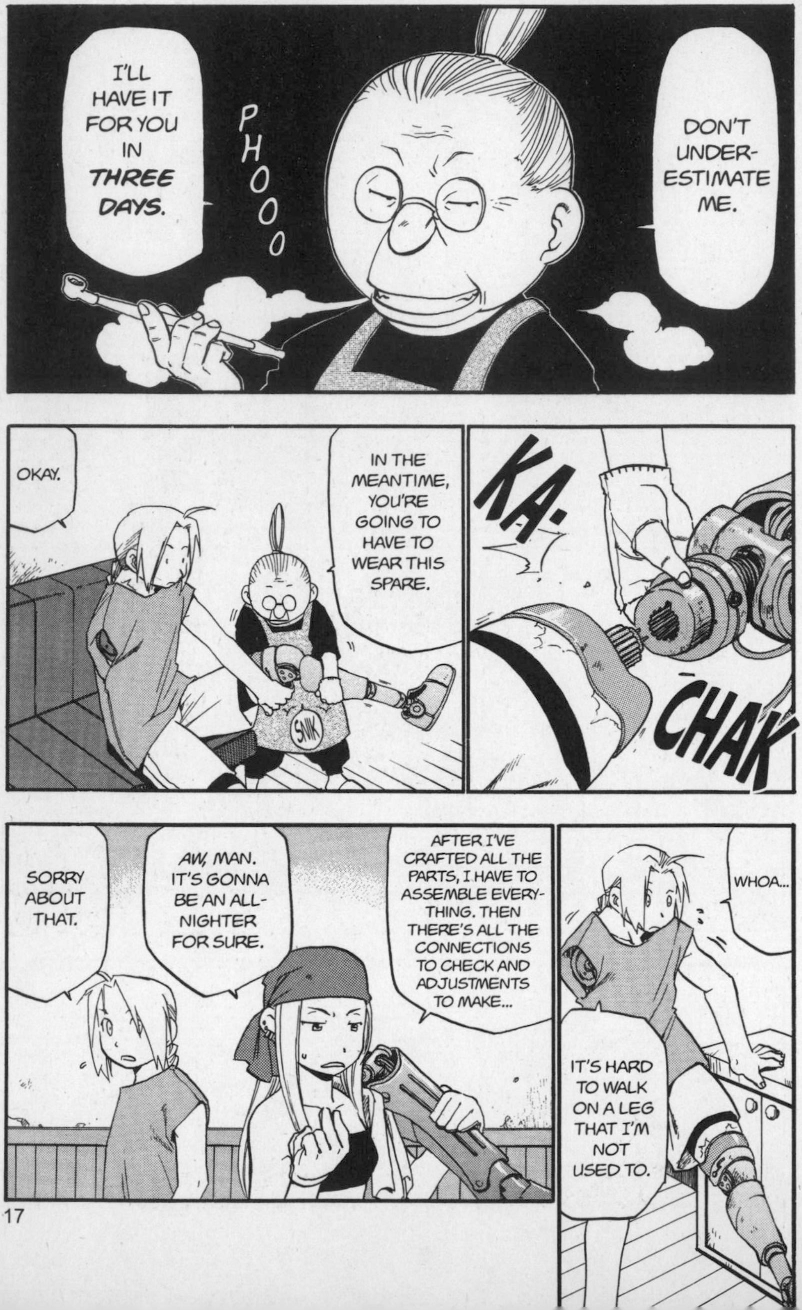
DON'T UNDER-ESTIMATE ME.
PHOOOO
I'LL HAVE IT FOR YOU IN *THREE DAYS.*
KA-
CHAK
IN THE MEANTIME, YOU'RE GOING TO HAVE TO WEAR THIS SPARE.
SNIK
OKAY.
WHOA...
IT'S HARD TO WALK ON A LEG THAT I'M NOT USED TO.
AFTER I'VE CRAFTED ALL THE PARTS, I HAVE TO ASSEMBLE EVERYTHING. THEN THERE'S ALL THE CONNECTIONS TO CHECK AND ADJUSTMENTS TO MAKE...
AW, MAN. IT'S GONNA BE AN ALL-NIGHTER FOR SURE.
SORRY ABOUT THAT.

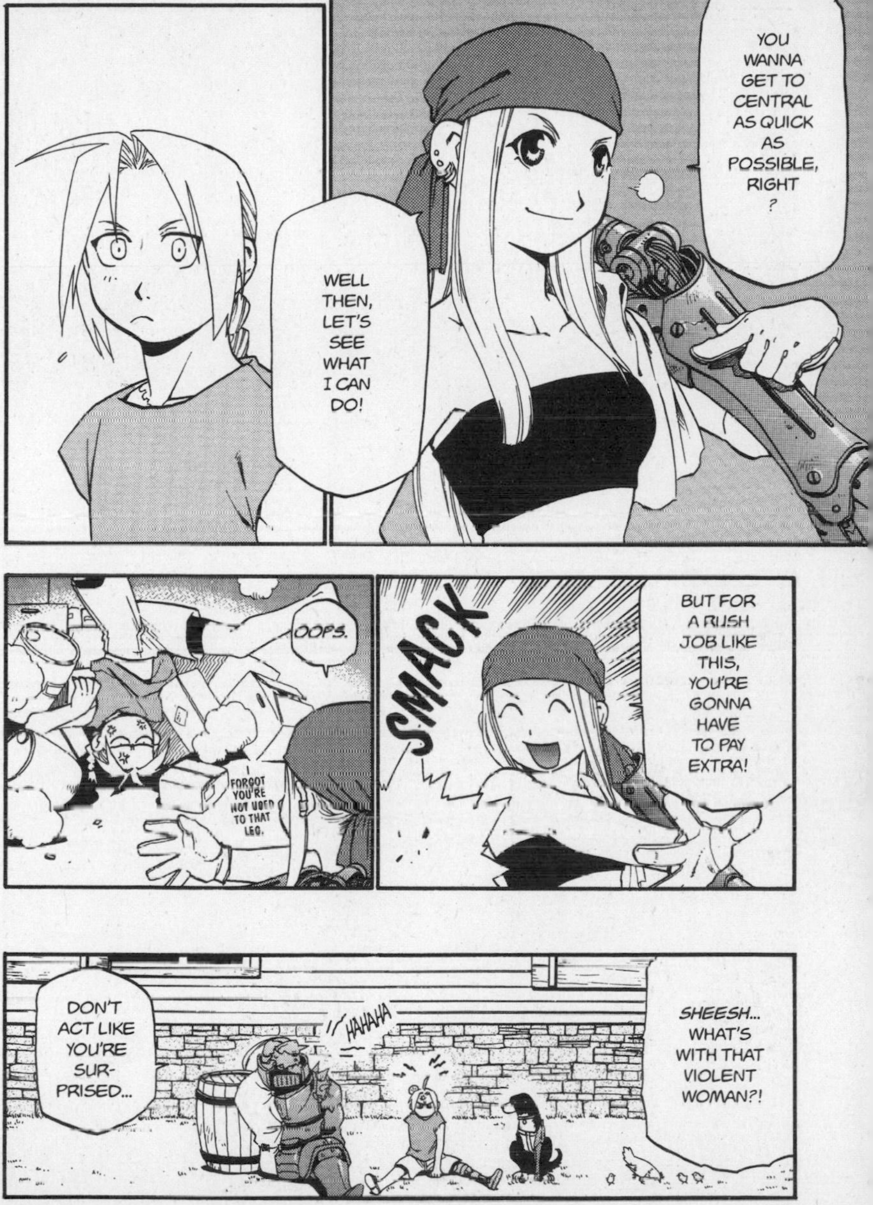
YOU WANNA GET TO CENTRAL AS QUICK AS POSSIBLE, RIGHT?
WELL THEN, LET'S SEE WHAT I CAN DO!
BUT FOR A RUSH JOB LIKE THIS, YOU'RE GONNA HAVE TO PAY EXTRA!
SMACK
OOPS.
I FORGOT YOU'RE NOT USED TO THAT LEG.
SHEESH... WHAT'S WITH THAT VIOLENT WOMAN?!
HAHAHA
DON'T ACT LIKE YOU'RE SURPRISED...

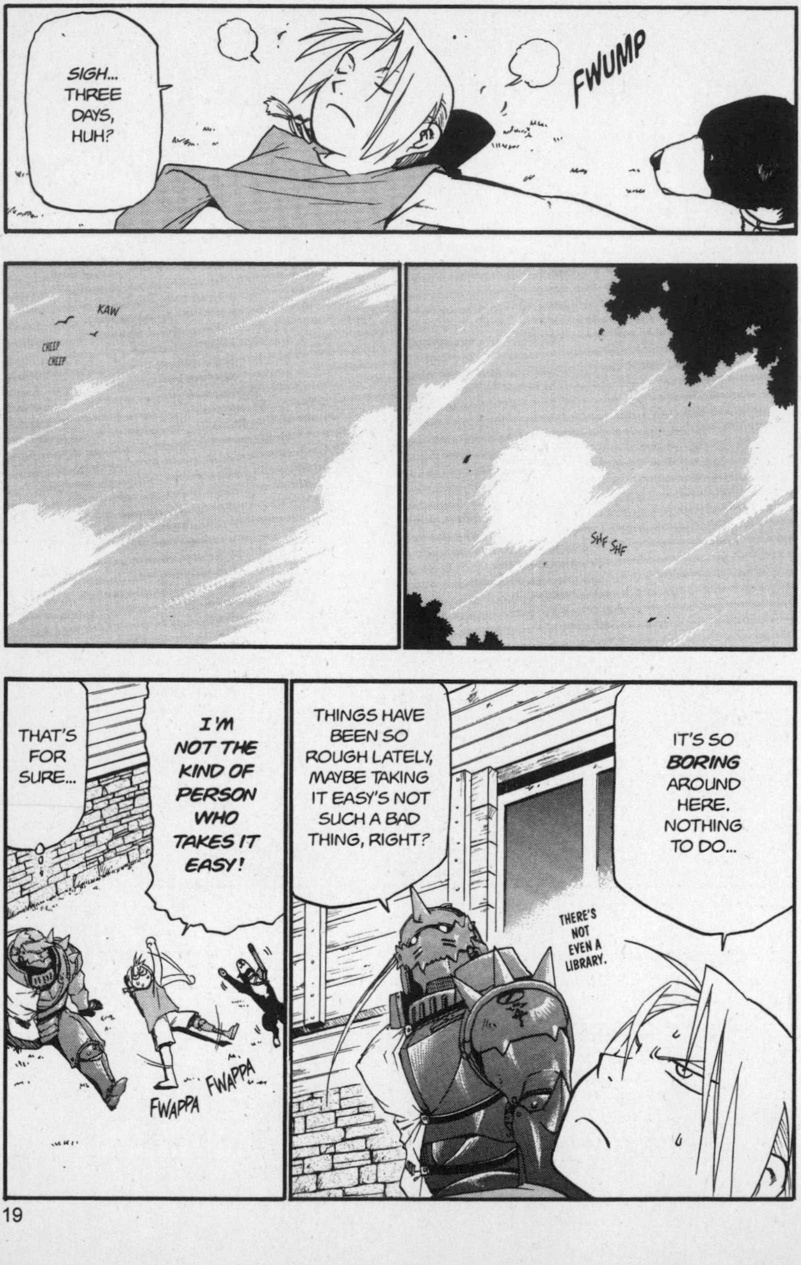
FWUMP
SIGH... THREE DAYS, HUH?
SHF SHF
KAW
CHEEP CHEEP
IT'S SO **BORING** AROUND HERE. NOTHING TO DO...
THINGS HAVE BEEN SO ROUGH LATELY, MAYBE TAKING IT EASY'S NOT SUCH A BAD THING, RIGHT?
THERE'S NOT EVEN A LIBRARY.
I'M NOT THE KIND OF PERSON WHO TAKES IT EASY!
THAT'S FOR SURE...
FWAPPA
FWAPPA

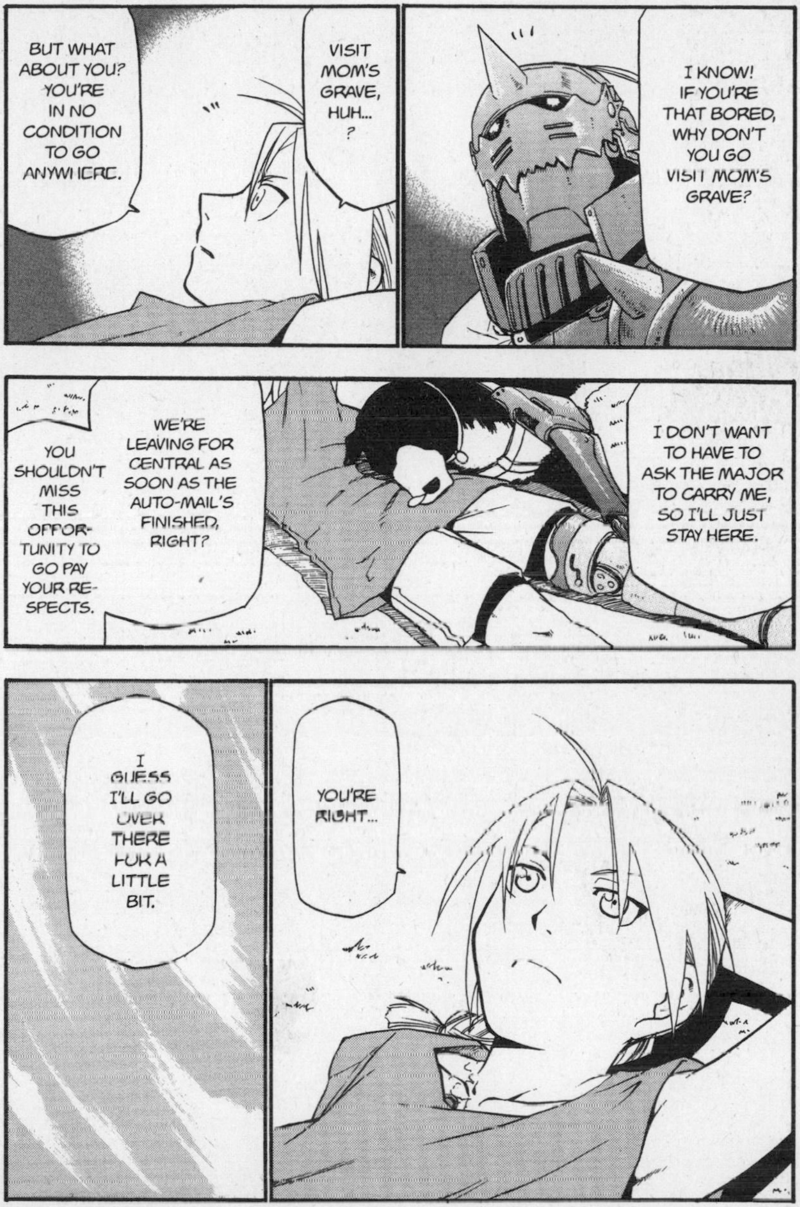
I KNOW! IF YOU'RE THAT BORED, WHY DON'T YOU GO VISIT MOM'S GRAVE?
VISIT MOM'S GRAVE, HUH... ?
BUT WHAT ABOUT YOU? YOU'RE IN NO CONDITION TO GO ANYWHERE.
I DON'T WANT TO HAVE TO ASK THE MAJOR TO CARRY ME, SO I'LL JUST STAY HERE.
WE'RE LEAVING FOR CENTRAL AS SOON AS THE AUTO-MAIL'S FINISHED, RIGHT?
YOU SHOULDN'T MISS THIS OPPOR-TUNITY TO GO PAY YOUR RE-SPECTS.
YOU'RE RIGHT...
I GUESS I'LL GO OVER THERE FOR A LITTLE BIT.

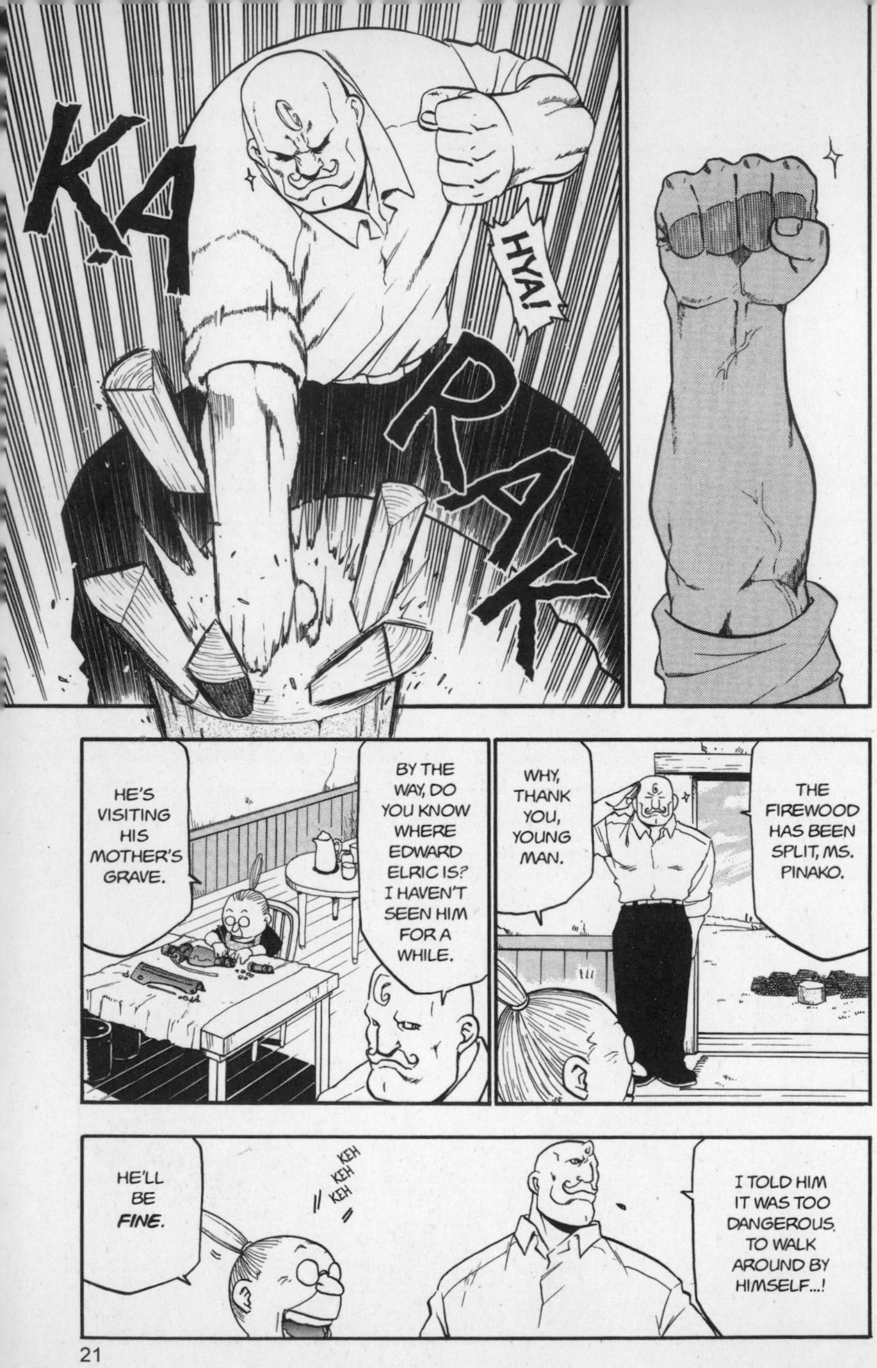
HYA!
KA
RAK
THE FIREWOOD HAS BEEN SPLIT, MS. PINAKO.
WHY, THANK YOU, YOUNG MAN.
BY THE WAY, DO YOU KNOW WHERE EDWARD ELRIC IS? I HAVEN'T SEEN HIM FOR A WHILE.
HE'S VISITING HIS MOTHER'S GRAVE.
I TOLD HIM IT WAS TOO DANGEROUS. TO WALK AROUND BY HIMSELF...!
KEH KEH KEH
HE'LL BE *FINE*.

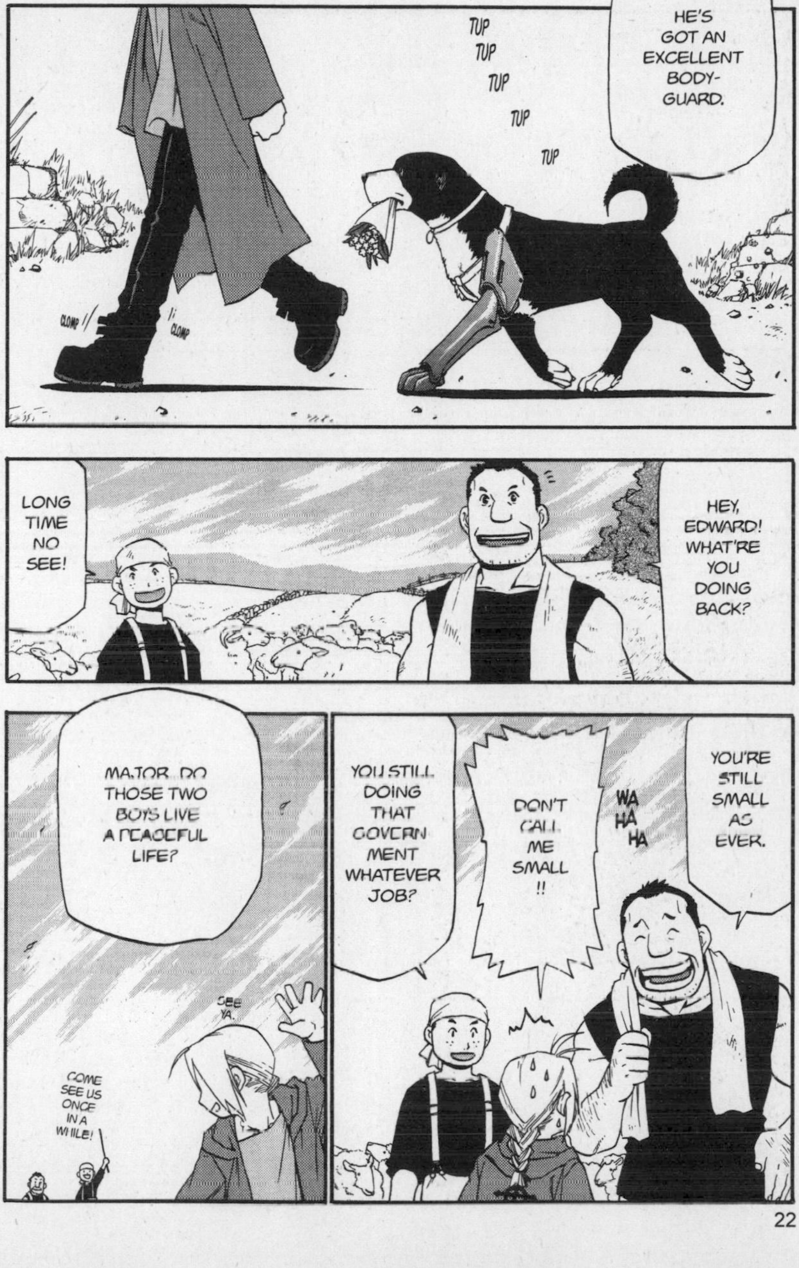
HE'S GOT AN EXCELLENT BODY-GUARD.
TUP TUP TUP TUP TUP
CLOMP
CLOMP
HEY, EDWARD! WHAT'RE YOU DOING BACK?
LONG TIME NO SEE!
YOU'RE STILL SMALL AS EVER.
WA HA HA
DON'T CALL ME SMALL!!
YOU STILL DOING THAT GOVERNMENT WHATEVER JOB?
MAJOR, DO THOSE TWO BOYS LIVE A PEACEFUL LIFE?
SEE YA.
COME SEE US ONCE IN A WHILE!

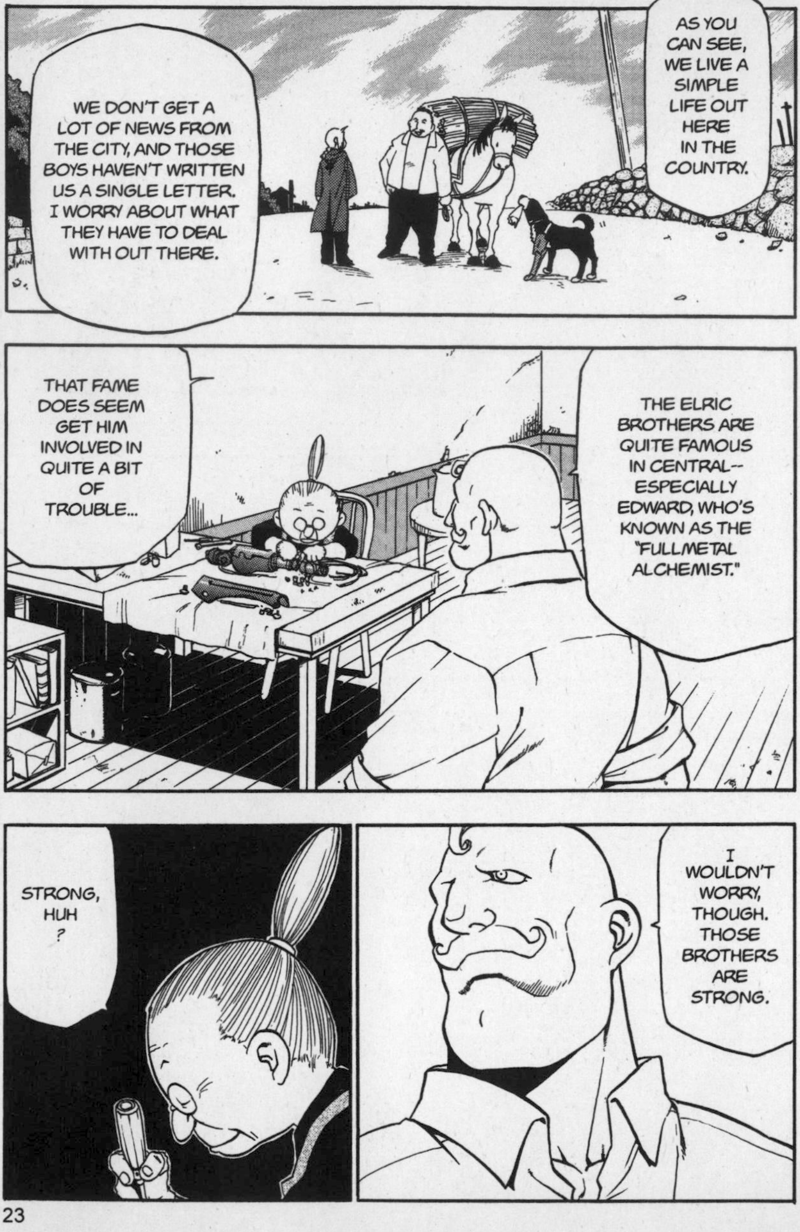
AS YOU CAN SEE, WE LIVE A SIMPLE LIFE OUT HERE IN THE COUNTRY.
WE DON'T GET A LOT OF NEWS FROM THE CITY, AND THOSE BOYS HAVEN'T WRITTEN US A SINGLE LETTER. I WORRY ABOUT WHAT THEY HAVE TO DEAL WITH OUT THERE.
THE ELRIC BROTHERS ARE QUITE FAMOUS IN CENTRAL-- ESPECIALLY EDWARD, WHO'S KNOWN AS THE "FULLMETAL ALCHEMIST."
THAT FAME DOES SEEM GET HIM INVOLVED IN QUITE A BIT OF TROUBLE...
I WOULDN'T WORRY, THOUGH. THOSE BROTHERS ARE STRONG.
STRONG, HUH?

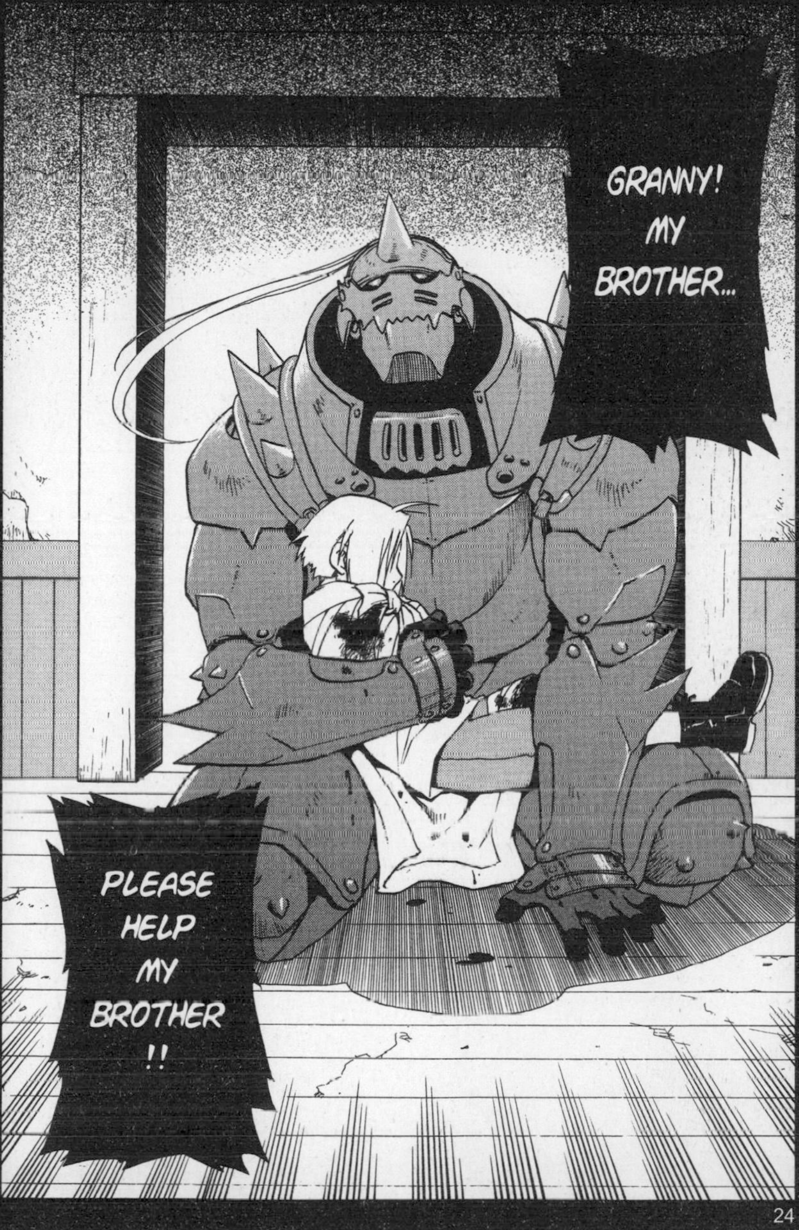
GRANNY! MY BROTHER...
PLEASE HELP MY BROTHER !!

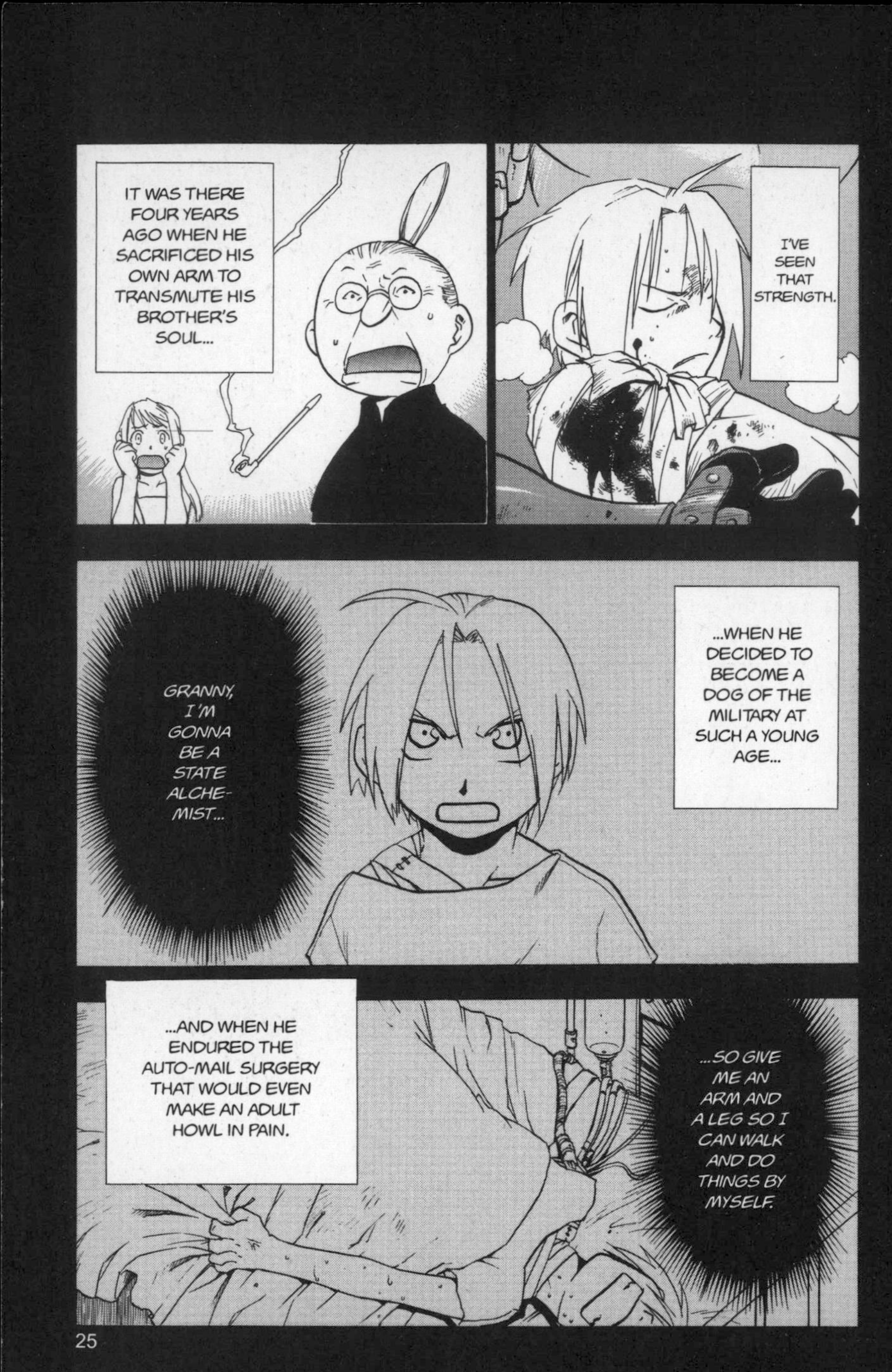
I'VE SEEN THAT STRENGTH.
IT WAS THERE FOUR YEARS AGO WHEN HE SACRIFICED HIS OWN ARM TO TRANSMUTE HIS BROTHER'S SOUL...
...WHEN HE DECIDED TO BECOME A DOG OF THE MILITARY AT SUCH A YOUNG AGE...
GRANNY, I'M GONNA BE A STATE ALCHE-MIST...
...SO GIVE ME AN ARM AND A LEG SO I CAN WALK AND DO THINGS BY MYSELF.
...AND WHEN HE ENDURED THE AUTO-MAIL SURGERY THAT WOULD EVEN MAKE AN ADULT HOWL IN PAIN.

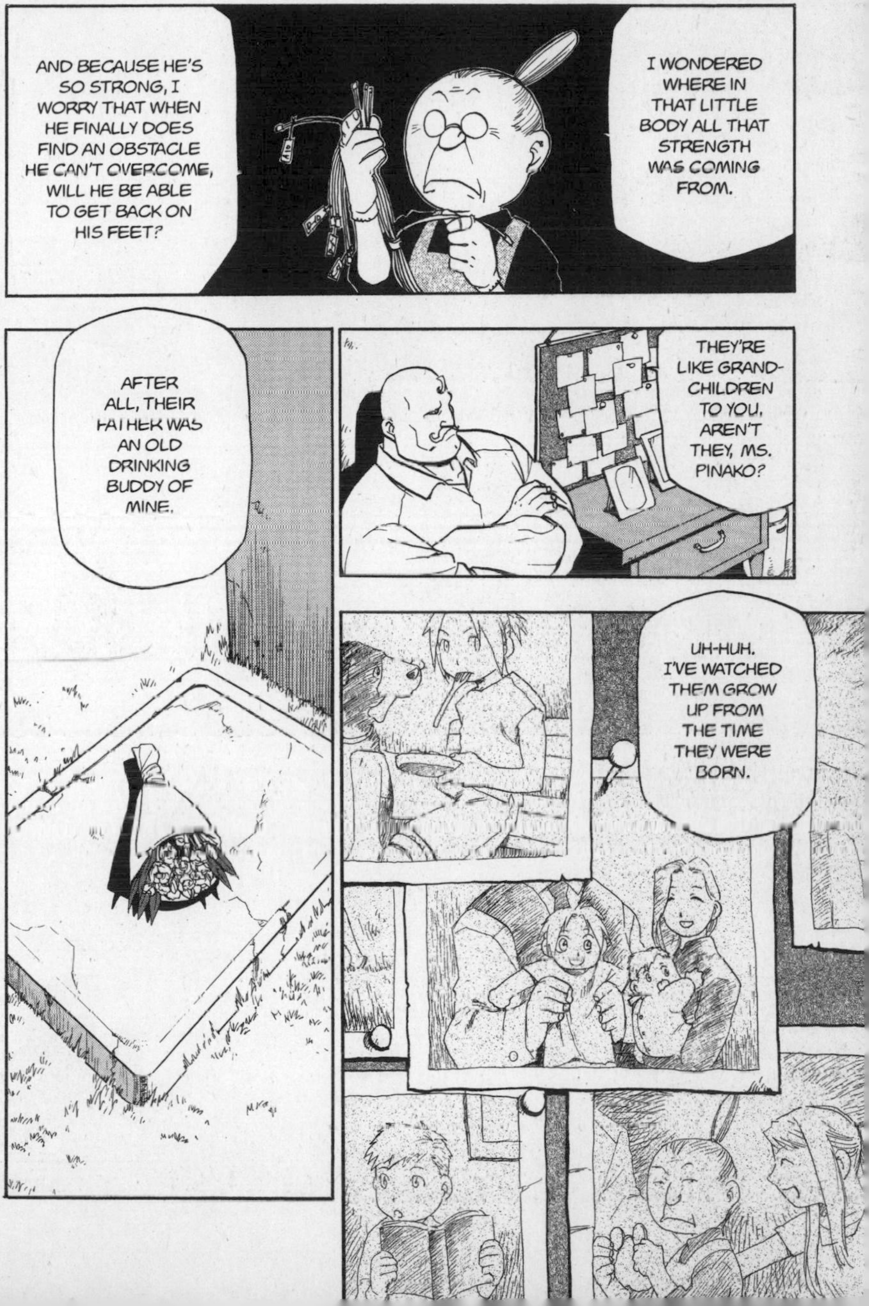
I WONDERED WHERE IN THAT LITTLE BODY ALL THAT STRENGTH WAS COMING FROM.
AND BECAUSE HE'S SO STRONG, I WORRY THAT WHEN HE FINALLY DOES FIND AN OBSTACLE HE CAN'T OVERCOME, WILL HE BE ABLE TO GET BACK ON HIS FEET?
THEY'RE LIKE GRAND-CHILDREN TO YOU, AREN'T THEY, MS. PINAKO?
UH-HUH. I'VE WATCHED THEM GROW UP FROM THE TIME THEY WERE BORN.
AFTER ALL, THEIR FATHER WAS AN OLD DRINKING BUDDY OF MINE.

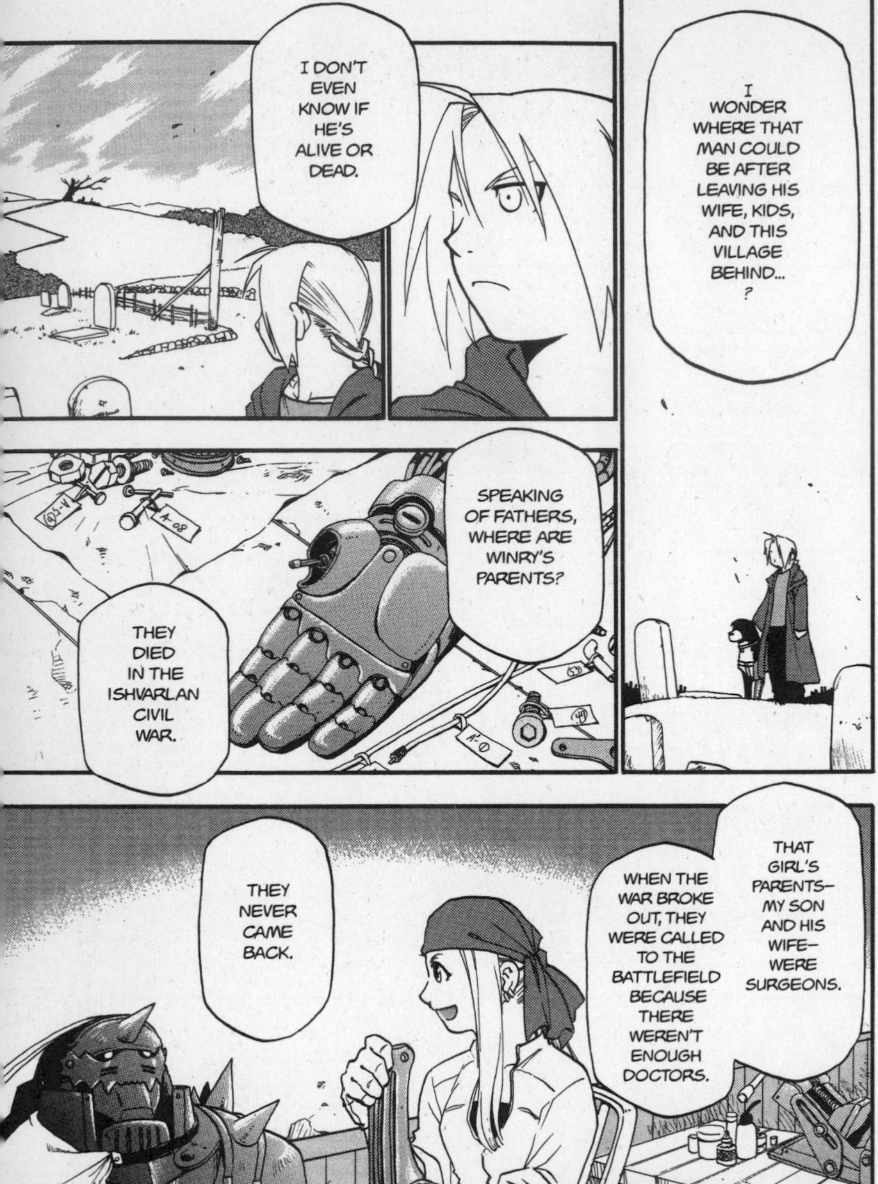
I WONDER WHERE THAT MAN COULD BE AFTER LEAVING HIS WIFE, KIDS, AND THIS VILLAGE BEHIND...?
I DON'T EVEN KNOW IF HE'S ALIVE OR DEAD.
SPEAKING OF FATHERS, WHERE ARE WINRY'S PARENTS?
THEY DIED IN THE ISHVARLAN CIVIL WAR.
THAT GIRL'S PARENTS— MY SON AND HIS WIFE— WERE SURGEONS.
WHEN THE WAR BROKE OUT, THEY WERE CALLED TO THE BATTLEFIELD BECAUSE THERE WEREN'T ENOUGH DOCTORS.
THEY NEVER CAME BACK.

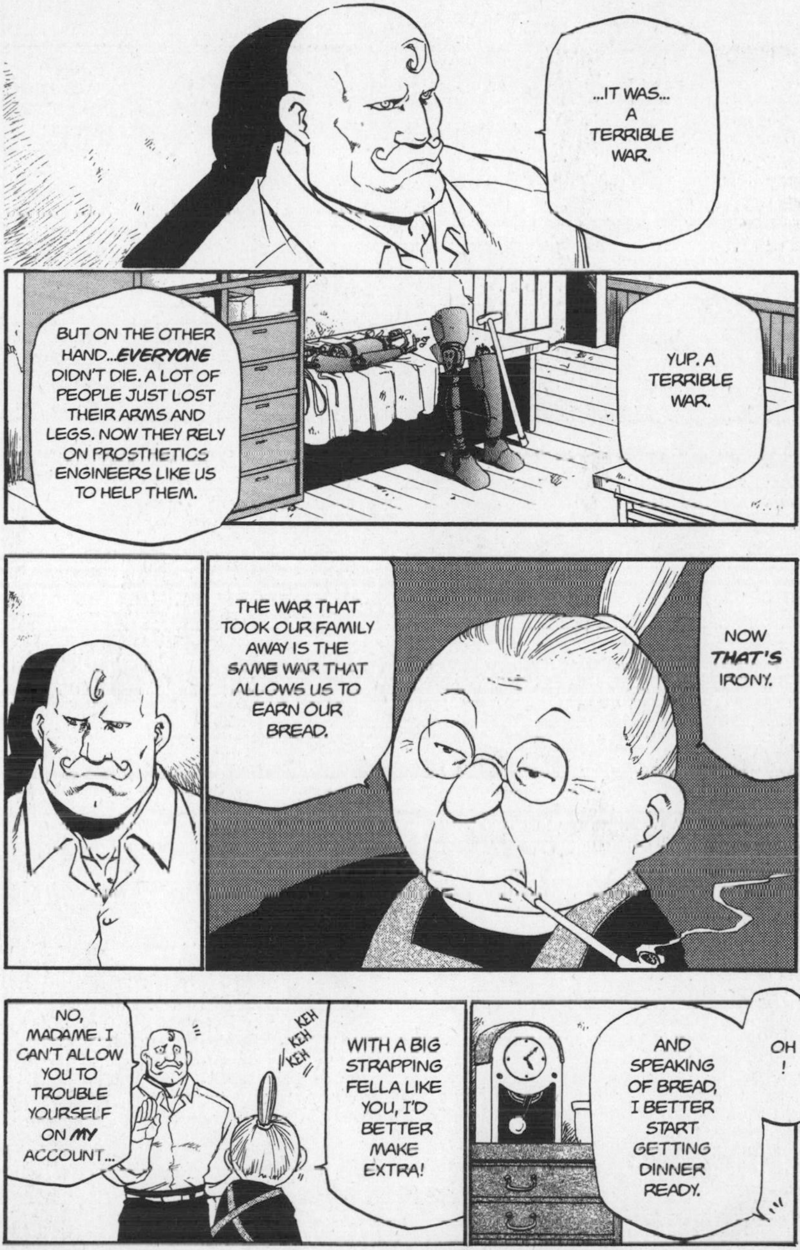

...IT WAS... A TERRIBLE WAR.
YUP. A TERRIBLE WAR.
BUT ON THE OTHER HAND... *EVERYONE* DIDN'T DIE. A LOT OF PEOPLE JUST LOST THEIR ARMS AND LEGS. NOW THEY RELY ON PROSTHETICS ENGINEERS LIKE US TO HELP THEM.
THE WAR THAT TOOK OUR FAMILY AWAY IS THE SAME WAR THAT ALLOWS US TO EARN OUR BREAD.
NOW *THAT'S* IRONY.
OH!
AND SPEAKING OF BREAD, I BETTER START GETTING DINNER READY.
WITH A BIG STRAPPING FELLA LIKE YOU, I'D BETTER MAKE EXTRA!
KEH KEH KEH
NO, MADAME. I CAN'T ALLOW YOU TO TROUBLE YOURSELF ON *MY* ACCOUNT...

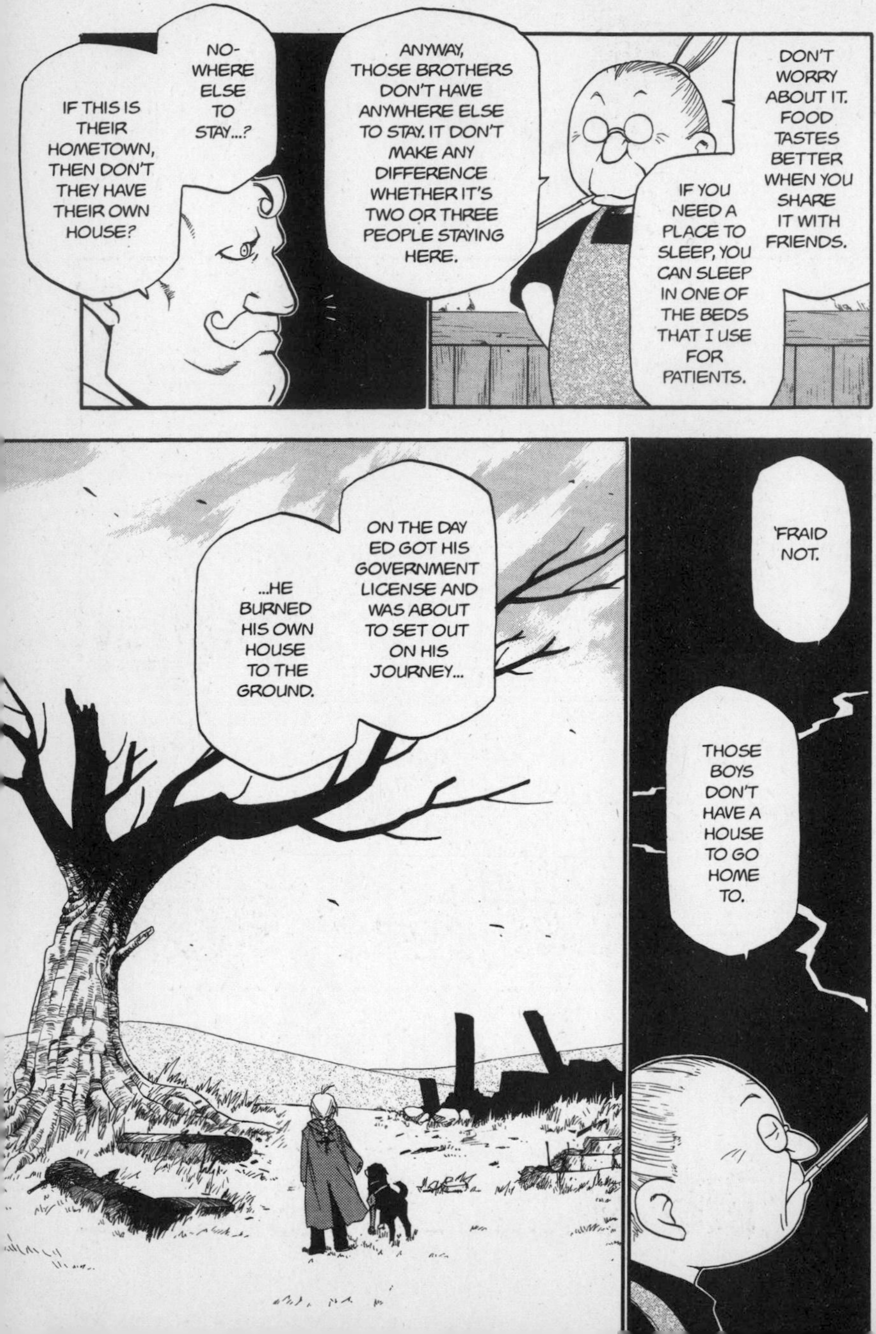
DON'T WORRY ABOUT IT. FOOD TASTES BETTER WHEN YOU SHARE IT WITH FRIENDS.
IF YOU NEED A PLACE TO SLEEP, YOU CAN SLEEP IN ONE OF THE BEDS THAT I USE FOR PATIENTS.
ANYWAY, THOSE BROTHERS DON'T HAVE ANYWHERE ELSE TO STAY. IT DON'T MAKE ANY DIFFERENCE WHETHER IT'S TWO OR THREE PEOPLE STAYING HERE.
NO-WHERE ELSE TO STAY...?
IF THIS IS THEIR HOMETOWN, THEN DON'T THEY HAVE THEIR OWN HOUSE?
'FRAID NOT.
THOSE BOYS DON'T HAVE A HOUSE TO GO HOME TO.
ON THE DAY ED GOT HIS GOVERNMENT LICENSE AND WAS ABOUT TO SET OUT ON HIS JOURNEY...
...HE BURNED HIS OWN HOUSE TO THE GROUND.

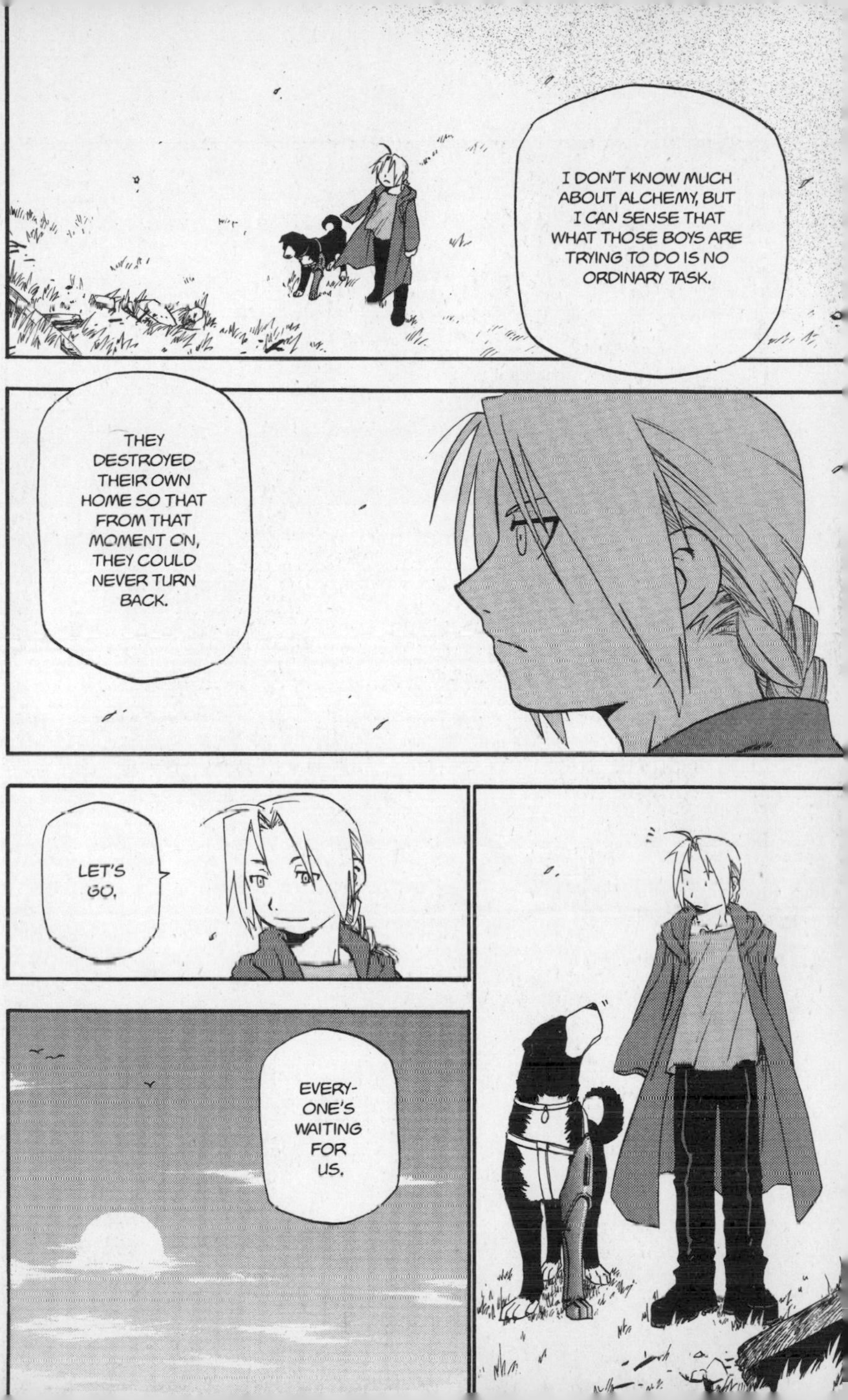
I DON'T KNOW MUCH ABOUT ALCHEMY, BUT I CAN SENSE THAT WHAT THOSE BOYS ARE TRYING TO DO IS NO ORDINARY TASK.
THEY DESTROYED THEIR OWN HOME SO THAT FROM THAT MOMENT ON, THEY COULD NEVER TURN BACK.
LET'S GO.
EVERY-ONE'S WAITING FOR US.

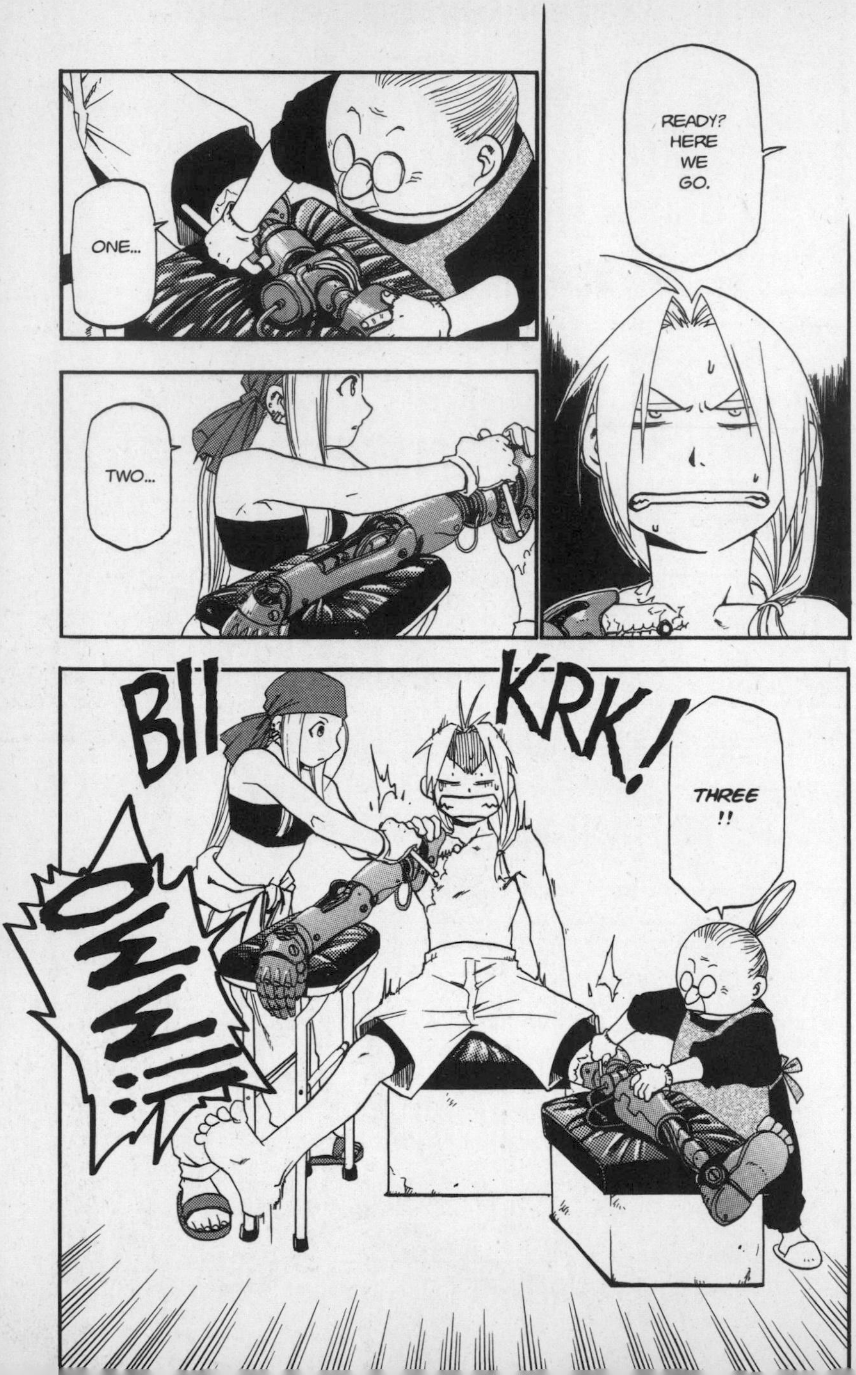
READY? HERE WE GO.
ONE...
TWO...
THREE!!
BII KRK!
OWW!!

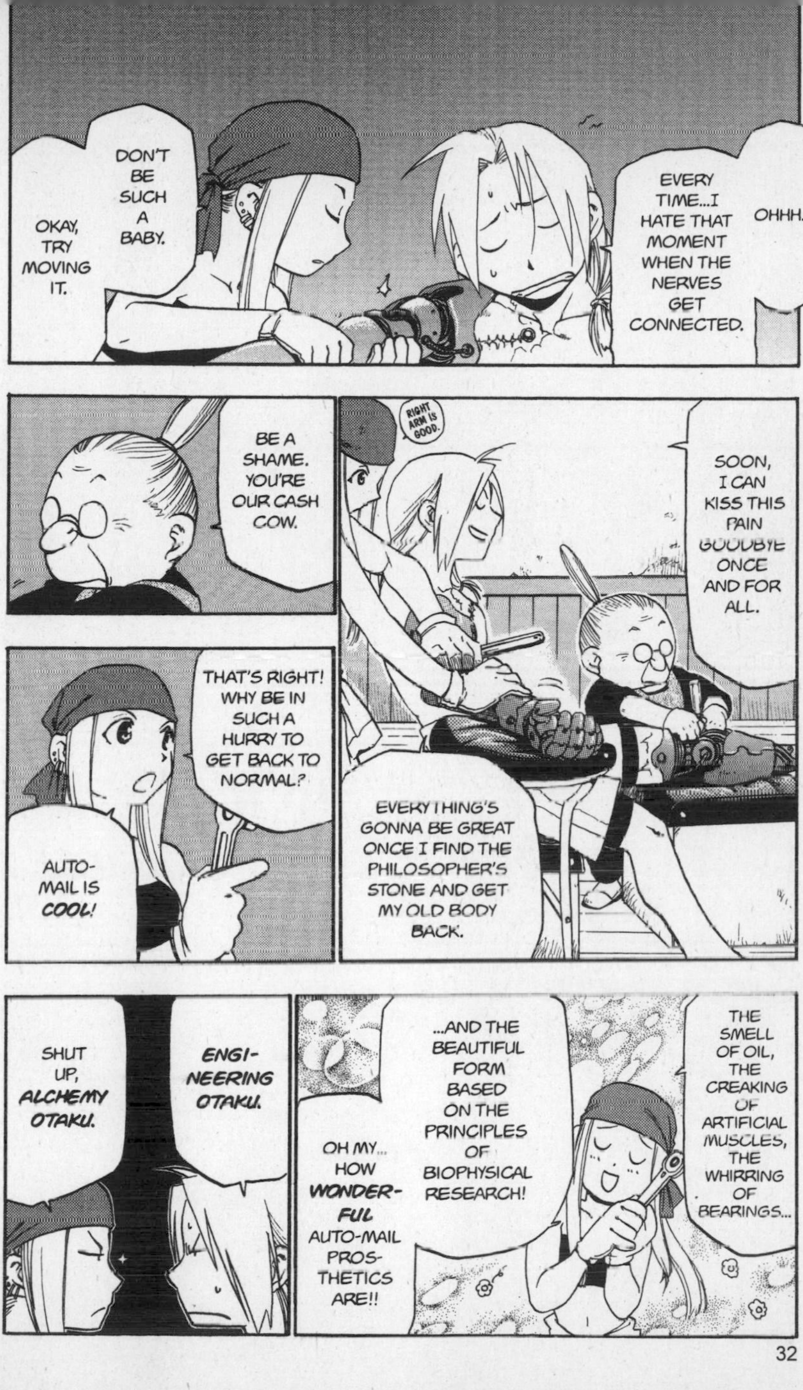

OHHH...
EVERY TIME...I HATE THAT MOMENT WHEN THE NERVES GET CONNECTED.
DON'T BE SUCH A BABY.
OKAY, TRY MOVING IT.
SOON, I CAN KISS THIS PAIN GOODBYE ONCE AND FOR ALL.
RIGHT ARM IS GOOD.
EVERYTHING'S GONNA BE GREAT ONCE I FIND THE PHILOSOPHER'S STONE AND GET MY OLD BODY BACK.
BE A SHAME. YOU'RE OUR CASH COW.
THAT'S RIGHT! WHY BE IN SUCH A HURRY TO GET BACK TO NORMAL?
AUTO-MAIL IS COOL!
THE SMELL OF OIL, THE CREAKING OF ARTIFICIAL MUSCLES, THE WHIRRING OF BEARINGS...
...AND THE BEAUTIFUL FORM BASED ON THE PRINCIPLES OF BIOPHYSICAL RESEARCH!
OH MY... HOW WONDERFUL AUTO-MAIL PROSTHETICS ARE!!
ENGINEERING OTAKU.
SHUT UP, ALCHEMY OTAKU.

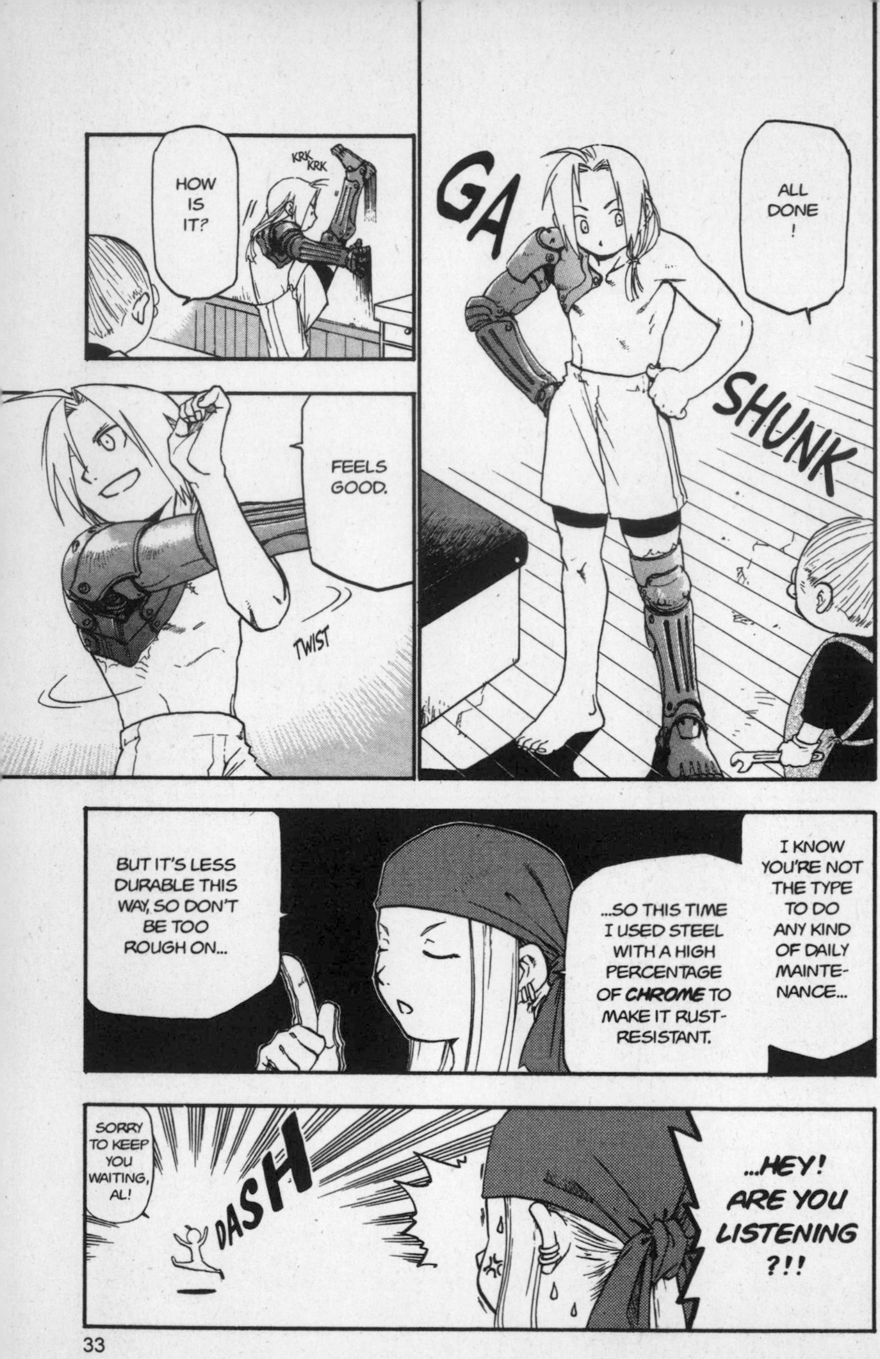
ALL DONE!
GA
SHUNK
HOW IS IT?
KRK KRK
FEELS GOOD.
TWIST
I KNOW YOU'RE NOT THE TYPE TO DO ANY KIND OF DAILY MAINTE-NANCE...
...SO THIS TIME I USED STEEL WITH A HIGH PERCENTAGE OF CHROME TO MAKE IT RUST-RESISTANT.
BUT IT'S LESS DURABLE THIS WAY, SO DON'T BE TOO ROUGH ON...
...HEY! ARE YOU LISTENING?!!
DASH
SORRY TO KEEP YOU WAITING, AL!

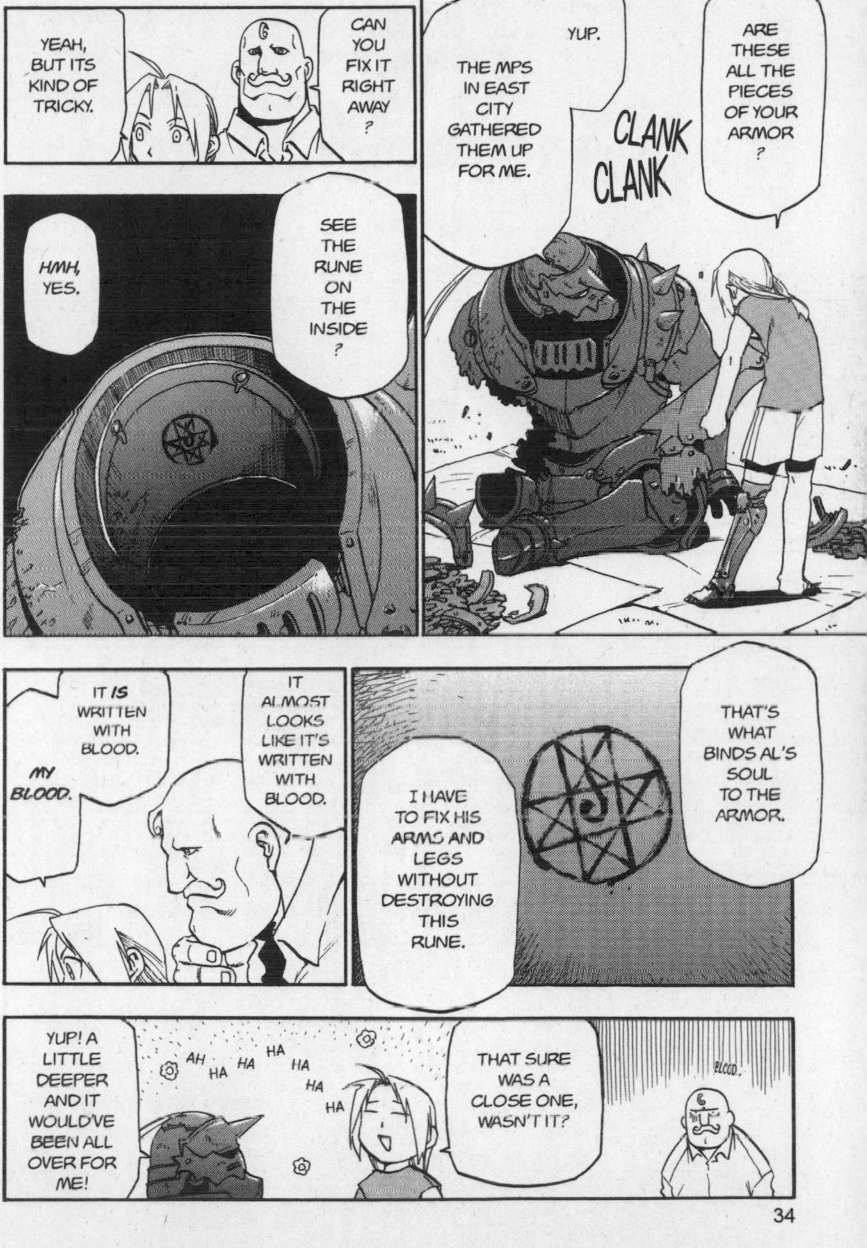
ARE THESE ALL THE PIECES OF YOUR ARMOR?
CLANK CLANK
YUP.
THE MPS IN EAST CITY GATHERED THEM UP FOR ME.
CAN YOU FIX IT RIGHT AWAY?
YEAH, BUT ITS KIND OF TRICKY.
SEE THE RUNE ON THE INSIDE?
HMH, YES.
THAT'S WHAT BINDS AL'S SOUL TO THE ARMOR.
I HAVE TO FIX HIS ARMS AND LEGS WITHOUT DESTROYING THIS RUNE.
IT ALMOST LOOKS LIKE IT'S WRITTEN WITH BLOOD.
IT *IS* WRITTEN WITH BLOOD.
MY BLOOD.
BLOOD.
THAT SURE WAS A CLOSE ONE, WASN'T IT?
AH HA HA HA HA HA HA
YUP! A LITTLE DEEPER AND IT WOULD'VE BEEN ALL OVER FOR ME!

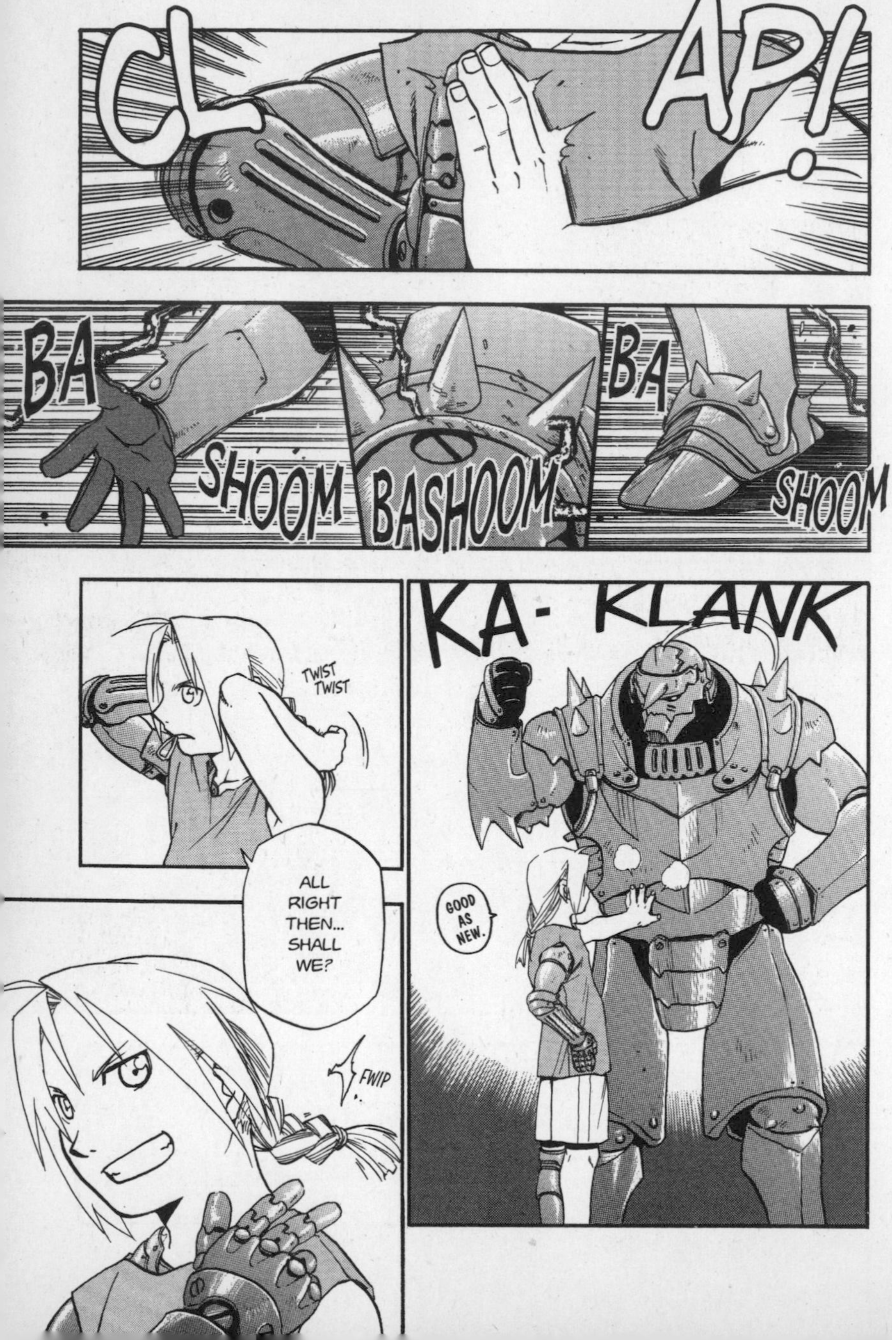
CLAP!
BA
SHOOM
BASHOOM
BA
SHOOM
KA-KLANK
GOOD AS NEW.
TWIST TWIST
ALL RIGHT THEN... SHALL WE?
FWIP

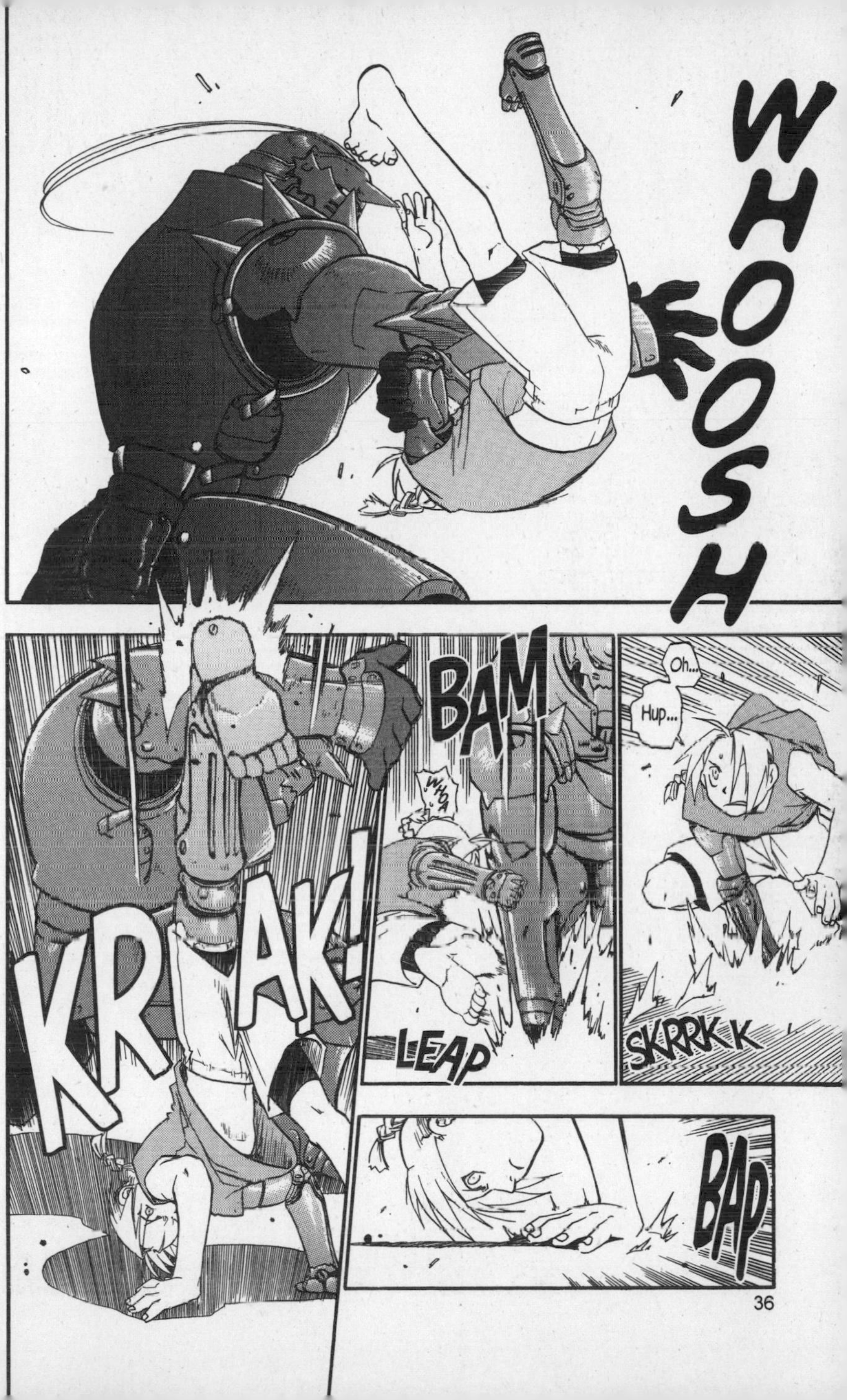
WHOOSH
Oh...
Hup...
SKRRK K
BAM
WHOA
LEAP
BAP
KRAK!

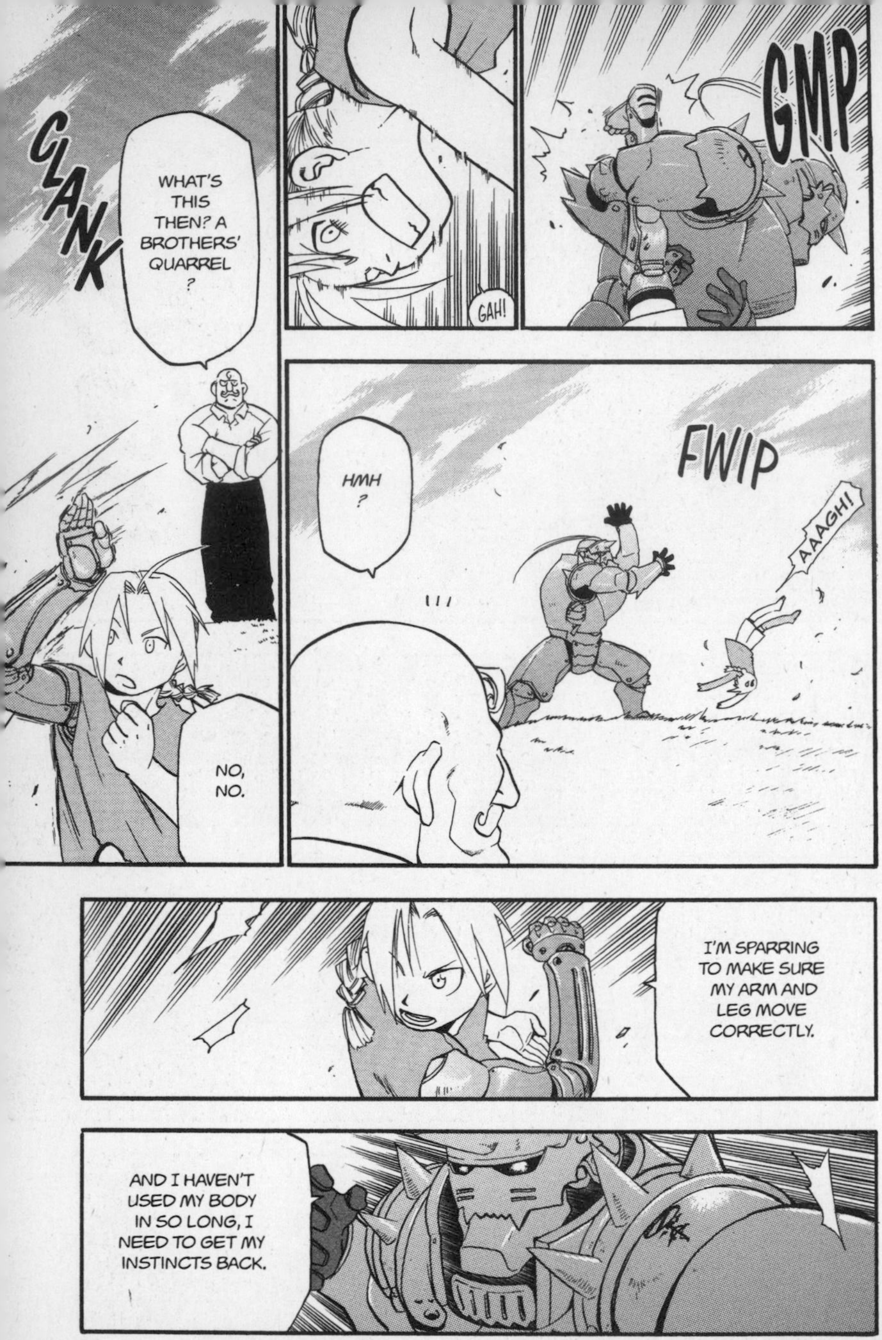
GMP
GAH!
FWIP
AAAGH!
HMH?
CLANK
WHAT'S THIS THEN? A BROTHERS' QUARREL?
NO, NO.
I'M SPARRING TO MAKE SURE MY ARM AND LEG MOVE CORRECTLY.
AND I HAVEN'T USED MY BODY IN SO LONG, I NEED TO GET MY INSTINCTS BACK.

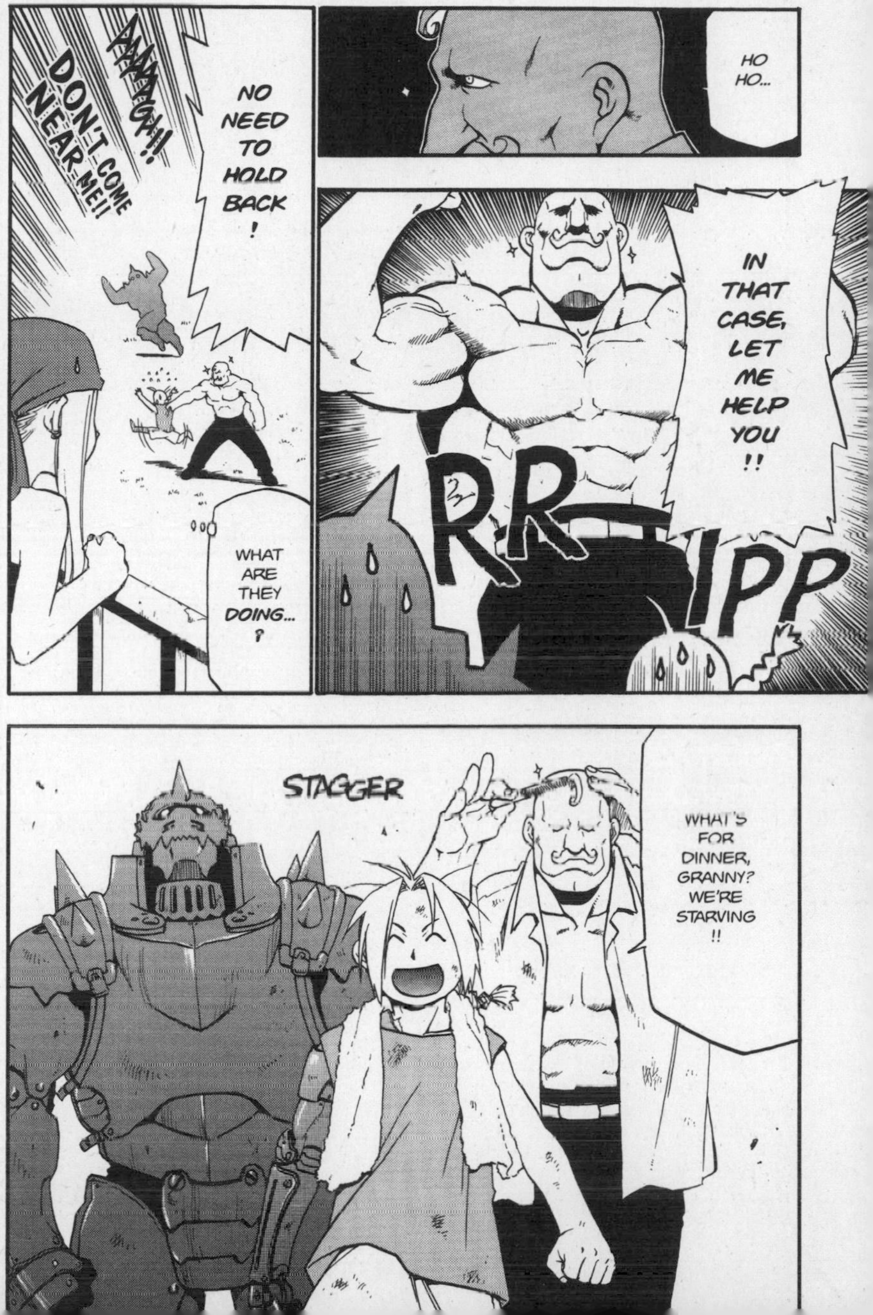
HO HO...
IN THAT CASE, LET ME HELP YOU!!
RRIPP
NO NEED TO HOLD BACK!
AAAAGH!!
DON'T COME NEAR ME!!
WHAT ARE THEY DOING...?
STAGGER
WHAT'S FOR DINNER, GRANNY? WE'RE STARVING!!

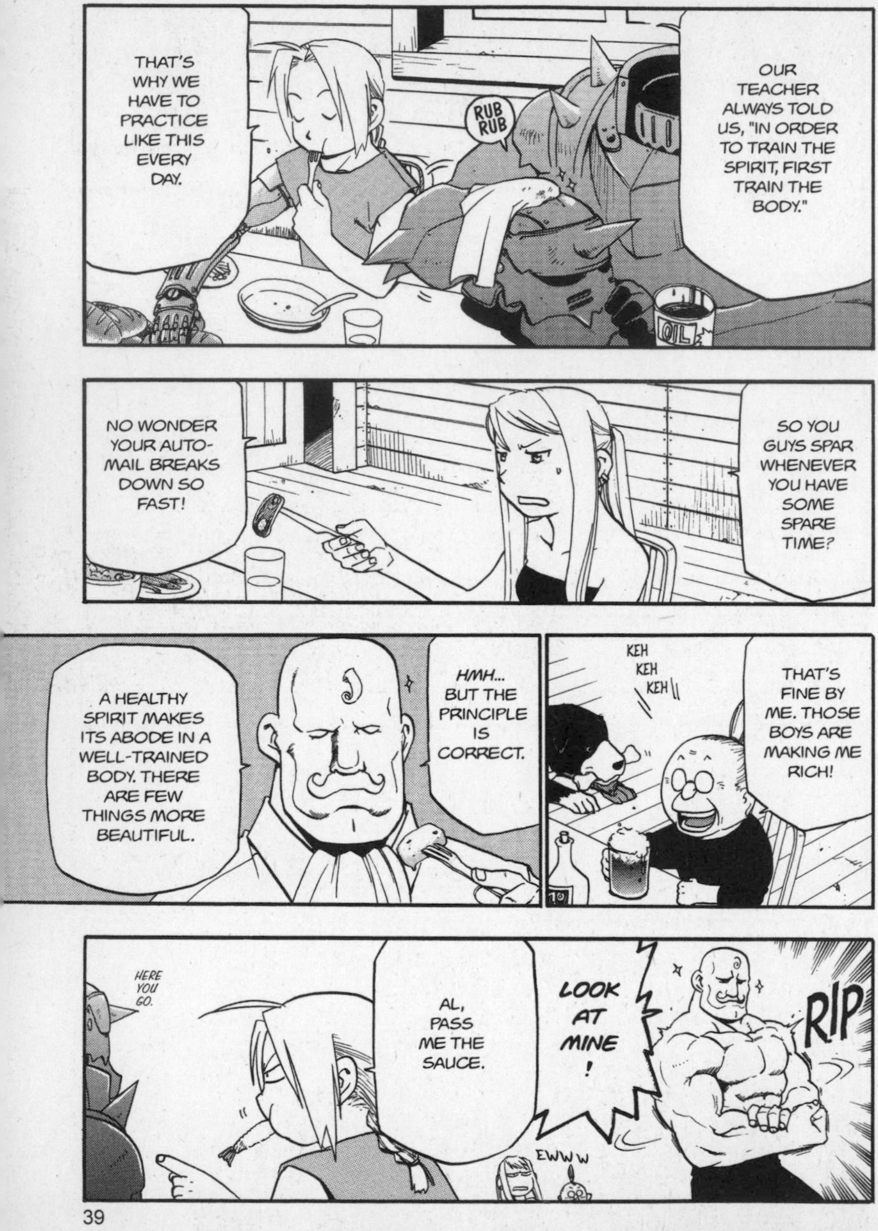
OUR TEACHER ALWAYS TOLD US, "IN ORDER TO TRAIN THE SPIRIT, FIRST TRAIN THE BODY."
RUB RUB
THAT'S WHY WE HAVE TO PRACTICE LIKE THIS EVERY DAY.
SO YOU GUYS SPAR WHENEVER YOU HAVE SOME SPARE TIME?
NO WONDER YOUR AUTO-MAIL BREAKS DOWN SO FAST!
THAT'S FINE BY ME. THOSE BOYS ARE MAKING ME RICH!
KEH KEH KEH
HMH... BUT THE PRINCIPLE IS CORRECT.
A HEALTHY SPIRIT MAKES ITS ABODE IN A WELL-TRAINED BODY. THERE ARE FEW THINGS MORE BEAUTIFUL.
RIP
LOOK AT MINE!
AL, PASS ME THE SAUCE.
EWWW
HERE YOU GO.

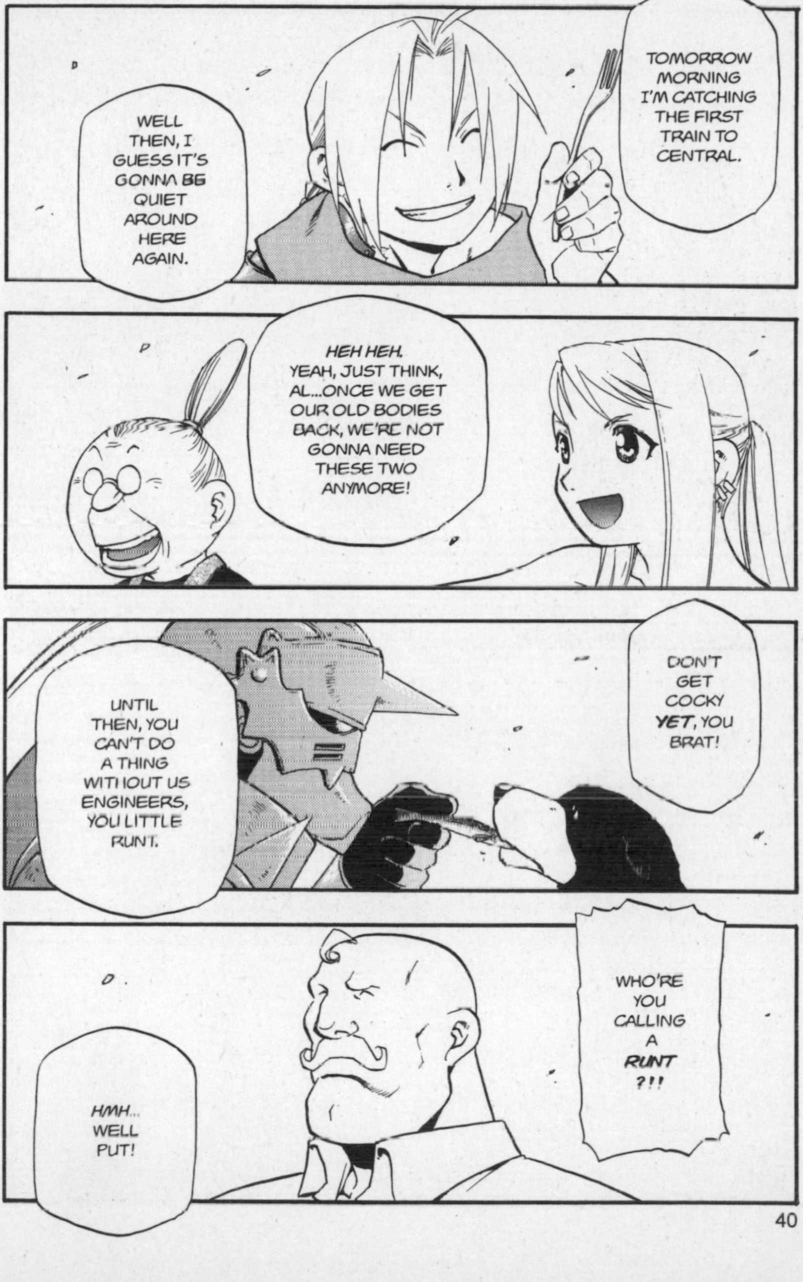
TOMORROW MORNING I'M CATCHING THE FIRST TRAIN TO CENTRAL.
WELL THEN, I GUESS IT'S GONNA BE QUIET AROUND HERE AGAIN.
HEH HEH. YEAH, JUST THINK, AL...ONCE WE GET OUR OLD BODIES BACK, WE'RE NOT GONNA NEED THESE TWO ANYMORE!
DON'T GET COCKY ***YET***, YOU BRAT!
UNTIL THEN, YOU CAN'T DO A THING WITHOUT US ENGINEERS, YOU LITTLE RUNT.
WHO'RE YOU CALLING A ***RUNT*** ?!!
HMH... WELL PUT!

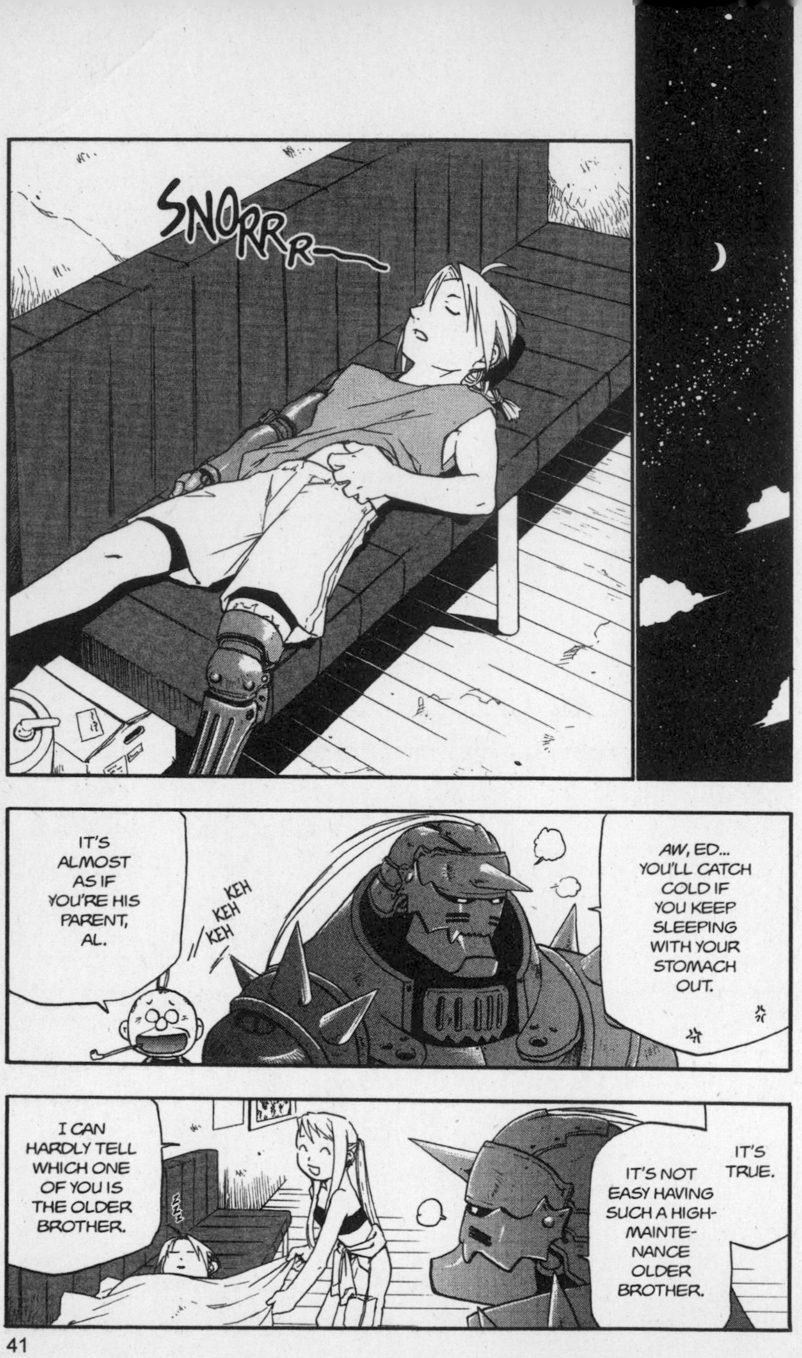
SNORRR—
AW, ED... YOU'LL CATCH COLD IF YOU KEEP SLEEPING WITH YOUR STOMACH OUT.
KEH KEH KEH
IT'S ALMOST AS IF YOU'RE HIS PARENT, AL.
IT'S TRUE.
IT'S NOT EASY HAVING SUCH A HIGH-MAINTENANCE OLDER BROTHER.
I CAN HARDLY TELL WHICH ONE OF YOU IS THE OLDER BROTHER.

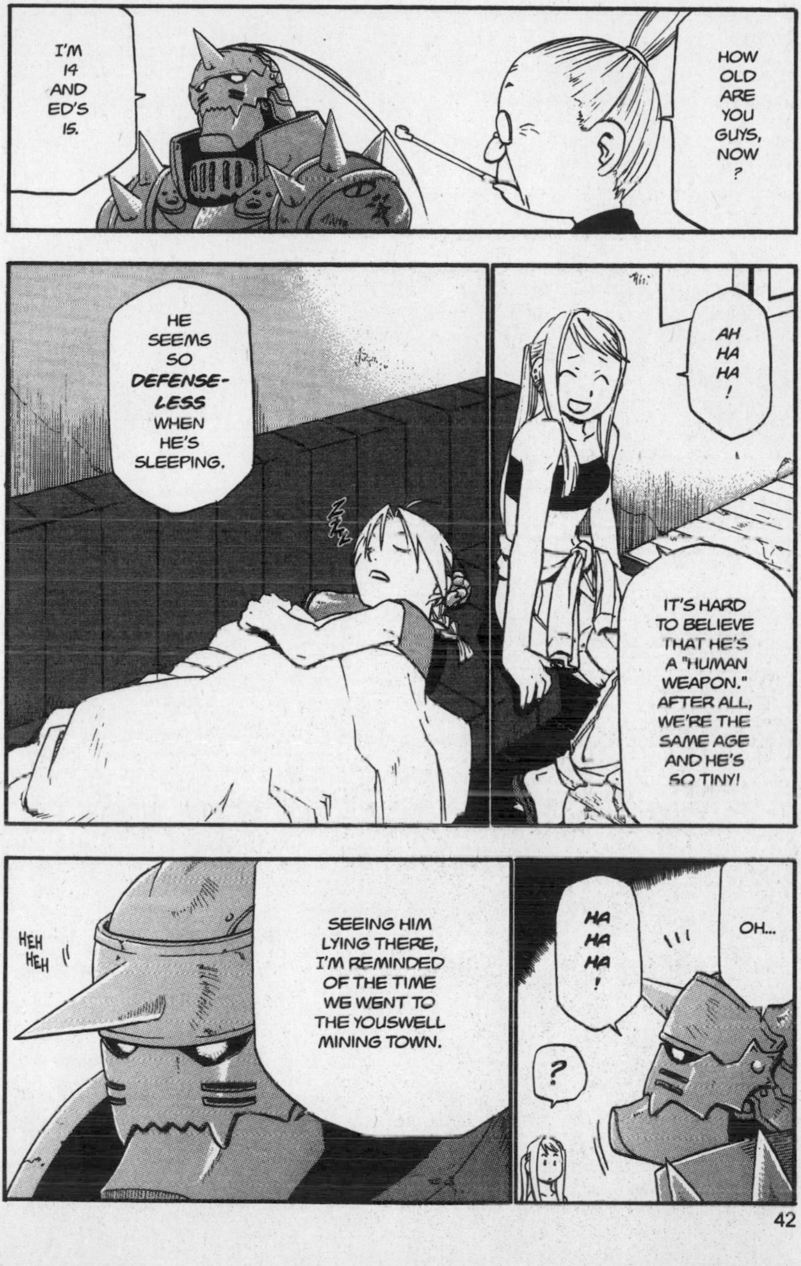
HOW OLD ARE YOU GUYS, NOW?
I'M 14 AND ED'S 15.
AH HA HA!
IT'S HARD TO BELIEVE THAT HE'S A "HUMAN WEAPON." AFTER ALL, WE'RE THE SAME AGE AND HE'S SO TINY!
HE SEEMS SO DEFENSE-LESS WHEN HE'S SLEEPING.
OH...
HA HA HA!
?
SEEING HIM LYING THERE, I'M REMINDED OF THE TIME WE WENT TO THE YOUSWELL MINING TOWN.
HEH HEH

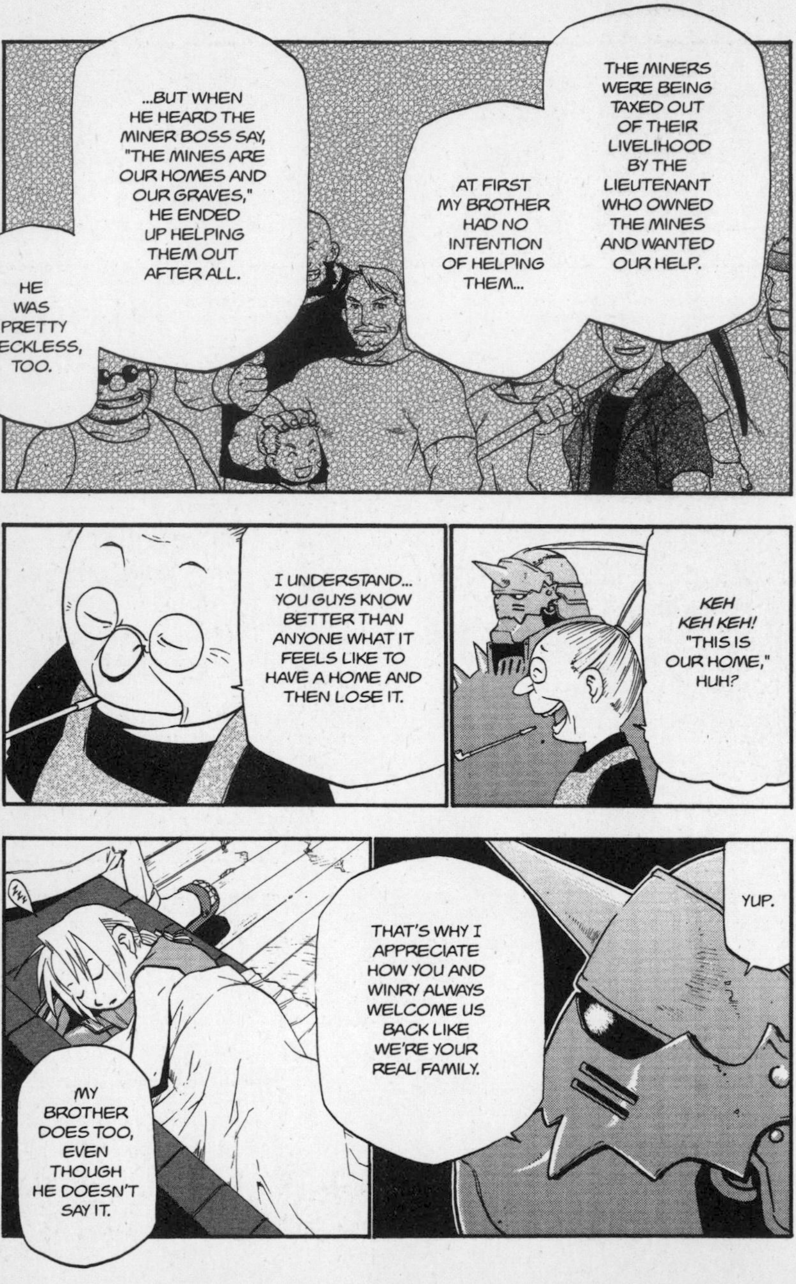
THE MINERS WERE BEING TAXED OUT OF THEIR LIVELIHOOD BY THE LIEUTENANT WHO OWNED THE MINES AND WANTED OUR HELP.
AT FIRST MY BROTHER HAD NO INTENTION OF HELPING THEM...
...BUT WHEN HE HEARD THE MINER BOSS SAY, "THE MINES ARE OUR HOMES AND OUR GRAVES," HE ENDED UP HELPING THEM OUT AFTER ALL.
HE WAS PRETTY RECKLESS, TOO.
KEH KEH KEH! "THIS IS OUR HOME," HUH?
I UNDERSTAND... YOU GUYS KNOW BETTER THAN ANYONE WHAT IT FEELS LIKE TO HAVE A HOME AND THEN LOSE IT.
YUP.
THAT'S WHY I APPRECIATE HOW YOU AND WINRY ALWAYS WELCOME US BACK LIKE WE'RE YOUR REAL FAMILY.
MY BROTHER DOES TOO, EVEN THOUGH HE DOESN'T SAY IT.

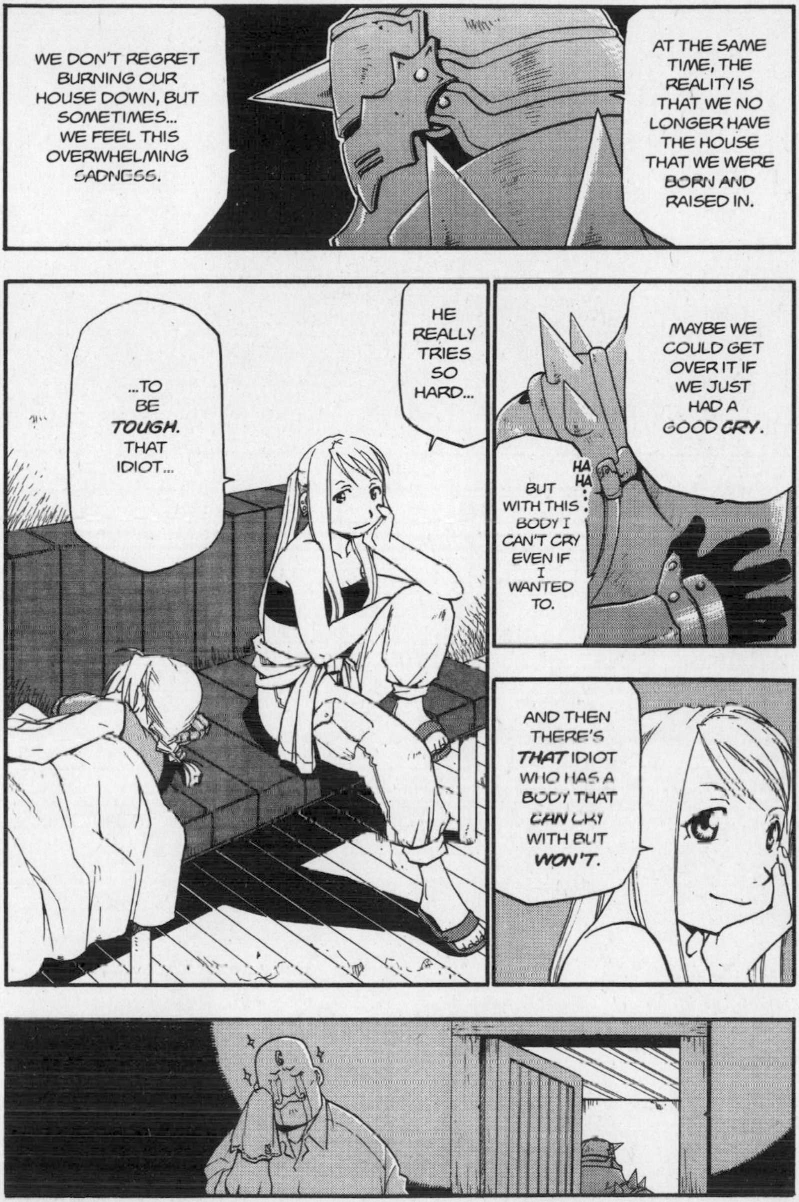
AT THE SAME TIME, THE REALITY IS THAT WE NO LONGER HAVE THE HOUSE THAT WE WERE BORN AND RAISED IN.
WE DON'T REGRET BURNING OUR HOUSE DOWN, BUT SOMETIMES... WE FEEL THIS OVERWHELMING SADNESS.
MAYBE WE COULD GET OVER IT IF WE JUST HAD A GOOD **CRY**.
HA HA...
BUT WITH THIS BODY I CAN'T CRY EVEN IF I WANTED TO.
AND THEN THERE'S **THAT** IDIOT WHO HAS A BODY THAT **CAN** CRY WITH BUT **WON'T**.
HE REALLY TRIES SO HARD...
...TO BE **TOUGH**. THAT IDIOT...

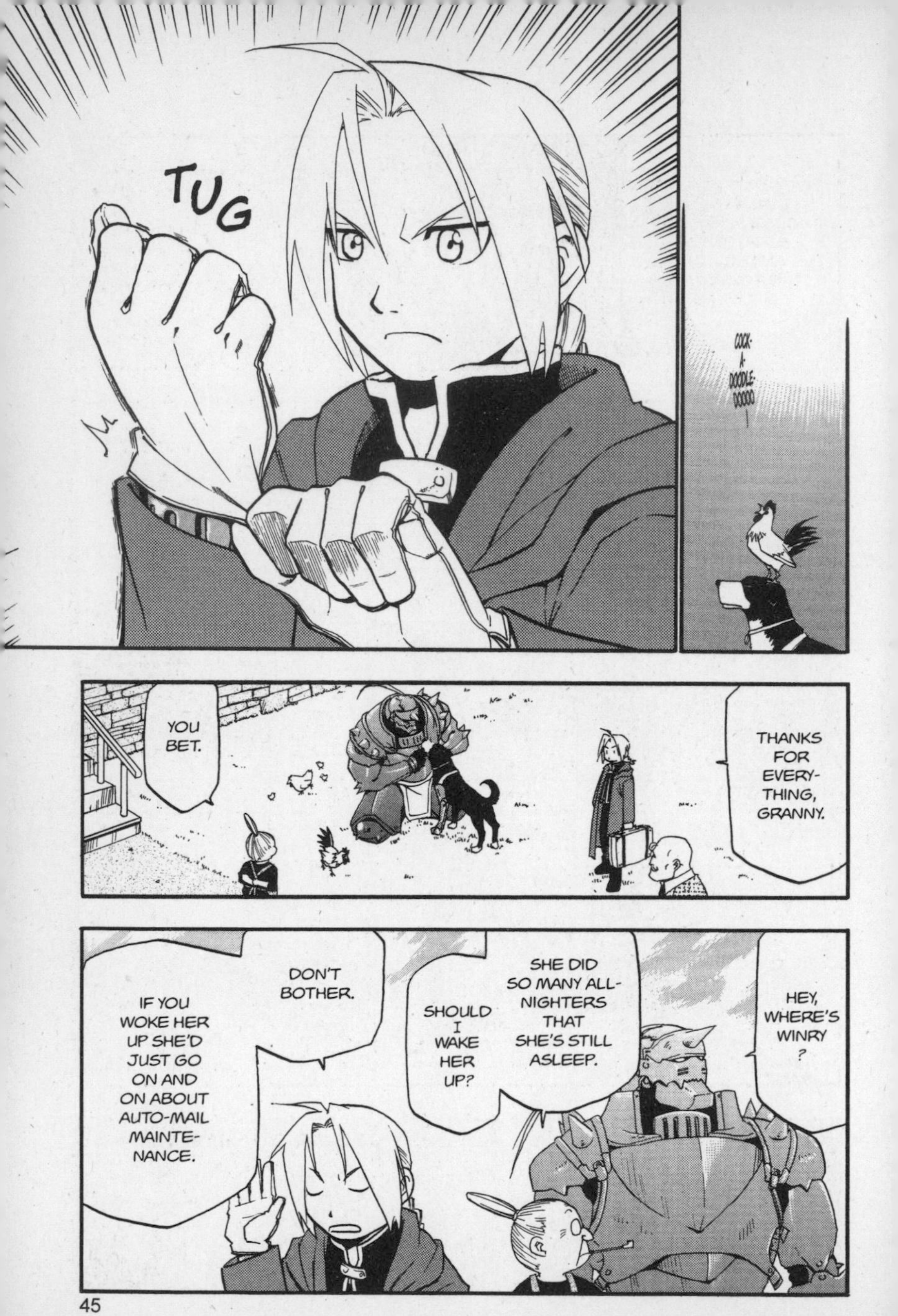
COCK-A-DOODLE-DOOOO
TUG
THANKS FOR EVERY-THING, GRANNY.
YOU BET.
HEY, WHERE'S WINRY?
SHE DID SO MANY ALL-NIGHTERS THAT SHE'S STILL ASLEEP.
SHOULD I WAKE HER UP?
DON'T BOTHER.
IF YOU WOKE HER UP SHE'D JUST GO ON AND ON ABOUT AUTO-MAIL MAINTE-NANCE.

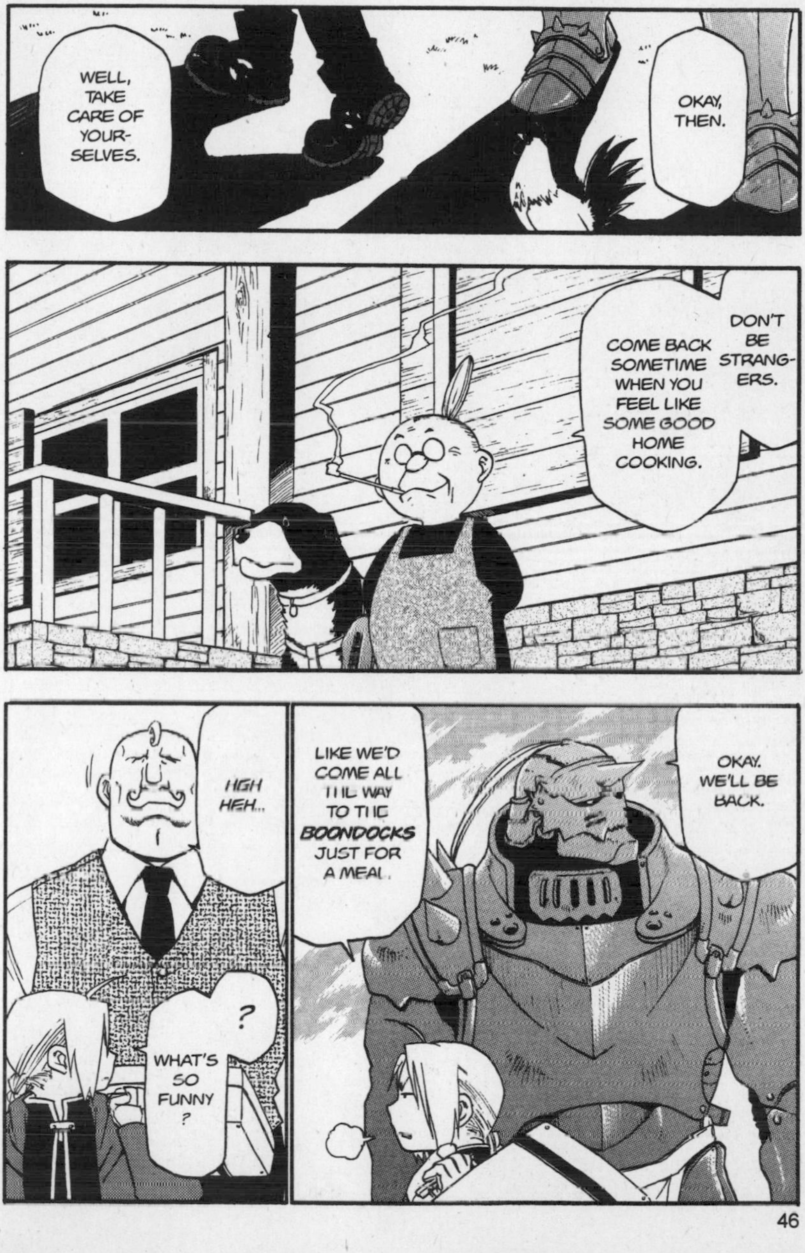
OKAY, THEN.
WELL, TAKE CARE OF YOUR-SELVES.
DON'T BE STRANG-ERS.
COME BACK SOMETIME WHEN YOU FEEL LIKE SOME GOOD HOME COOKING.
OKAY. WE'LL BE BACK.
LIKE WE'D COME ALL THE WAY TO THE BOONDOCKS JUST FOR A MEAL.
HEH HEH...
?
WHAT'S SO FUNNY ?

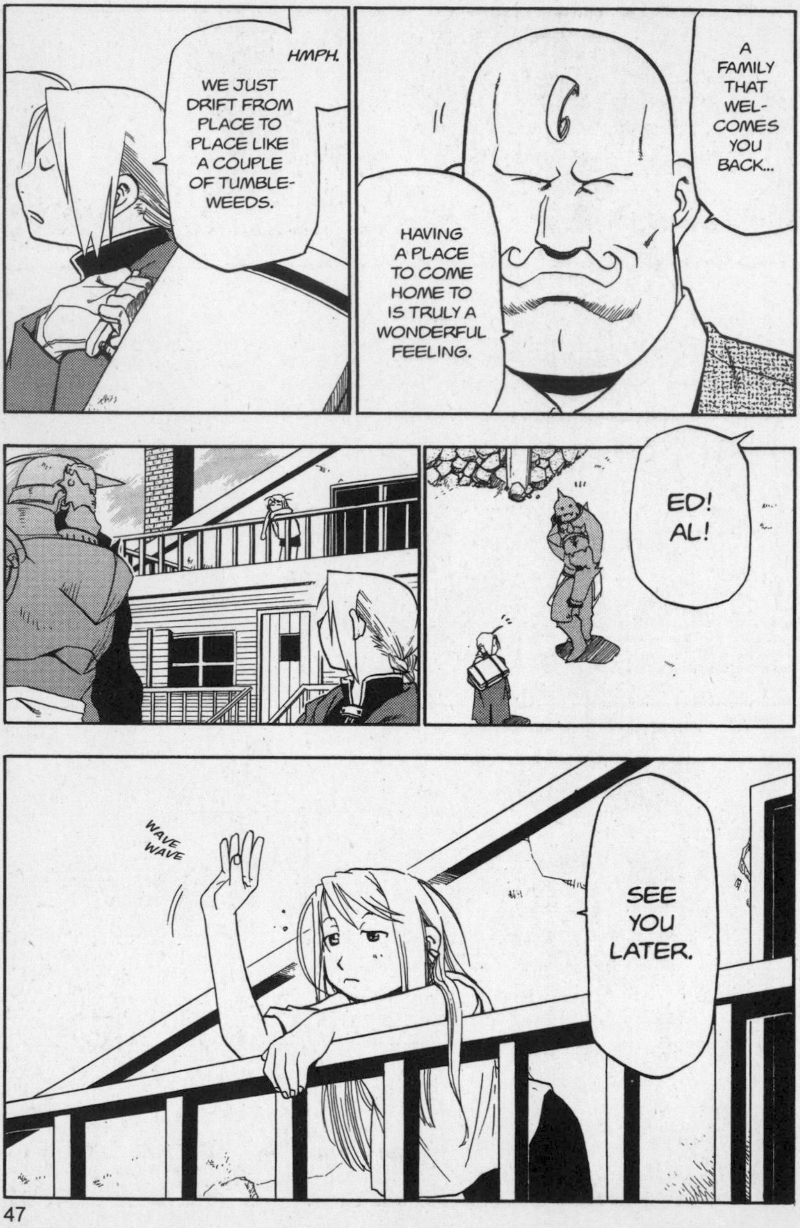
A FAMILY THAT WEL-COMES YOU BACK...
HAVING A PLACE TO COME HOME TO IS TRULY A WONDERFUL FEELING.
HMPH.
WE JUST DRIFT FROM PLACE TO PLACE LIKE A COUPLE OF TUMBLE-WEEDS.
ED! AL!
SEE YOU LATER.
WAVE WAVE

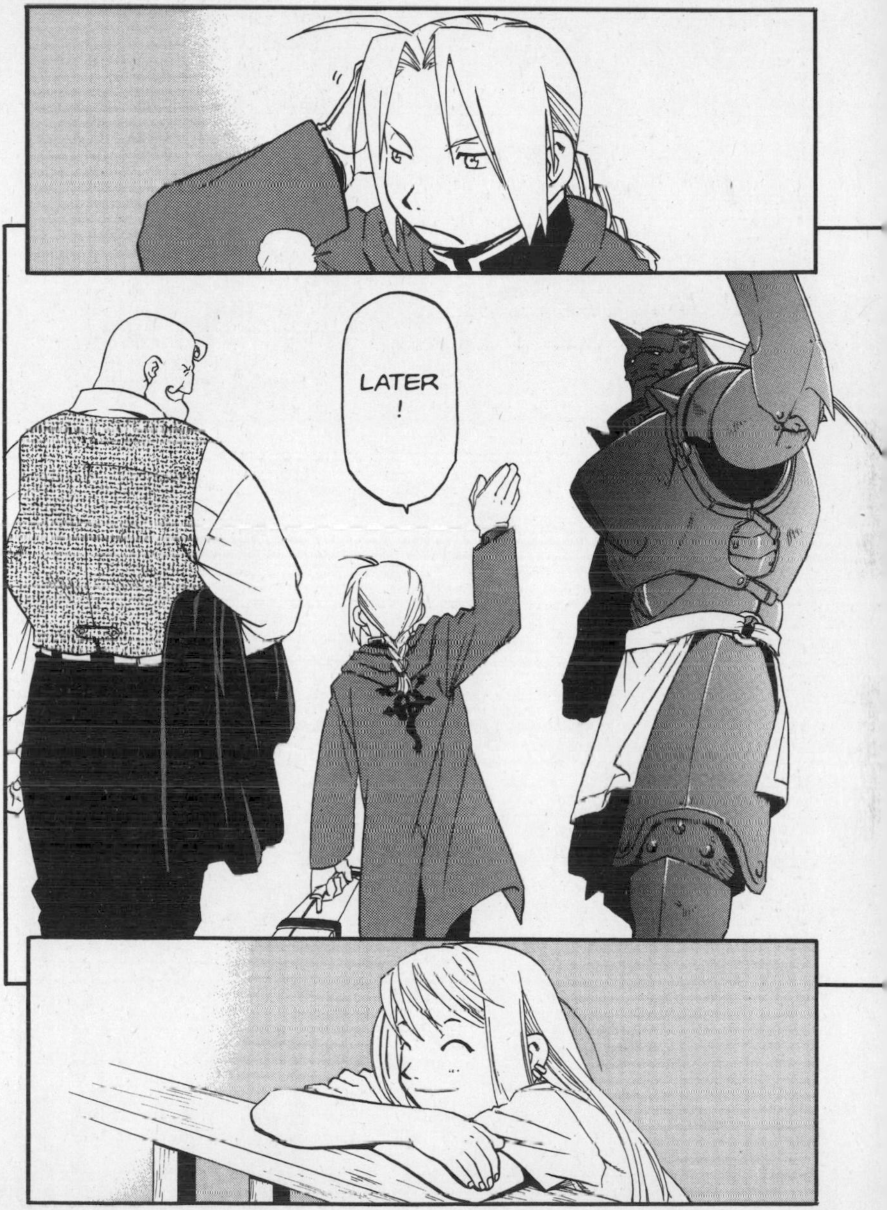
LATER
!

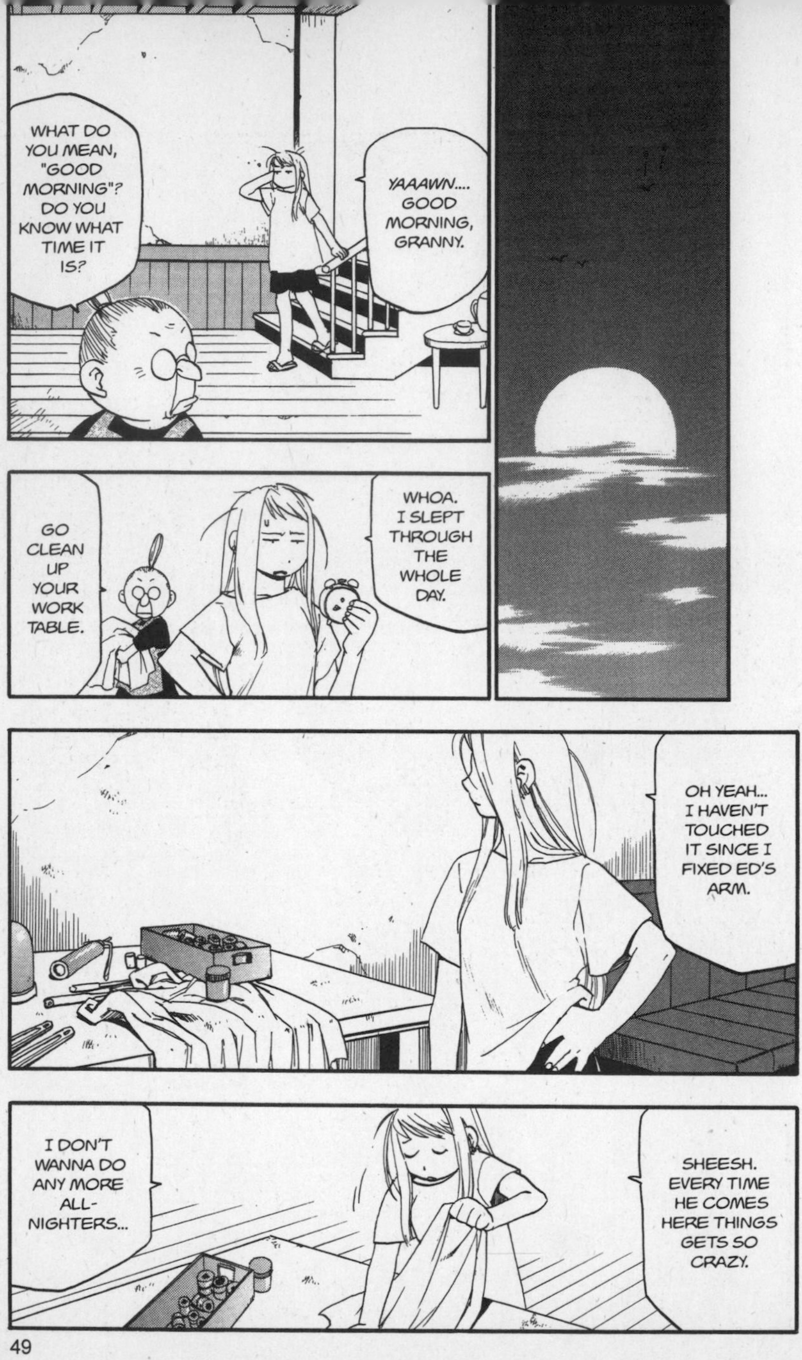
YAAAWN.... GOOD MORNING, GRANNY.
WHAT DO YOU MEAN, "GOOD MORNING"? DO YOU KNOW WHAT TIME IT IS?
WHOA. I SLEPT THROUGH THE WHOLE DAY.
GO CLEAN UP YOUR WORK TABLE.
OH YEAH... I HAVEN'T TOUCHED IT SINCE I FIXED ED'S ARM.
SHEESH. EVERY TIME HE COMES HERE THINGS GETS SO CRAZY.
I DON'T WANNA DO ANY MORE ALL-NIGHTERS...

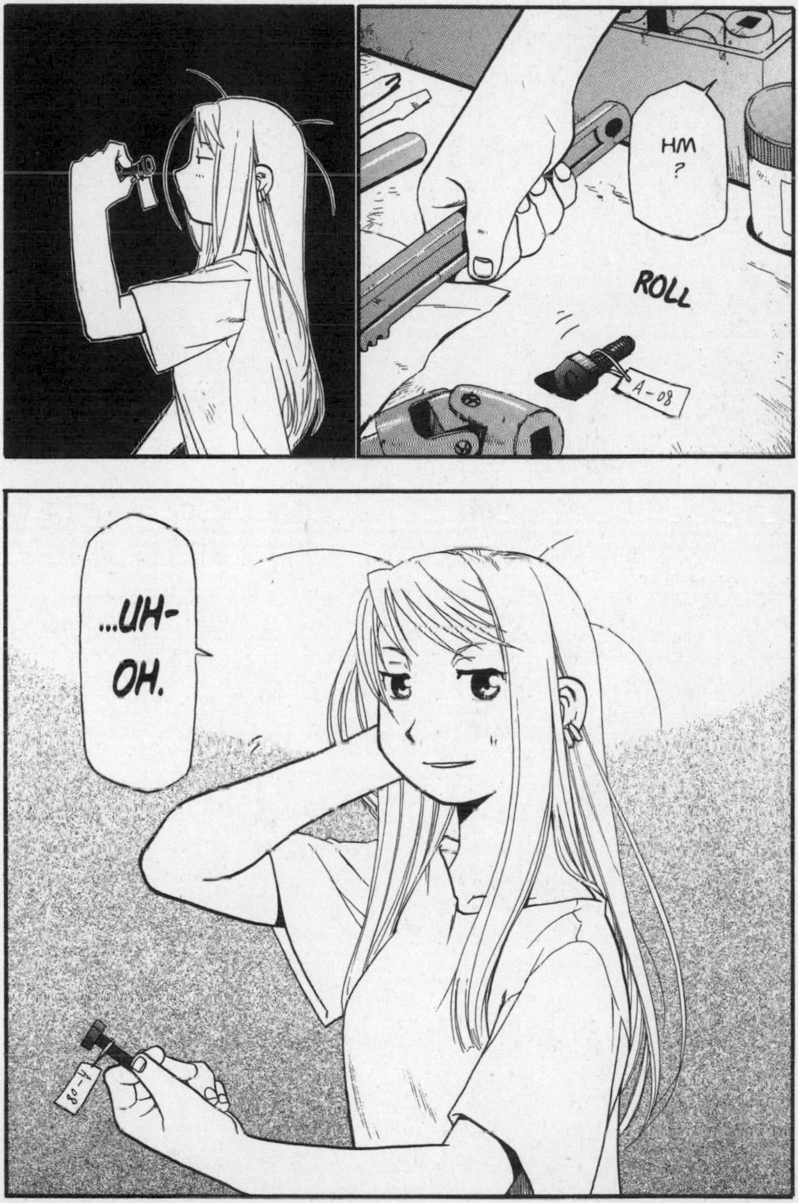
HM ?
ROLL
A-08
...UH-OH.

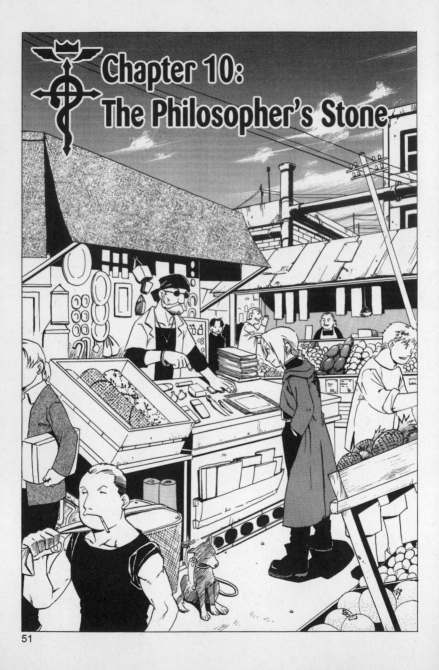

Chapter 10:
The Philosopher's Stone

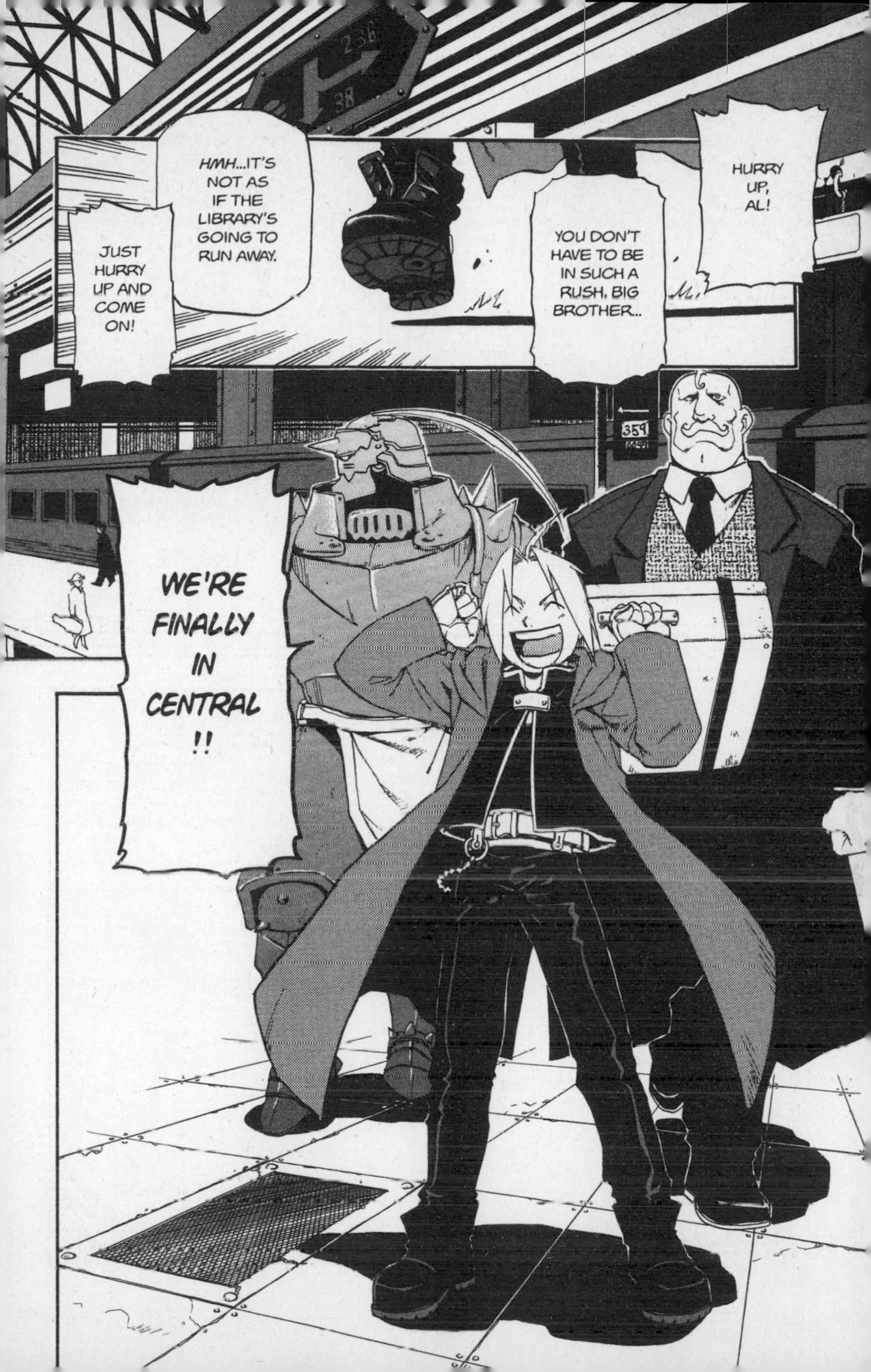
HURRY UP, AL!
YOU DON'T HAVE TO BE IN SUCH A RUSH, BIG BROTHER...
HMH...IT'S NOT AS IF THE LIBRARY'S GOING TO RUN AWAY.
JUST HURRY UP AND COME ON!
WE'RE FINALLY IN CENTRAL !!

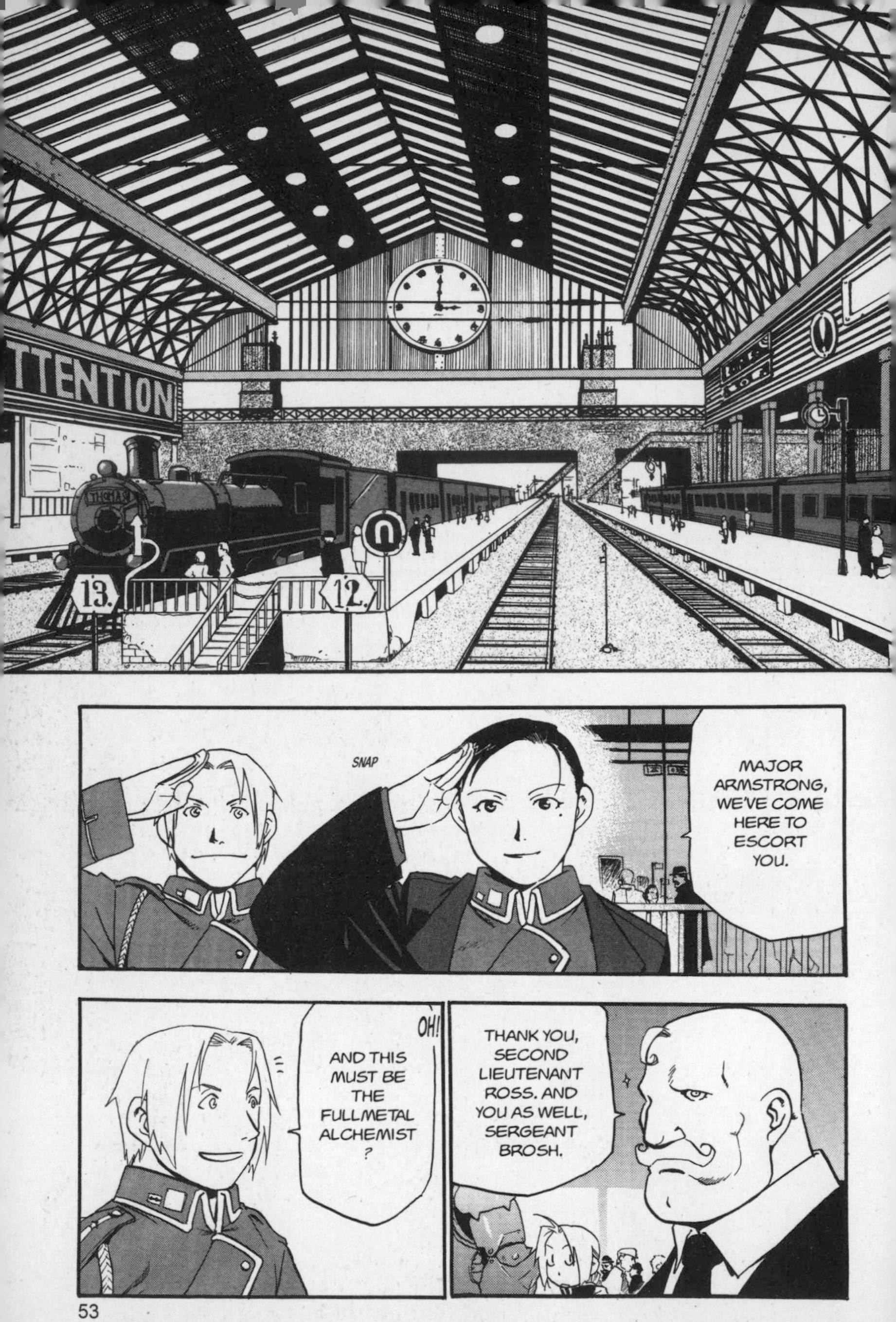
TTENTION
13.
12.
MAJOR ARMSTRONG, WE'VE COME HERE TO ESCORT YOU.
SNAP
THANK YOU, SECOND LIEUTENANT ROSS. AND YOU AS WELL, SERGEANT BROSH.
OH!
AND THIS MUST BE THE FULLMETAL ALCHEMIST?

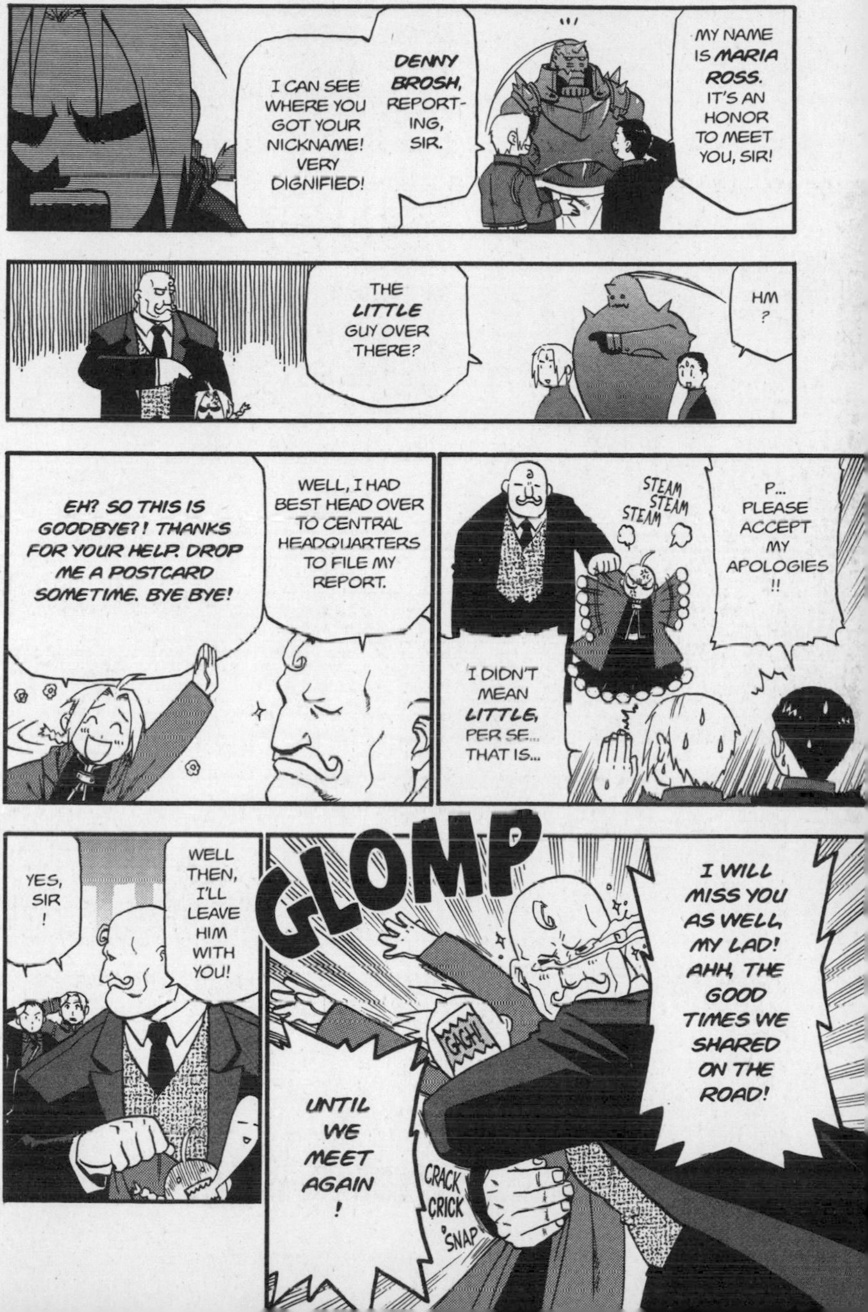
MY NAME IS MARIA ROSS. IT'S AN HONOR TO MEET YOU, SIR!
DENNY BROSH, REPORTING, SIR.
I CAN SEE WHERE YOU GOT YOUR NICKNAME! VERY DIGNIFIED!
HM?
THE LITTLE GUY OVER THERE?
P... PLEASE ACCEPT MY APOLOGIES!!
STEAM STEAM STEAM
I DIDN'T MEAN LITTLE, PER SE... THAT IS...
WELL, I HAD BEST HEAD OVER TO CENTRAL HEADQUARTERS TO FILE MY REPORT.
EH? SO THIS IS GOODBYE?! THANKS FOR YOUR HELP. DROP ME A POSTCARD SOMETIME. BYE BYE!
I WILL MISS YOU AS WELL, MY LAD! AHH, THE GOOD TIMES WE SHARED ON THE ROAD!
GLOMP
GAGH!
UNTIL WE MEET AGAIN!
CRACK
CRICK
SNAP
WELL THEN, I'LL LEAVE HIM WITH YOU!
YES, SIR!

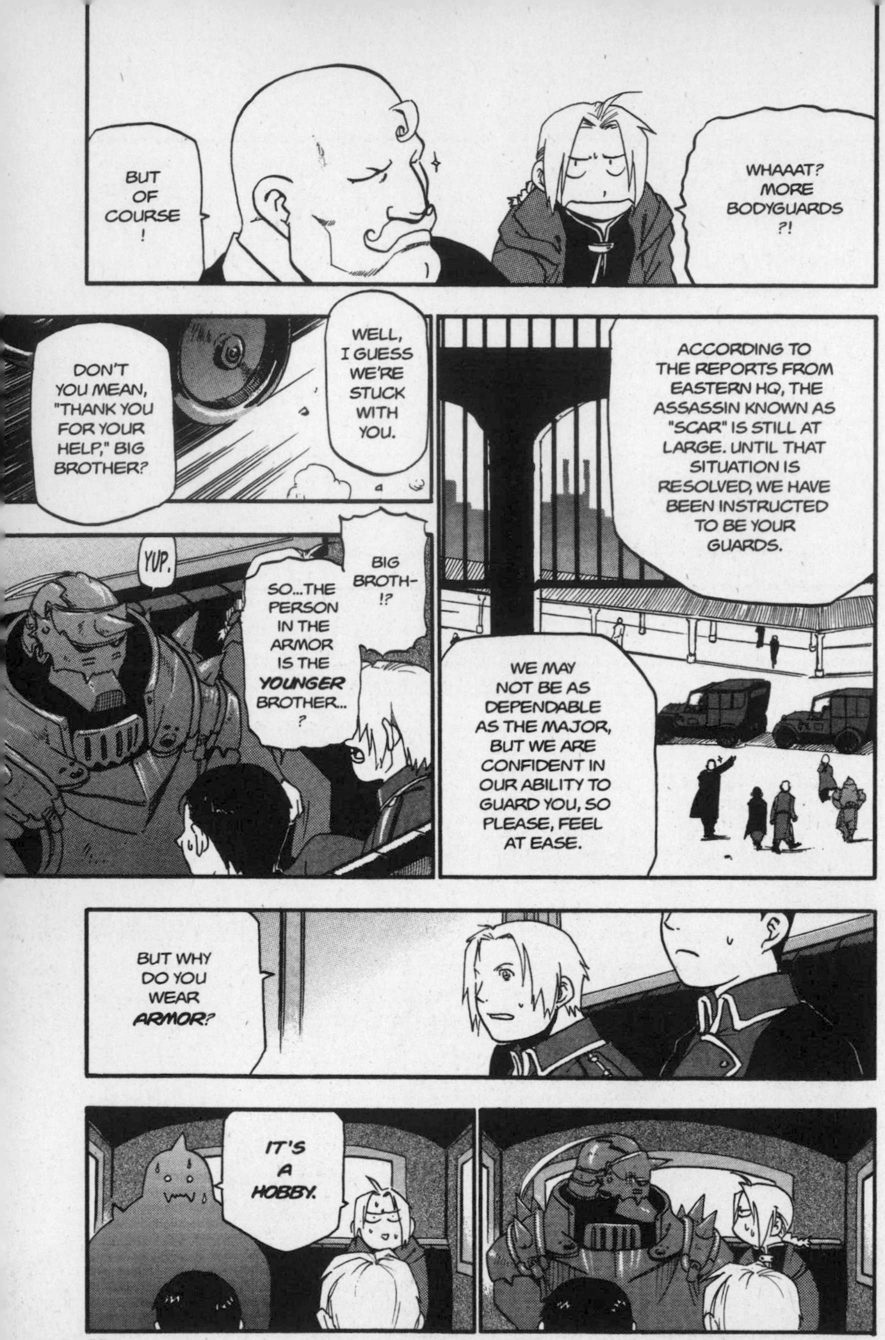
WHAAAT? MORE BODYGUARDS?!
BUT OF COURSE!
ACCORDING TO THE REPORTS FROM EASTERN HQ, THE ASSASSIN KNOWN AS "SCAR" IS STILL AT LARGE. UNTIL THAT SITUATION IS RESOLVED, WE HAVE BEEN INSTRUCTED TO BE YOUR GUARDS.
WE MAY NOT BE AS DEPENDABLE AS THE MAJOR, BUT WE ARE CONFIDENT IN OUR ABILITY TO GUARD YOU, SO PLEASE, FEEL AT EASE.
WELL, I GUESS WE'RE STUCK WITH YOU.
DON'T YOU MEAN, "THANK YOU FOR YOUR HELP," BIG BROTHER?
BIG BROTH-!?
SO...THE PERSON IN THE ARMOR IS THE YOUNGER BROTHER...?
YUP.
BUT WHY DO YOU WEAR ARMOR?
IT'S A HOBBY.

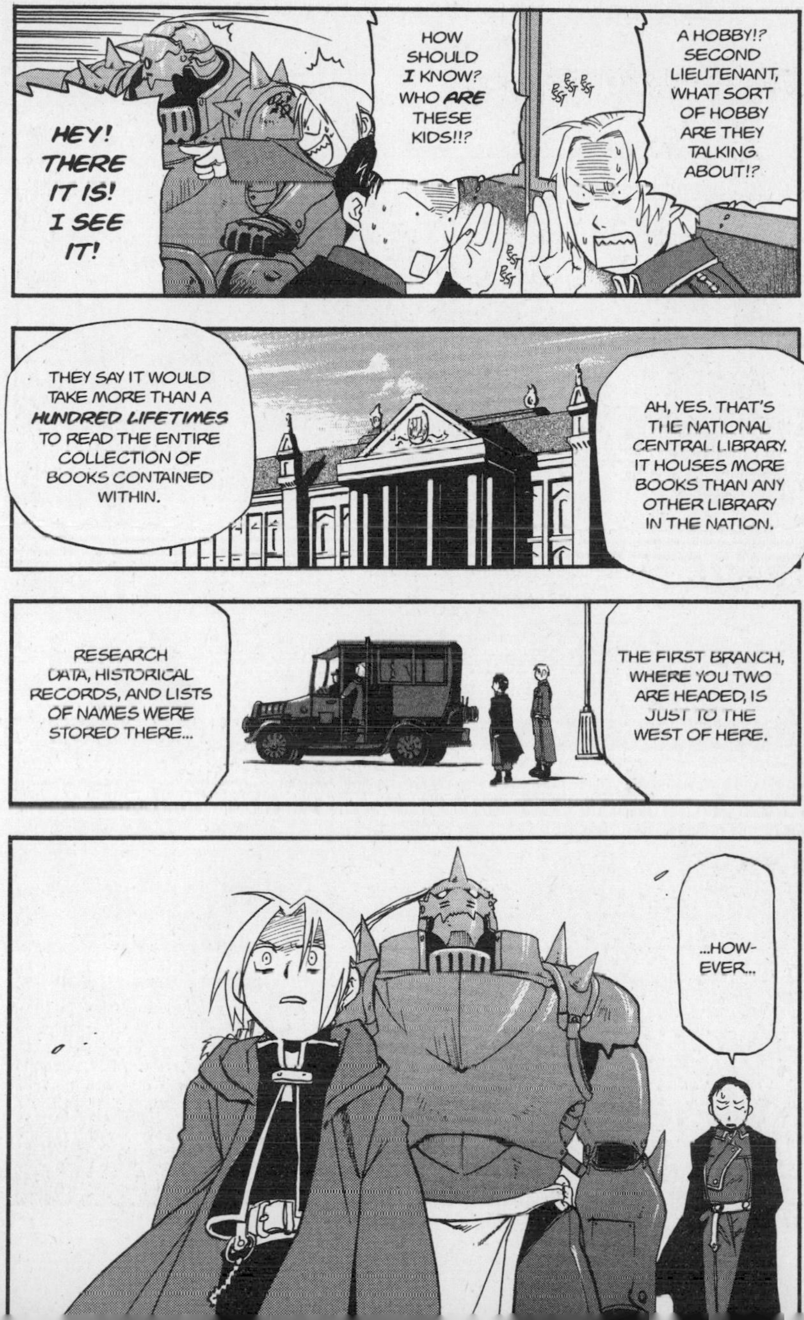
A HOBBY!? SECOND LIEUTENANT, WHAT SORT OF HOBBY ARE THEY TALKING ABOUT!?
PSST PSST PSST
HOW SHOULD I KNOW? WHO ARE THESE KIDS!!?
PSST PSST
HEY! THERE IT IS! I SEE IT!
AH, YES. THAT'S THE NATIONAL CENTRAL LIBRARY. IT HOUSES MORE BOOKS THAN ANY OTHER LIBRARY IN THE NATION.
THEY SAY IT WOULD TAKE MORE THAN A HUNDRED LIFETIMES TO READ THE ENTIRE COLLECTION OF BOOKS CONTAINED WITHIN.
THE FIRST BRANCH, WHERE YOU TWO ARE HEADED, IS JUST TO THE WEST OF HERE.
RESEARCH DATA, HISTORICAL RECORDS, AND LISTS OF NAMES WERE STORED THERE...
...HOW-EVER...

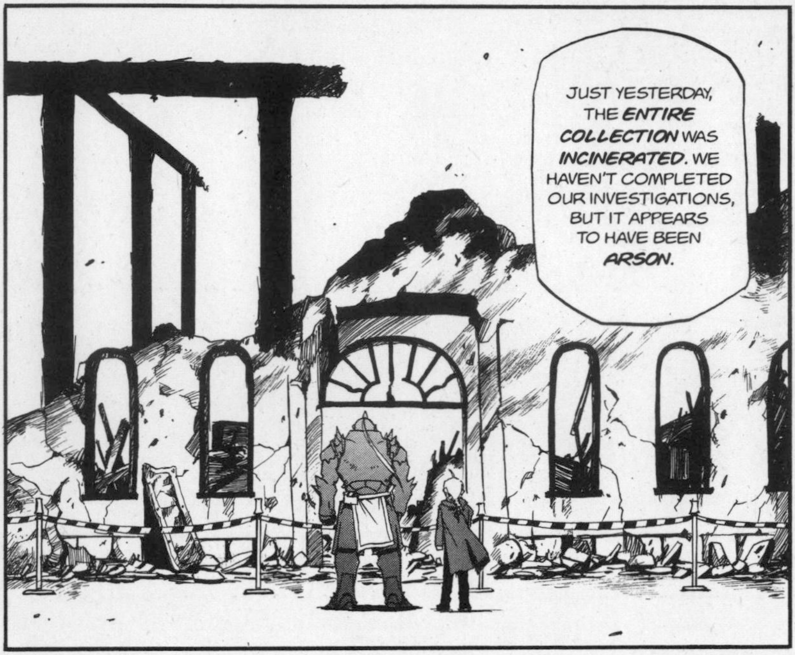
JUST YESTERDAY, THE ENTIRE COLLECTION WAS INCINERATED. WE HAVEN'T COMPLETED OUR INVESTIGATIONS, BUT IT APPEARS TO HAVE BEEN ARSON.

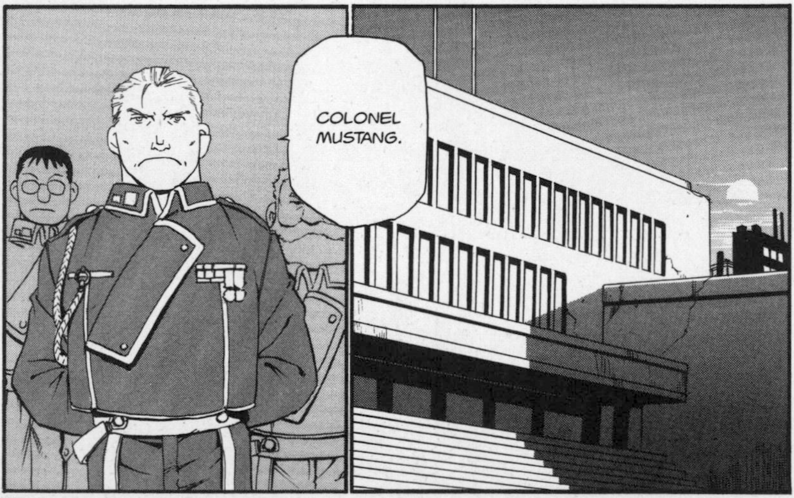
COLONEL MUSTANG.

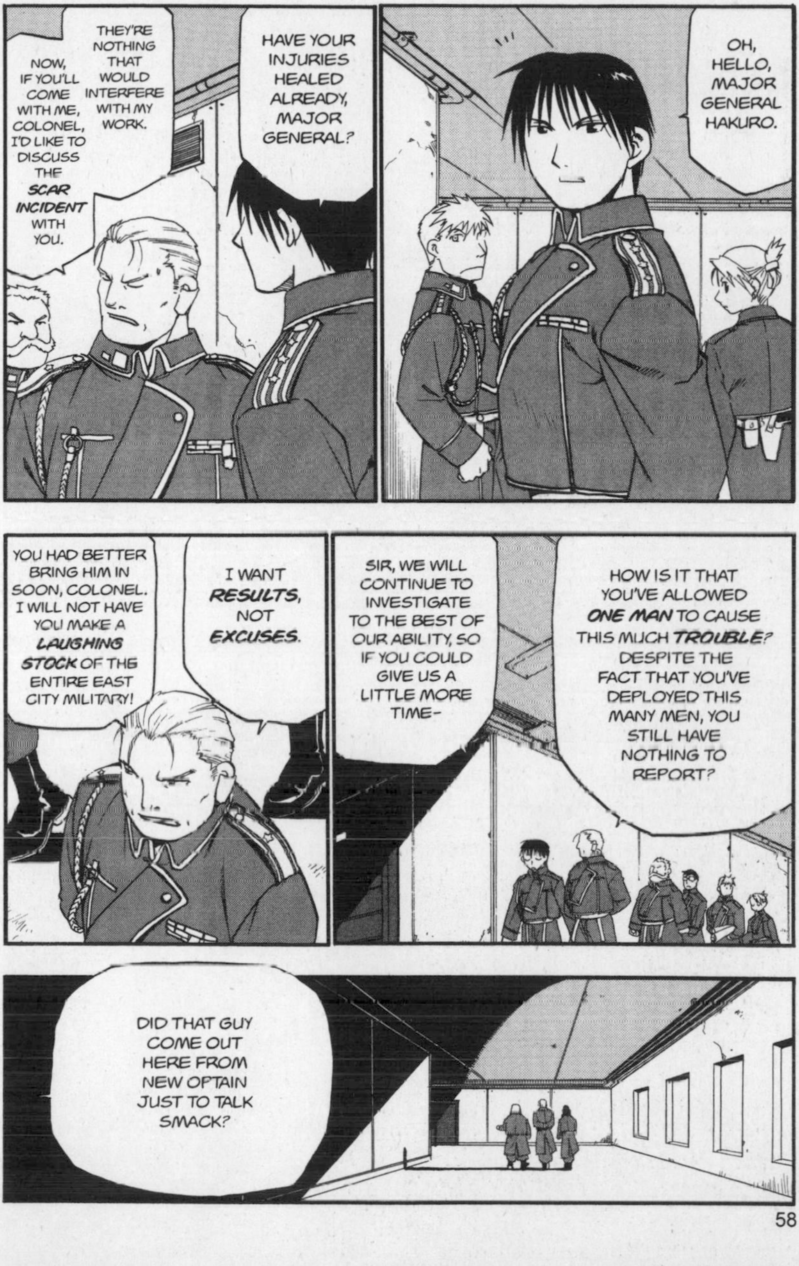
OH, HELLO, MAJOR GENERAL HAKURO.
HAVE YOUR INJURIES HEALED ALREADY, MAJOR GENERAL?
THEY'RE NOTHING THAT WOULD INTERFERE WITH MY WORK.
NOW, IF YOU'LL COME WITH ME, COLONEL, I'D LIKE TO DISCUSS THE SCAR INCIDENT WITH YOU.
HOW IS IT THAT YOU'VE ALLOWED ONE MAN TO CAUSE THIS MUCH TROUBLE? DESPITE THE FACT THAT YOU'VE DEPLOYED THIS MANY MEN, YOU STILL HAVE NOTHING TO REPORT?
SIR, WE WILL CONTINUE TO INVESTIGATE TO THE BEST OF OUR ABILITY, SO IF YOU COULD GIVE US A LITTLE MORE TIME-
I WANT RESULTS, NOT EXCUSES.
YOU HAD BETTER BRING HIM IN SOON, COLONEL. I WILL NOT HAVE YOU MAKE A LAUGHING STOCK OF THE ENTIRE EAST CITY MILITARY!
DID THAT GUY COME OUT HERE FROM NEW OPTAIN JUST TO TALK SMACK?

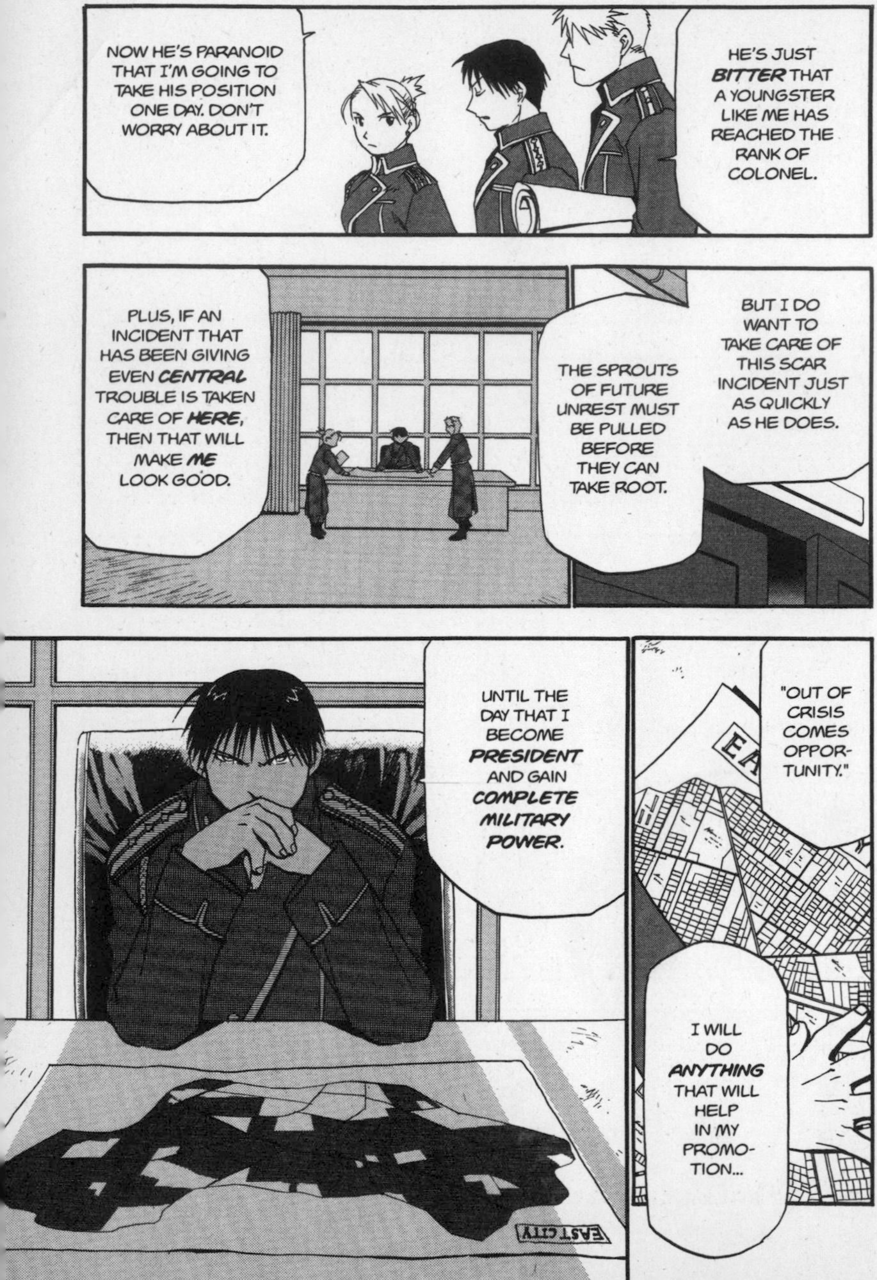
HE'S JUST BITTER THAT A YOUNGSTER LIKE ME HAS REACHED THE RANK OF COLONEL.
NOW HE'S PARANOID THAT I'M GOING TO TAKE HIS POSITION ONE DAY. DON'T WORRY ABOUT IT.
BUT I DO WANT TO TAKE CARE OF THIS SCAR INCIDENT JUST AS QUICKLY AS HE DOES.
THE SPROUTS OF FUTURE UNREST MUST BE PULLED BEFORE THEY CAN TAKE ROOT.
PLUS, IF AN INCIDENT THAT HAS BEEN GIVING EVEN CENTRAL TROUBLE IS TAKEN CARE OF HERE, THEN THAT WILL MAKE ME LOOK GOOD.
"OUT OF CRISIS COMES OPPORTUNITY."
I WILL DO ANYTHING THAT WILL HELP IN MY PROMOTION...
UNTIL THE DAY THAT I BECOME PRESIDENT AND GAIN COMPLETE MILITARY POWER.
EAST CITY

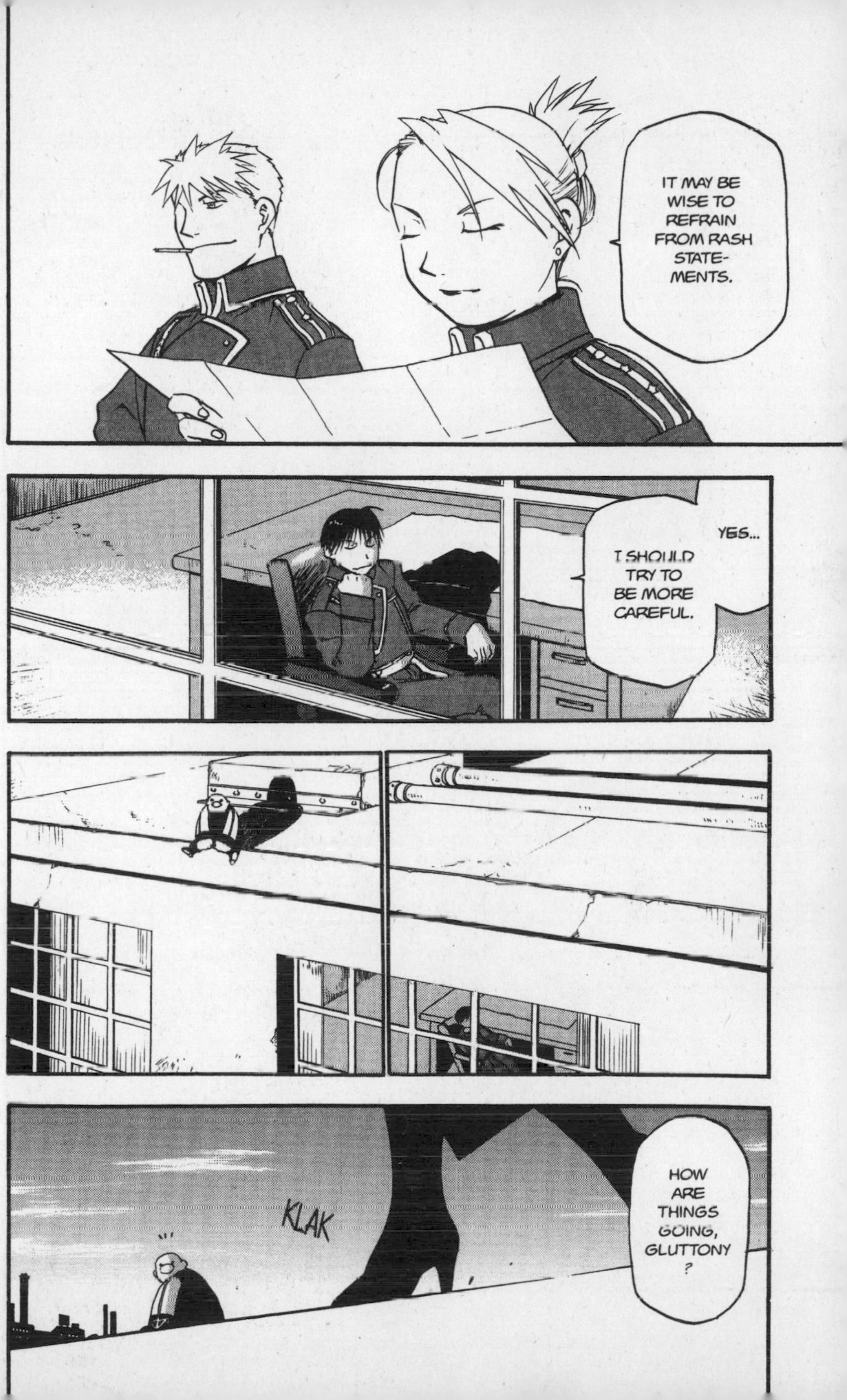
IT MAY BE WISE TO REFRAIN FROM RASH STATE-MENTS.
YES... I SHOULD TRY TO BE MORE CAREFUL.
KLAK
HOW ARE THINGS GOING, GLUTTONY?

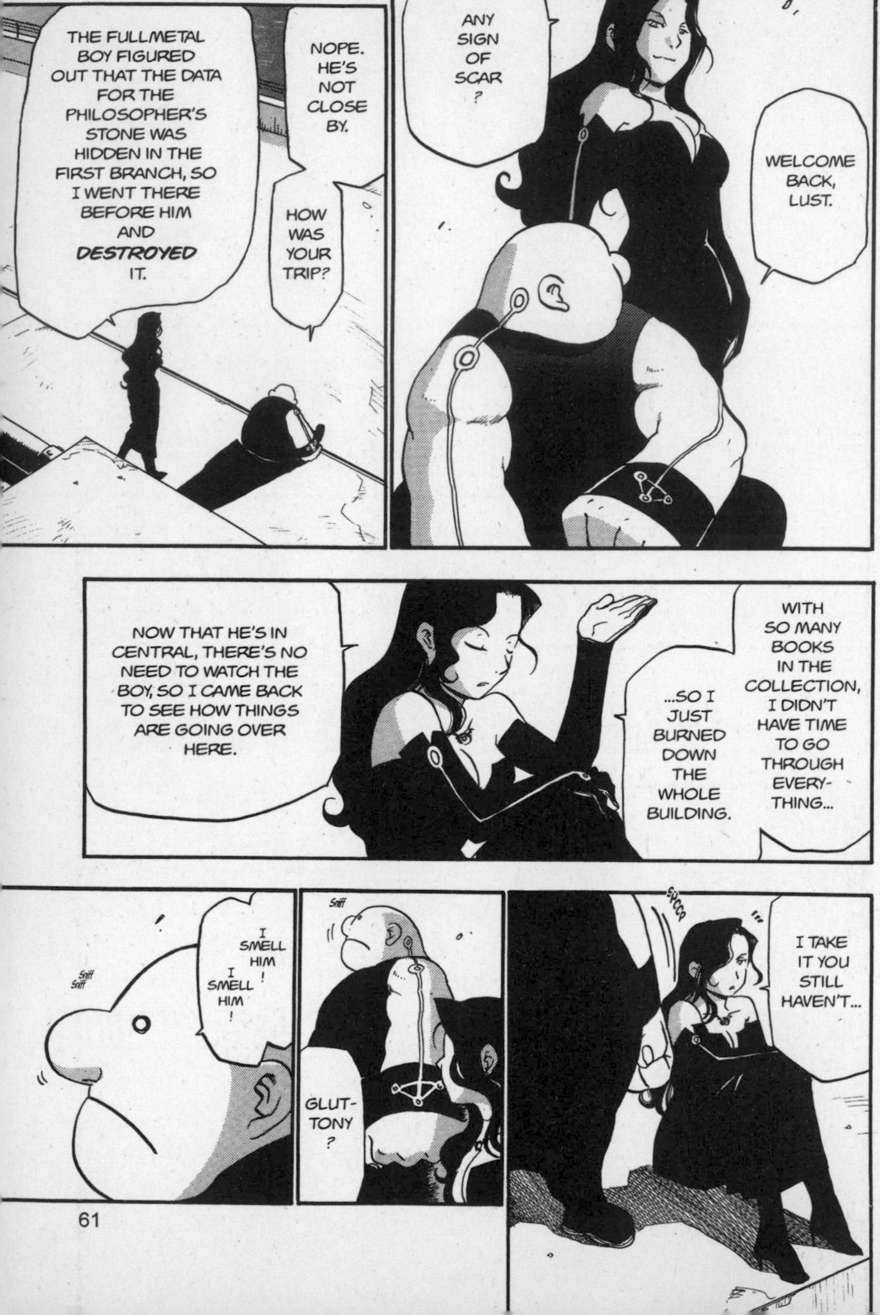
WELCOME BACK, LUST.
ANY SIGN OF SCAR?
NOPE. HE'S NOT CLOSE BY.
HOW WAS YOUR TRIP?
THE FULLMETAL BOY FIGURED OUT THAT THE DATA FOR THE PHILOSOPHER'S STONE WAS HIDDEN IN THE FIRST BRANCH, SO I WENT THERE BEFORE HIM AND ***DESTROYED*** IT.
WITH SO MANY BOOKS IN THE COLLECTION, I DIDN'T HAVE TIME TO GO THROUGH EVERY-THING...
...SO I JUST BURNED DOWN THE WHOLE BUILDING.
NOW THAT HE'S IN CENTRAL, THERE'S NO NEED TO WATCH THE BOY, SO I CAME BACK TO SEE HOW THINGS ARE GOING OVER HERE.
I TAKE IT YOU STILL HAVEN'T...
Sniff
GLUT-TONY?
I SMELL HIM! I SMELL HIM!
Sniff Sniff

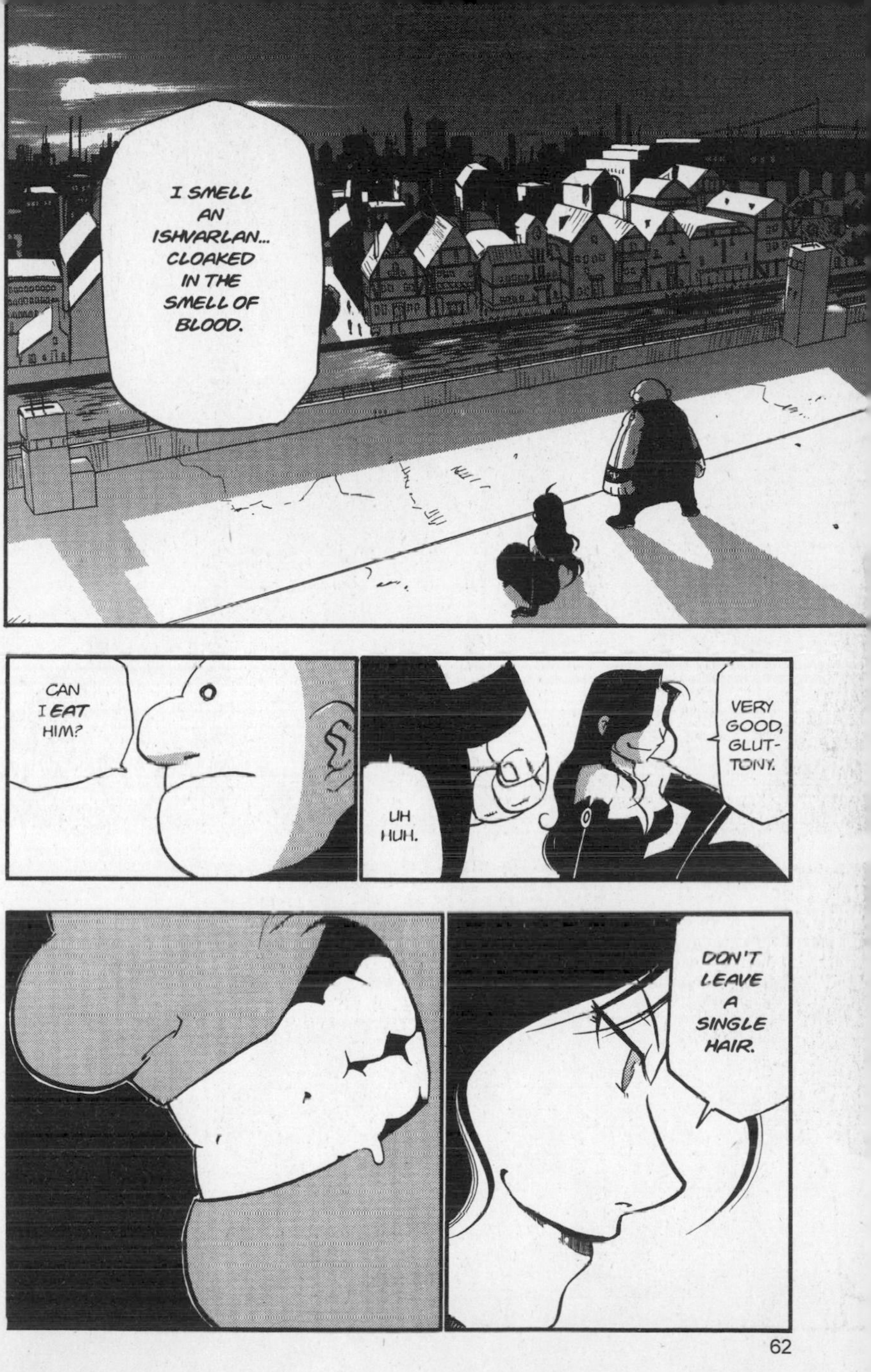
I SMELL AN ISHVARLAN... CLOAKED IN THE SMELL OF BLOOD.
VERY GOOD, GLUTTONY.
UH HUH.
CAN I EAT HIM?
DON'T LEAVE A SINGLE HAIR.

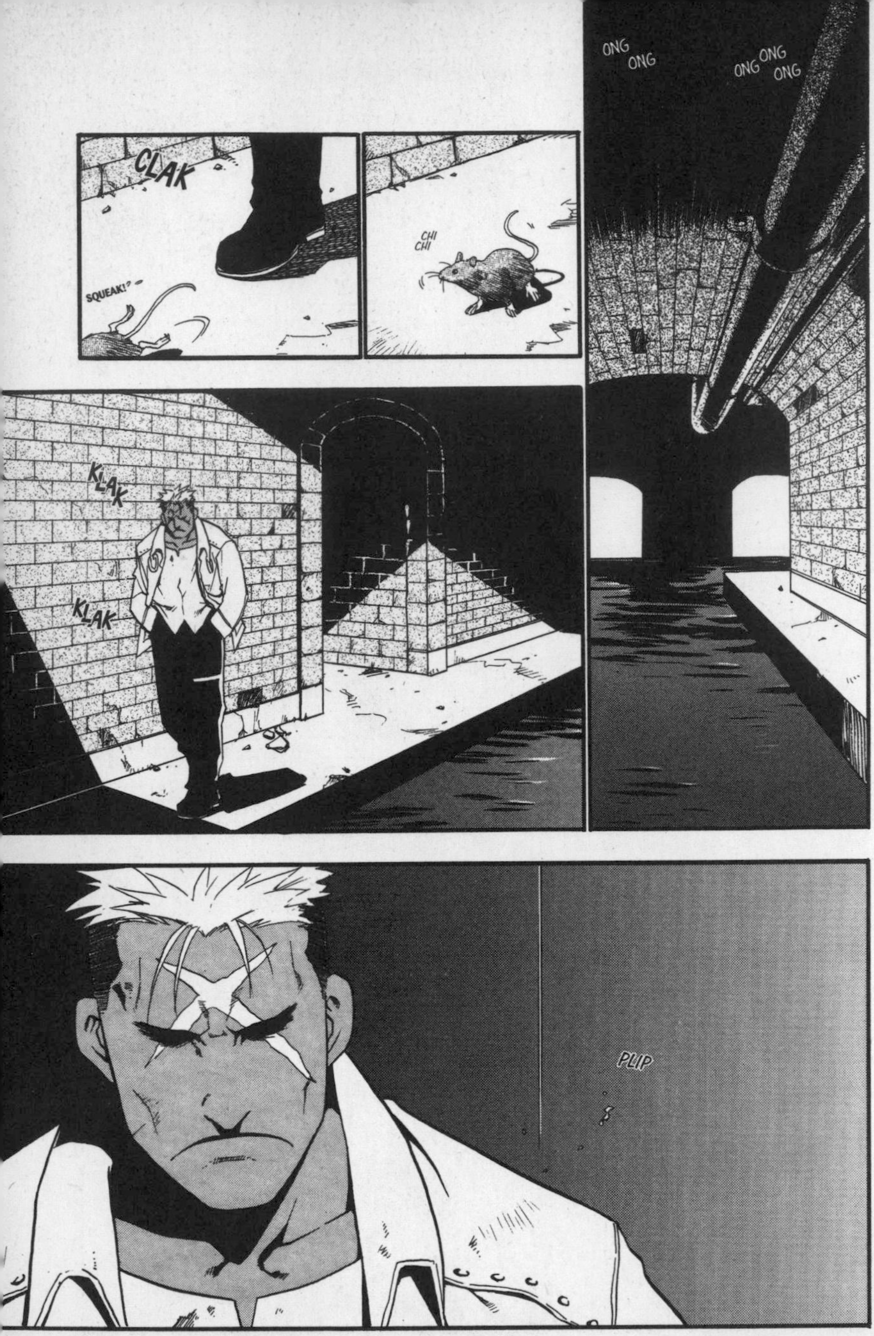
ONG ONG
ONG ONG ONG
CHI CHI
CLAK
SQUEAK!?
KLAK
KLAK
PLIP

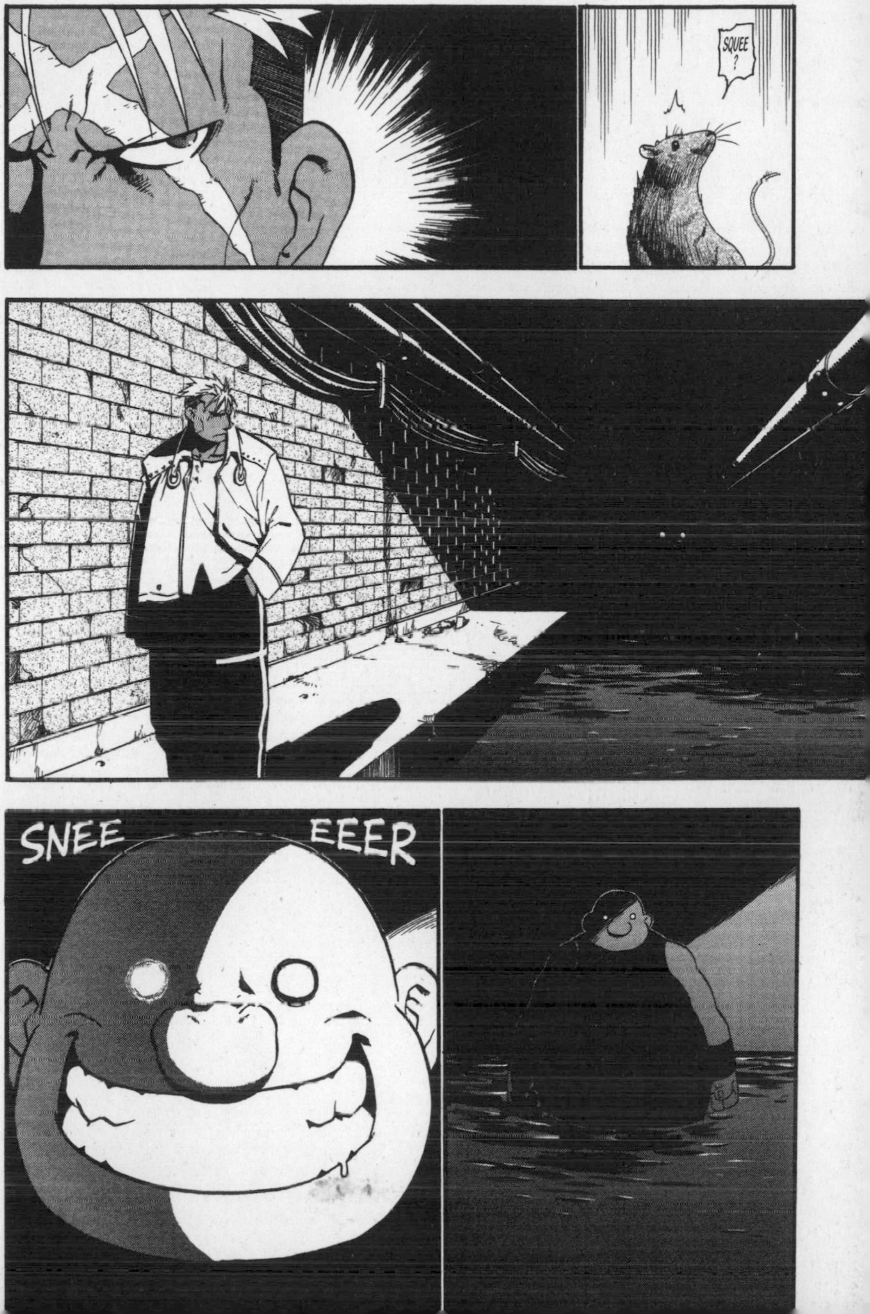
SQUEE ?
SNEE EEER

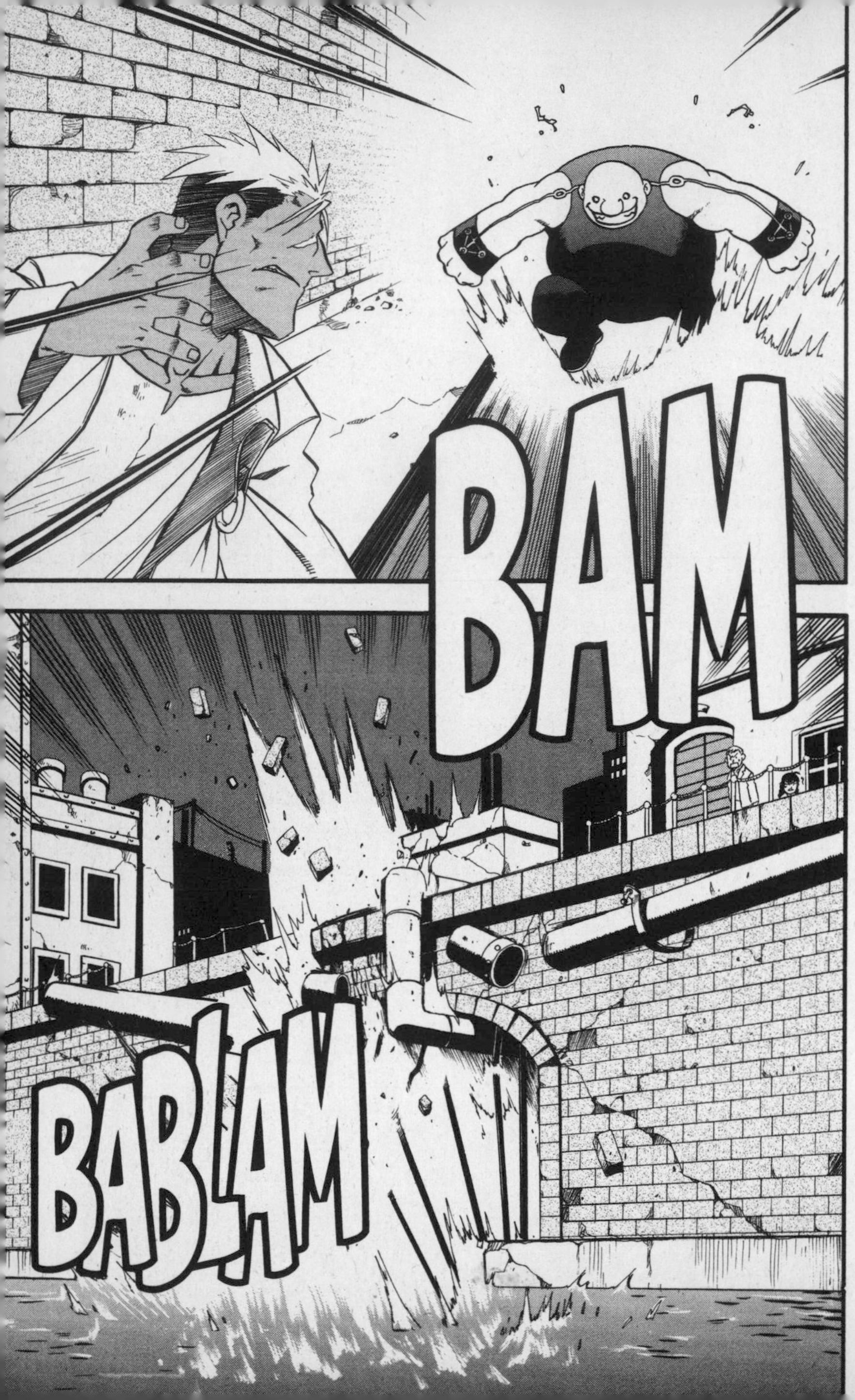
BAM
BABLAM

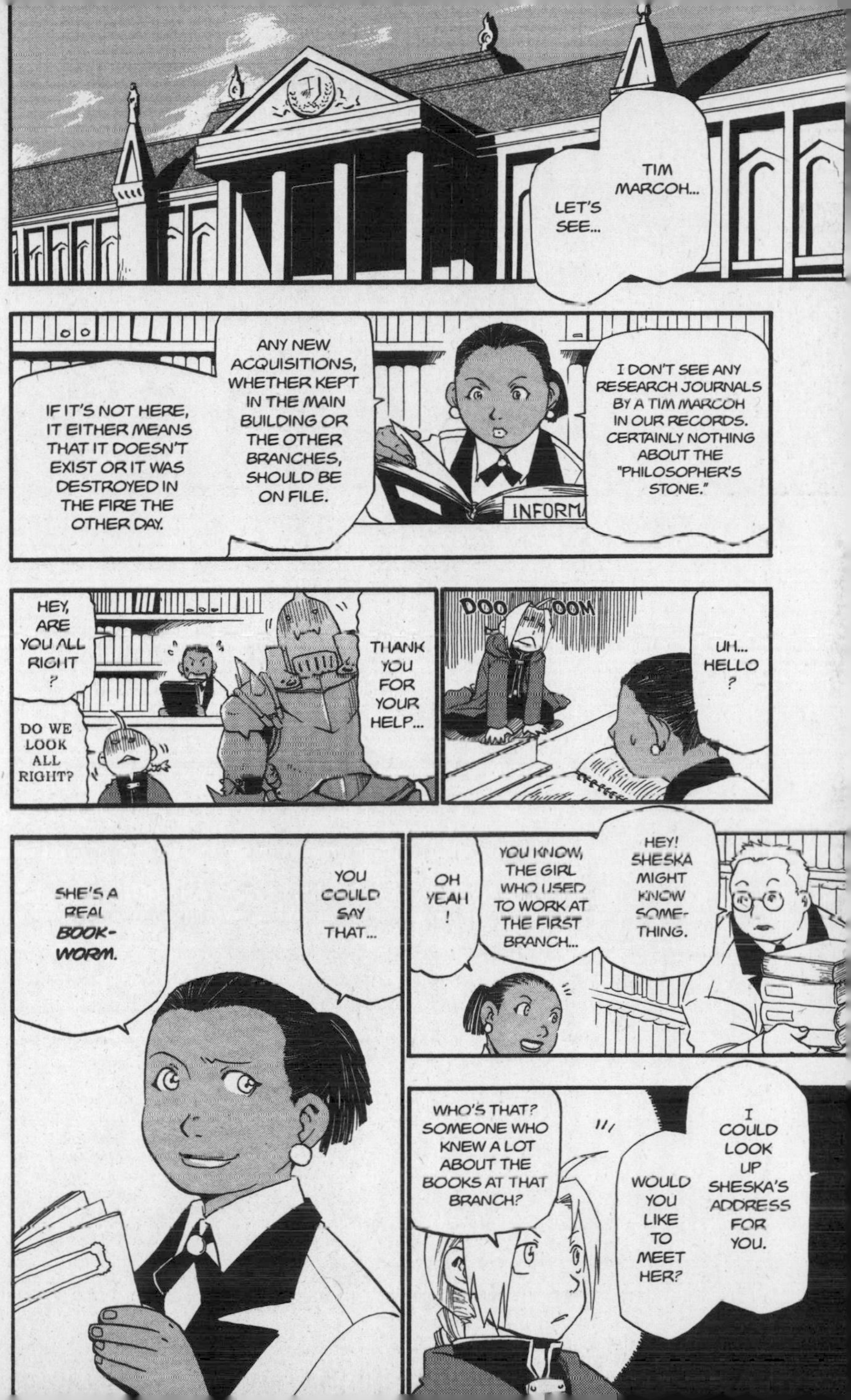
LET'S SEE... TIM MARCOH...
I DON'T SEE ANY RESEARCH JOURNALS BY A TIM MARCOH IN OUR RECORDS. CERTAINLY NOTHING ABOUT THE "PHILOSOPHER'S STONE."
INFORM
ANY NEW ACQUISITIONS, WHETHER KEPT IN THE MAIN BUILDING OR THE OTHER BRANCHES, SHOULD BE ON FILE.
IF IT'S NOT HERE, IT EITHER MEANS THAT IT DOESN'T EXIST OR IT WAS DESTROYED IN THE FIRE THE OTHER DAY.
UH... HELLO ?
DOO OOM
THANK YOU FOR YOUR HELP...
HEY, ARE YOU ALL RIGHT ?
DO WE LOOK ALL RIGHT?
HEY! SHESKA MIGHT KNOW SOME-THING.
YOU KNOW, THE GIRL WHO USED TO WORK AT THE FIRST BRANCH...
OH YEAH !
I COULD LOOK UP SHESKA'S ADDRESS FOR YOU.
WOULD YOU LIKE TO MEET HER?
WHO'S THAT? SOMEONE WHO KNEW A LOT ABOUT THE BOOKS AT THAT BRANCH?
YOU COULD SAY THAT...
SHE'S A REAL BOOK-WORM.

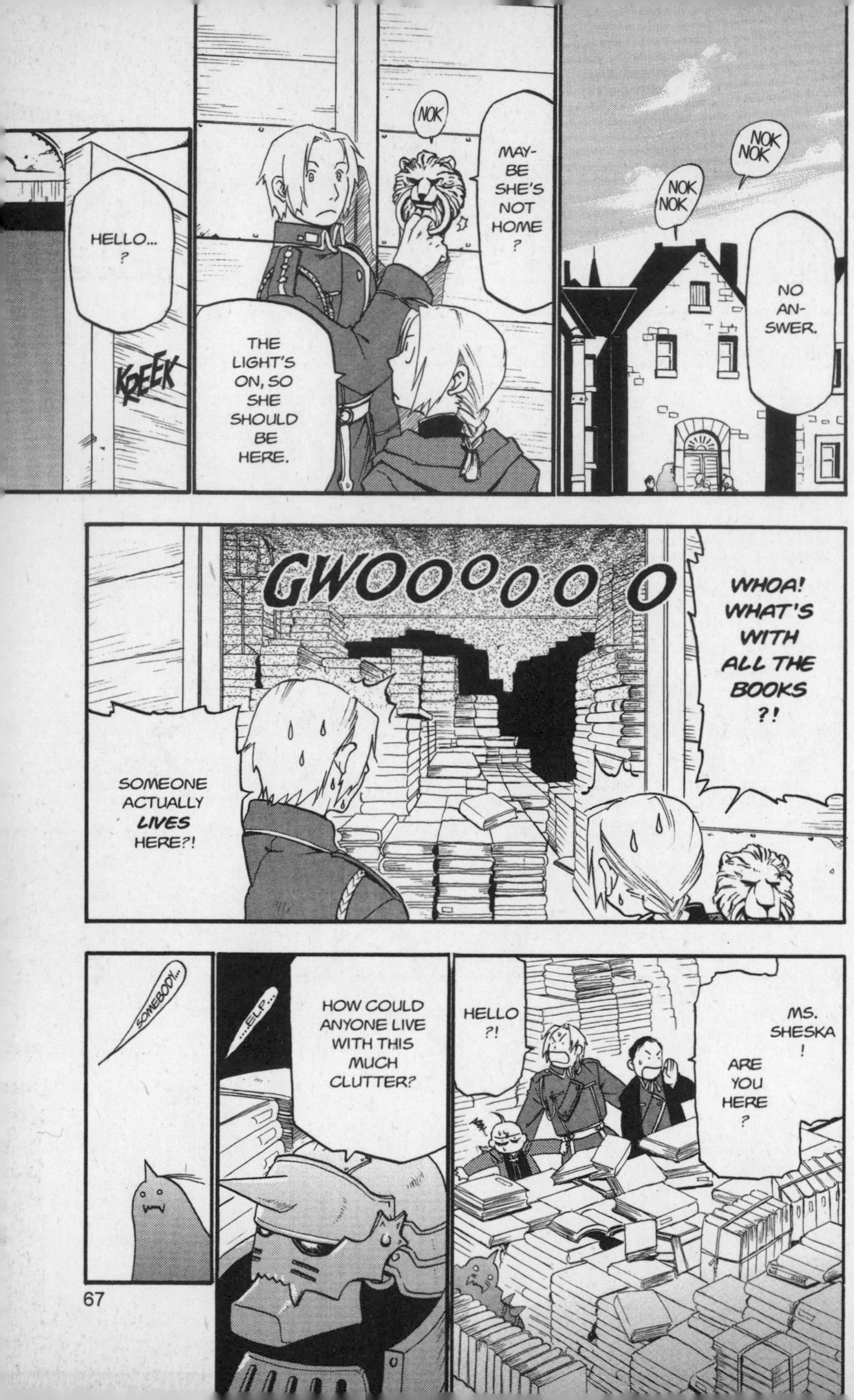
NOK NOK
NOK NOK
NO AN-SWER.
NOK
MAY-BE SHE'S NOT HOME?
THE LIGHT'S ON, SO SHE SHOULD BE HERE.
HELLO...?
KREEK
GWOOOOOO
WHOA! WHAT'S WITH ALL THE BOOKS?!
SOMEONE ACTUALLY *LIVES* HERE?!
MS. SHESKA!
ARE YOU HERE?
HELLO?!
HOW COULD ANYONE LIVE WITH THIS MUCH CLUTTER?
...ELP...
SOMEBODY...

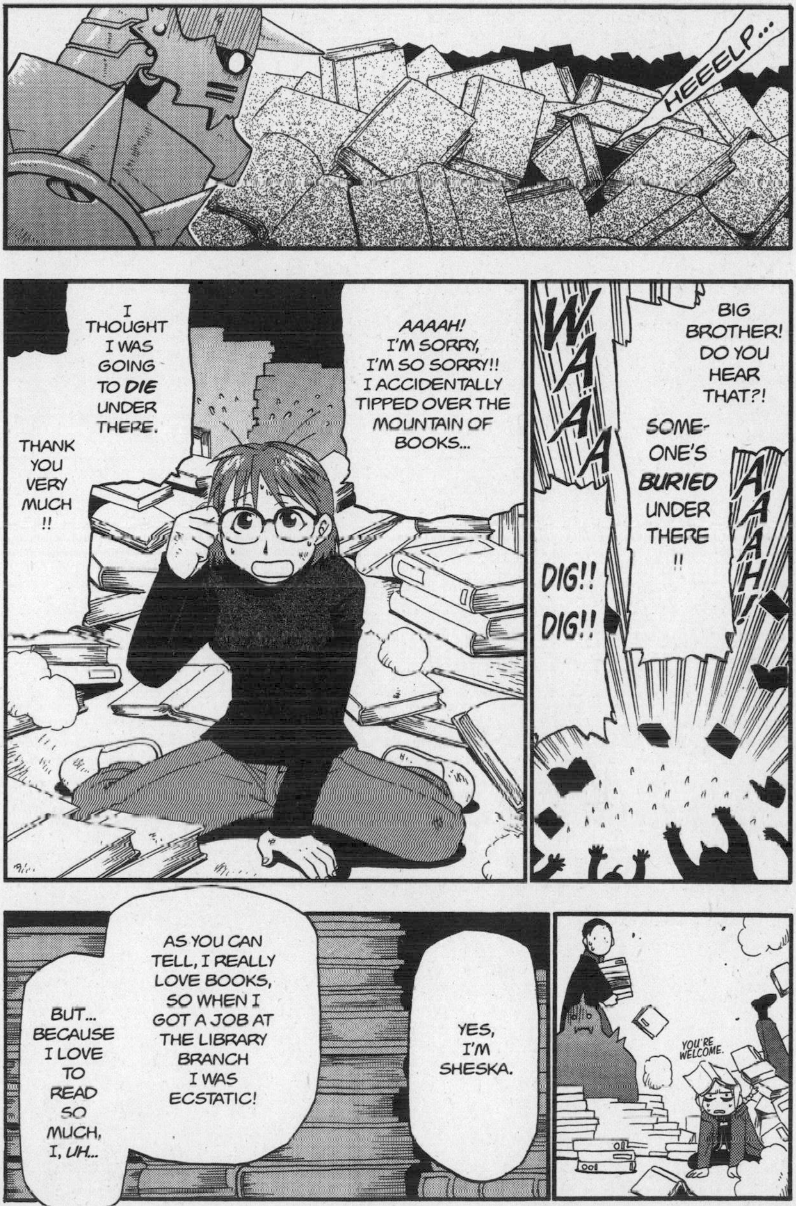
HEEELP...
BIG BROTHER! DO YOU HEAR THAT?!
SOME-ONE'S *BURIED* UNDER THERE!!
WAAAA
AAAAH!
DIG!! DIG!!
AAAAH! I'M SORRY, I'M SO SORRY!! I ACCIDENTALLY TIPPED OVER THE MOUNTAIN OF BOOKS...
I THOUGHT I WAS GOING TO *DIE* UNDER THERE.
THANK YOU VERY MUCH!!
YOU'RE WELCOME.
YES, I'M SHESKA.
AS YOU CAN TELL, I REALLY LOVE BOOKS, SO WHEN I GOT A JOB AT THE LIBRARY BRANCH I WAS ECSTATIC!
BUT... BECAUSE I LOVE TO READ SO MUCH, I, *UH*...

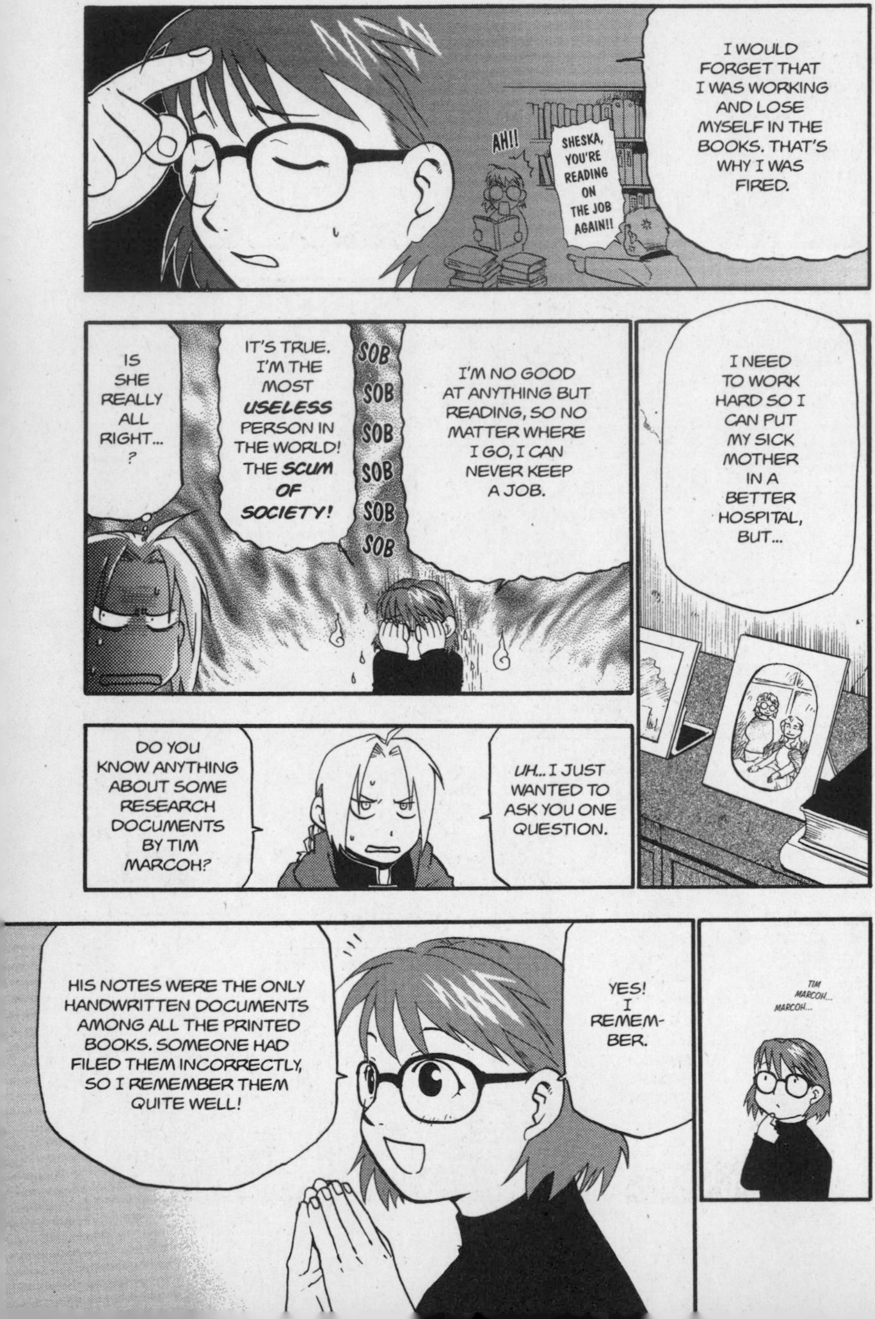
I WOULD FORGET THAT I WAS WORKING AND LOSE MYSELF IN THE BOOKS. THAT'S WHY I WAS FIRED.
SHESKA, YOU'RE READING ON THE JOB AGAIN!!
AH!!
I NEED TO WORK HARD SO I CAN PUT MY SICK MOTHER IN A BETTER HOSPITAL, BUT...
I'M NO GOOD AT ANYTHING BUT READING, SO NO MATTER WHERE I GO, I CAN NEVER KEEP A JOB.
SOB SOB SOB SOB SOB SOB
IT'S TRUE. I'M THE MOST USELESS PERSON IN THE WORLD! THE SCUM OF SOCIETY!
IS SHE REALLY ALL RIGHT...?
UH... I JUST WANTED TO ASK YOU ONE QUESTION.
DO YOU KNOW ANYTHING ABOUT SOME RESEARCH DOCUMENTS BY TIM MARCOH?
TIM MARCOH... MARCOH...
YES! I REMEMBER.
HIS NOTES WERE THE ONLY HANDWRITTEN DOCUMENTS AMONG ALL THE PRINTED BOOKS. SOMEONE HAD FILED THEM INCORRECTLY, SO I REMEMBER THEM QUITE WELL!

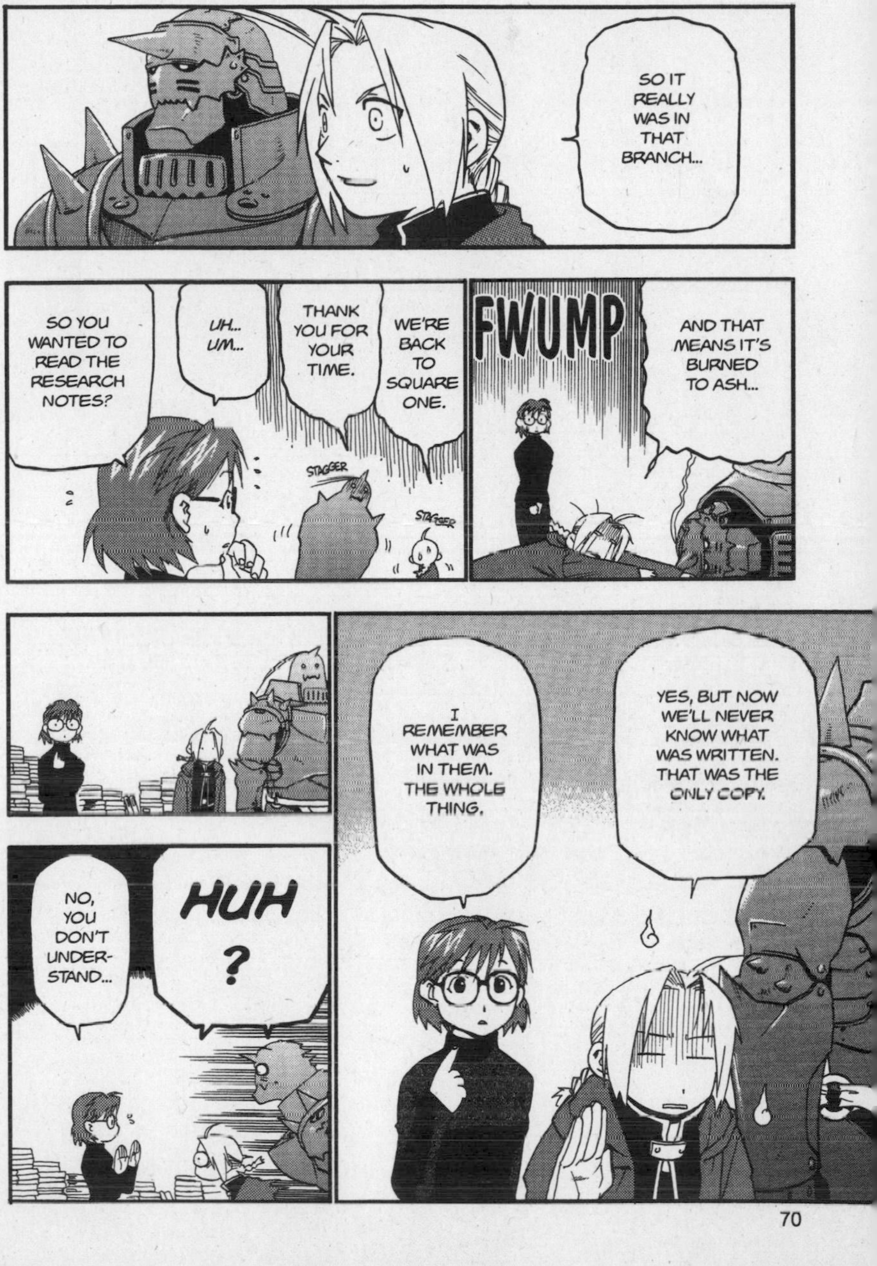
SO IT REALLY WAS IN THAT BRANCH...
AND THAT MEANS IT'S BURNED TO ASH...
FWUMP
WE'RE BACK TO SQUARE ONE.
THANK YOU FOR YOUR TIME.
UH... UM...
SO YOU WANTED TO READ THE RESEARCH NOTES?
STAGGER
STAGGER
YES, BUT NOW WE'LL NEVER KNOW WHAT WAS WRITTEN. THAT WAS THE ONLY COPY.
I REMEMBER WHAT WAS IN THEM. THE WHOLE THING.
HUH ?
NO, YOU DON'T UNDER-STAND...

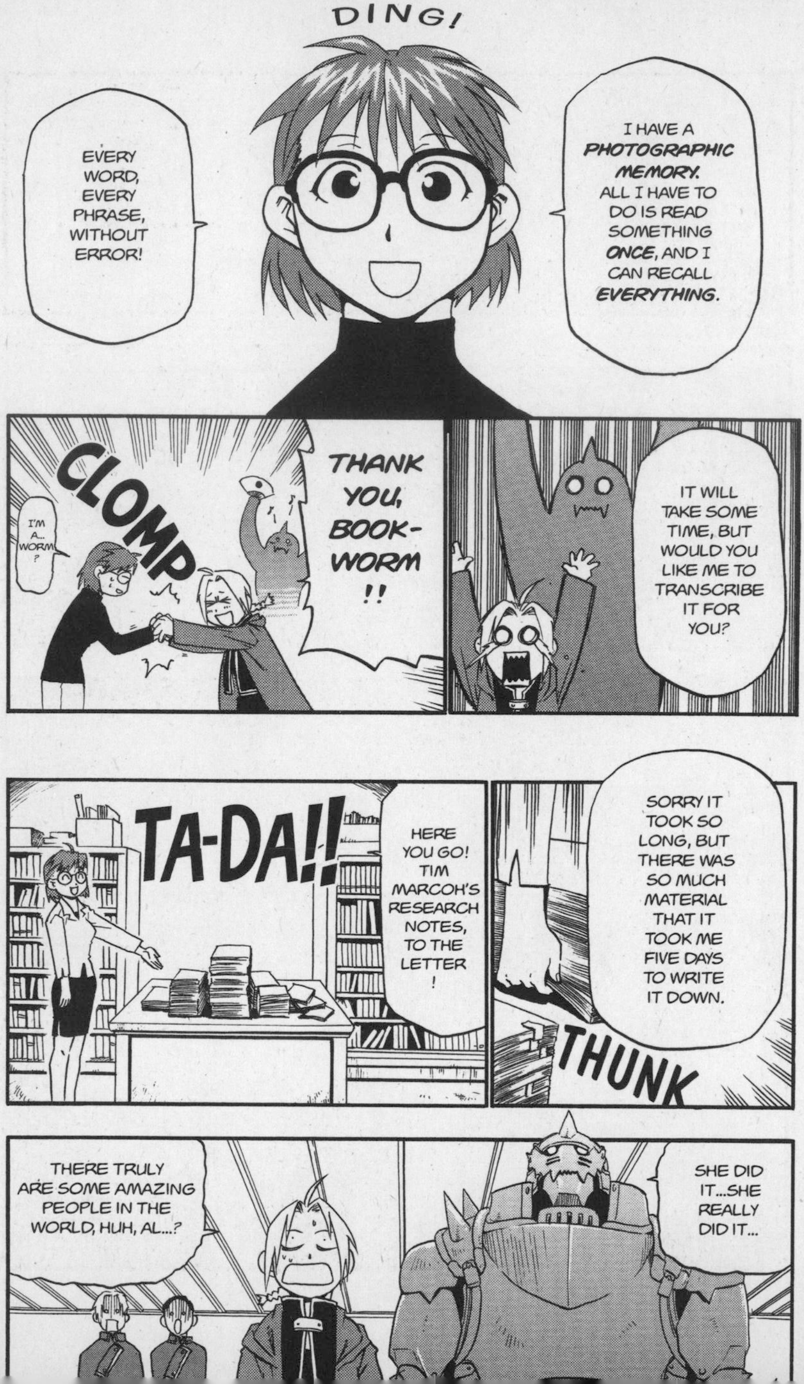
DING!
I HAVE A PHOTOGRAPHIC MEMORY. ALL I HAVE TO DO IS READ SOMETHING ONCE, AND I CAN RECALL EVERYTHING.
EVERY WORD, EVERY PHRASE, WITHOUT ERROR!
IT WILL TAKE SOME TIME, BUT WOULD YOU LIKE ME TO TRANSCRIBE IT FOR YOU?
THANK YOU, BOOK-WORM!!
CLOMP
I'M A... WORM?
SORRY IT TOOK SO LONG, BUT THERE WAS SO MUCH MATERIAL THAT IT TOOK ME FIVE DAYS TO WRITE IT DOWN.
THUNK
HERE YOU GO! TIM MARCOH'S RESEARCH NOTES, TO THE LETTER!
TA-DA!!
SHE DID IT...SHE REALLY DID IT...
THERE TRULY ARE SOME AMAZING PEOPLE IN THE WORLD, HUH, AL...?

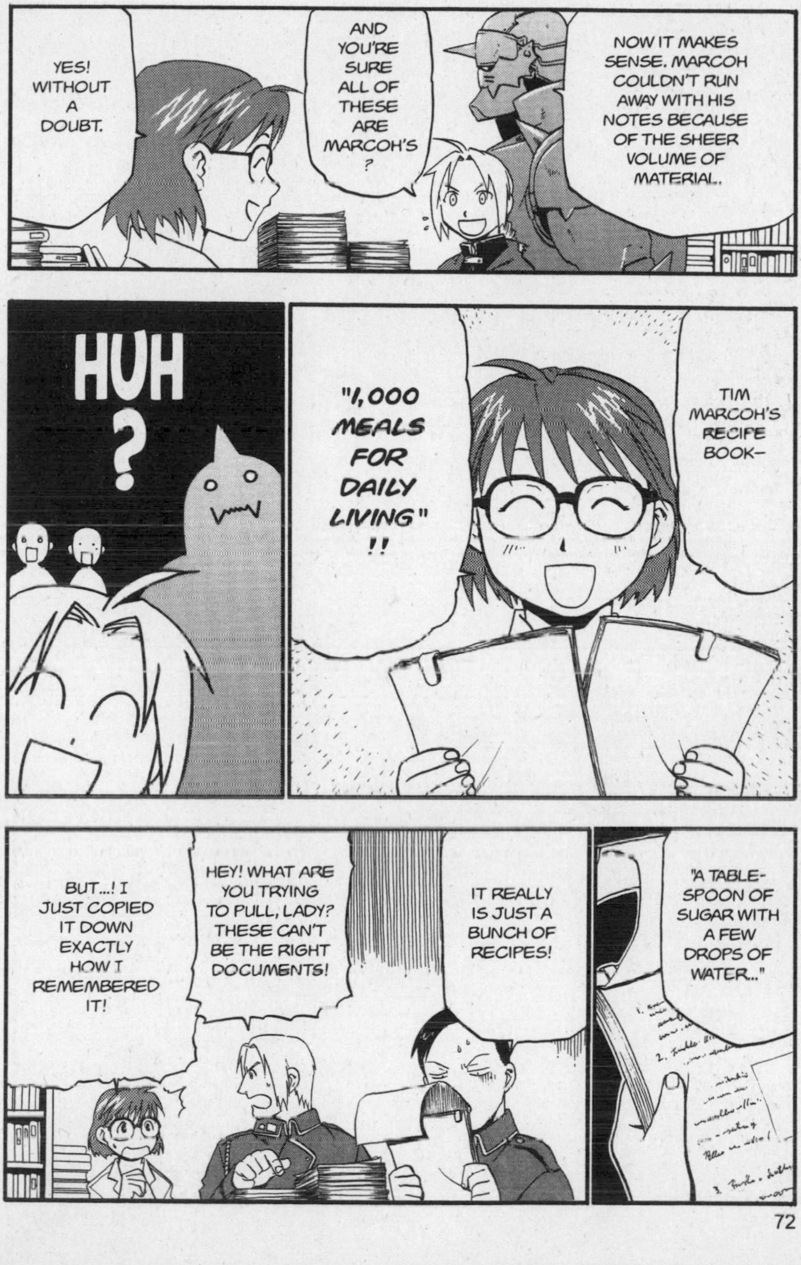
NOW IT MAKES SENSE. MARCOH COULDN'T RUN AWAY WITH HIS NOTES BECAUSE OF THE SHEER VOLUME OF MATERIAL.
AND YOU'RE SURE ALL OF THESE ARE MARCOH'S?
YES! WITHOUT A DOUBT.
TIM MARCOH'S RECIPE BOOK—
"1,000 MEALS FOR DAILY LIVING"!!
HUH?
"A TABLESPOON OF SUGAR WITH A FEW DROPS OF WATER..."
IT REALLY IS JUST A BUNCH OF RECIPES!
HEY! WHAT ARE YOU TRYING TO PULL, LADY? THESE CAN'T BE THE RIGHT DOCUMENTS!
BUT...! I JUST COPIED IT DOWN EXACTLY HOW I REMEMBERED IT!

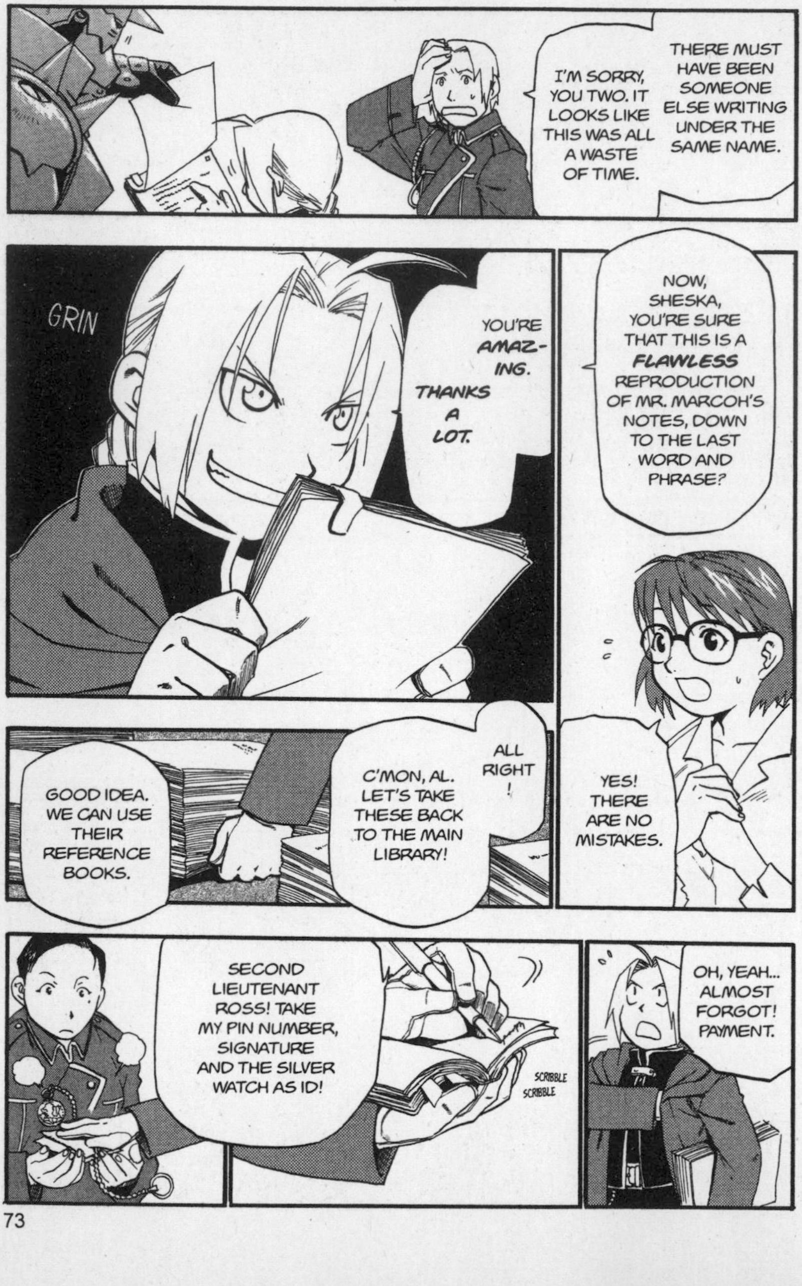
THERE MUST HAVE BEEN SOMEONE ELSE WRITING UNDER THE SAME NAME.
I'M SORRY, YOU TWO. IT LOOKS LIKE THIS WAS ALL A WASTE OF TIME.
NOW, SHESKA, YOU'RE SURE THAT THIS IS A ***FLAWLESS*** REPRODUCTION OF MR. MARCOH'S NOTES, DOWN TO THE LAST WORD AND PHRASE?
YES! THERE ARE NO MISTAKES.
YOU'RE ***AMAZ-ING.***
THANKS A LOT.
GRIN
ALL RIGHT!
C'MON, AL. LET'S TAKE THESE BACK TO THE MAIN LIBRARY!
GOOD IDEA. WE CAN USE THEIR REFERENCE BOOKS.
OH, YEAH... ALMOST FORGOT! PAYMENT.
SECOND LIEUTENANT ROSS! TAKE MY PIN NUMBER, SIGNATURE AND THE SILVER WATCH AS ID!
SCRIBBLE SCRIBBLE

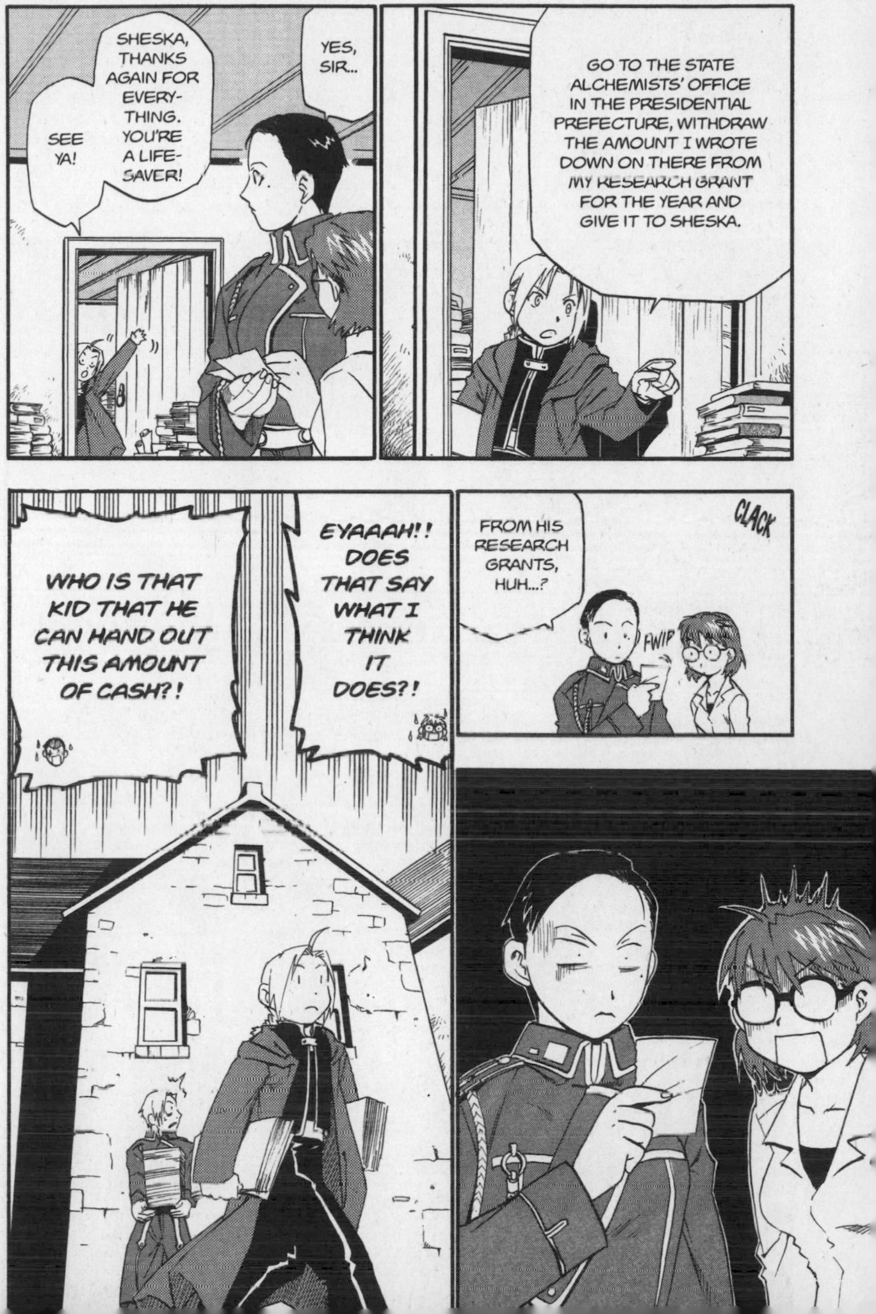
GO TO THE STATE ALCHEMISTS' OFFICE IN THE PRESIDENTIAL PREFECTURE, WITHDRAW THE AMOUNT I WROTE DOWN ON THERE FROM MY RESEARCH GRANT FOR THE YEAR AND GIVE IT TO SHESKA.
YES, SIR...
SHESKA, THANKS AGAIN FOR EVERY-THING. YOU'RE A LIFE-SAVER!
SEE YA!
CLACK
FROM HIS RESEARCH GRANTS, HUH...?
FWIP
EYAAAH!! DOES THAT SAY WHAT I THINK IT DOES?!
WHO IS THAT KID THAT HE CAN HAND OUT THIS AMOUNT OF CASH?!

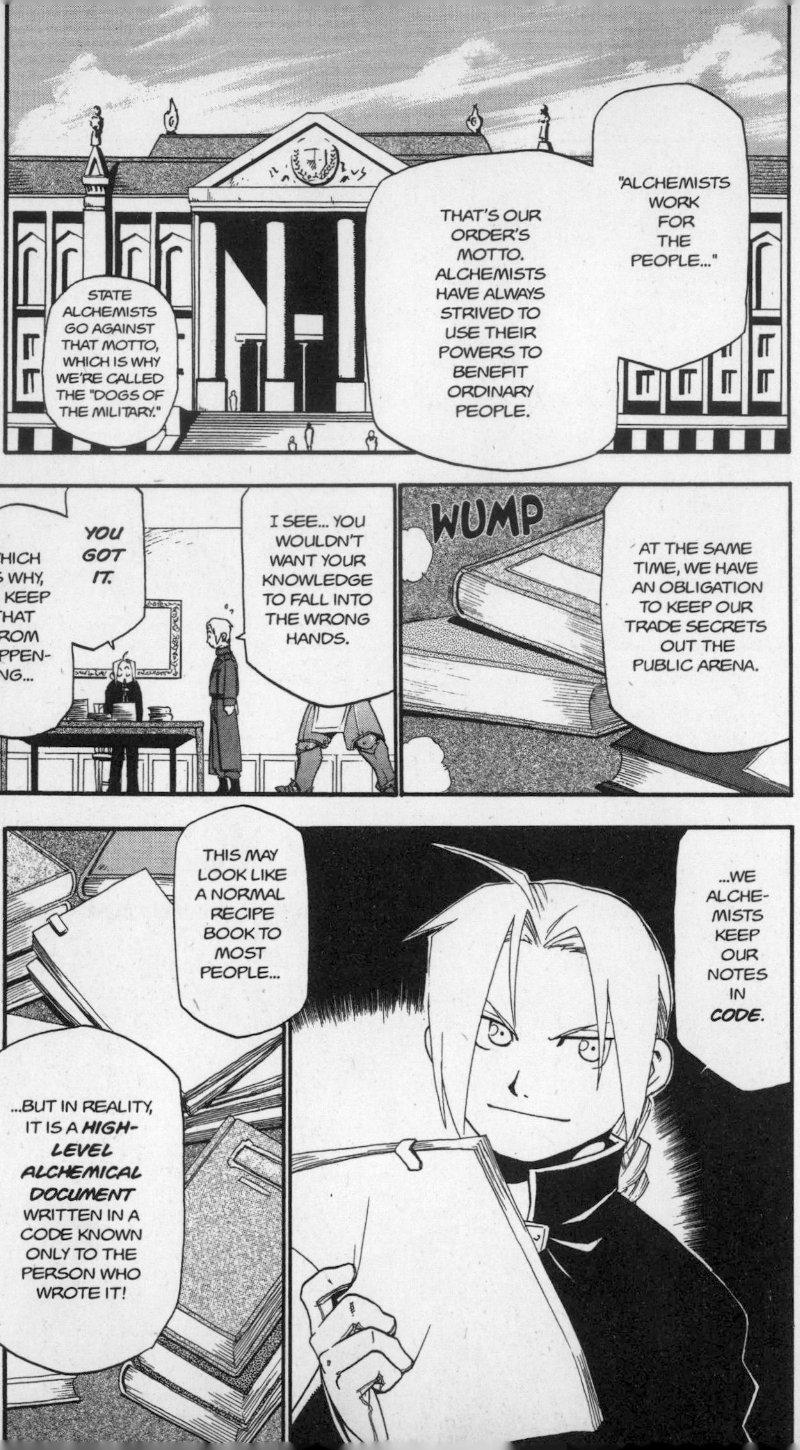
"ALCHEMISTS WORK FOR THE PEOPLE..."
THAT'S OUR ORDER'S MOTTO. ALCHEMISTS HAVE ALWAYS STRIVED TO USE THEIR POWERS TO BENEFIT ORDINARY PEOPLE.
STATE ALCHEMISTS GO AGAINST THAT MOTTO, WHICH IS WHY WE'RE CALLED THE "DOGS OF THE MILITARY."
WUMP
AT THE SAME TIME, WE HAVE AN OBLIGATION TO KEEP OUR TRADE SECRETS OUT THE PUBLIC ARENA.
I SEE... YOU WOULDN'T WANT YOUR KNOWLEDGE TO FALL INTO THE WRONG HANDS.
YOU GOT IT.
WHICH IS WHY, TO KEEP THAT FROM HAPPEN-ING...
...WE ALCHE-MISTS KEEP OUR NOTES IN CODE.
THIS MAY LOOK LIKE A NORMAL RECIPE BOOK TO MOST PEOPLE...
...BUT IN REALITY, IT IS A HIGH-LEVEL ALCHEMICAL DOCUMENT WRITTEN IN A CODE KNOWN ONLY TO THE PERSON WHO WROTE IT!

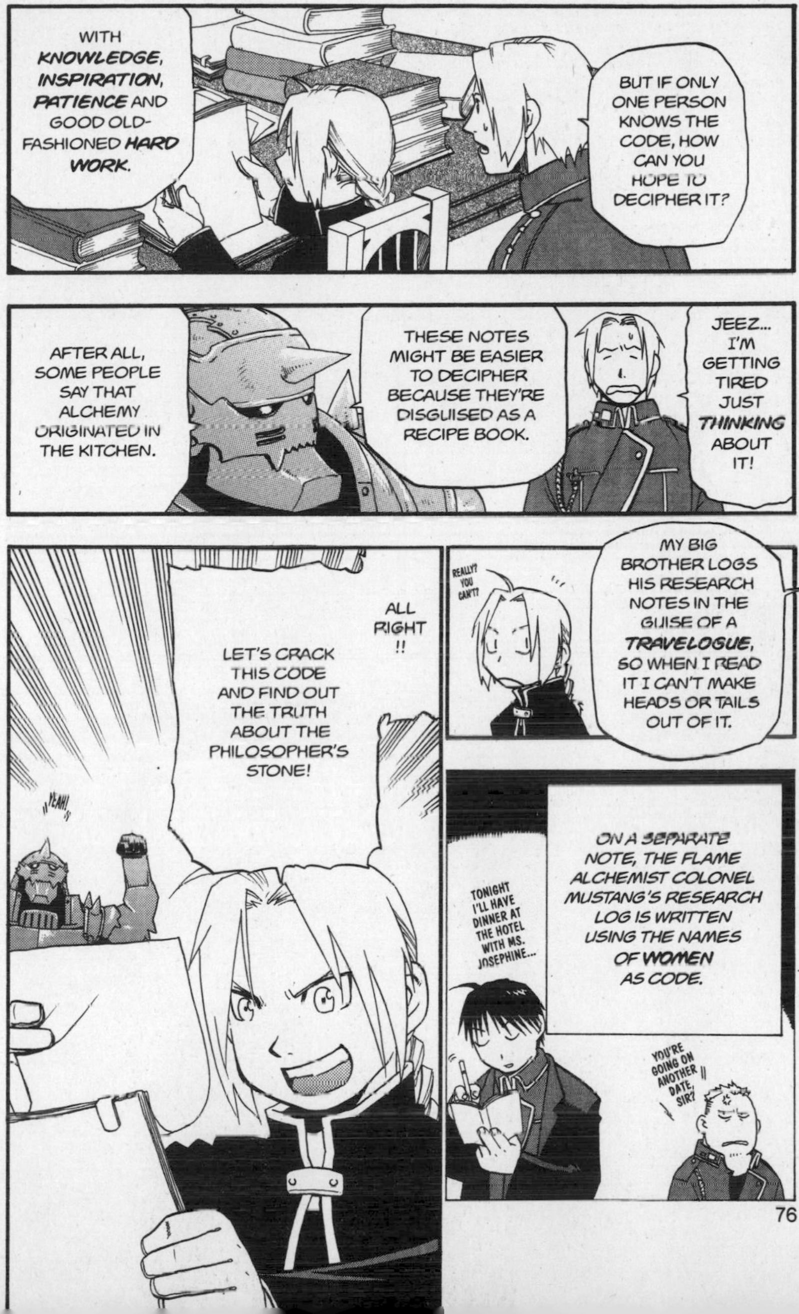
BUT IF ONLY ONE PERSON KNOWS THE CODE, HOW CAN YOU HOPE TO DECIPHER IT?
WITH KNOWLEDGE, INSPIRATION, PATIENCE AND GOOD OLD-FASHIONED HARD WORK.
JEEZ... I'M GETTING TIRED JUST THINKING ABOUT IT!
THESE NOTES MIGHT BE EASIER TO DECIPHER BECAUSE THEY'RE DISGUISED AS A RECIPE BOOK.
AFTER ALL, SOME PEOPLE SAY THAT ALCHEMY ORIGINATED IN THE KITCHEN.
MY BIG BROTHER LOGS HIS RESEARCH NOTES IN THE GUISE OF A TRAVELOGUE, SO WHEN I READ IT I CAN'T MAKE HEADS OR TAILS OUT OF IT.
REALLY? YOU CAN'T?
ON A SEPARATE NOTE, THE FLAME ALCHEMIST COLONEL MUSTANG'S RESEARCH LOG IS WRITTEN USING THE NAMES OF WOMEN AS CODE.
TONIGHT I'LL HAVE DINNER AT THE HOTEL WITH MS. JOSEPHINE...
YOU'RE GOING ON ANOTHER DATE, SIR?
ALL RIGHT !!
LET'S CRACK THIS CODE AND FIND OUT THE TRUTH ABOUT THE PHILOSOPHER'S STONE!
YEAH!

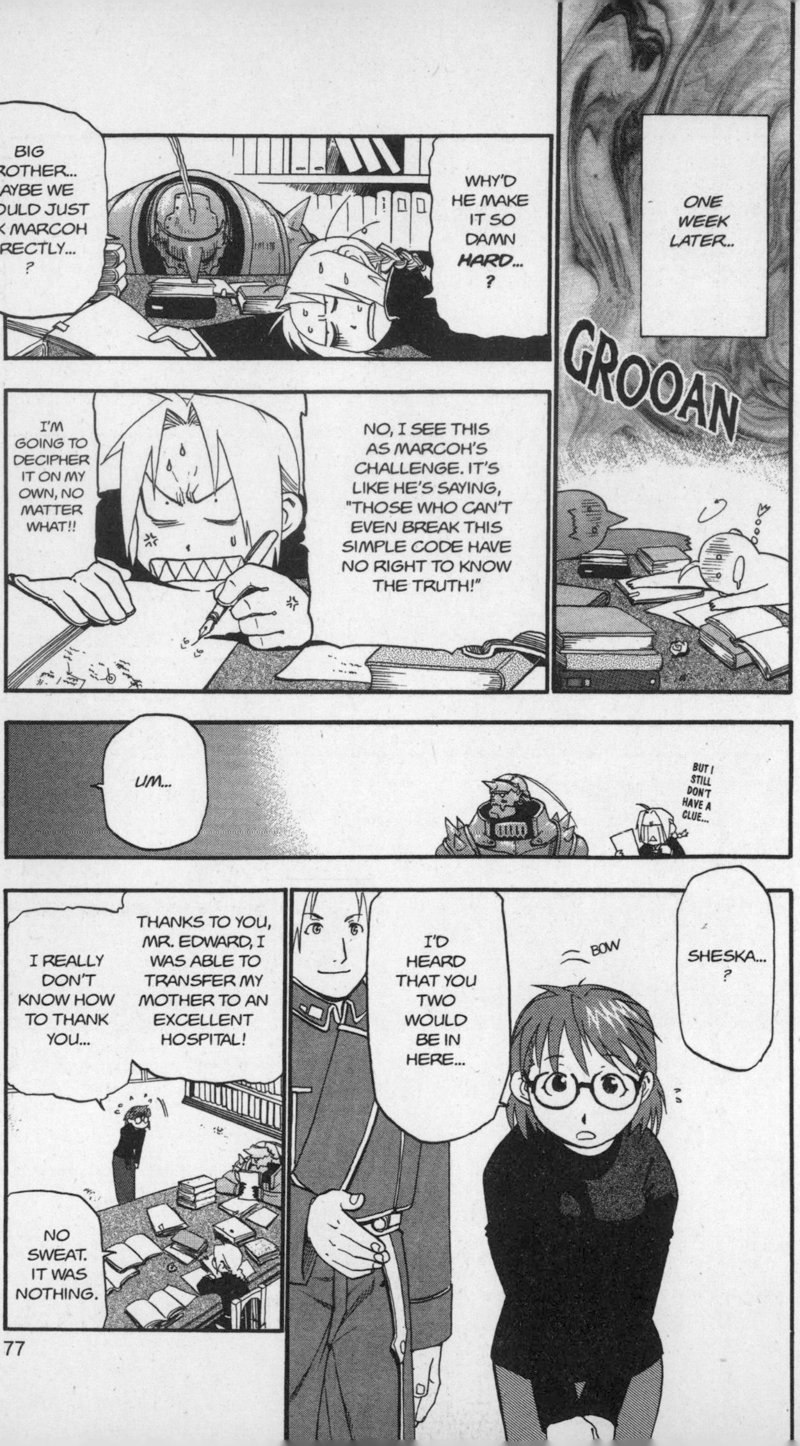
ONE WEEK LATER...
GROOAN
WHY'D HE MAKE IT SO DAMN *HARD*...?
BIG BROTHER... MAYBE WE SHOULD JUST ASK MARCOH DIRECTLY...?
NO, I SEE THIS AS MARCOH'S CHALLENGE. IT'S LIKE HE'S SAYING, "THOSE WHO CAN'T EVEN BREAK THIS SIMPLE CODE HAVE NO RIGHT TO KNOW THE TRUTH!"
I'M GOING TO DECIPHER IT ON MY OWN, NO MATTER WHAT!!
BUT I STILL DON'T HAVE A CLUE...
UM...
SHESKA...?
BOW
I'D HEARD THAT YOU TWO WOULD BE IN HERE...
THANKS TO YOU, MR. EDWARD, I WAS ABLE TO TRANSFER MY MOTHER TO AN EXCELLENT HOSPITAL!
I REALLY DON'T KNOW HOW TO THANK YOU...
NO SWEAT. IT WAS NOTHING.

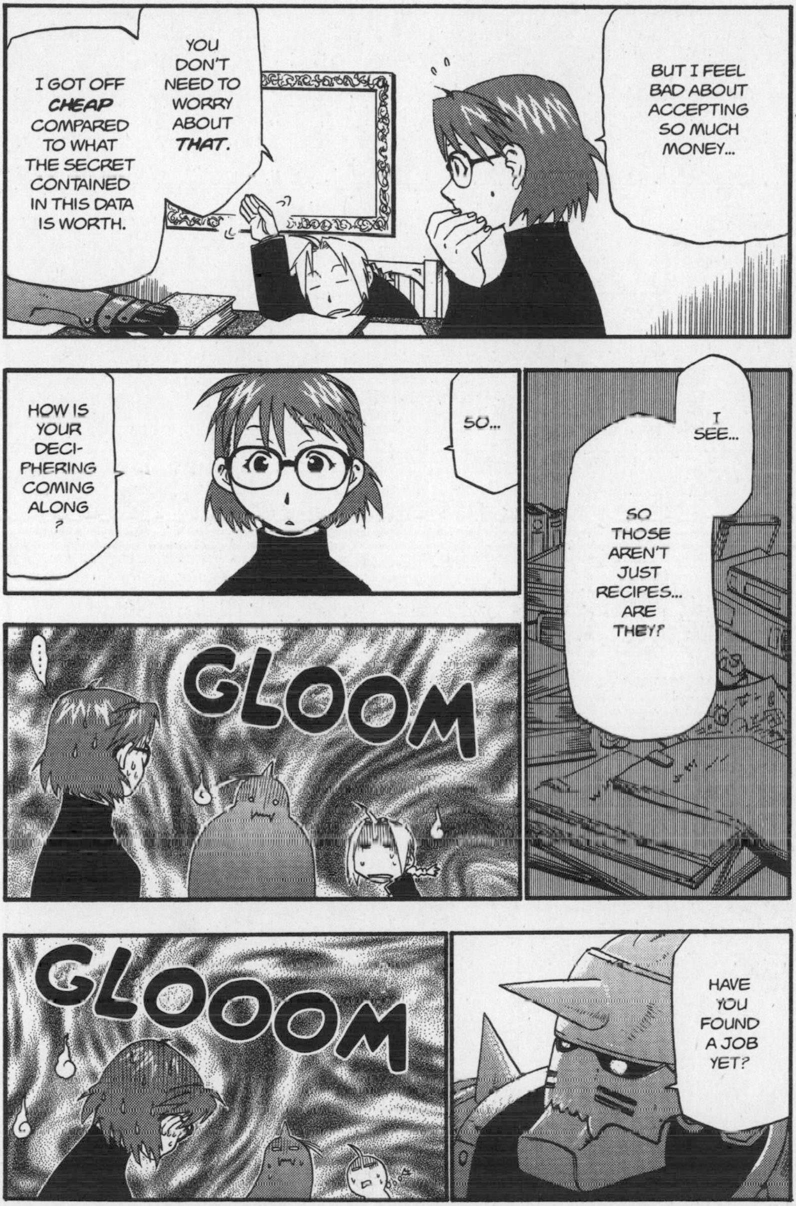
BUT I FEEL BAD ABOUT ACCEPTING SO MUCH MONEY...
YOU DON'T NEED TO WORRY ABOUT THAT.
I GOT OFF CHEAP COMPARED TO WHAT THE SECRET CONTAINED IN THIS DATA IS WORTH.
I SEE...
SO THOSE AREN'T JUST RECIPES... ARE THEY?
SO...
HOW IS YOUR DECIPHERING COMING ALONG?
....
GLOOM
HAVE YOU FOUND A JOB YET?
GLOOOM

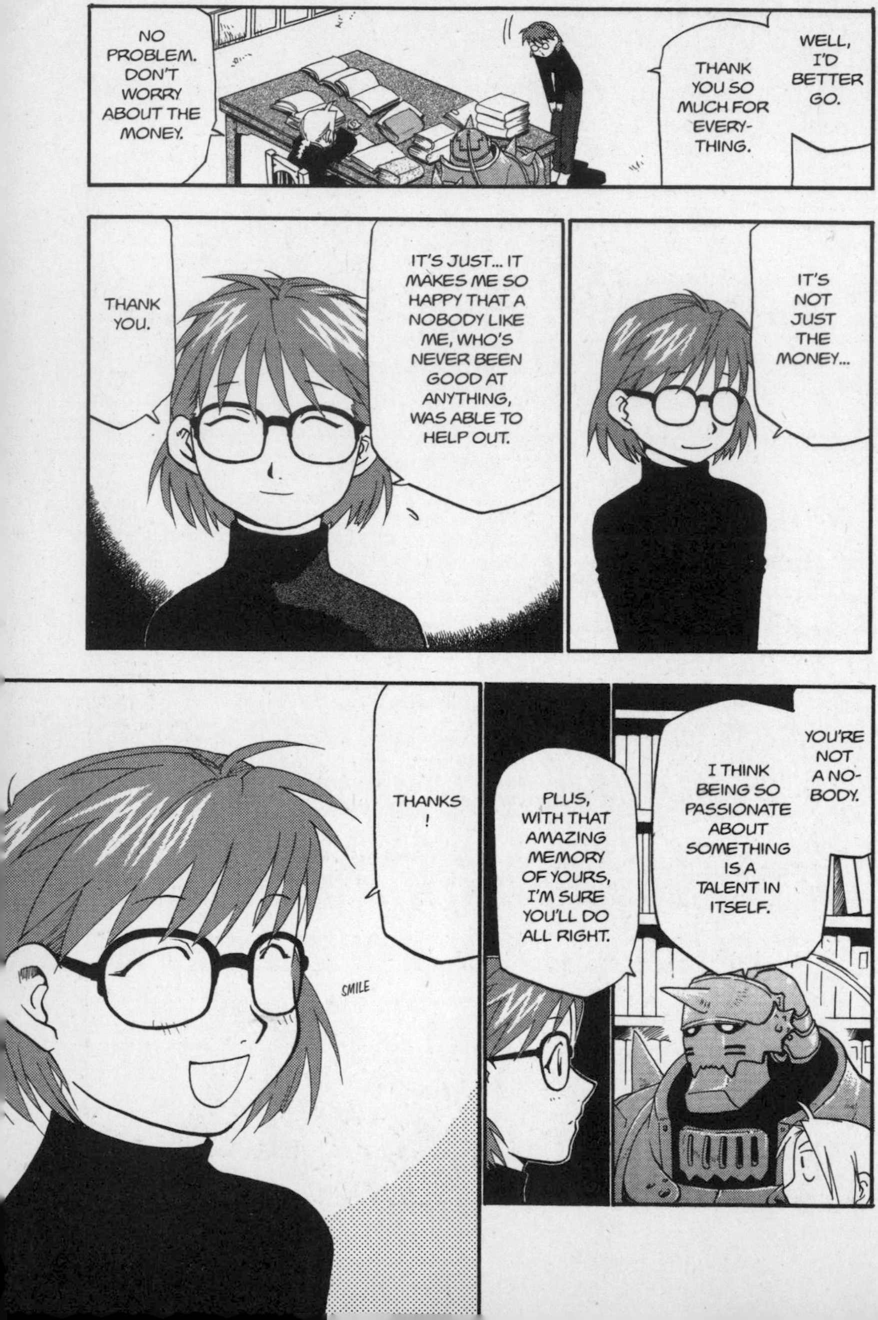
WELL, I'D BETTER GO.
THANK YOU SO MUCH FOR EVERYTHING.
NO PROBLEM. DON'T WORRY ABOUT THE MONEY.
IT'S NOT JUST THE MONEY...
IT'S JUST... IT MAKES ME SO HAPPY THAT A NOBODY LIKE ME, WHO'S NEVER BEEN GOOD AT ANYTHING, WAS ABLE TO HELP OUT.
THANK YOU.
YOU'RE NOT A NO-BODY.
I THINK BEING SO PASSIONATE ABOUT SOMETHING IS A TALENT IN ITSELF.
PLUS, WITH THAT AMAZING MEMORY OF YOURS, I'M SURE YOU'LL DO ALL RIGHT.
THANKS!
SMILE

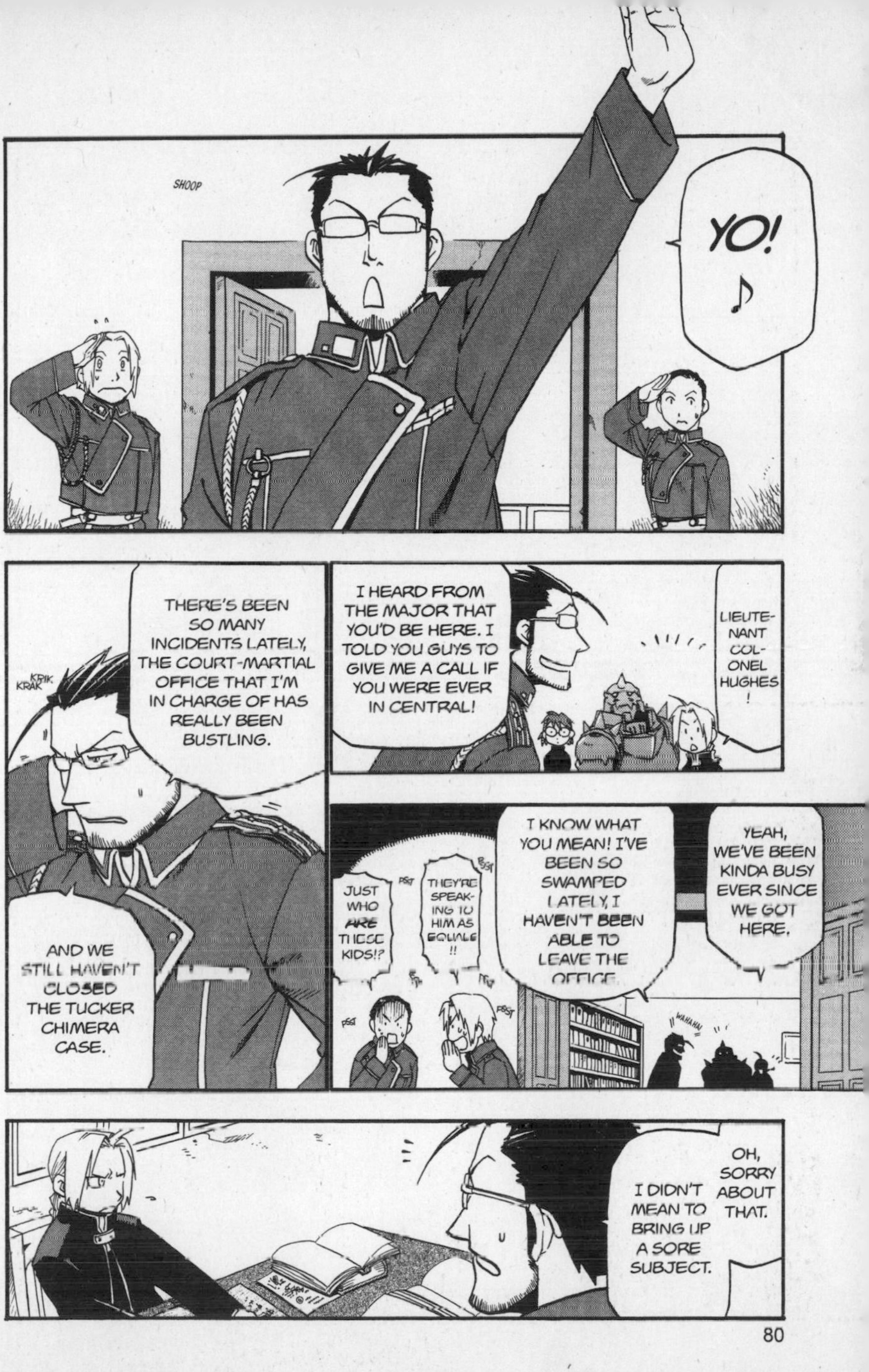
SHOOP
YO! ♪
LIEUTENANT COLONEL HUGHES!
I HEARD FROM THE MAJOR THAT YOU'D BE HERE. I TOLD YOU GUYS TO GIVE ME A CALL IF YOU WERE EVER IN CENTRAL!
YEAH, WE'VE BEEN KINDA BUSY EVER SINCE WE GOT HERE.
I KNOW WHAT YOU MEAN! I'VE BEEN SO SWAMPED LATELY, I HAVEN'T BEEN ABLE TO LEAVE THE OFFICE.
WAHAHA
PSST
THEY'RE SPEAKING TO HIM AS EQUALS!!
PSST
JUST WHO ARE THESE KIDS!?
PSST
KRIK KRAK
THERE'S BEEN SO MANY INCIDENTS LATELY, THE COURT-MARTIAL OFFICE THAT I'M IN CHARGE OF HAS REALLY BEEN BUSTLING.
AND WE STILL HAVEN'T CLOSED THE TUCKER CHIMERA CASE.
OH, SORRY ABOUT THAT.
I DIDN'T MEAN TO BRING UP A SORE SUBJECT.

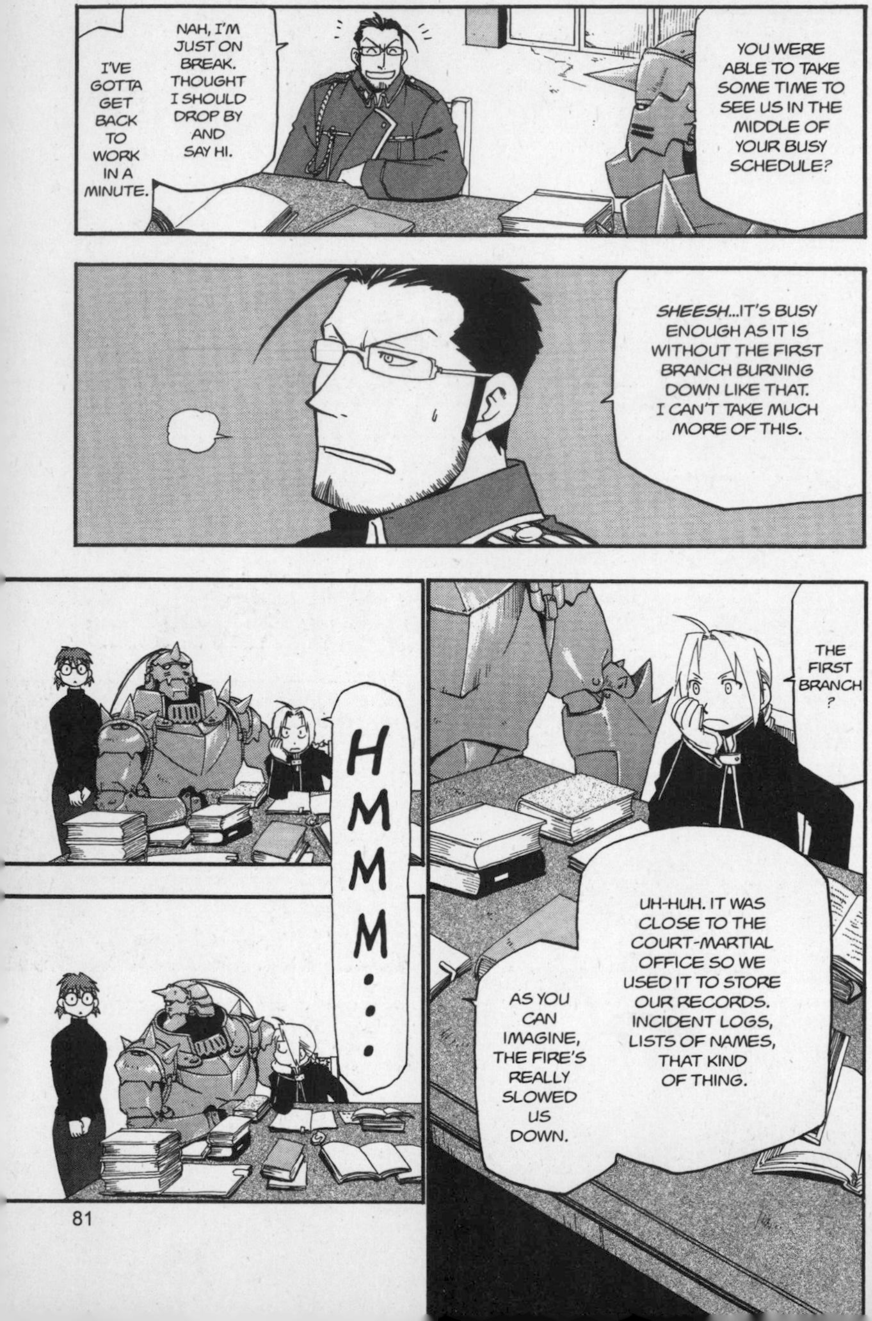
YOU WERE ABLE TO TAKE SOME TIME TO SEE US IN THE MIDDLE OF YOUR BUSY SCHEDULE?
NAH, I'M JUST ON BREAK. THOUGHT I SHOULD DROP BY AND SAY HI.
I'VE GOTTA GET BACK TO WORK IN A MINUTE.
SHEESH...IT'S BUSY ENOUGH AS IT IS WITHOUT THE FIRST BRANCH BURNING DOWN LIKE THAT. I CAN'T TAKE MUCH MORE OF THIS.
THE FIRST BRANCH?
UH-HUH. IT WAS CLOSE TO THE COURT-MARTIAL OFFICE SO WE USED IT TO STORE OUR RECORDS. INCIDENT LOGS, LISTS OF NAMES, THAT KIND OF THING.
AS YOU CAN IMAGINE, THE FIRE'S REALLY SLOWED US DOWN.
HMMM...

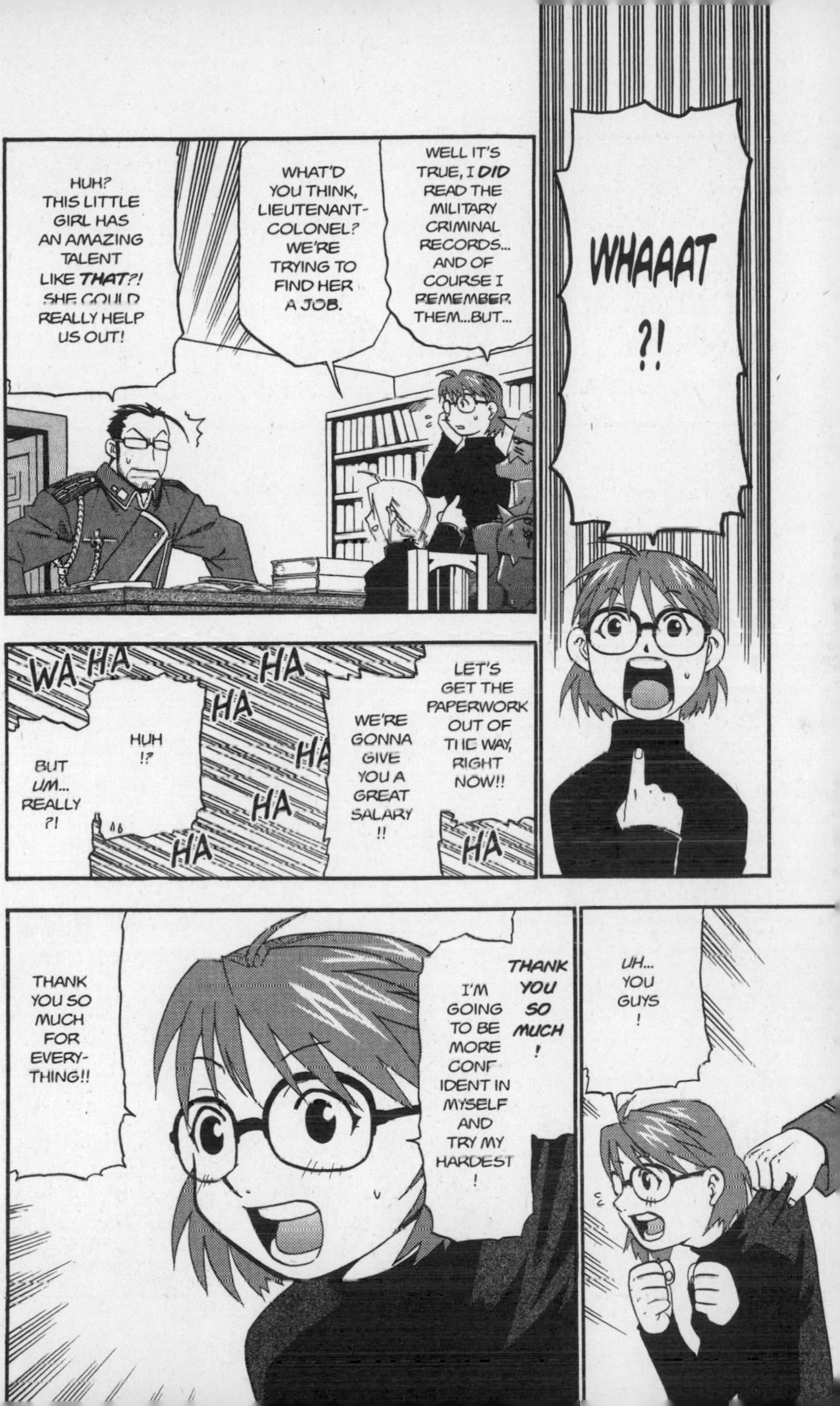
WHAAAT ?!
WELL IT'S TRUE, I DID READ THE MILITARY CRIMINAL RECORDS... AND OF COURSE I REMEMBER THEM...BUT...
WHAT'D YOU THINK, LIEUTENANT-COLONEL? WE'RE TRYING TO FIND HER A JOB.
HUH? THIS LITTLE GIRL HAS AN AMAZING TALENT LIKE THAT?! SHE COULD REALLY HELP US OUT!
HA
LET'S GET THE PAPERWORK OUT OF THE WAY, RIGHT NOW!!
WE'RE GONNA GIVE YOU A GREAT SALARY !!
WA HA HA HA HA HA HA
HUH !?
BUT UM... REALLY ?!
UH... YOU GUYS !
THANK YOU SO MUCH !
I'M GOING TO BE MORE CONFIDENT IN MYSELF AND TRY MY HARDEST !
THANK YOU SO MUCH FOR EVERYTHING!!

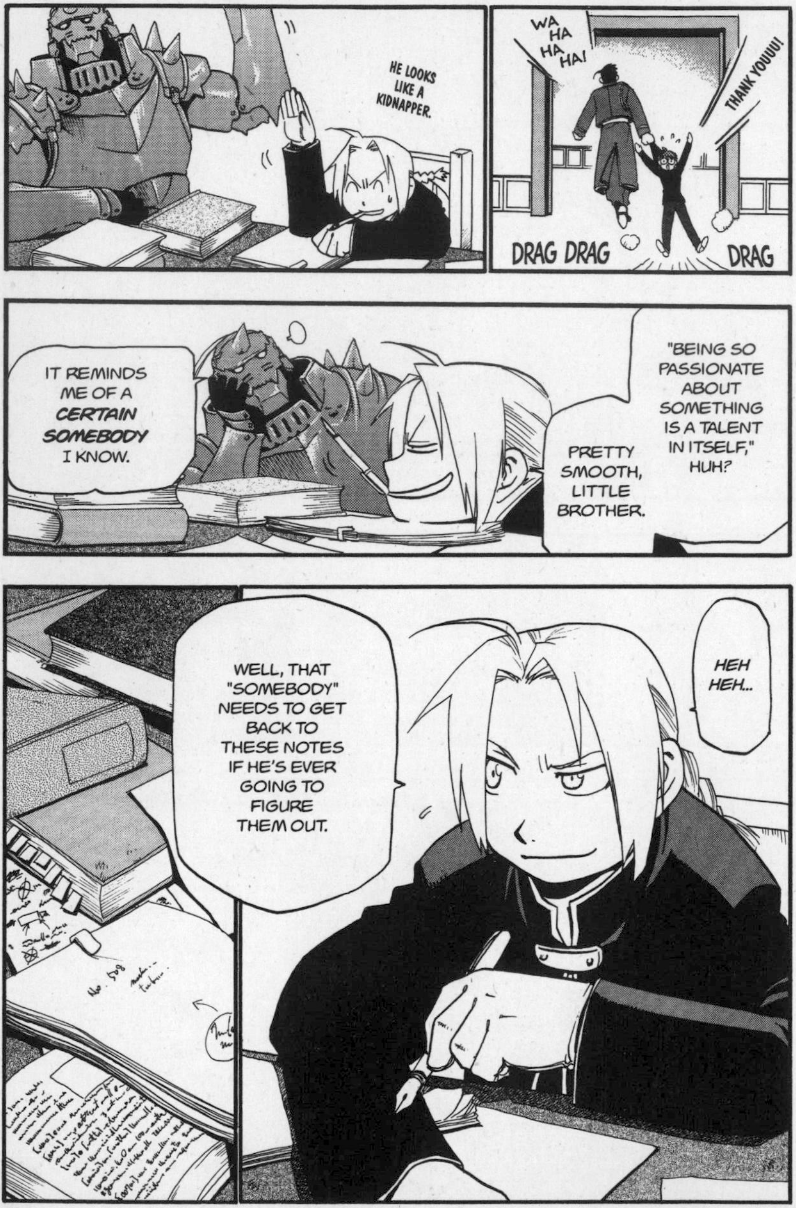
WA HA HA HA!
THANK YOUUU!
DRAG DRAG
DRAG
HE LOOKS LIKE A KIDNAPPER.
"BEING SO PASSIONATE ABOUT SOMETHING IS A TALENT IN ITSELF," HUH?
PRETTY SMOOTH, LITTLE BROTHER.
IT REMINDS ME OF A *CERTAIN SOMEBODY* I KNOW.
HEH HEH...
WELL, THAT "SOMEBODY" NEEDS TO GET BACK TO THESE NOTES IF HE'S EVER GOING TO FIGURE THEM OUT.

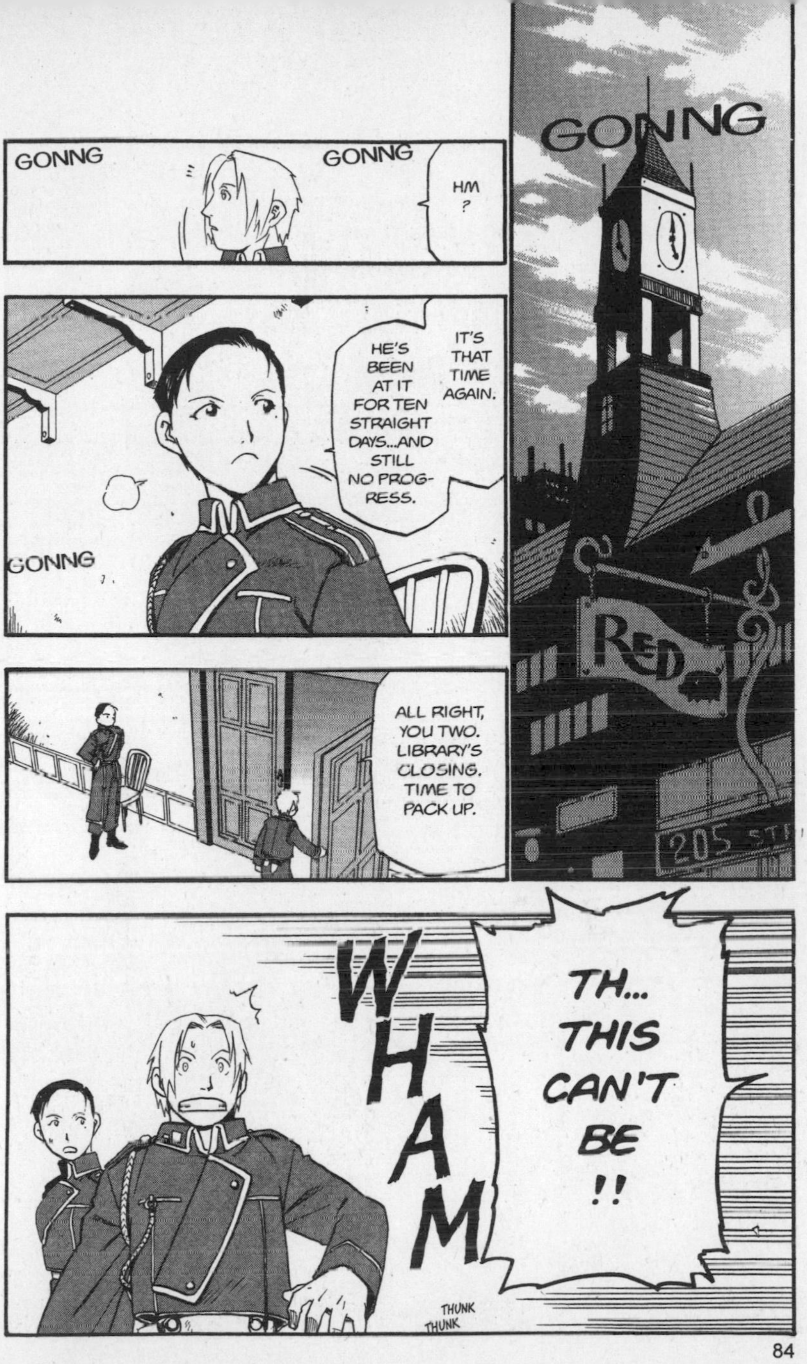

GONNG
RED
205
HM?
GONNG
GONNG
IT'S THAT TIME AGAIN.
HE'S BEEN AT IT FOR TEN STRAIGHT DAYS...AND STILL NO PROG-RESS.
GONNG
ALL RIGHT, YOU TWO. LIBRARY'S CLOSING. TIME TO PACK UP.
TH... THIS CAN'T BE!!
WHAM
THUNK
THUNK

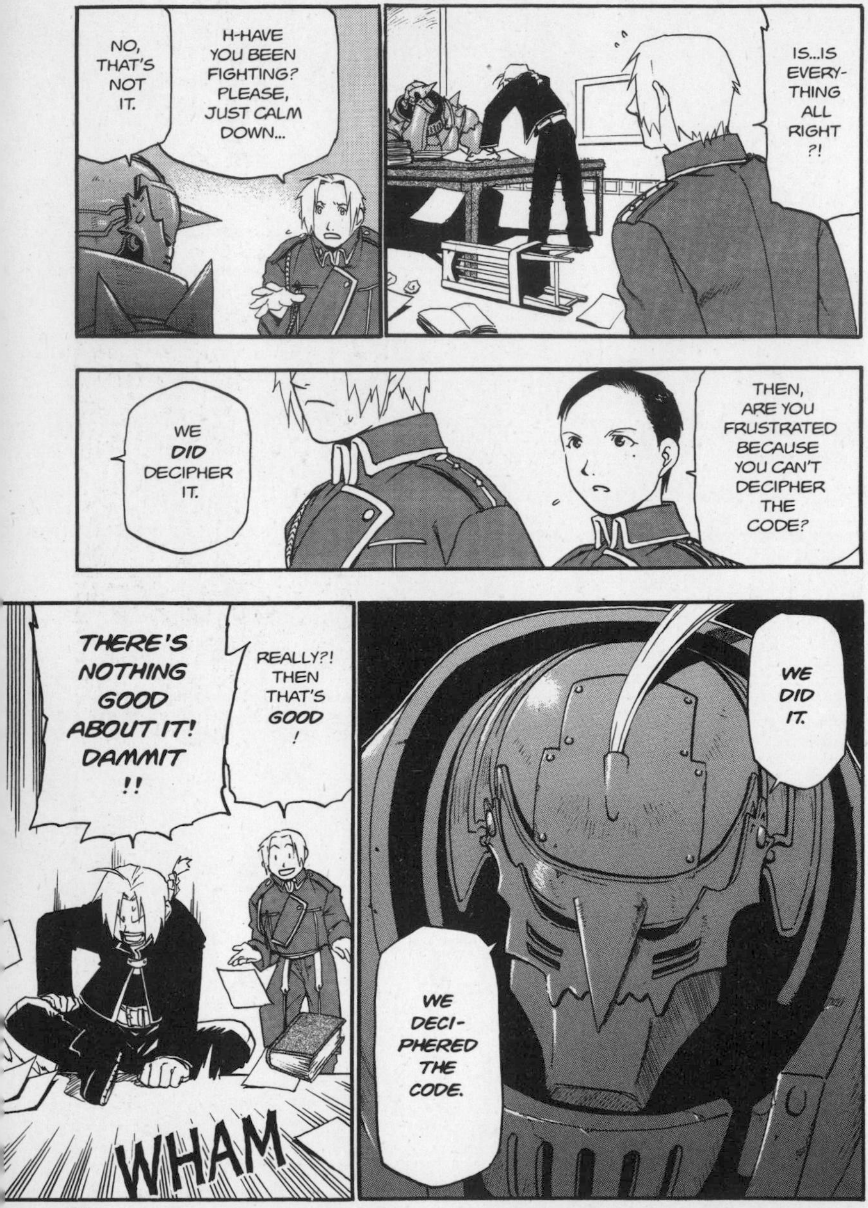
IS...IS EVERYTHING ALL RIGHT?!
H-HAVE YOU BEEN FIGHTING? PLEASE, JUST CALM DOWN...
NO, THAT'S NOT IT.
THEN, ARE YOU FRUSTRATED BECAUSE YOU CAN'T DECIPHER THE CODE?
WE DID DECIPHER IT.
WE DID IT.
WE DECIPHERED THE CODE.
REALLY?! THEN THAT'S GOOD!
THERE'S NOTHING GOOD ABOUT IT! DAMMIT!!
WHAM

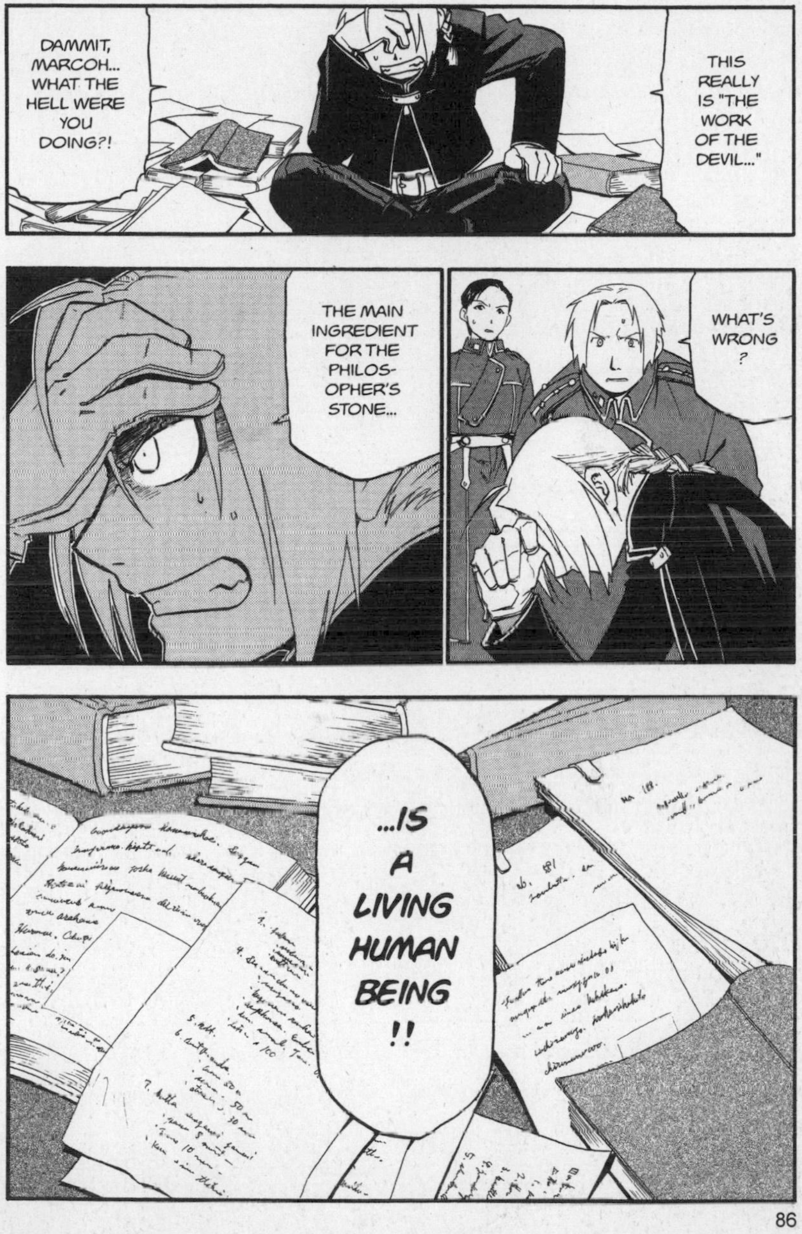
THIS REALLY IS "THE WORK OF THE DEVIL..."
DAMMIT, MARCOH... WHAT THE HELL WERE YOU DOING?!
WHAT'S WRONG ?
THE MAIN INGREDIENT FOR THE PHILOS-OPHER'S STONE...
...IS A LIVING HUMAN BEING !!

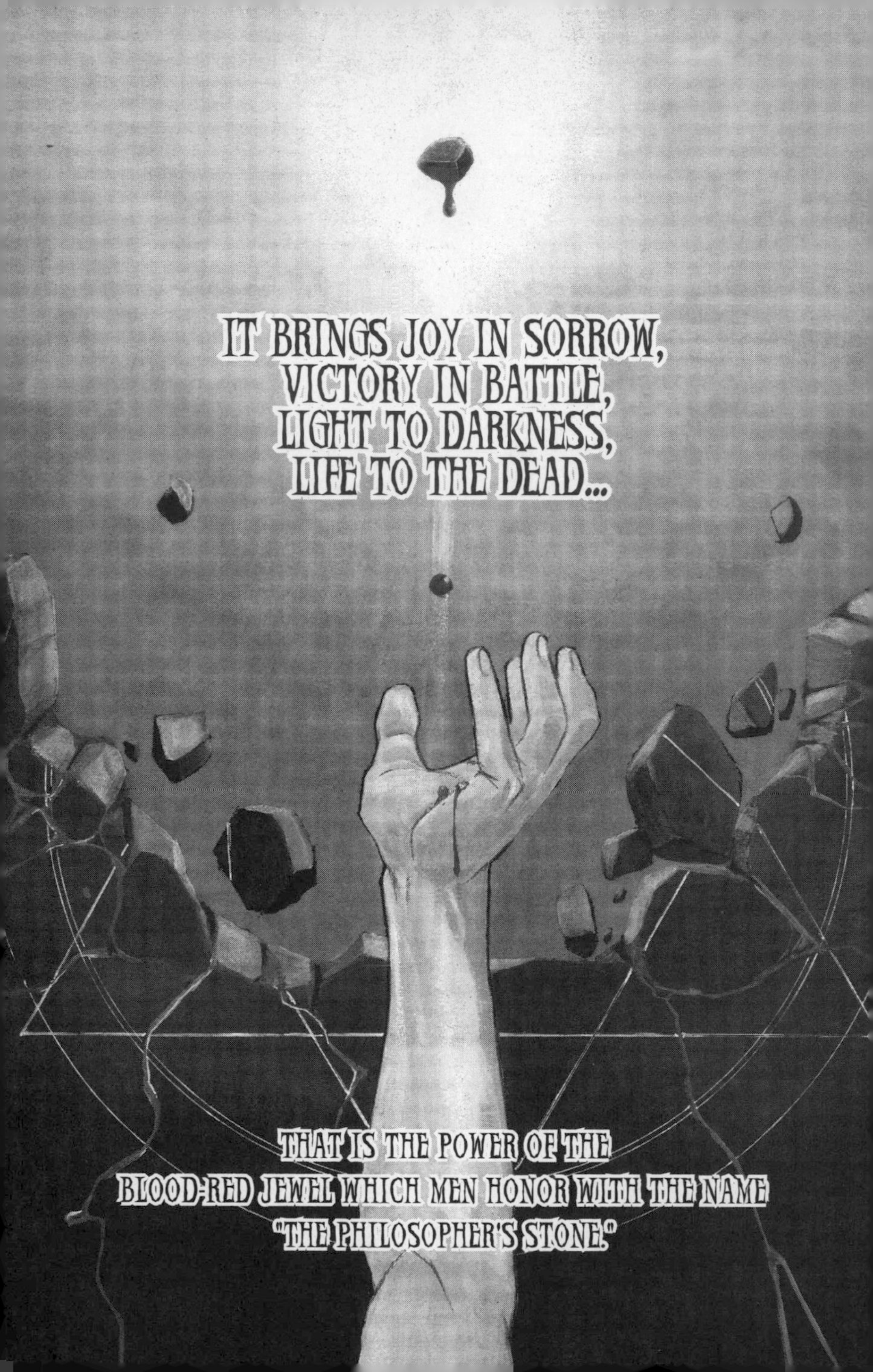
IT BRINGS JOY IN SORROW, VICTORY IN BATTLE, LIGHT TO DARKNESS, LIFE TO THE DEAD...
THAT IS THE POWER OF THE BLOOD-RED JEWEL WHICH MEN HONOR WITH THE NAME "THE PHILOSOPHER'S STONE."

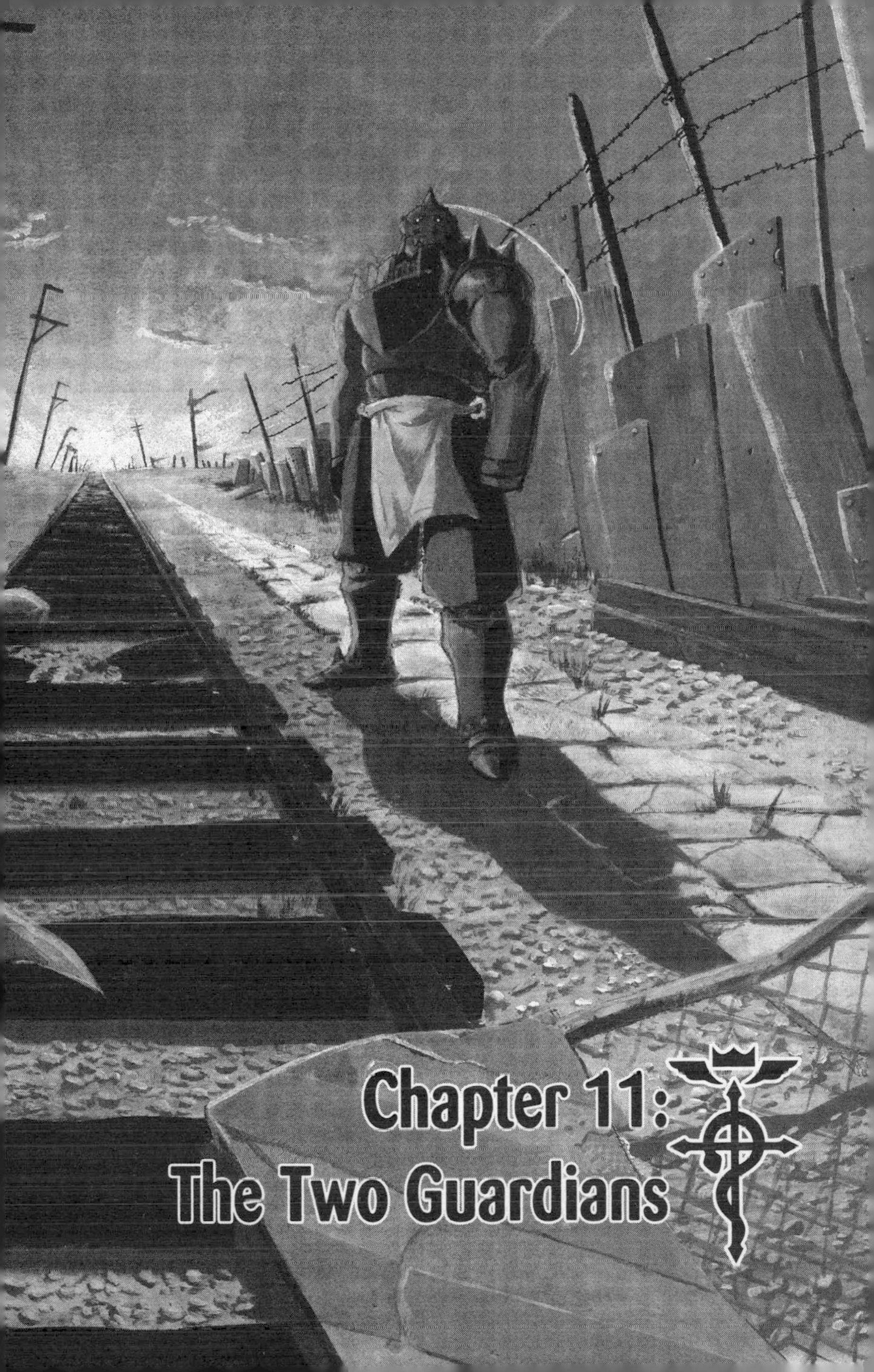
Chapter 11:
The Two Guardians

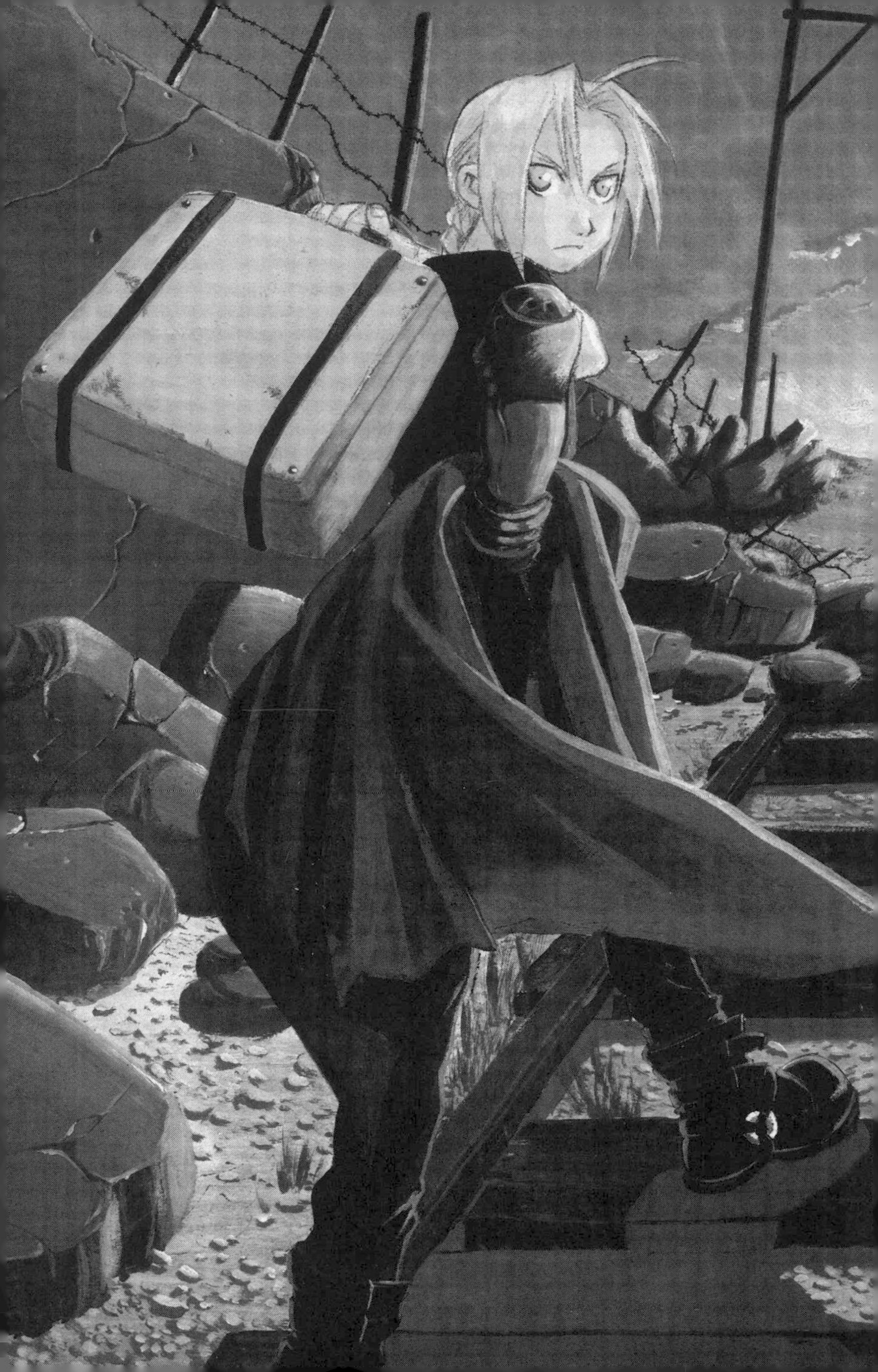

FULLMETAL
ALCHEMIST

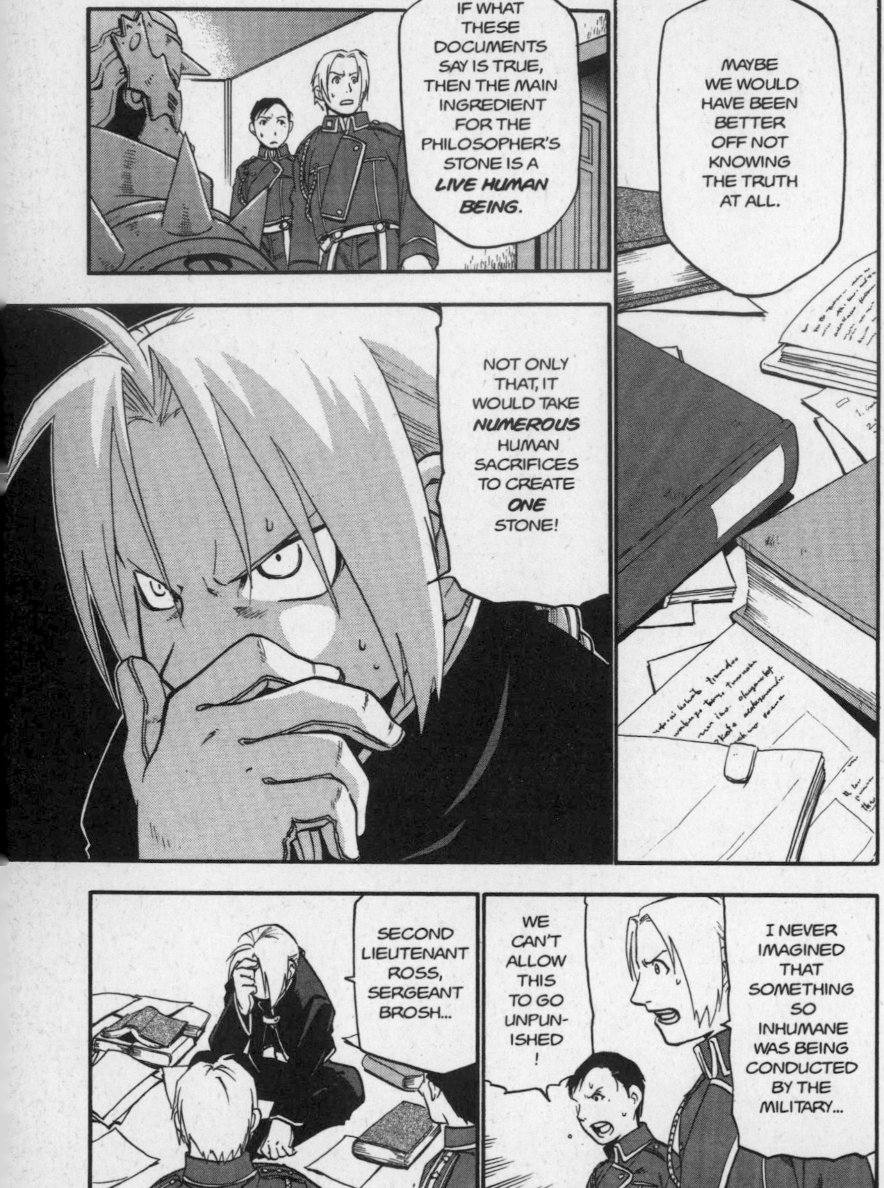
MAYBE WE WOULD HAVE BEEN BETTER OFF NOT KNOWING THE TRUTH AT ALL.
IF WHAT THESE DOCUMENTS SAY IS TRUE, THEN THE MAIN INGREDIENT FOR THE PHILOSOPHER'S STONE IS A *LIVE HUMAN BEING*.
NOT ONLY THAT, IT WOULD TAKE *NUMEROUS* HUMAN SACRIFICES TO CREATE *ONE* STONE!
I NEVER IMAGINED THAT SOMETHING SO INHUMANE WAS BEING CONDUCTED BY THE MILITARY...
WE CAN'T ALLOW THIS TO GO UNPUNISHED!
SECOND LIEUTENANT ROSS, SERGEANT BROSH...

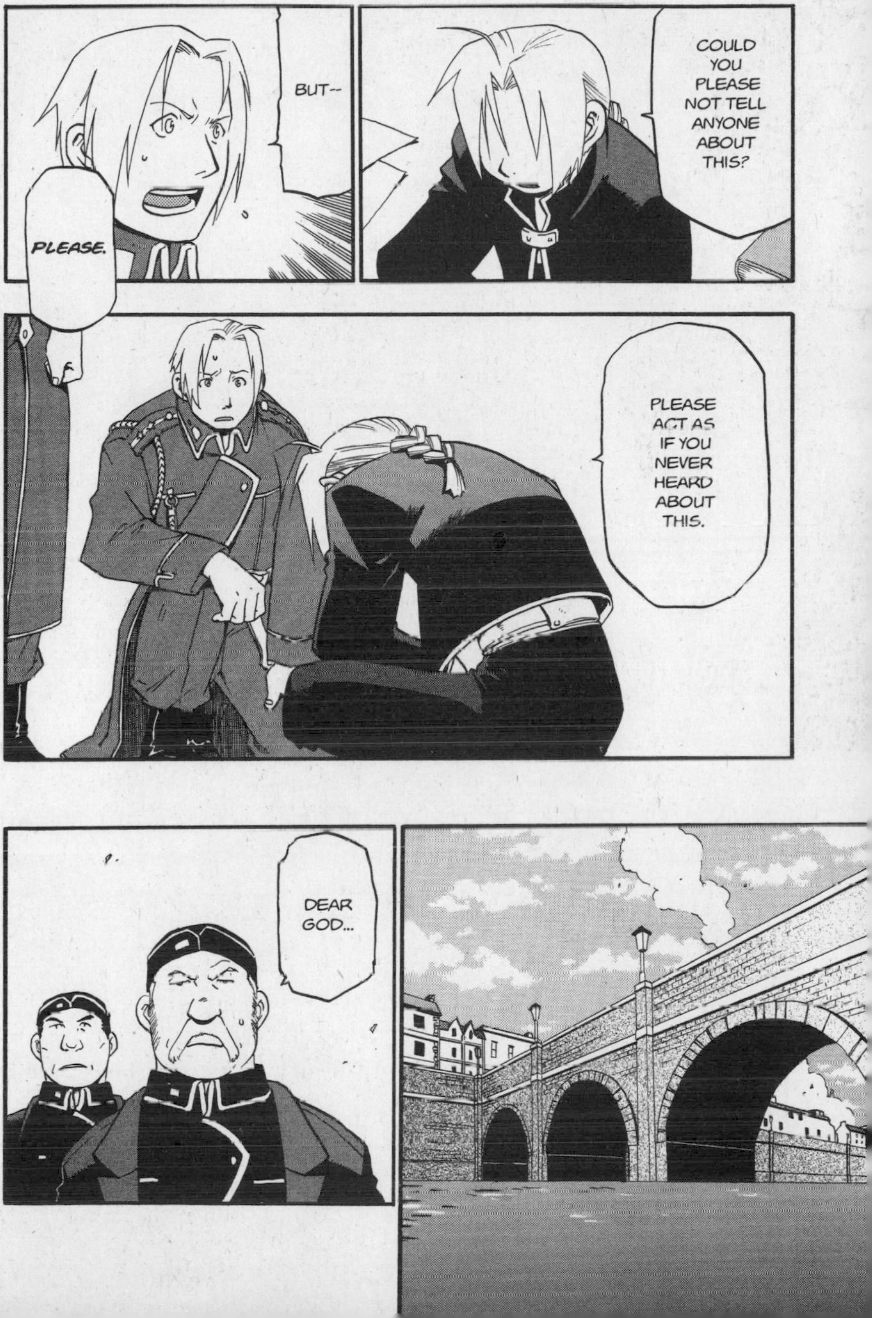
COULD YOU PLEASE NOT TELL ANYONE ABOUT THIS?
BUT--
PLEASE.
PLEASE ACT AS IF YOU NEVER HEARD ABOUT THIS.
DEAR GOD...

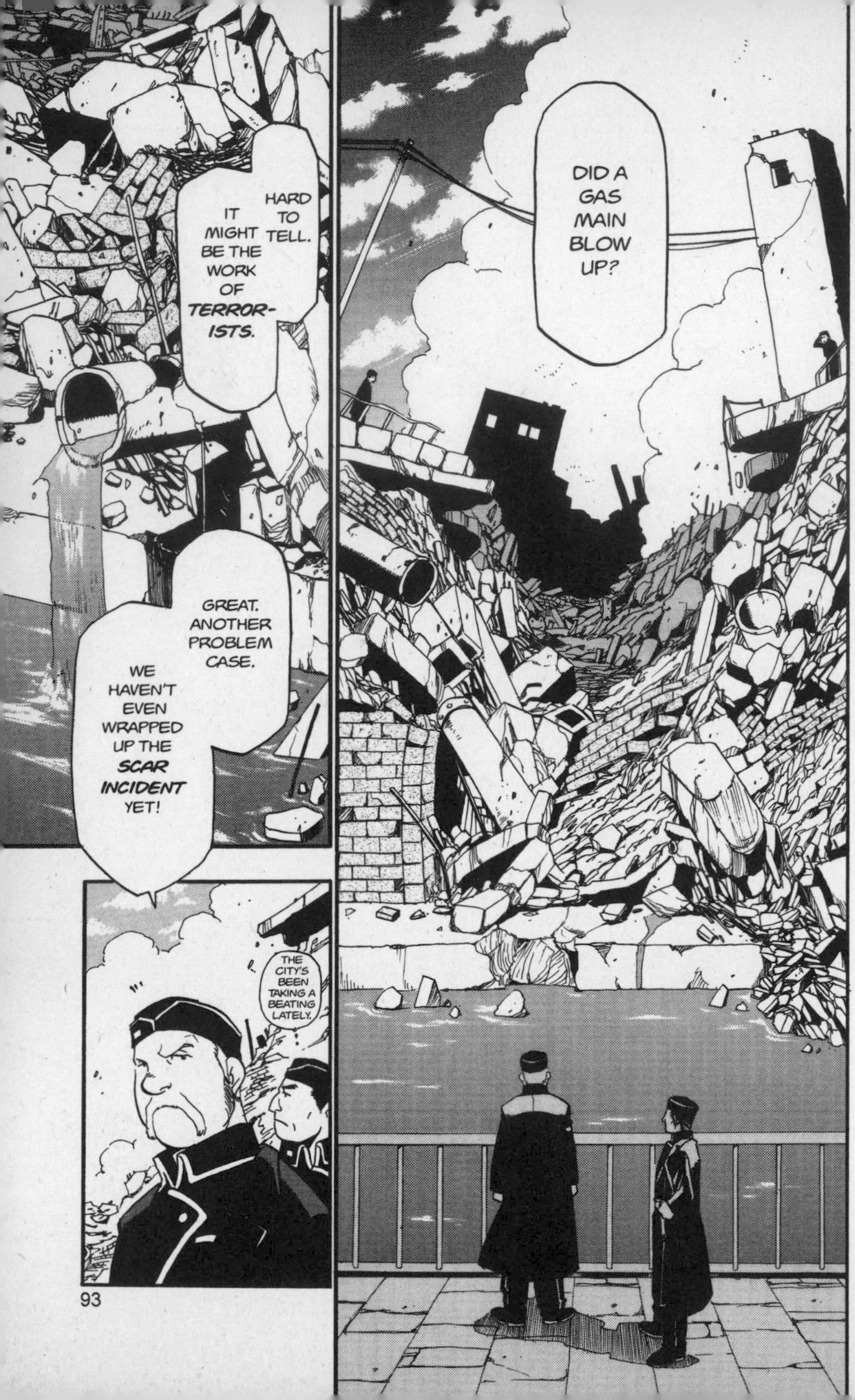
DID A GAS MAIN BLOW UP?
HARD TO TELL.
IT MIGHT BE THE WORK OF TERRORISTS.
GREAT. ANOTHER PROBLEM CASE.
WE HAVEN'T EVEN WRAPPED UP THE SCAR INCIDENT YET!
THE CITY'S BEEN TAKING A BEATING LATELY.

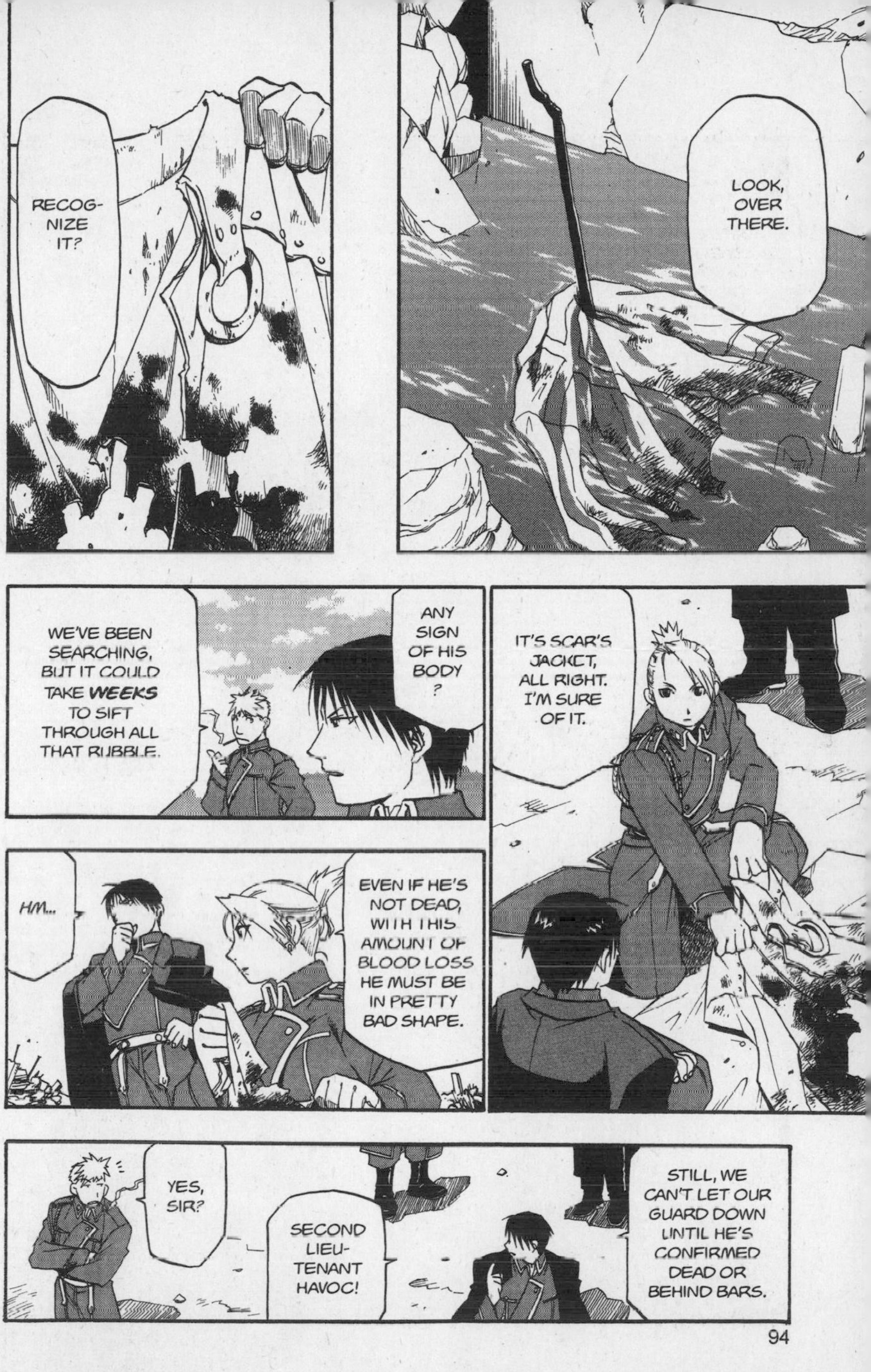
LOOK, OVER THERE.
RECOG-NIZE IT?
IT'S SCAR'S JACKET, ALL RIGHT. I'M SURE OF IT.
ANY SIGN OF HIS BODY?
WE'VE BEEN SEARCHING, BUT IT COULD TAKE **WEEKS** TO SIFT THROUGH ALL THAT RUBBLE.
EVEN IF HE'S NOT DEAD, WITH THIS AMOUNT OF BLOOD LOSS HE MUST BE IN PRETTY BAD SHAPE.
HM...
STILL, WE CAN'T LET OUR GUARD DOWN UNTIL HE'S CONFIRMED DEAD OR BEHIND BARS.
SECOND LIEU-TENANT HAVOC!
YES, SIR?

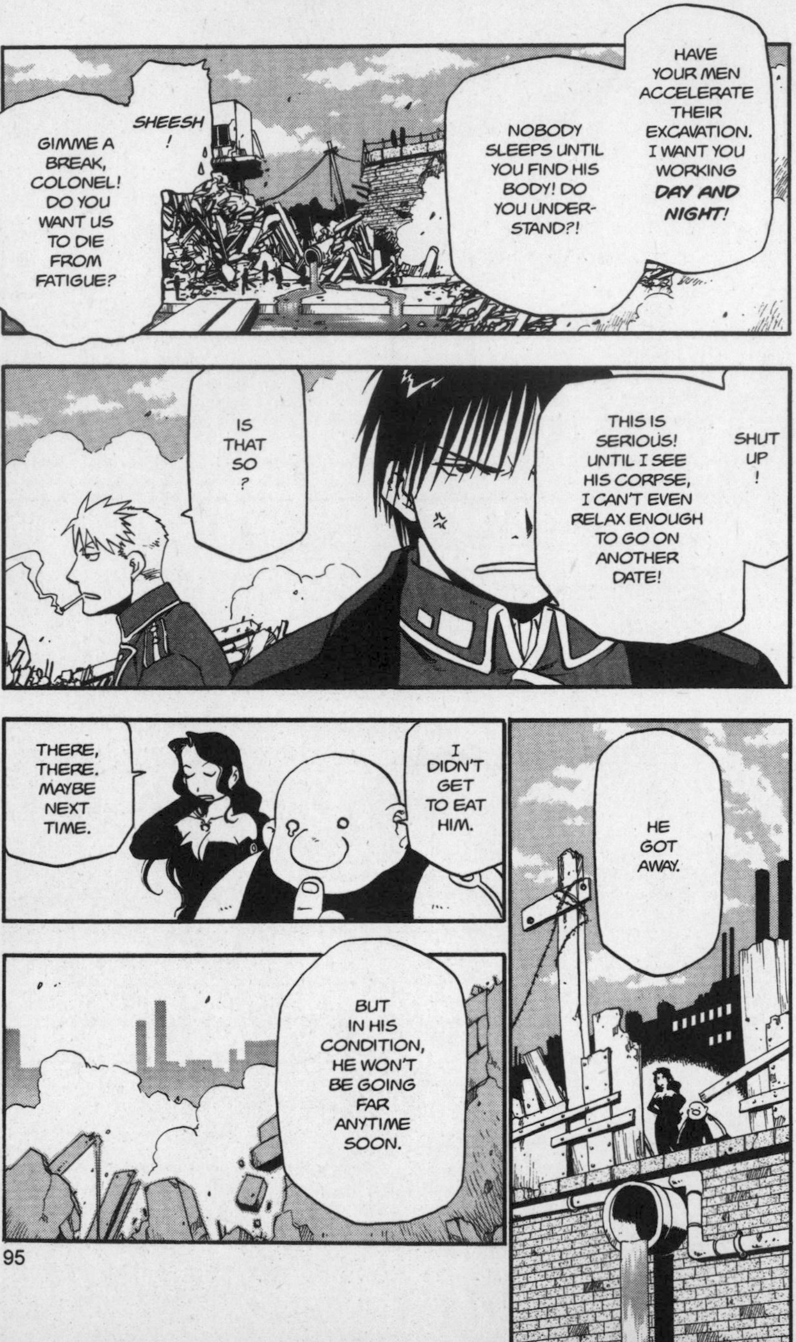
HAVE YOUR MEN ACCELERATE THEIR EXCAVATION. I WANT YOU WORKING **DAY AND NIGHT!**
NOBODY SLEEPS UNTIL YOU FIND HIS BODY! DO YOU UNDER-STAND?!
SHEESH!
GIMME A BREAK, COLONEL! DO YOU WANT US TO DIE FROM FATIGUE?
SHUT UP!
THIS IS SERIOUS! UNTIL I SEE HIS CORPSE, I CAN'T EVEN RELAX ENOUGH TO GO ON ANOTHER DATE!
IS THAT SO?
HE GOT AWAY.
I DIDN'T GET TO EAT HIM.
THERE, THERE. MAYBE NEXT TIME.
BUT IN HIS CONDITION, HE WON'T BE GOING FAR ANYTIME SOON.

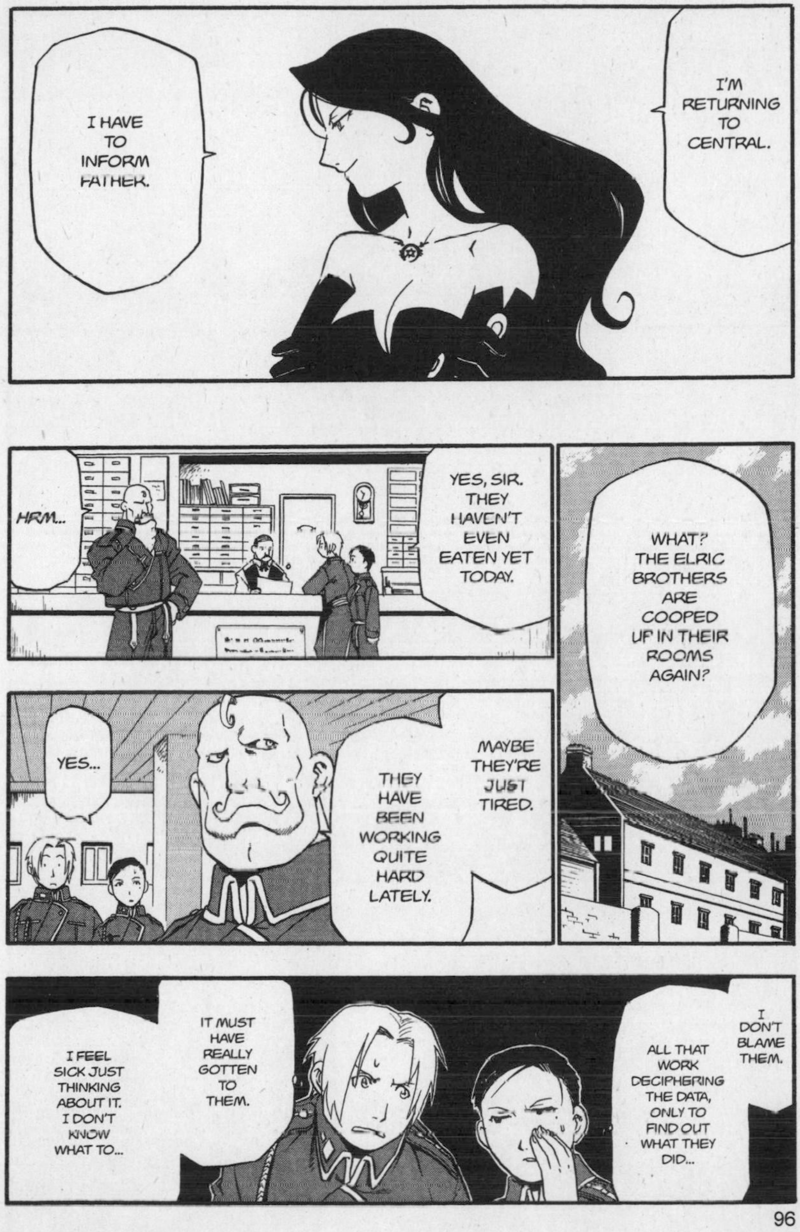
I'M RETURNING TO CENTRAL.
I HAVE TO INFORM FATHER.
WHAT? THE ELRIC BROTHERS ARE COOPED UP IN THEIR ROOMS AGAIN?
YES, SIR. THEY HAVEN'T EVEN EATEN YET TODAY.
HRM...
MAYBE THEY'RE JUST TIRED.
THEY HAVE BEEN WORKING QUITE HARD LATELY.
YES...
I DON'T BLAME THEM.
ALL THAT WORK DECIPHERING THE DATA, ONLY TO FIND OUT WHAT THEY DID...
IT MUST HAVE REALLY GOTTEN TO THEM.
I FEEL SICK JUST THINKING ABOUT IT. I DON'T KNOW WHAT TO...

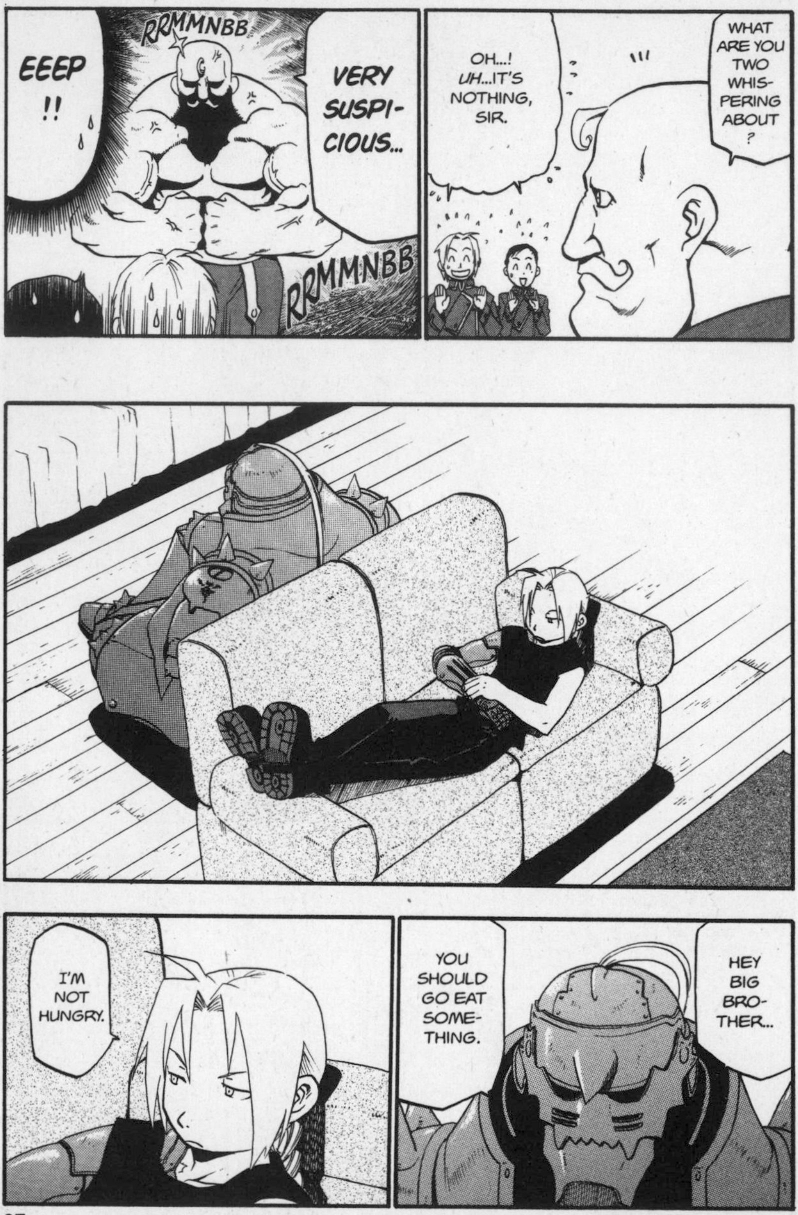
WHAT ARE YOU TWO WHISPERING ABOUT?
OH...! UH...IT'S NOTHING, SIR.
VERY SUSPICIOUS...
RRMMNBB
EEEP!!
RRMMNBB
HEY BIG BROTHER...
YOU SHOULD GO EAT SOMETHING.
I'M NOT HUNGRY.

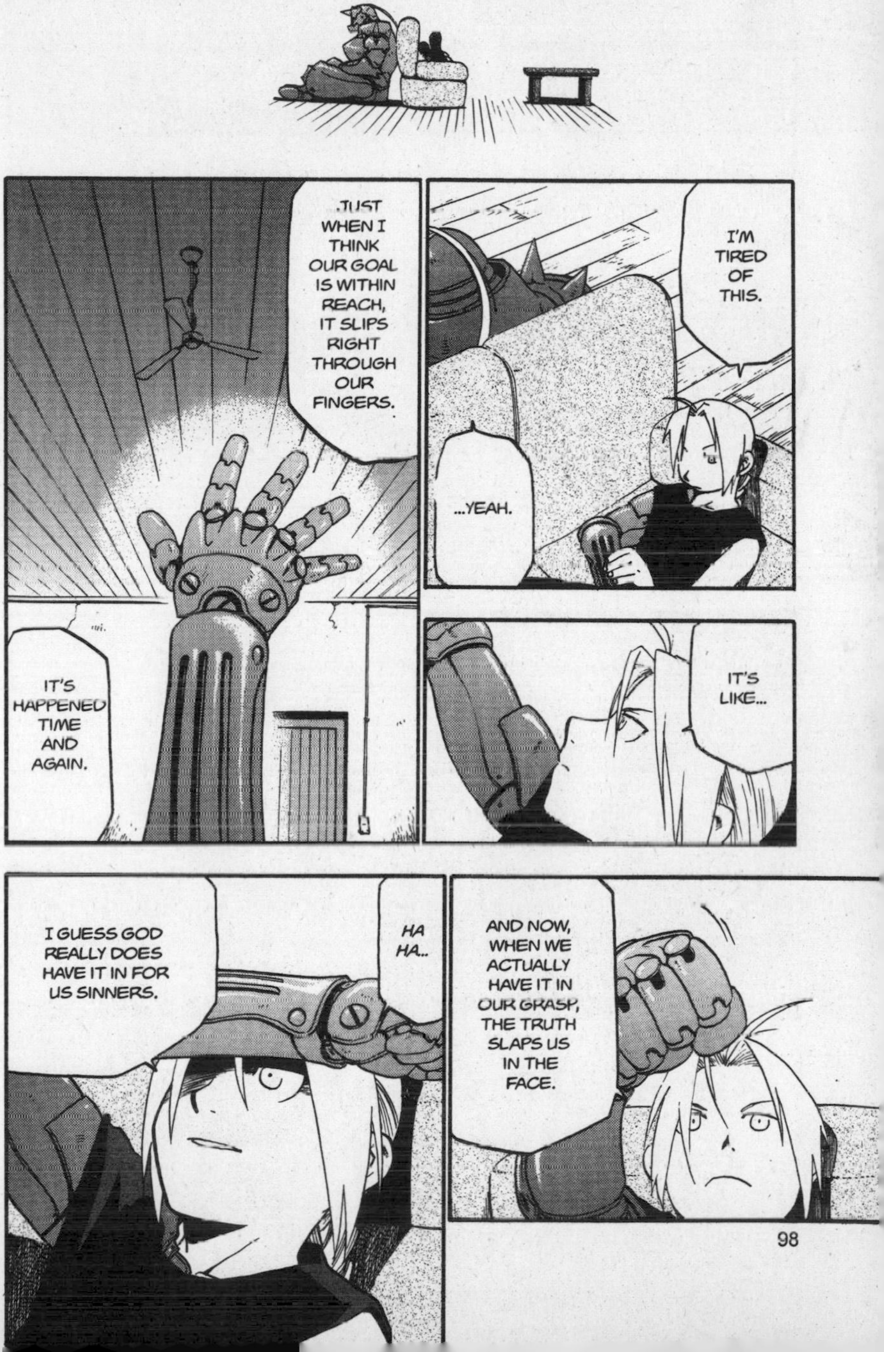
I'M TIRED OF THIS.
...YEAH.
IT'S LIKE...
...JUST WHEN I THINK OUR GOAL IS WITHIN REACH, IT SLIPS RIGHT THROUGH OUR FINGERS.
IT'S HAPPENED TIME AND AGAIN.
AND NOW, WHEN WE ACTUALLY HAVE IT IN OUR GRASP, THE TRUTH SLAPS US IN THE FACE.
HA HA...
I GUESS GOD REALLY DOES HAVE IT IN FOR US SINNERS.

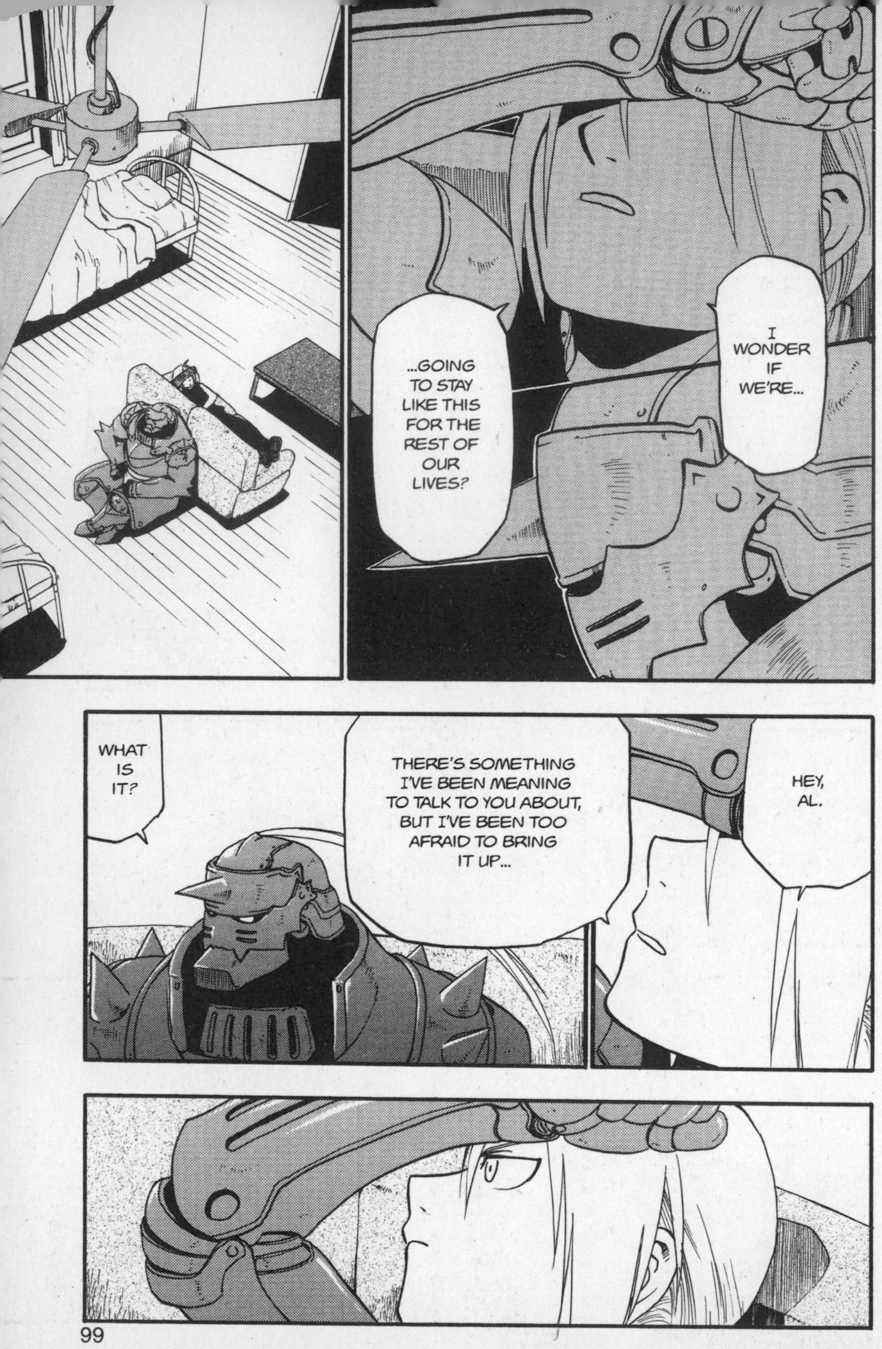
I WONDER IF WE'RE...
...GOING TO STAY LIKE THIS FOR THE REST OF OUR LIVES?
HEY, AL.
THERE'S SOMETHING I'VE BEEN MEANING TO TALK TO YOU ABOUT, BUT I'VE BEEN TOO AFRAID TO BRING IT UP...
WHAT IS IT?

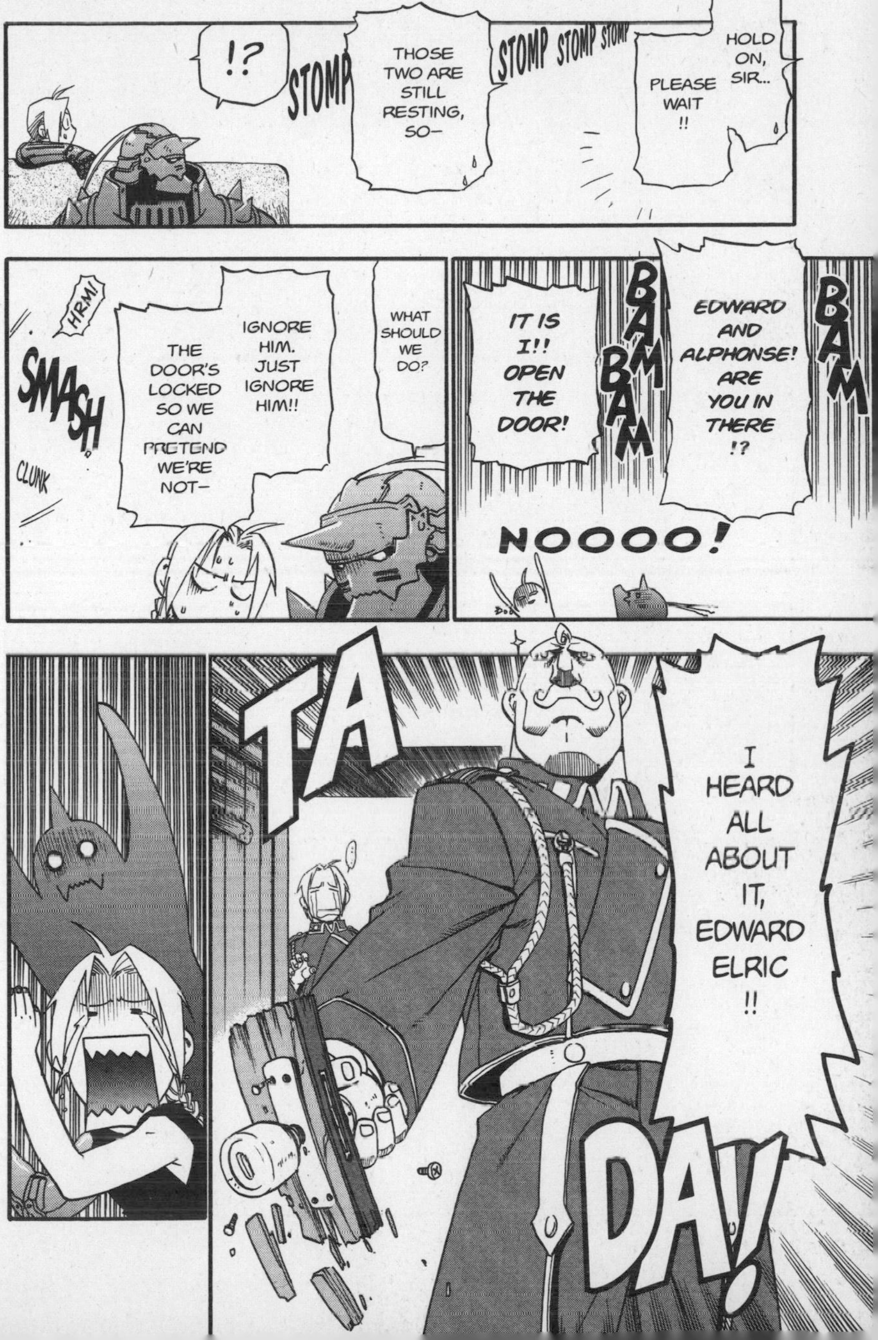
HOLD ON, SIR...
PLEASE WAIT !!
STOMP STOMP STOMP
THOSE TWO ARE STILL RESTING, SO—
STOMP
!?
BAM BAM
EDWARD AND ALPHONSE! ARE YOU IN THERE !?
BAM BAM
IT IS I!! OPEN THE DOOR!
NOOOO!
WHAT SHOULD WE DO?
IGNORE HIM. JUST IGNORE HIM!!
THE DOOR'S LOCKED SO WE CAN PRETEND WE'RE NOT—
HRM!
SMASH
CLUNK
I HEARD ALL ABOUT IT, EDWARD ELRIC !!
TA
DA!

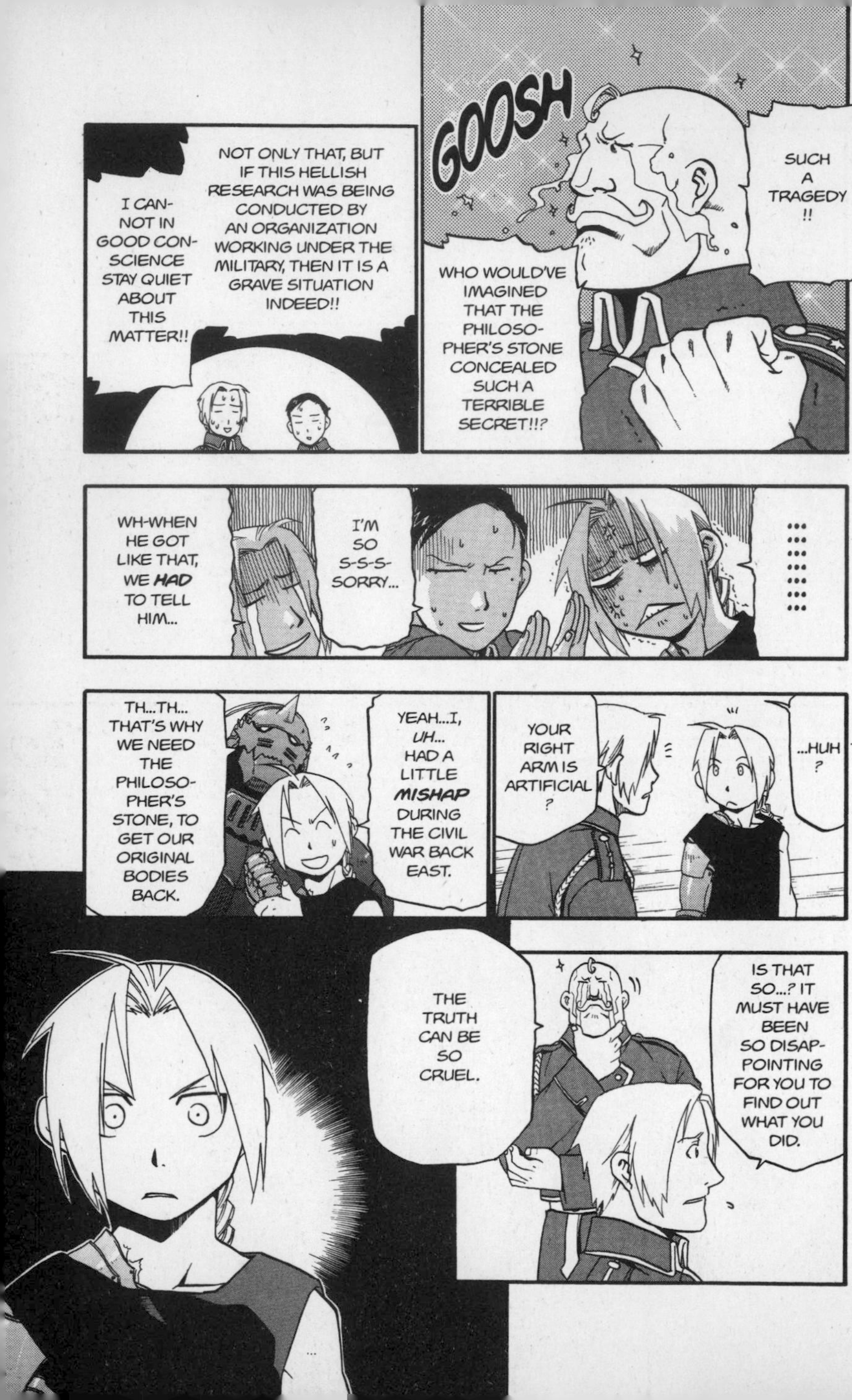
SUCH A TRAGEDY!!
GOOSH
WHO WOULD'VE IMAGINED THAT THE PHILOSOPHER'S STONE CONCEALED SUCH A TERRIBLE SECRET!!?
NOT ONLY THAT, BUT IF THIS HELLISH RESEARCH WAS BEING CONDUCTED BY AN ORGANIZATION WORKING UNDER THE MILITARY, THEN IT IS A GRAVE SITUATION INDEED!!
I CANNOT IN GOOD CONSCIENCE STAY QUIET ABOUT THIS MATTER!!
......
I'M SO S-S-S-SORRY...
WH-WHEN HE GOT LIKE THAT, WE *HAD* TO TELL HIM...
...HUH?
YOUR RIGHT ARM IS ARTIFICIAL?
YEAH...I, *UH*... HAD A LITTLE *MISHAP* DURING THE CIVIL WAR BACK EAST.
TH...TH... THAT'S WHY WE NEED THE PHILOSOPHER'S STONE, TO GET OUR ORIGINAL BODIES BACK.
IS THAT SO...? IT MUST HAVE BEEN SO DISAPPOINTING FOR YOU TO FIND OUT WHAT YOU DID.
THE TRUTH CAN BE SO CRUEL.
...

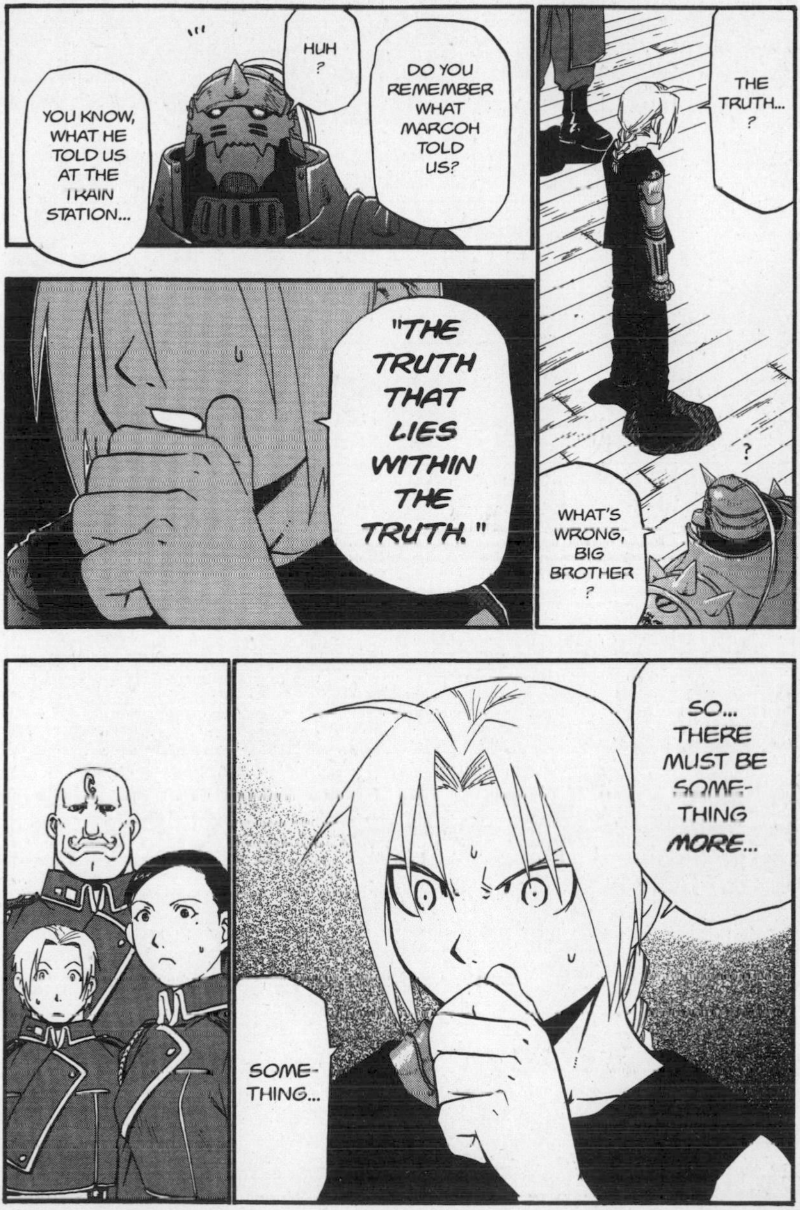
THE TRUTH... ?
WHAT'S WRONG, BIG BROTHER ?
DO YOU REMEMBER WHAT MARCOH TOLD US?
HUH ?
YOU KNOW, WHAT HE TOLD US AT THE TRAIN STATION...
"THE TRUTH THAT LIES WITHIN THE TRUTH."
SO... THERE MUST BE SOME-THING MORE...
SOME-THING...

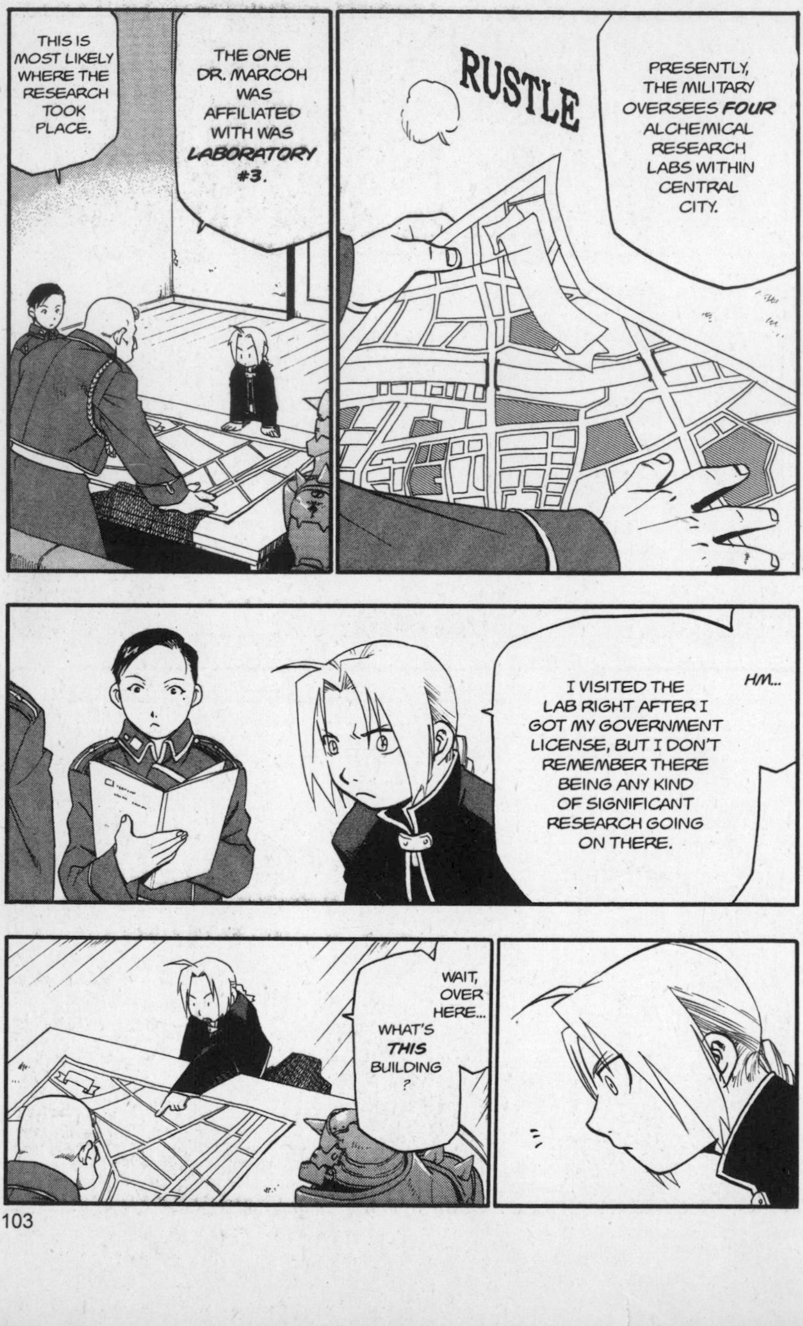
PRESENTLY, THE MILITARY OVERSEES **FOUR** ALCHEMICAL RESEARCH LABS WITHIN CENTRAL CITY.
RUSTLE
THE ONE DR. MARCOH WAS AFFILIATED WITH WAS **LABORATORY #3.**
THIS IS MOST LIKELY WHERE THE RESEARCH TOOK PLACE.
HM...
I VISITED THE LAB RIGHT AFTER I GOT MY GOVERNMENT LICENSE, BUT I DON'T REMEMBER THERE BEING ANY KIND OF SIGNIFICANT RESEARCH GOING ON THERE.
WAIT, OVER HERE... WHAT'S **THIS** BUILDING?

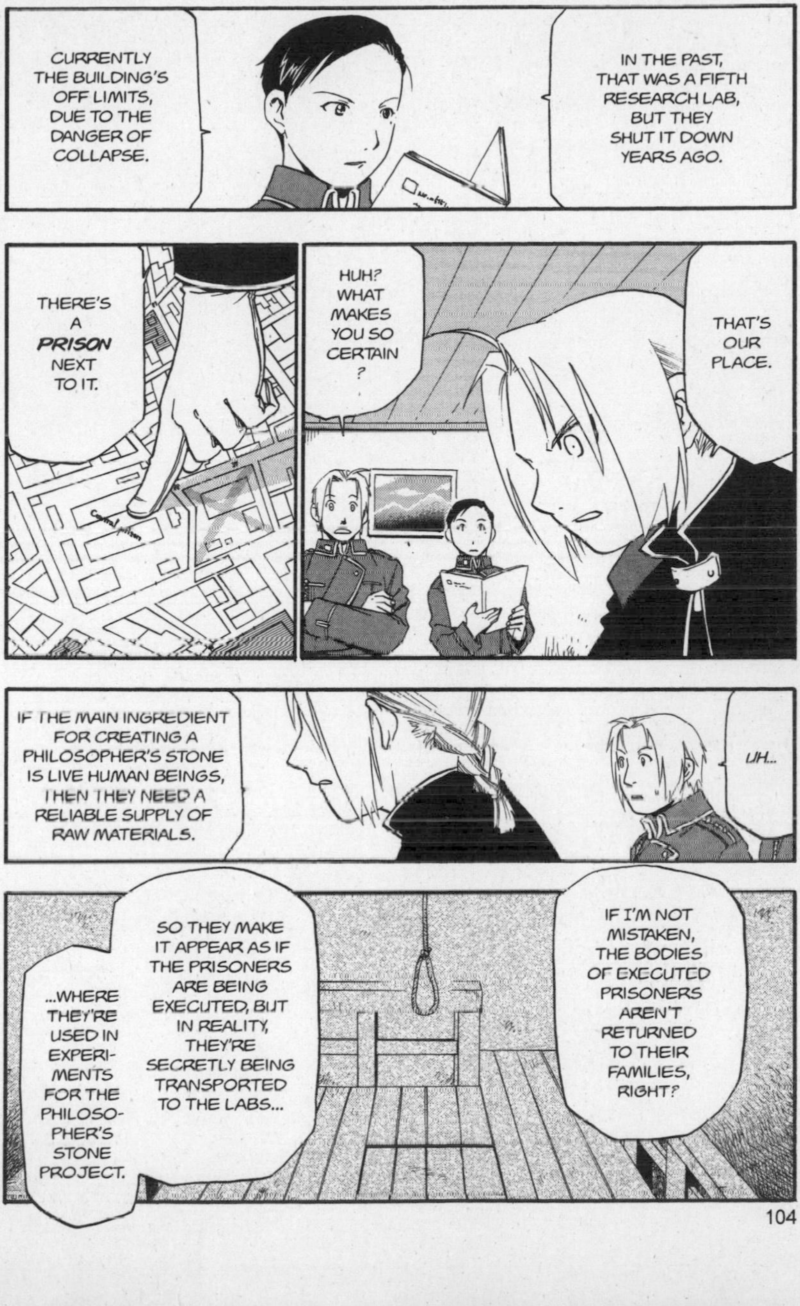
IN THE PAST, THAT WAS A FIFTH RESEARCH LAB, BUT THEY SHUT IT DOWN YEARS AGO.
CURRENTLY THE BUILDING'S OFF LIMITS, DUE TO THE DANGER OF COLLAPSE.
THAT'S OUR PLACE.
HUH? WHAT MAKES YOU SO CERTAIN?
THERE'S A **PRISON** NEXT TO IT.
Central prison
UH...
IF THE MAIN INGREDIENT FOR CREATING A PHILOSOPHER'S STONE IS LIVE HUMAN BEINGS, THEN THEY NEED A RELIABLE SUPPLY OF RAW MATERIALS.
IF I'M NOT MISTAKEN, THE BODIES OF EXECUTED PRISONERS AREN'T RETURNED TO THEIR FAMILIES, RIGHT?
SO THEY MAKE IT APPEAR AS IF THE PRISONERS ARE BEING EXECUTED, BUT IN REALITY, THEY'RE SECRETLY BEING TRANSPORTED TO THE LABS...
...WHERE THEY'RE USED IN EXPERIMENTS FOR THE PHILOSOPHER'S STONE PROJECT.

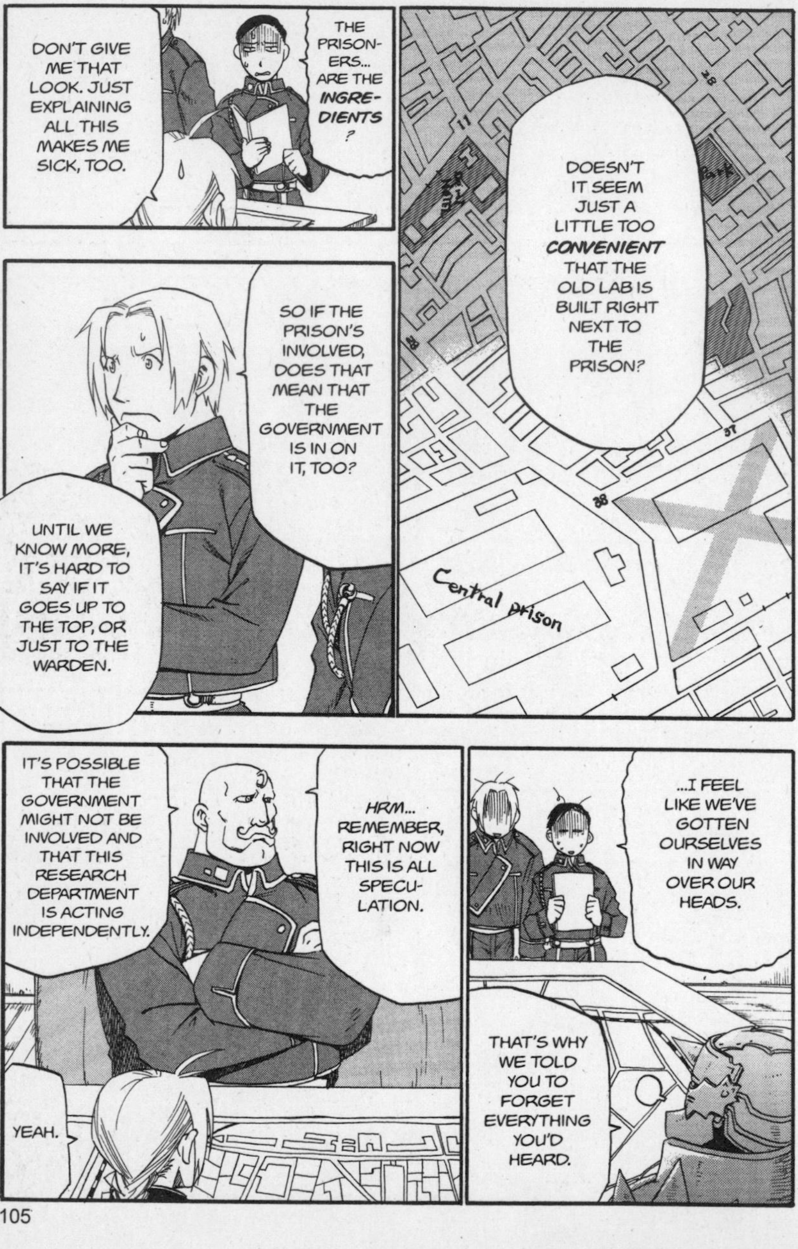
DOESN'T IT SEEM JUST A LITTLE TOO **CONVENIENT** THAT THE OLD LAB IS BUILT RIGHT NEXT TO THE PRISON?
Park
Central prison
THE PRISONERS... ARE THE ***INGREDIENTS***?
DON'T GIVE ME THAT LOOK. JUST EXPLAINING ALL THIS MAKES ME SICK, TOO.
SO IF THE PRISON'S INVOLVED, DOES THAT MEAN THAT THE GOVERNMENT IS IN ON IT, TOO?
UNTIL WE KNOW MORE, IT'S HARD TO SAY IF IT GOES UP TO THE TOP, OR JUST TO THE WARDEN.
...I FEEL LIKE WE'VE GOTTEN OURSELVES IN WAY OVER OUR HEADS.
THAT'S WHY WE TOLD YOU TO FORGET EVERYTHING YOU'D HEARD.
HRM... REMEMBER, RIGHT NOW THIS IS ALL SPECULATION.
IT'S POSSIBLE THAT THE GOVERNMENT MIGHT NOT BE INVOLVED AND THAT THIS RESEARCH DEPARTMENT IS ACTING INDEPENDENTLY.
YEAH.

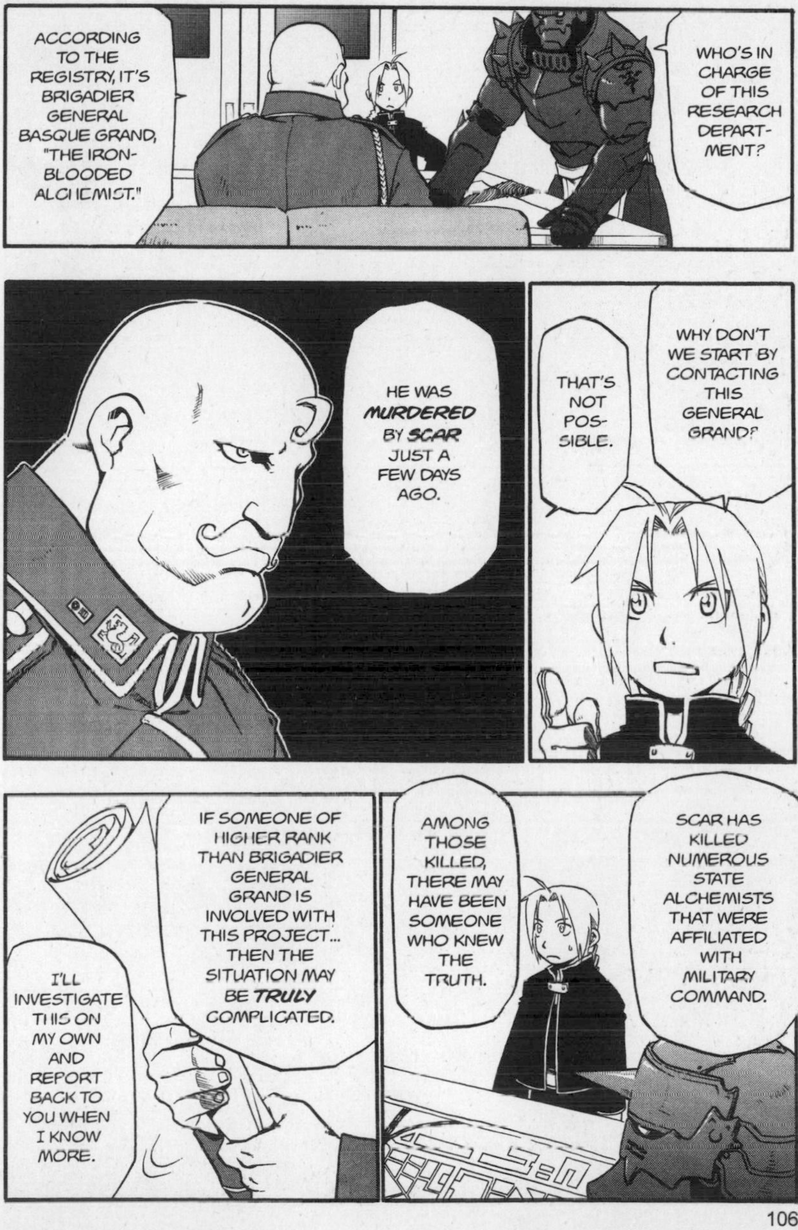
WHO'S IN CHARGE OF THIS RESEARCH DEPARTMENT?
ACCORDING TO THE REGISTRY, IT'S BRIGADIER GENERAL BASQUE GRAND, "THE IRON-BLOODED ALCHEMIST."
WHY DON'T WE START BY CONTACTING THIS GENERAL GRAND?
THAT'S NOT POSSIBLE.
HE WAS MURDERED BY SCAR JUST A FEW DAYS AGO.
SCAR HAS KILLED NUMEROUS STATE ALCHEMISTS THAT WERE AFFILIATED WITH MILITARY COMMAND.
AMONG THOSE KILLED, THERE MAY HAVE BEEN SOMEONE WHO KNEW THE TRUTH.
IF SOMEONE OF HIGHER RANK THAN BRIGADIER GENERAL GRAND IS INVOLVED WITH THIS PROJECT... THEN THE SITUATION MAY BE TRULY COMPLICATED.
I'LL INVESTIGATE THIS ON MY OWN AND REPORT BACK TO YOU WHEN I KNOW MORE.

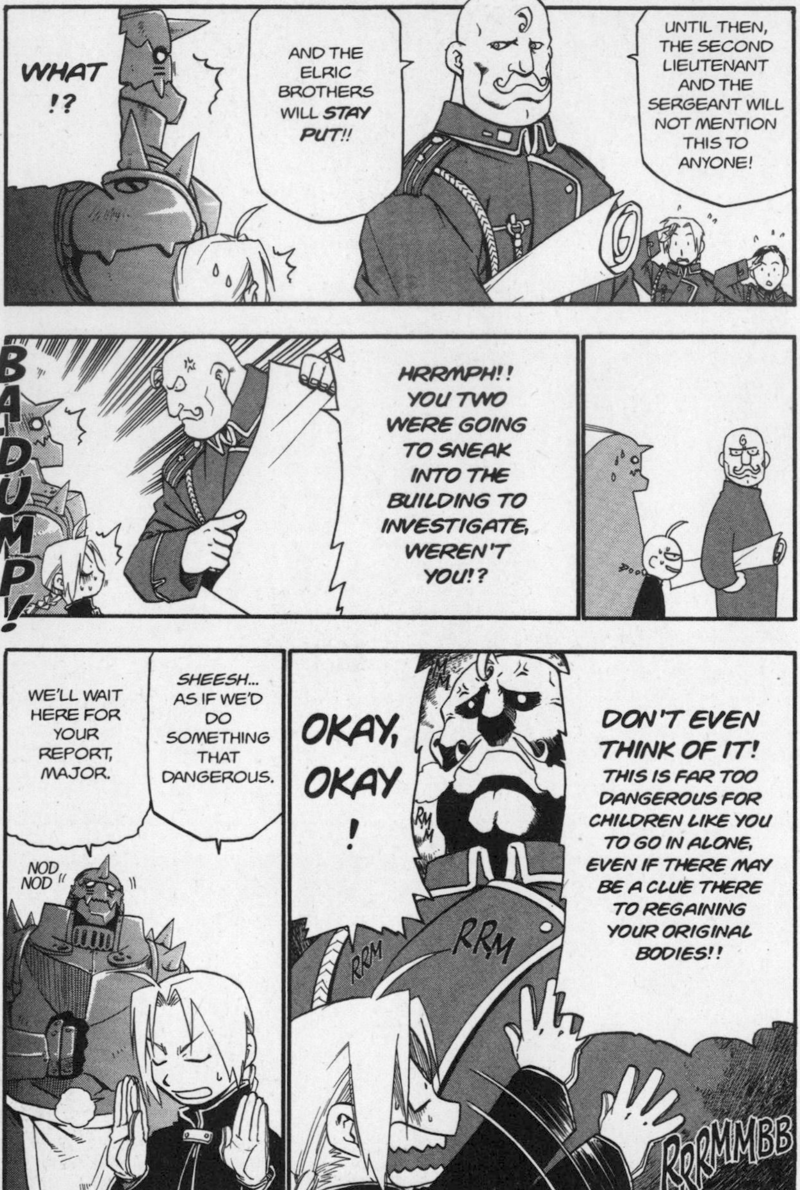
UNTIL THEN, THE SECOND LIEUTENANT AND THE SERGEANT WILL NOT MENTION THIS TO ANYONE!
AND THE ELRIC BROTHERS WILL STAY PUT!!
WHAT!?
HRRMPH!! YOU TWO WERE GOING TO SNEAK INTO THE BUILDING TO INVESTIGATE, WEREN'T YOU!?
BA-DUMP!
DON'T EVEN THINK OF IT! THIS IS FAR TOO DANGEROUS FOR CHILDREN LIKE YOU TO GO IN ALONE, EVEN IF THERE MAY BE A CLUE THERE TO REGAINING YOUR ORIGINAL BODIES!!
OKAY, OKAY!
RRM
RRM
RRM
RRM
RRRMMBB
SHEESH... AS IF WE'D DO SOMETHING THAT DANGEROUS.
WE'LL WAIT HERE FOR YOUR REPORT, MAJOR.
NOD NOD

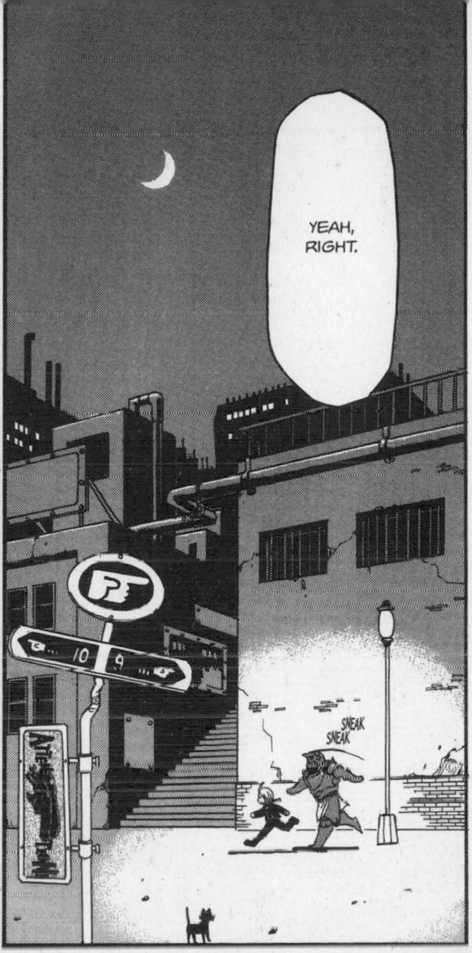
YEAH, RIGHT.
SNEAK SNEAK

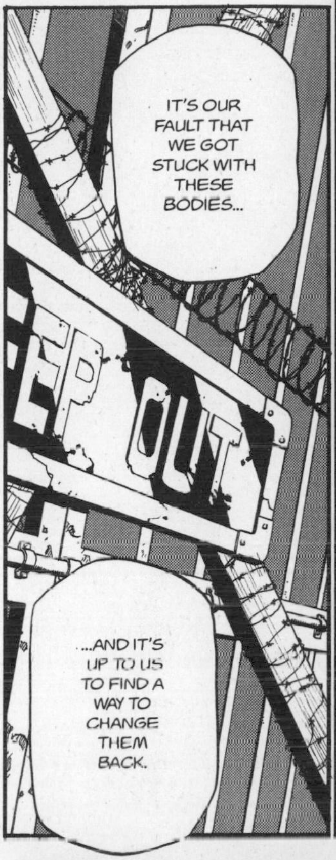
IT'S OUR FAULT THAT WE GOT STUCK WITH THESE BODIES...
EP OUT
...AND IT'S UP TO US TO FIND A WAY TO CHANGE THEM BACK.

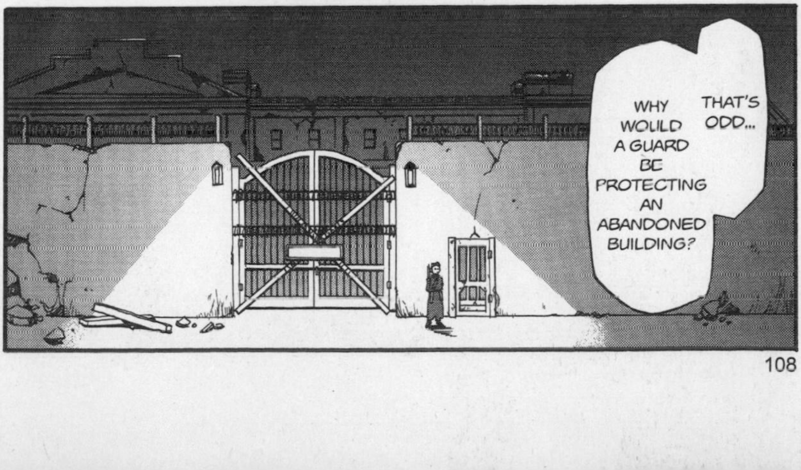
THAT'S ODD...
WHY WOULD A GUARD BE PROTECTING AN ABANDONED BUILDING?

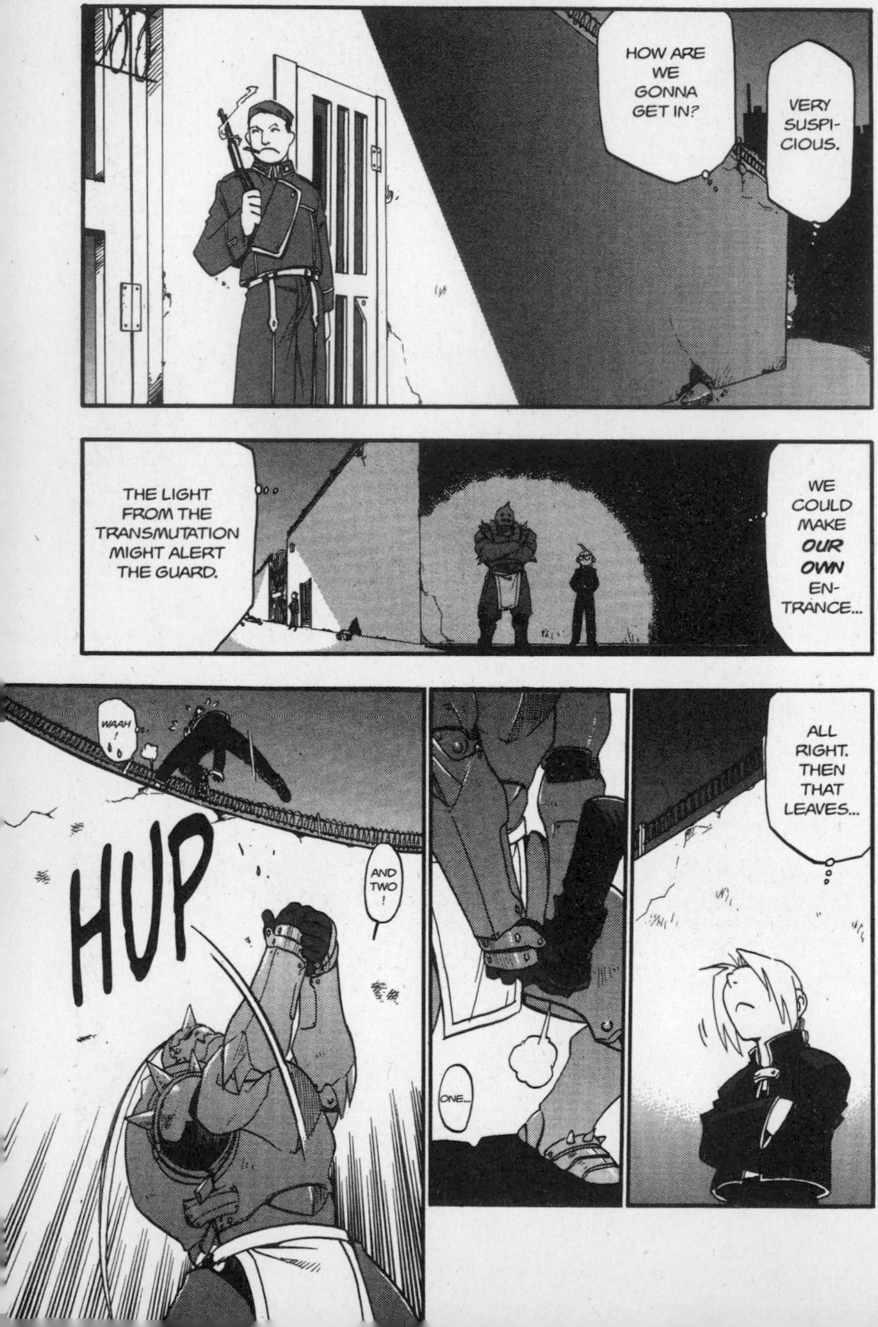
VERY SUSPICIOUS.
HOW ARE WE GONNA GET IN?
WE COULD MAKE ***OUR OWN*** ENTRANCE...
THE LIGHT FROM THE TRANSMUTATION MIGHT ALERT THE GUARD.
ALL RIGHT. THEN THAT LEAVES...
ONE...
AND TWO!
HUP
WAAH!

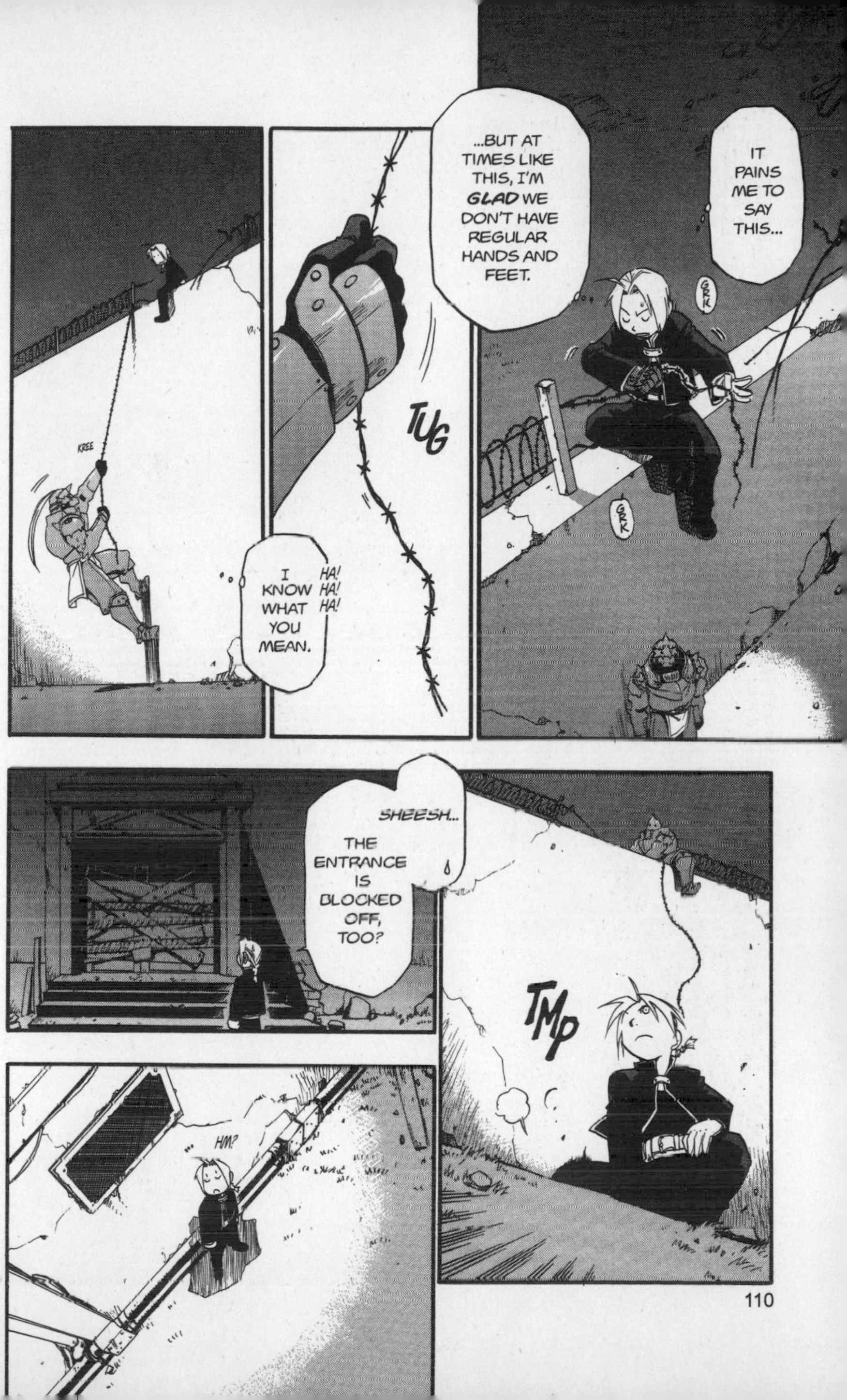
IT PAINS ME TO SAY THIS...
...BUT AT TIMES LIKE THIS, I'M **GLAD** WE DON'T HAVE REGULAR HANDS AND FEET.
GRK
GRK
TUG
HA! HA! HA!
I KNOW WHAT YOU MEAN.
KREE
TMP
SHEESH... THE ENTRANCE IS BLOCKED OFF, TOO?
HM?

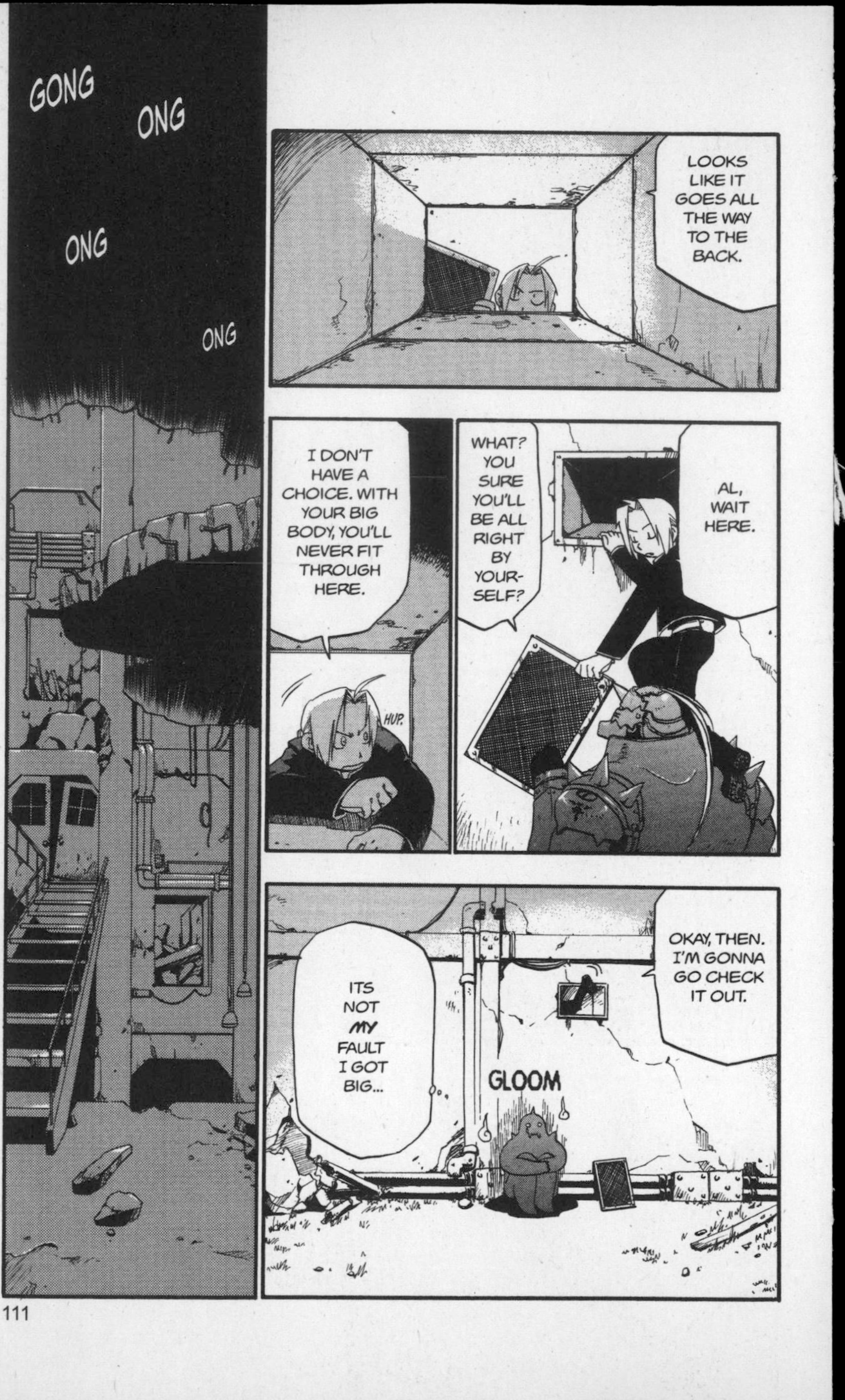
LOOKS LIKE IT GOES ALL THE WAY TO THE BACK.
AL, WAIT HERE.
WHAT? YOU SURE YOU'LL BE ALL RIGHT BY YOUR-SELF?
I DON'T HAVE A CHOICE. WITH YOUR BIG BODY, YOU'LL NEVER FIT THROUGH HERE.
HUP.
OKAY, THEN. I'M GONNA GO CHECK IT OUT.
ITS NOT MY FAULT I GOT BIG...
GLOOM
GONG
ONG
ONG
ONG

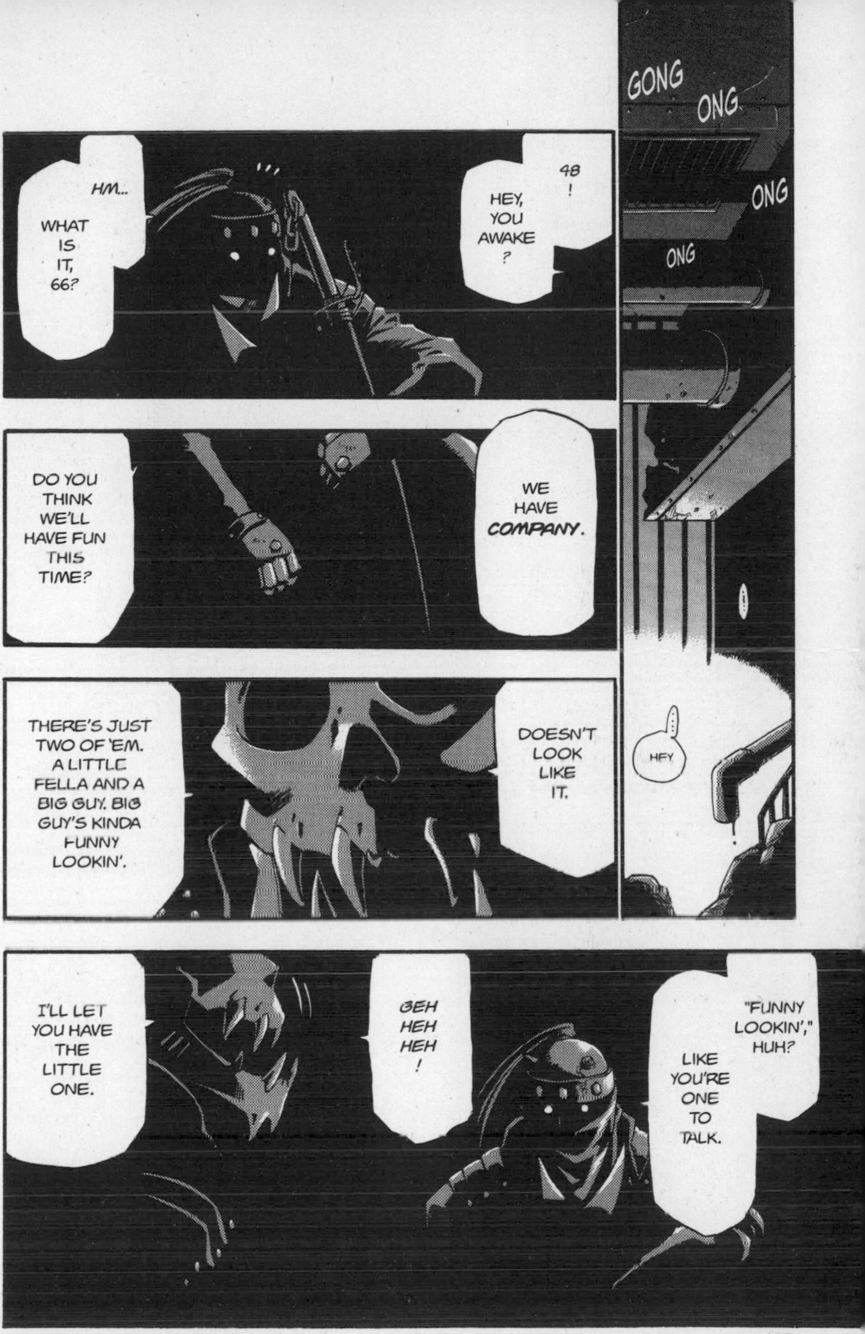
GONG ONG ONG ONG
HEY
48! HEY, YOU AWAKE?
HM... WHAT IS IT, 66?
WE HAVE COMPANY.
DO YOU THINK WE'LL HAVE FUN THIS TIME?
DOESN'T LOOK LIKE IT.
THERE'S JUST TWO OF 'EM. A LITTLE FELLA AND A BIG GUY. BIG GUY'S KINDA FUNNY LOOKIN'.
"FUNNY LOOKIN'," HUH?
LIKE YOU'RE ONE TO TALK.
GEH HEH HEH!
I'LL LET YOU HAVE THE LITTLE ONE.

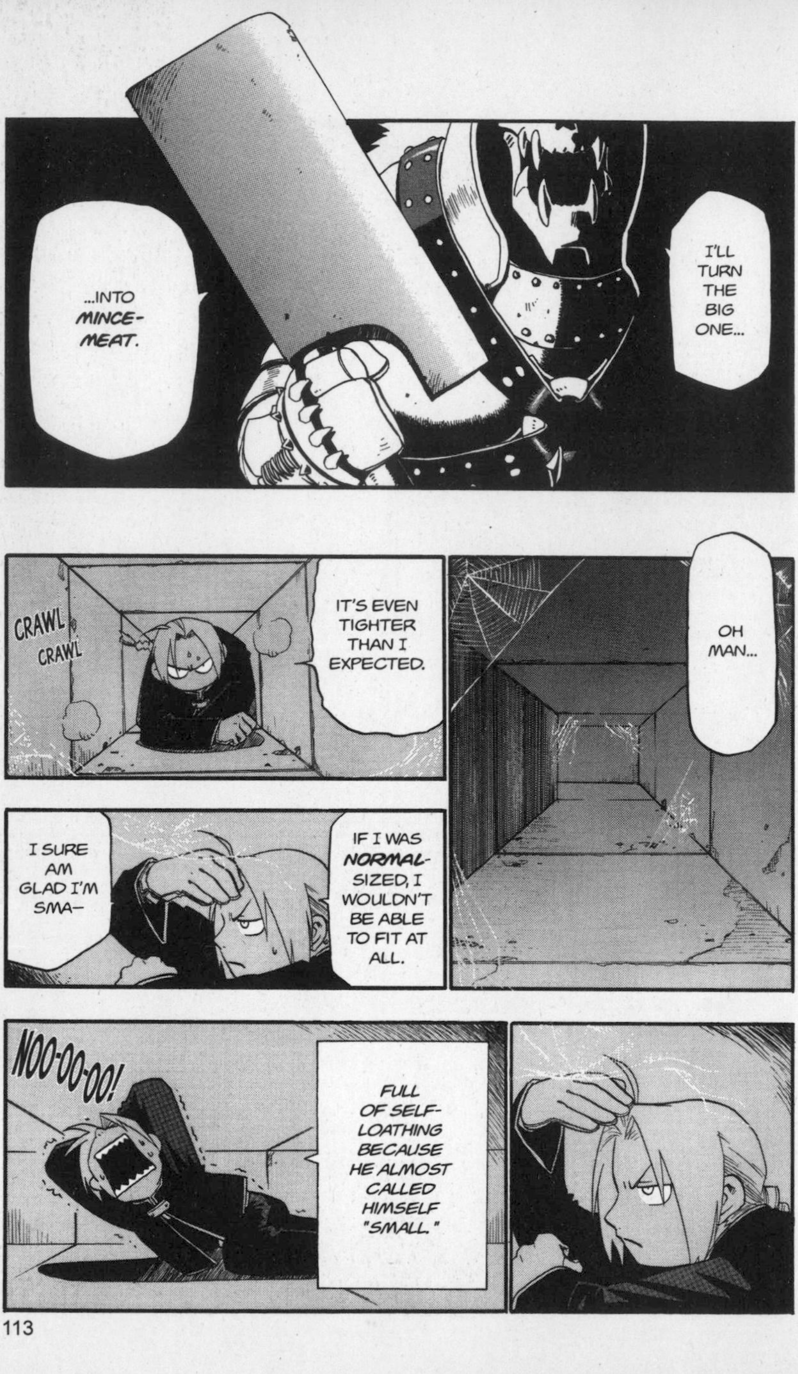
I'LL TURN THE BIG ONE...
...INTO MINCE-MEAT.
OH MAN...
IT'S EVEN TIGHTER THAN I EXPECTED.
CRAWL CRAWL
IF I WAS NORMAL-SIZED, I WOULDN'T BE ABLE TO FIT AT ALL.
I SURE AM GLAD I'M SMA—
FULL OF SELF-LOATHING BECAUSE HE ALMOST CALLED HIMSELF "SMALL."
NOO-OO-OO!

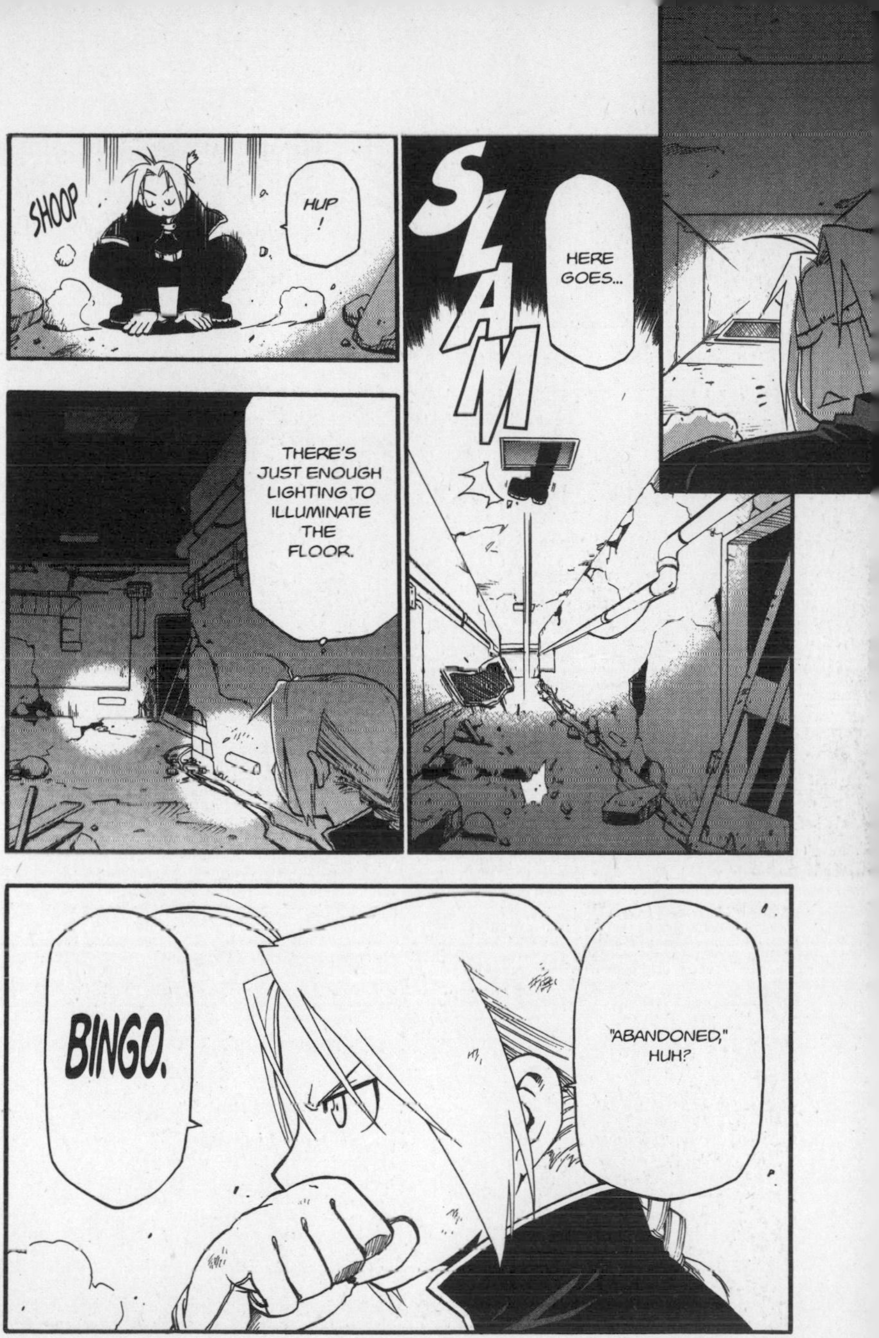
SLAM
HERE GOES...
SHOOP
HUP!
THERE'S JUST ENOUGH LIGHTING TO ILLUMINATE THE FLOOR.
"ABANDONED," HUH?
BINGO.

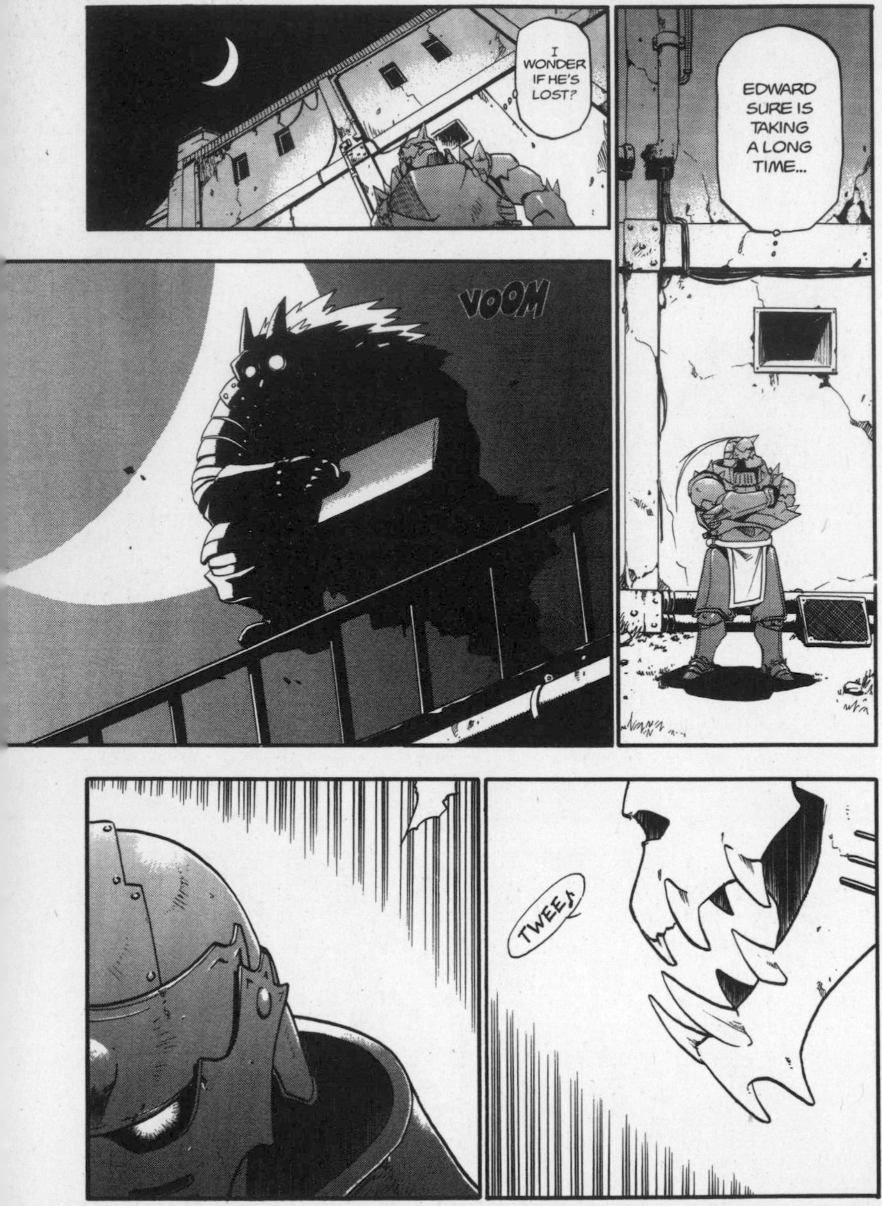
EDWARD SURE IS TAKING A LONG TIME...
I WONDER IF HE'S LOST?
VOOM
TWEE♪

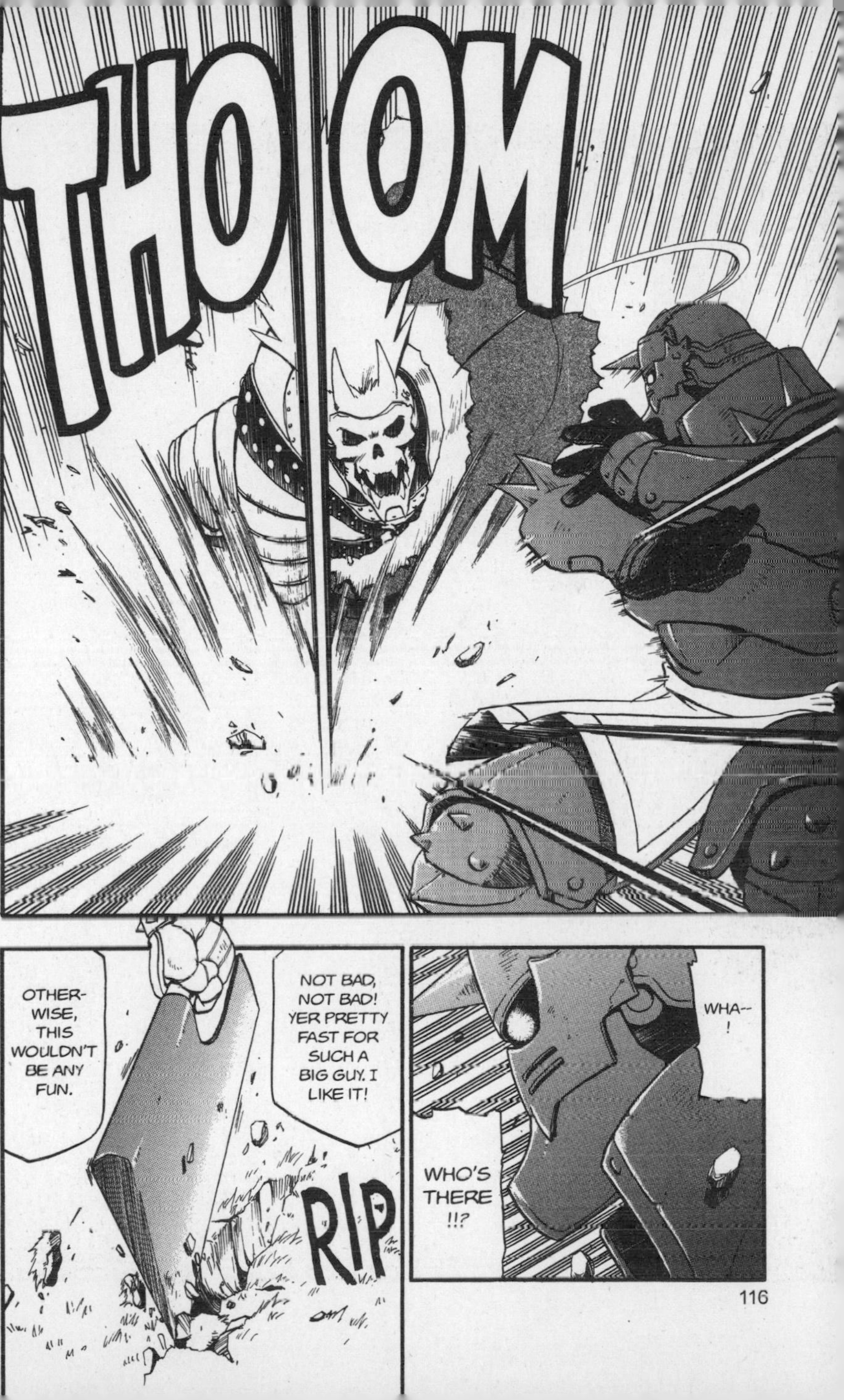
THOOM
WHA--!
WHO'S THERE!!?
NOT BAD, NOT BAD! YER PRETTY FAST FOR SUCH A BIG GUY. I LIKE IT!
OTHER-WISE, THIS WOULDN'T BE ANY FUN.
RIP

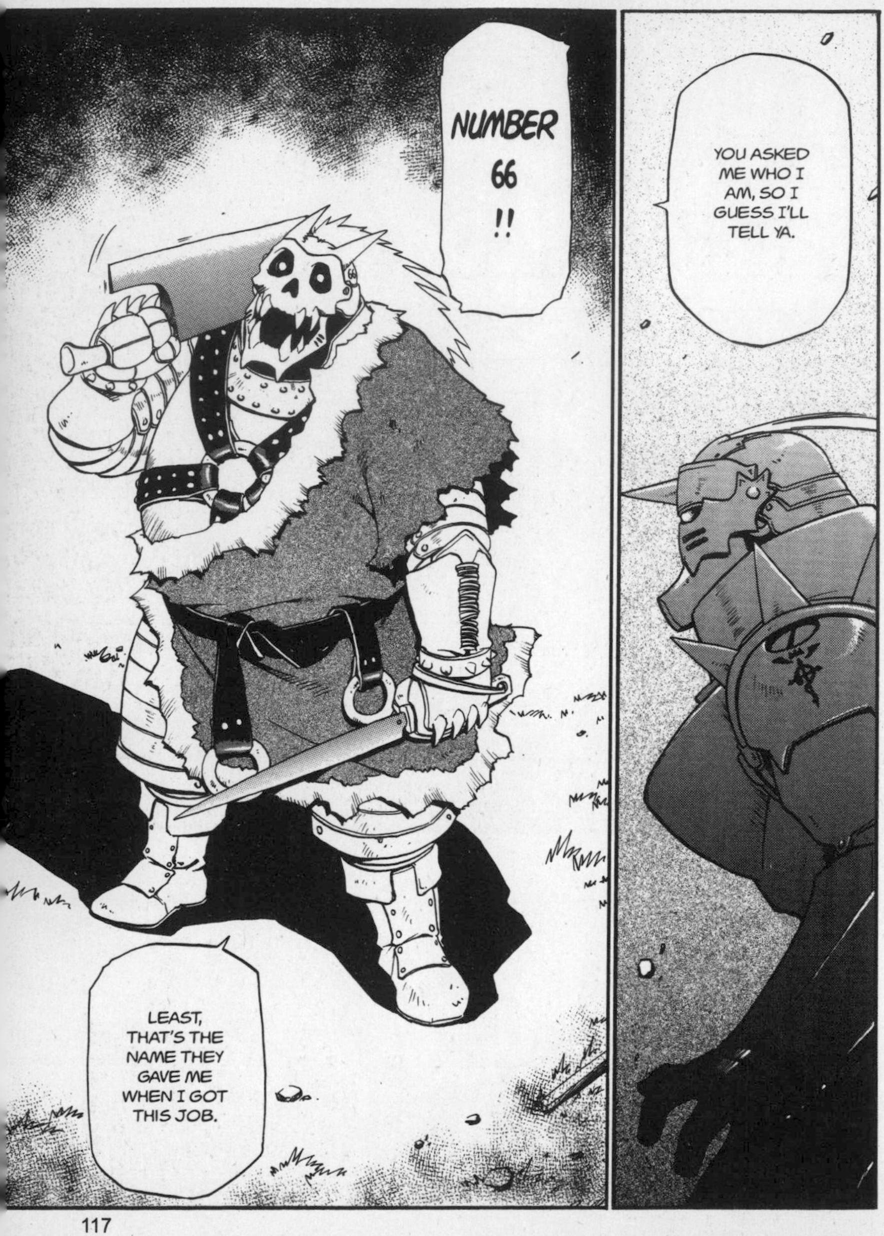
YOU ASKED ME WHO I AM, SO I GUESS I'LL TELL YA.
NUMBER 66 !!
LEAST, THAT'S THE NAME THEY GAVE ME WHEN I GOT THIS JOB.

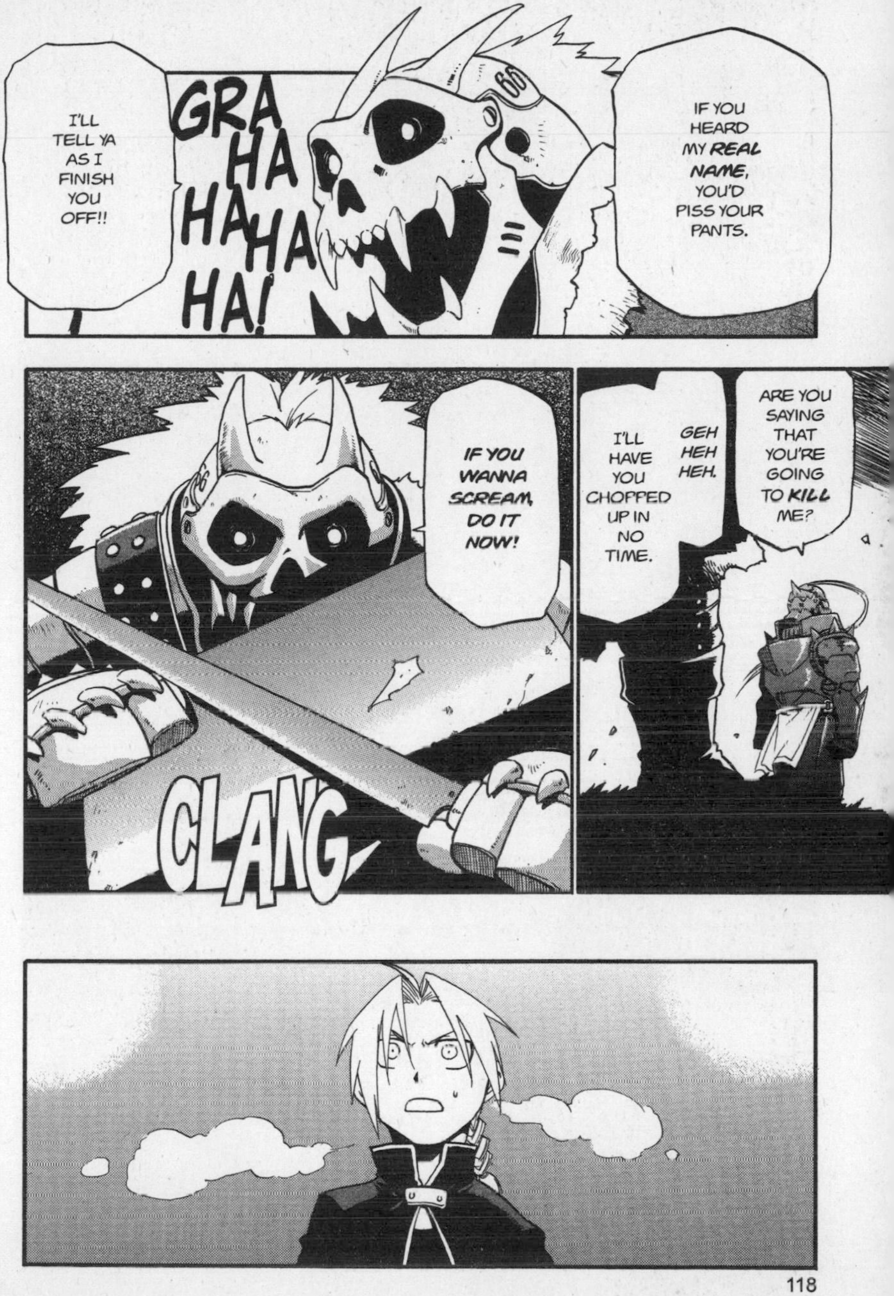
IF YOU HEARD MY REAL NAME, YOU'D PISS YOUR PANTS.
GRA HA HA HA HA HA!
I'LL TELL YA AS I FINISH YOU OFF!!
ARE YOU SAYING THAT YOU'RE GOING TO KILL ME?
GEH HEH HEH.
I'LL HAVE YOU CHOPPED UP IN NO TIME.
IF YOU WANNA SCREAM, DO IT NOW!
CLANG

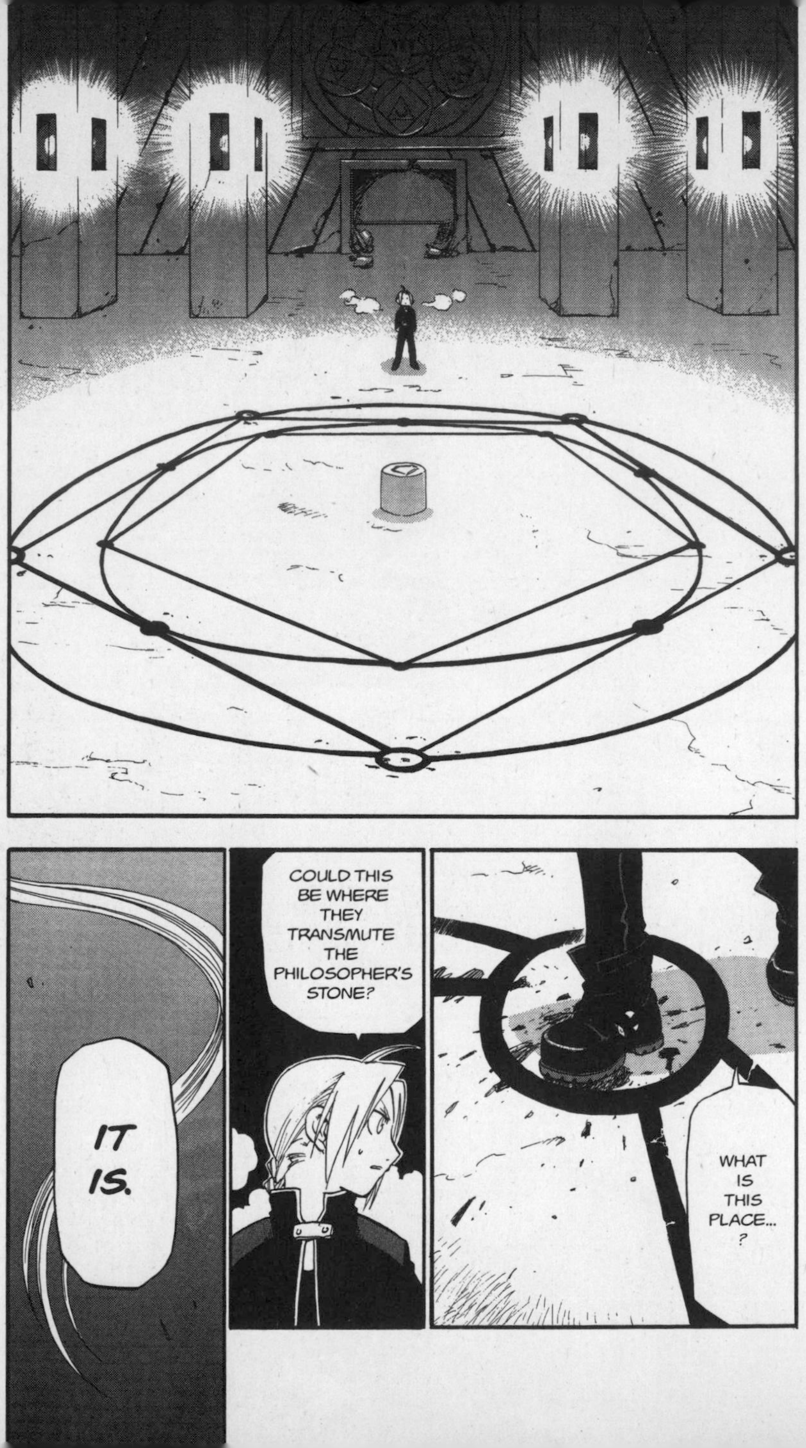
WHAT IS THIS PLACE...?
COULD THIS BE WHERE THEY TRANSMUTE THE PHILOSOPHER'S STONE?
IT IS.

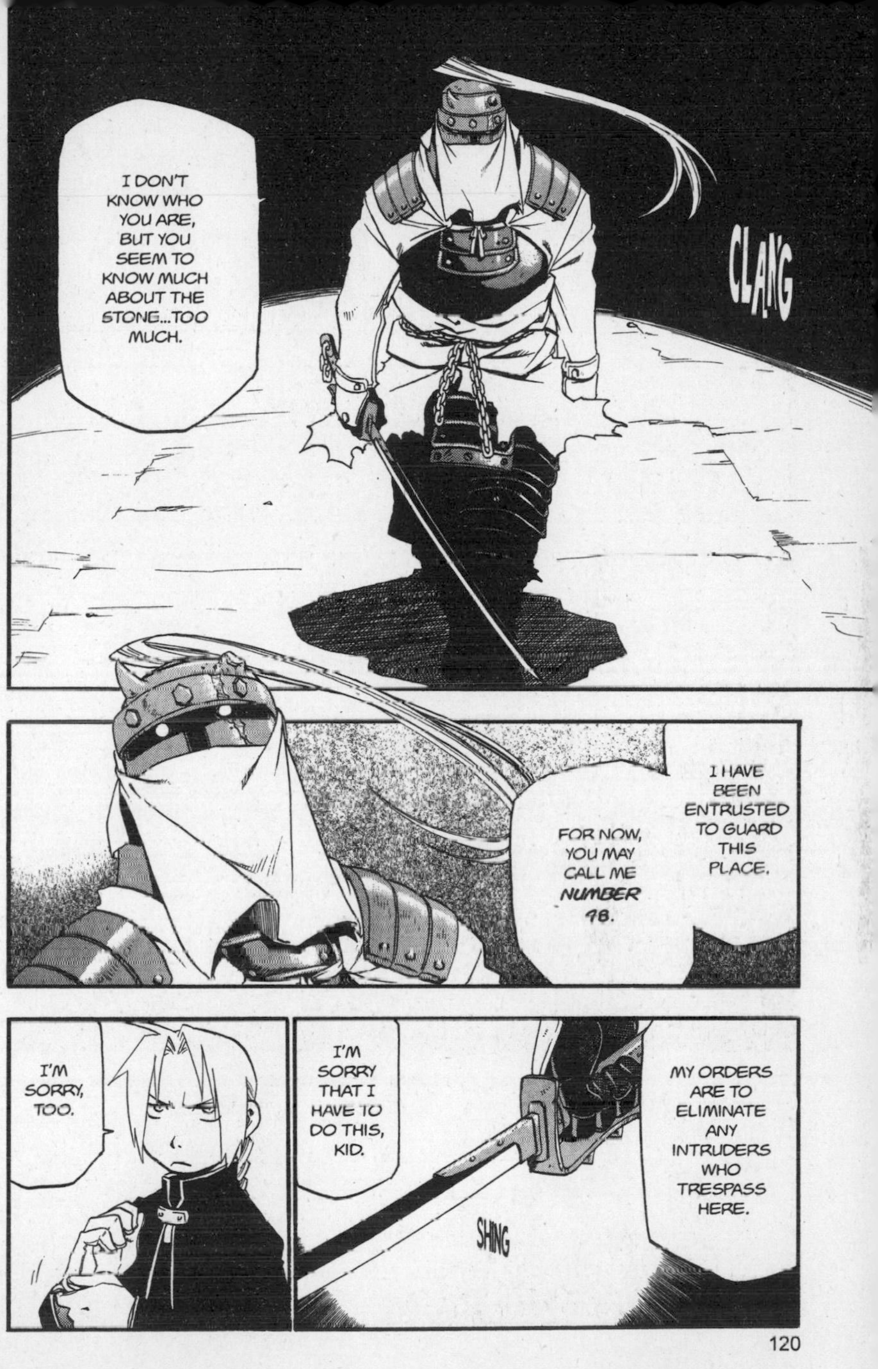
I DON'T KNOW WHO YOU ARE, BUT YOU SEEM TO KNOW MUCH ABOUT THE STONE...TOO MUCH.
CLANG
I HAVE BEEN ENTRUSTED TO GUARD THIS PLACE.
FOR NOW, YOU MAY CALL ME NUMBER 48.
MY ORDERS ARE TO ELIMINATE ANY INTRUDERS WHO TRESPASS HERE.
I'M SORRY THAT I HAVE TO DO THIS, KID.
SHING
I'M SORRY, TOO.

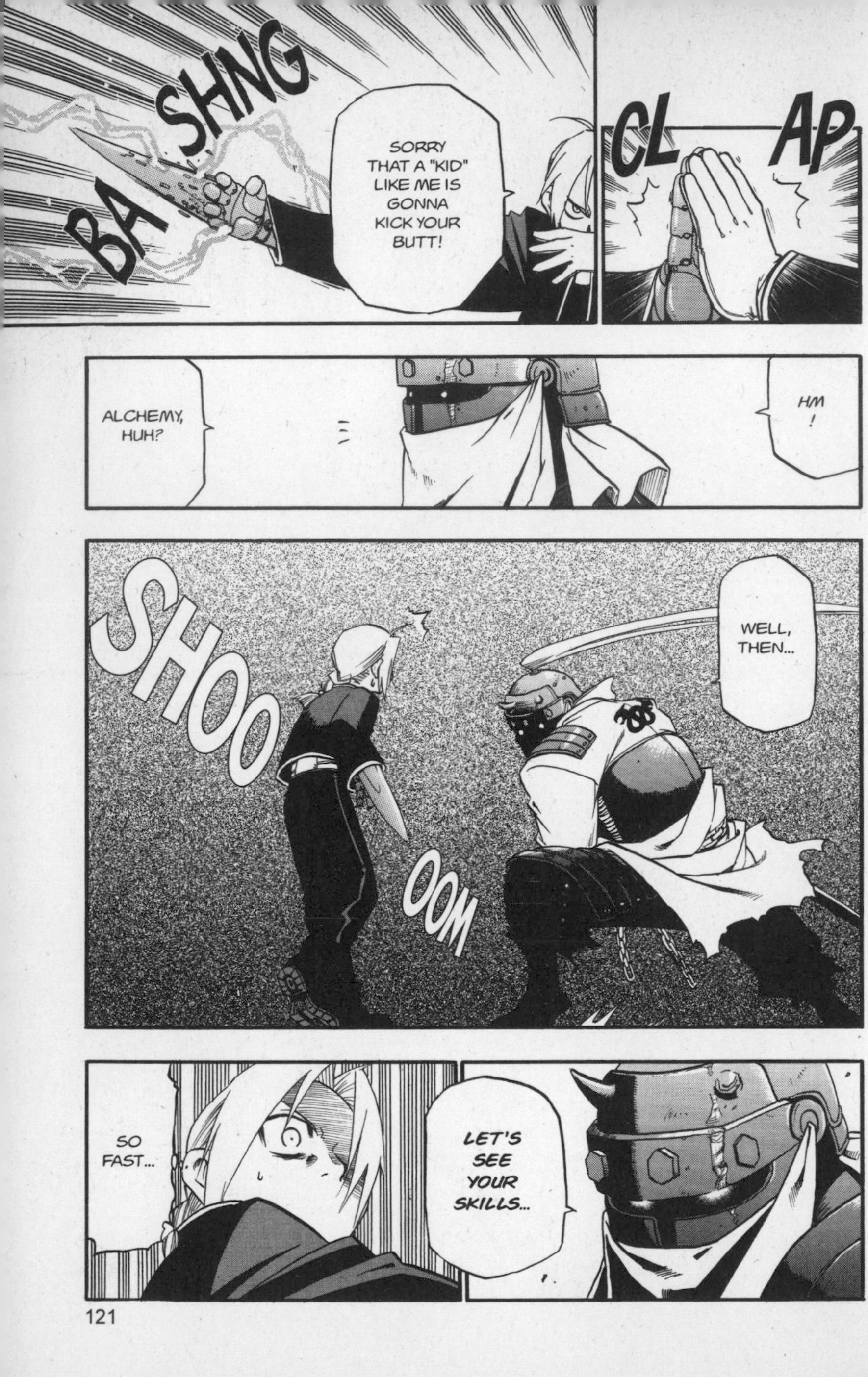
CL AP
SORRY THAT A "KID" LIKE ME IS GONNA KICK YOUR BUTT!
BASHNG
HM!
ALCHEMY, HUH?
WELL, THEN...
SHOOOOM
LET'S SEE YOUR SKILLS...
SO FAST...

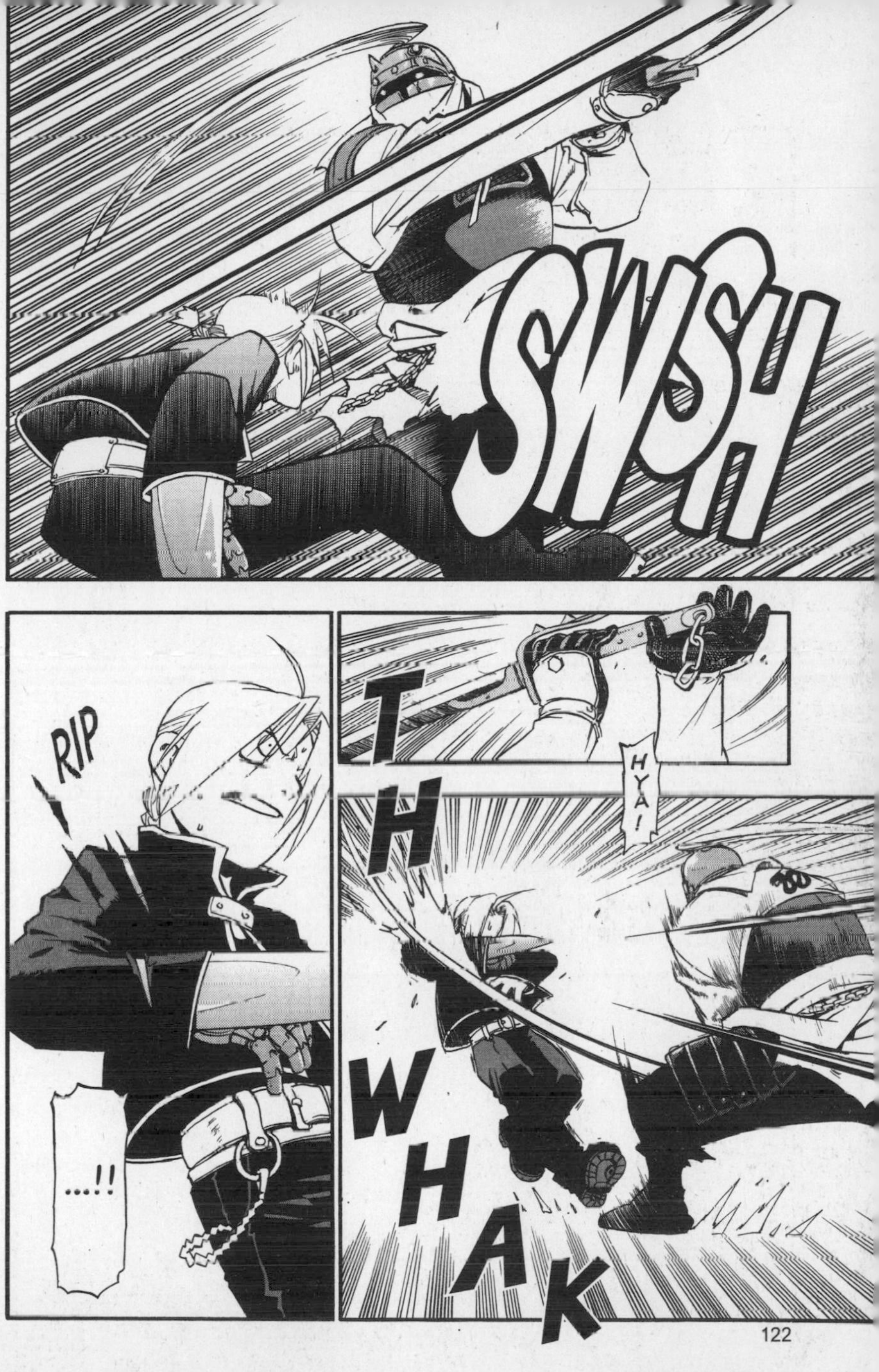
SWSH
THWHAK
HYA!
RIP
...!!

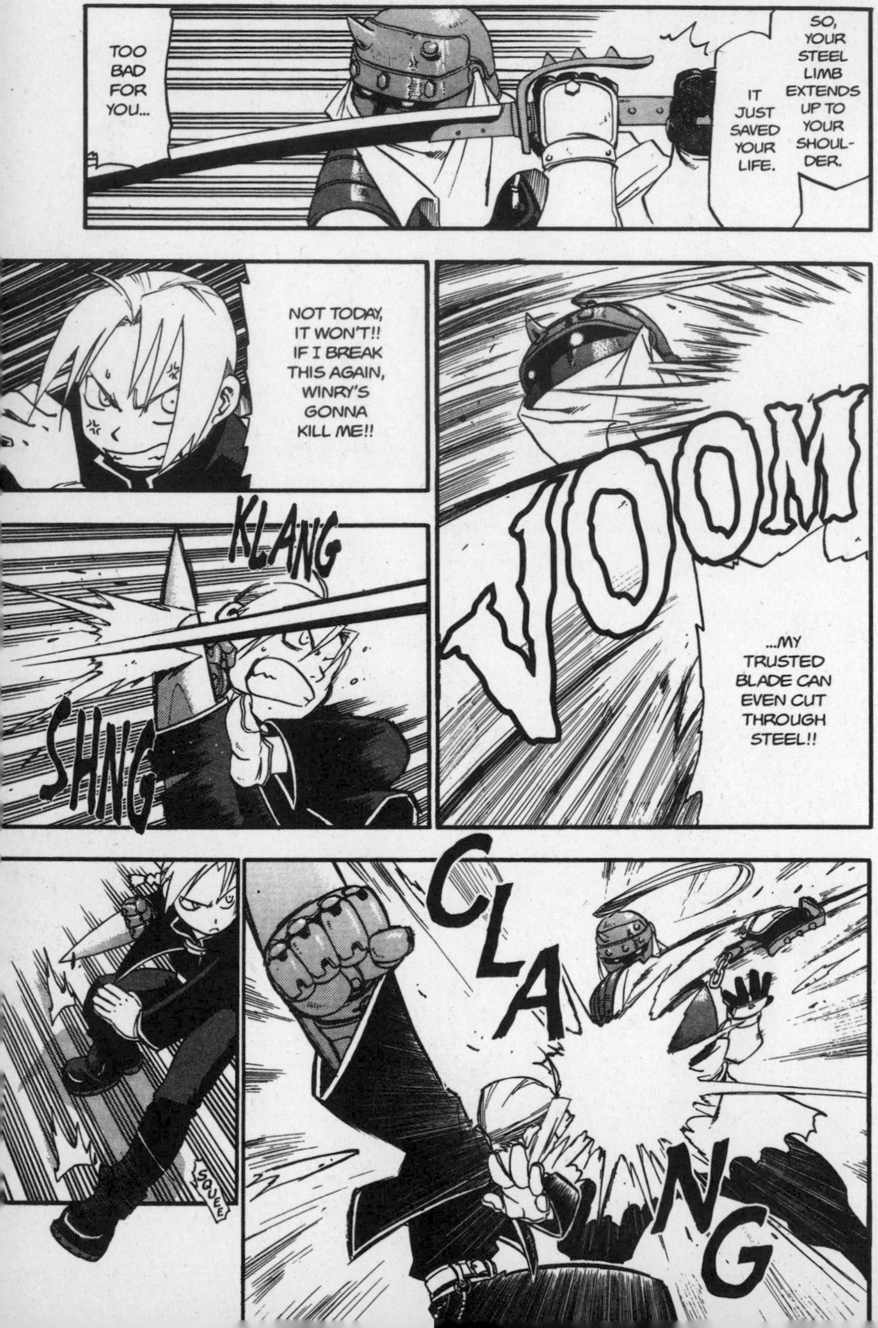
SO, YOUR STEEL LIMB EXTENDS UP TO YOUR SHOULDER.
IT JUST SAVED YOUR LIFE.
TOO BAD FOR YOU...
VOOM
...MY TRUSTED BLADE CAN EVEN CUT THROUGH STEEL!!
NOT TODAY, IT WON'T!! IF I BREAK THIS AGAIN, WINRY'S GONNA KILL ME!!
KLANG
SHNG
CLANG
SQUEE

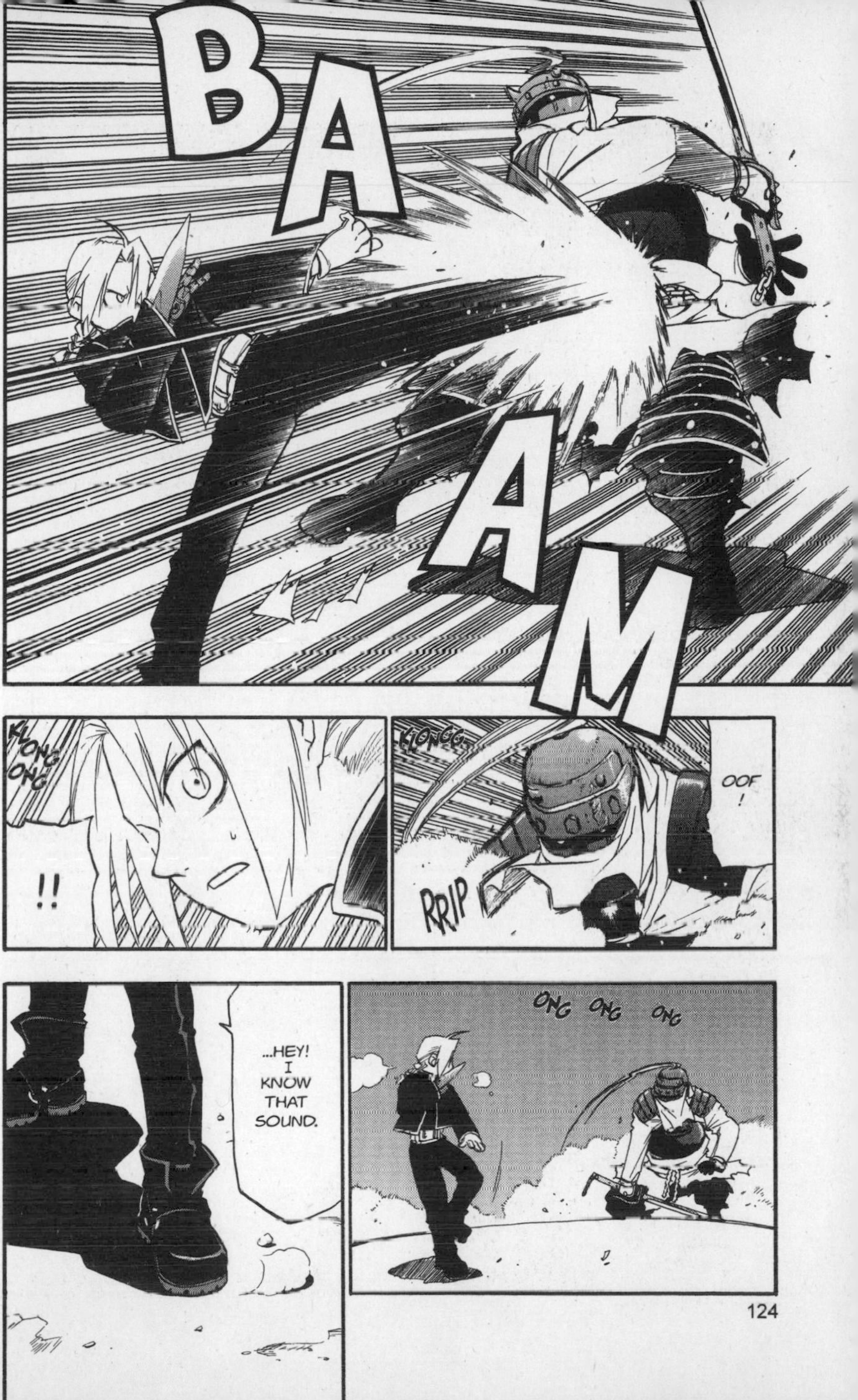
BAAM
KLONGG
OOF!
RRIP
KLONG ONG
!!
ONG ONG ONG
...HEY! I KNOW THAT SOUND.

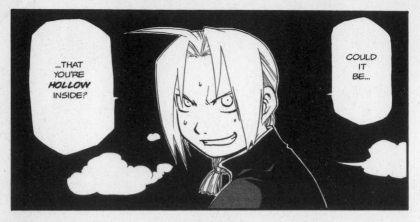

COULD IT BE...
...THAT YOU'RE **HOLLOW** INSIDE?
...VERY GOOD.
HOW DID YOU KNOW ?
I SPAR ALL THE TIME WITH A GUY LIKE YOU.
I COULD JUST TELL BY THE FEEL.
OH ?
SO THERE ARE OTHERS LIKE MYSELF ON THE OUTSIDE ?
IT MAKES ME SICK...
...KNOWING THAT THERE ARE IDIOTS OUT THERE BESIDES ME WHO WOULD EVEN THINK OF BINDING A **SOUL** TO A **SUIT OF ARMOR**.

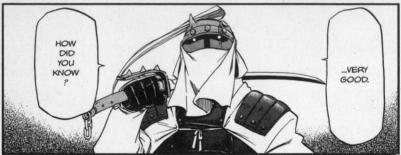

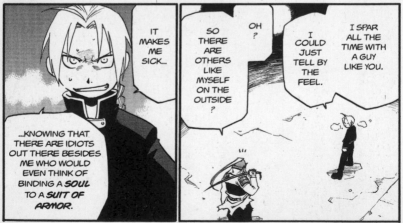

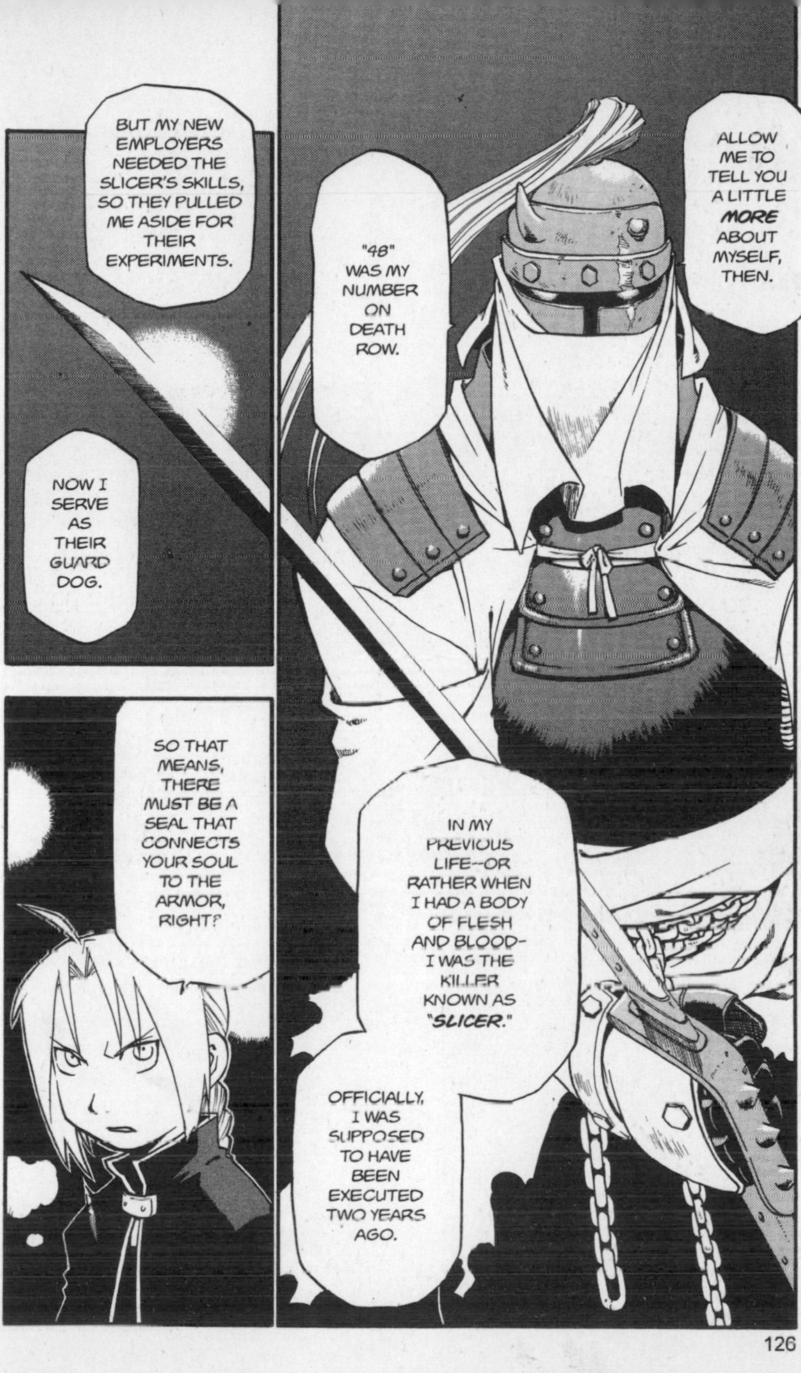
ALLOW ME TO TELL YOU A LITTLE MORE ABOUT MYSELF, THEN.
"48" WAS MY NUMBER ON DEATH ROW.
IN MY PREVIOUS LIFE--OR RATHER WHEN I HAD A BODY OF FLESH AND BLOOD-I WAS THE KILLER KNOWN AS "SLICER."
OFFICIALLY, I WAS SUPPOSED TO HAVE BEEN EXECUTED TWO YEARS AGO.
BUT MY NEW EMPLOYERS NEEDED THE SLICER'S SKILLS, SO THEY PULLED ME ASIDE FOR THEIR EXPERIMENTS.
NOW I SERVE AS THEIR GUARD DOG.
SO THAT MEANS, THERE MUST BE A SEAL THAT CONNECTS YOUR SOUL TO THE ARMOR, RIGHT?

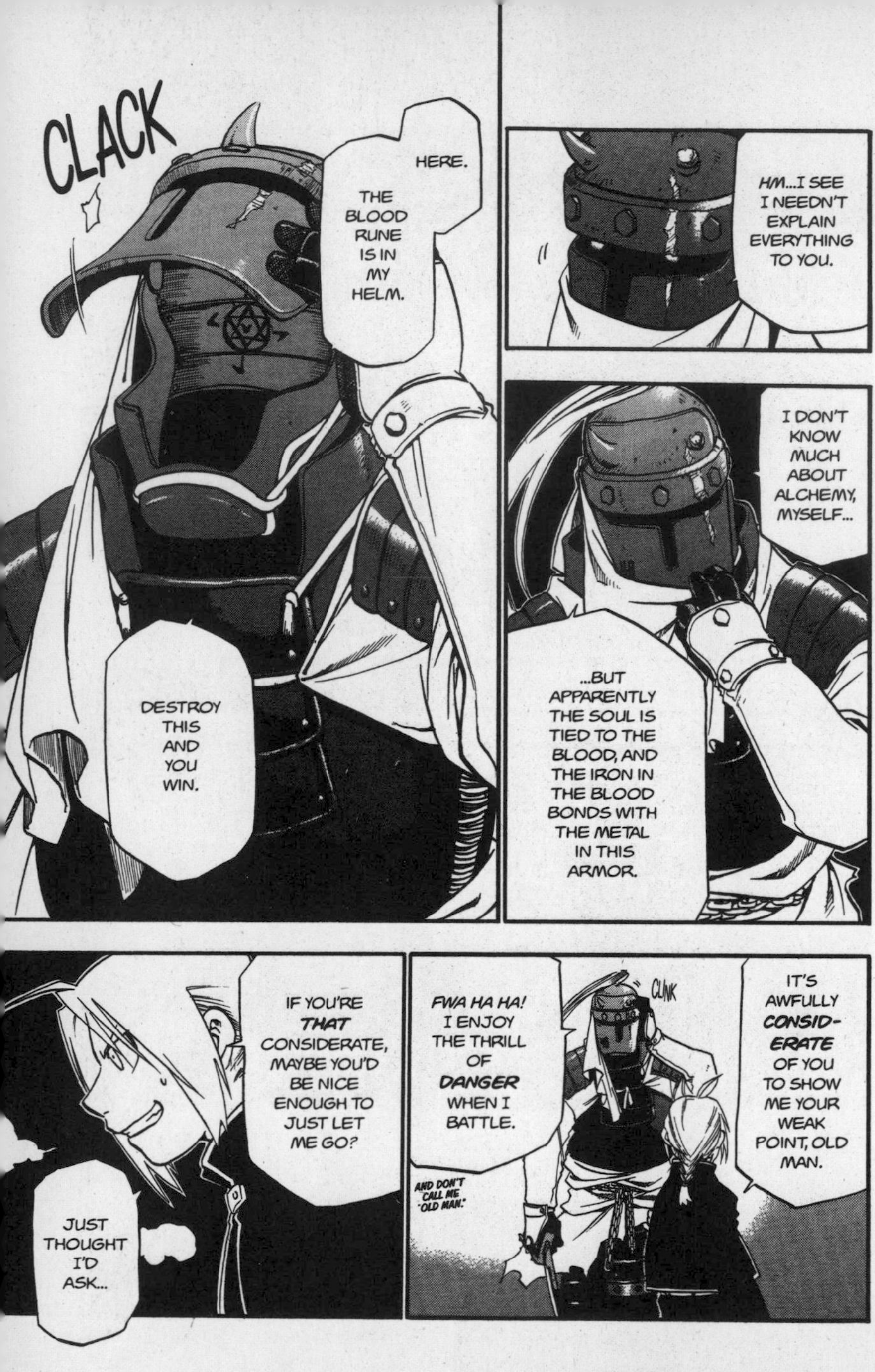
HM...I SEE I NEEDN'T EXPLAIN EVERYTHING TO YOU.
I DON'T KNOW MUCH ABOUT ALCHEMY, MYSELF...
...BUT APPARENTLY THE SOUL IS TIED TO THE BLOOD, AND THE IRON IN THE BLOOD BONDS WITH THE METAL IN THIS ARMOR.
CLACK
HERE.
THE BLOOD RUNE IS IN MY HELM.
DESTROY THIS AND YOU WIN.
IT'S AWFULLY CONSIDERATE OF YOU TO SHOW ME YOUR WEAK POINT, OLD MAN.
CLINK
FWA HA HA! I ENJOY THE THRILL OF DANGER WHEN I BATTLE.
AND DON'T CALL ME "OLD MAN."
IF YOU'RE THAT CONSIDERATE, MAYBE YOU'D BE NICE ENOUGH TO JUST LET ME GO?
JUST THOUGHT I'D ASK...

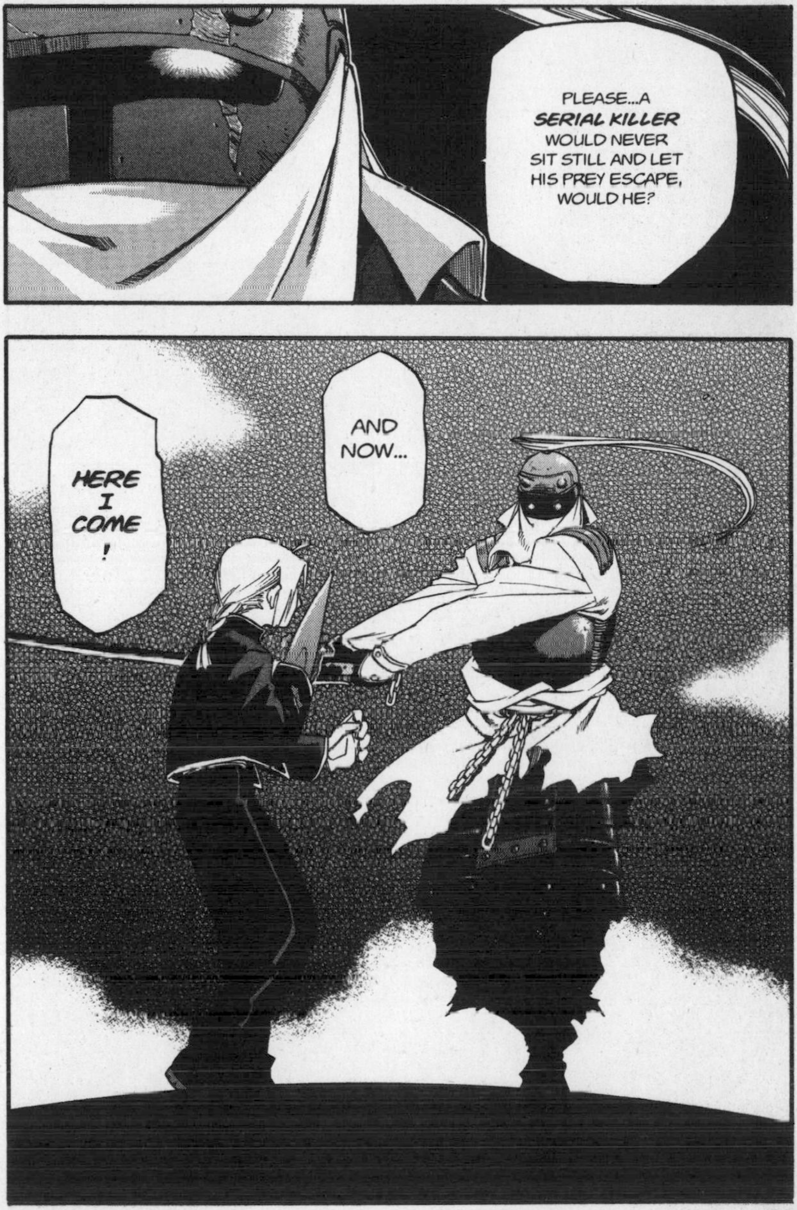
PLEASE...A **SERIAL KILLER** WOULD NEVER SIT STILL AND LET HIS PREY ESCAPE, WOULD HE?
AND NOW...
HERE I COME!

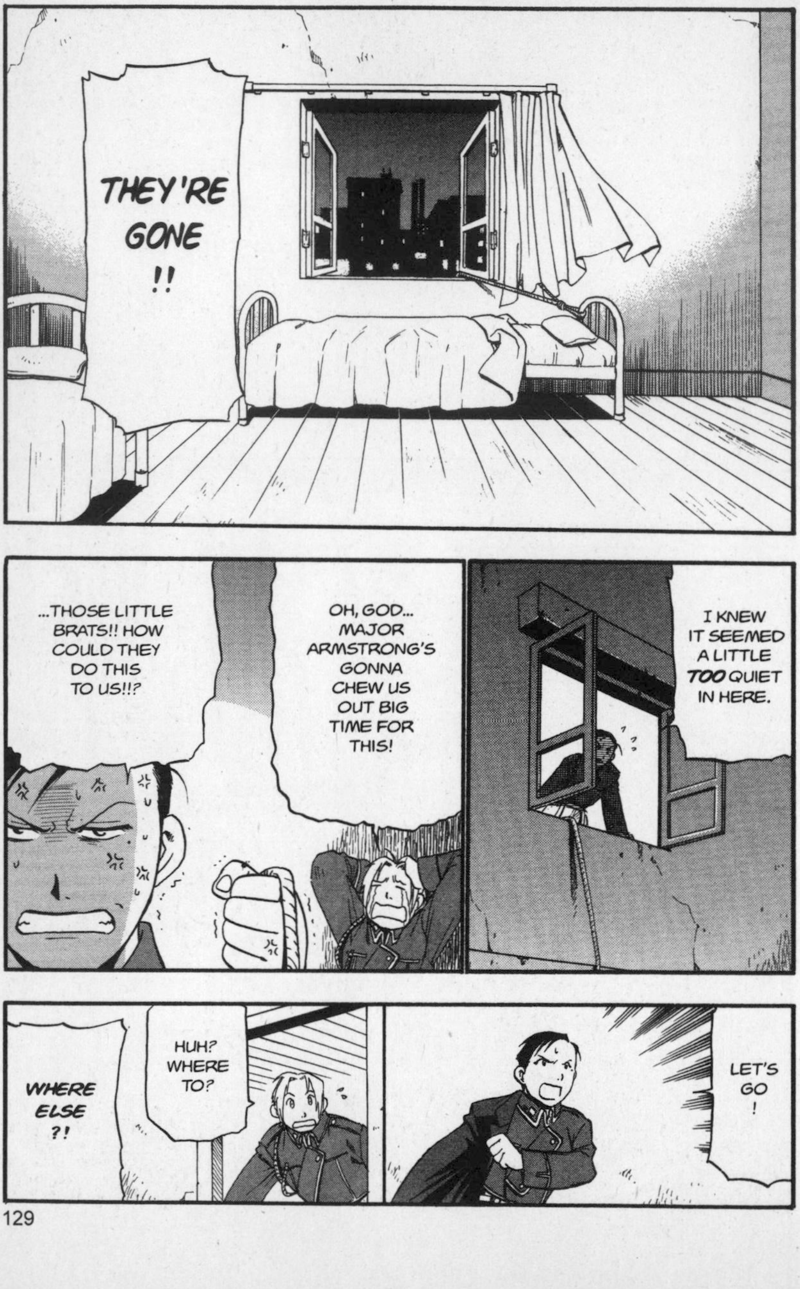
THEY'RE GONE !!
I KNEW IT SEEMED A LITTLE TOO QUIET IN HERE.
OH, GOD... MAJOR ARMSTRONG'S GONNA CHEW US OUT BIG TIME FOR THIS!
...THOSE LITTLE BRATS!! HOW COULD THEY DO THIS TO US!!?
LET'S GO !
HUH? WHERE TO?
WHERE ELSE ?!

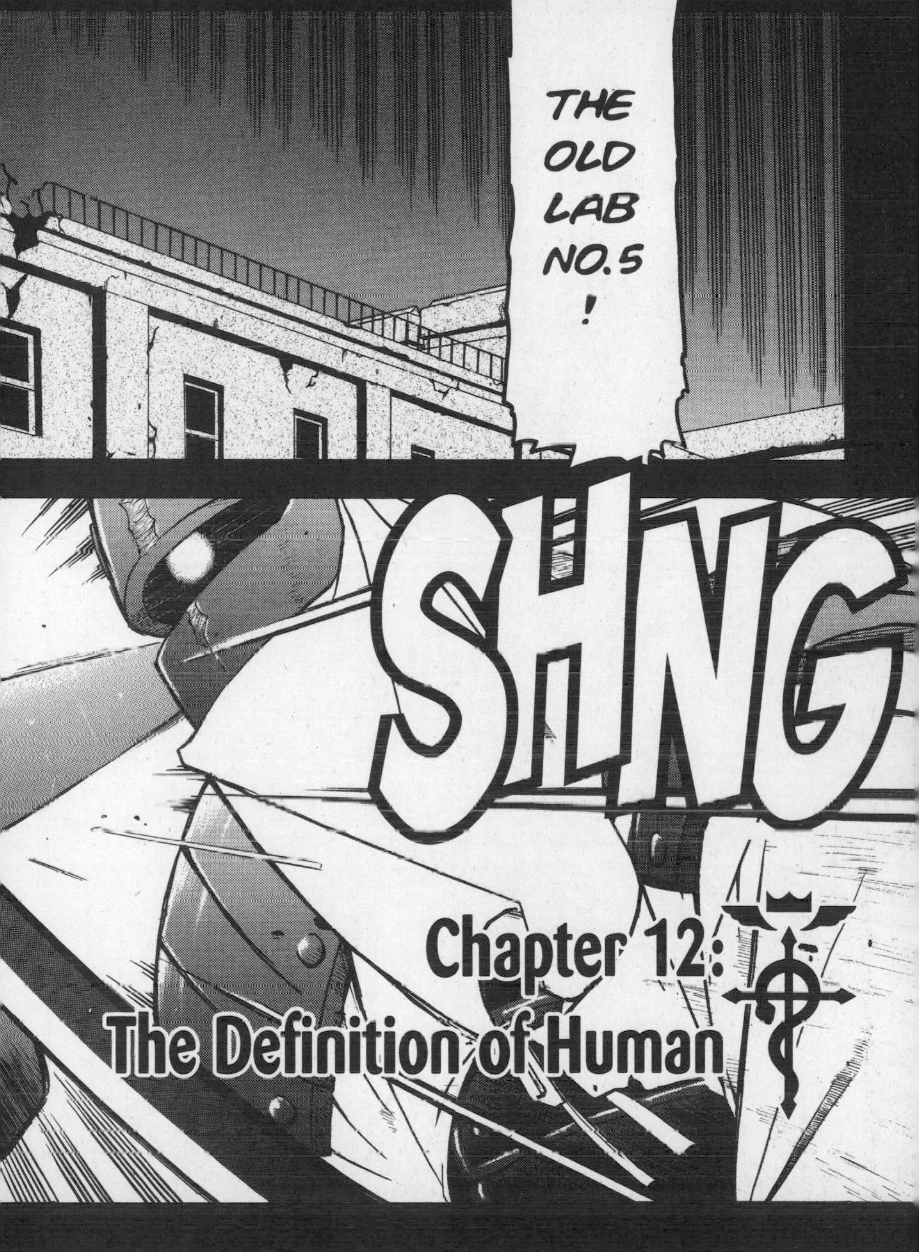
THE OLD LAB NO.5 !
SHNG

Chapter 12: The Definition of Human

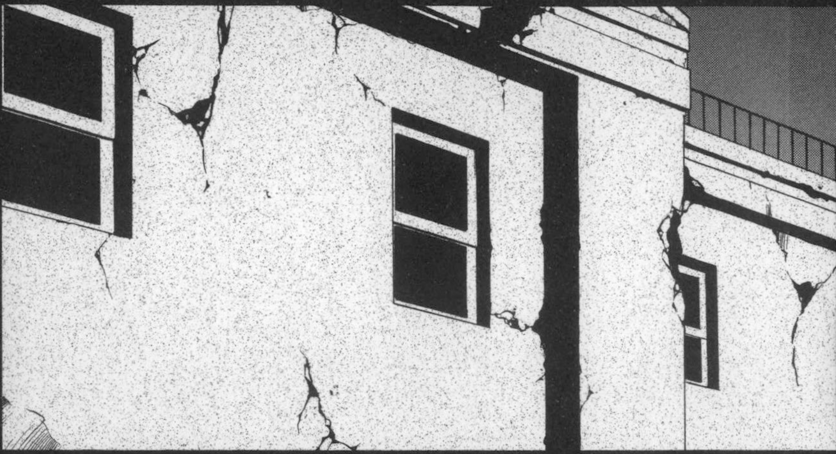
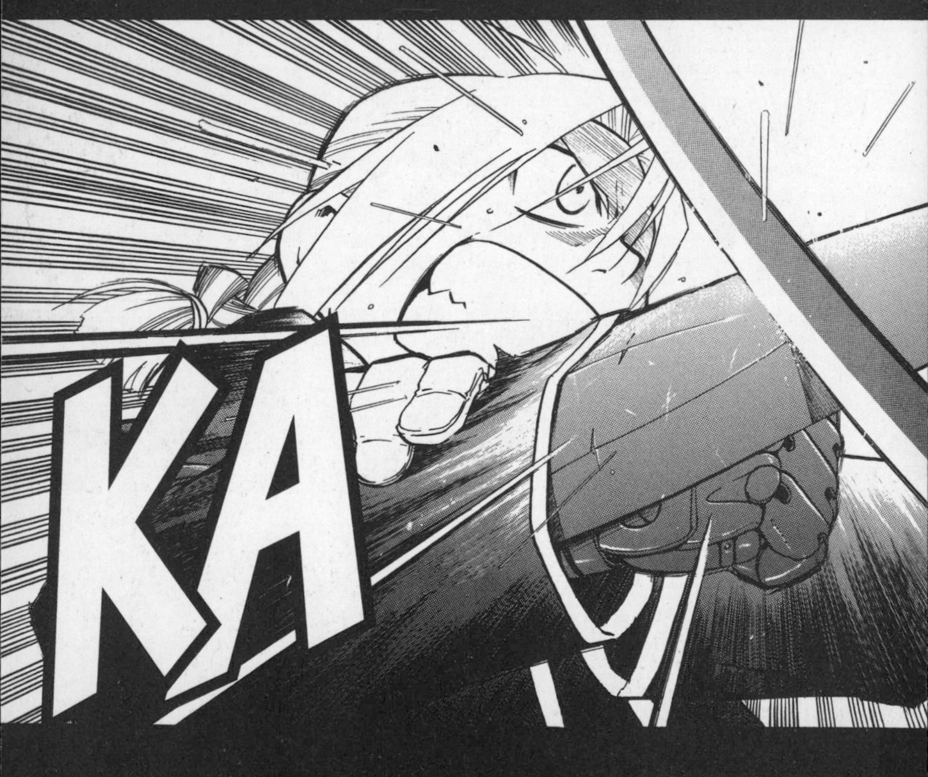
KA

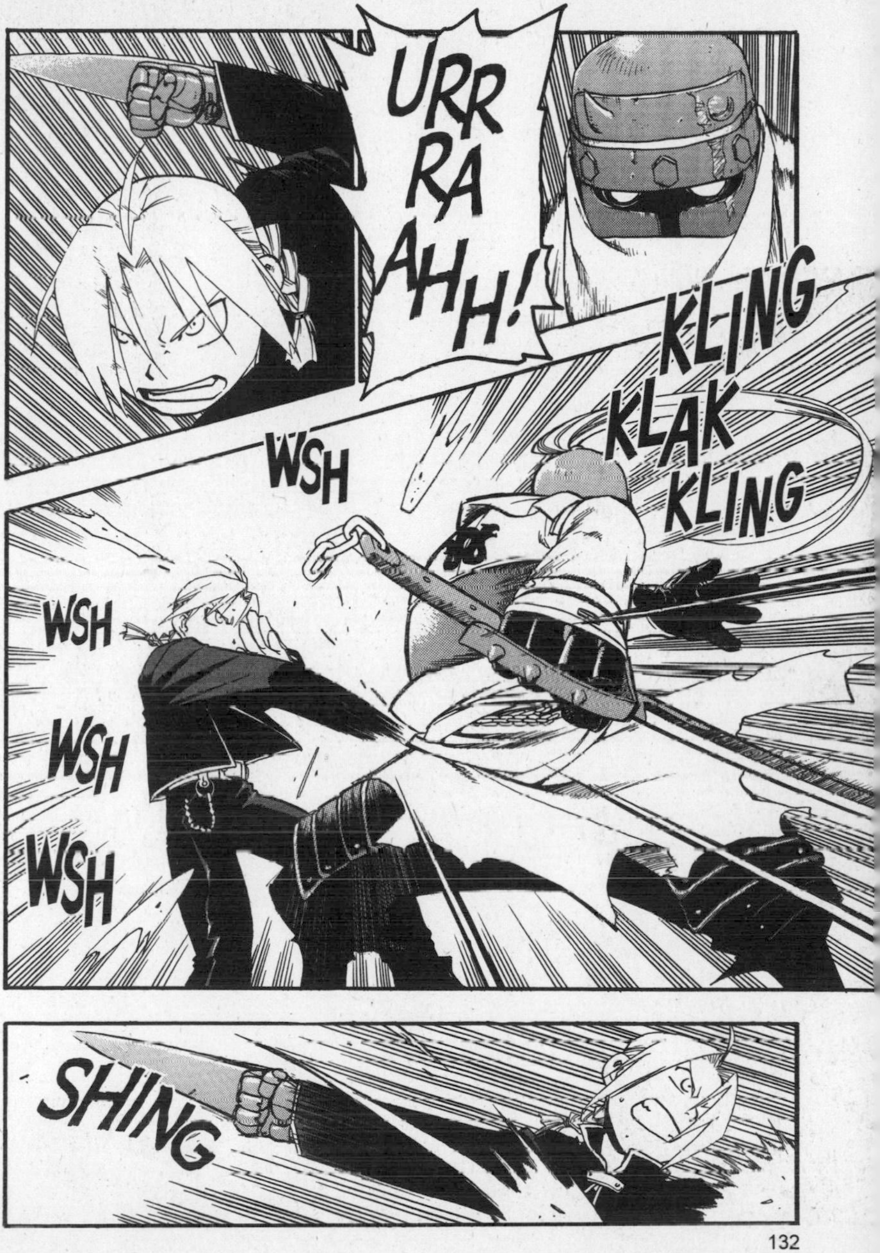
URRRAAHH!
KLING KLAK KLING
WSH
WSH
WSH
WSH
SHING

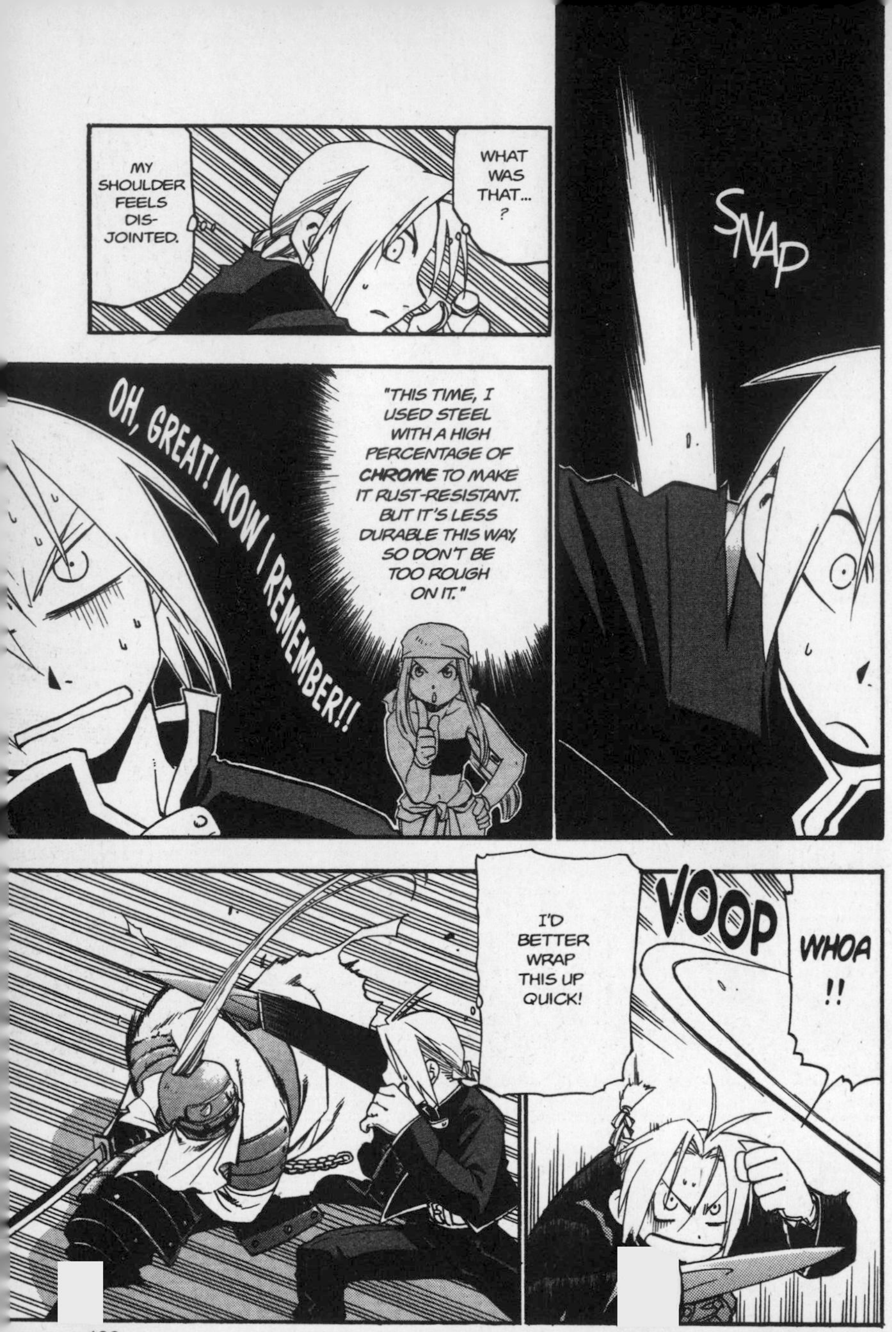
SNAP
WHAT WAS THAT...?
MY SHOULDER FEELS DIS-JOINTED.
"THIS TIME, I USED STEEL WITH A HIGH PERCENTAGE OF CHROME TO MAKE IT RUST-RESISTANT. BUT IT'S LESS DURABLE THIS WAY, SO DON'T BE TOO ROUGH ON IT."
OH, GREAT! NOW I REMEMBER!!
WHOA!!
VOOP
I'D BETTER WRAP THIS UP QUICK!

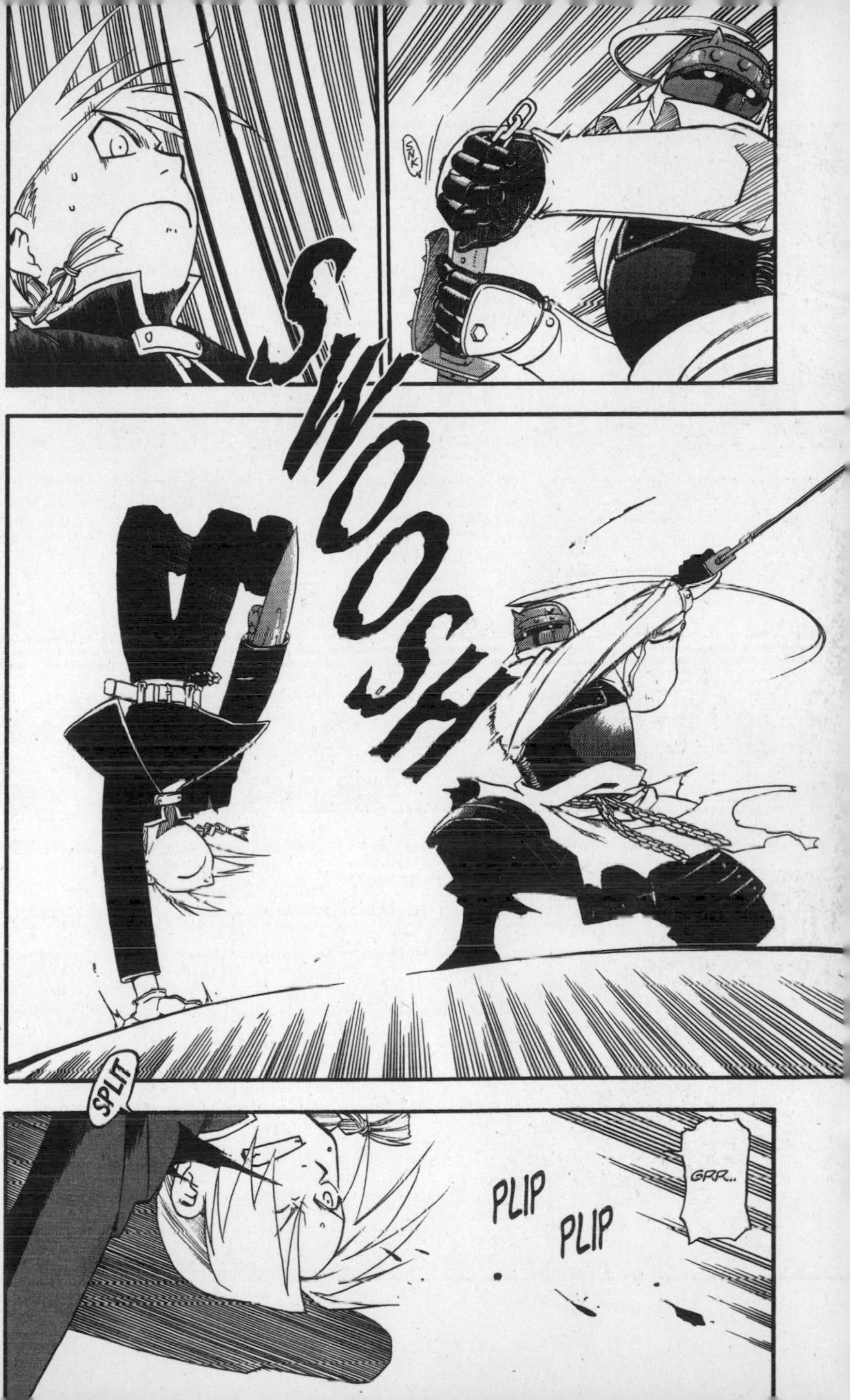
SNK
SWOOSH
GRR...
PLIP
PLIP
SPLIT

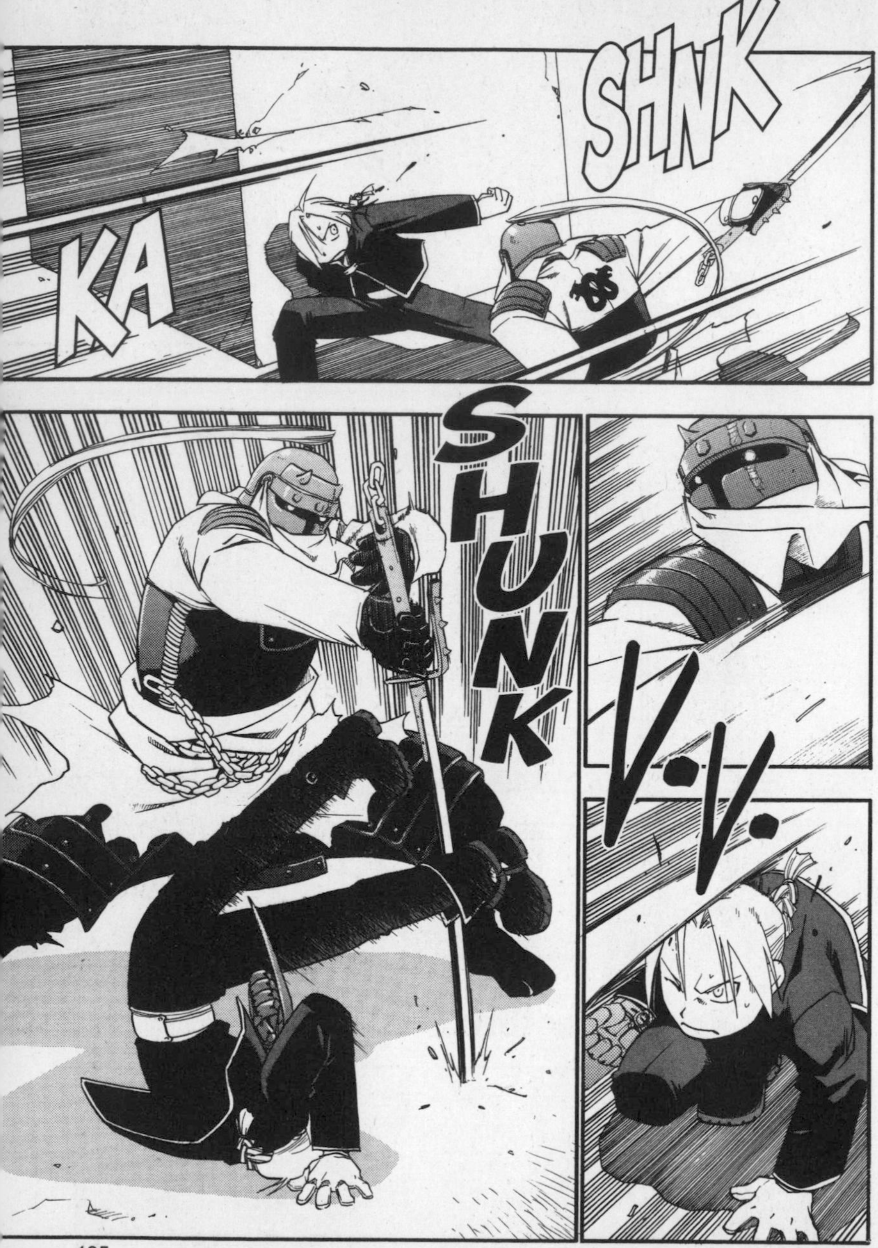
SHNK
KA
SHUNK

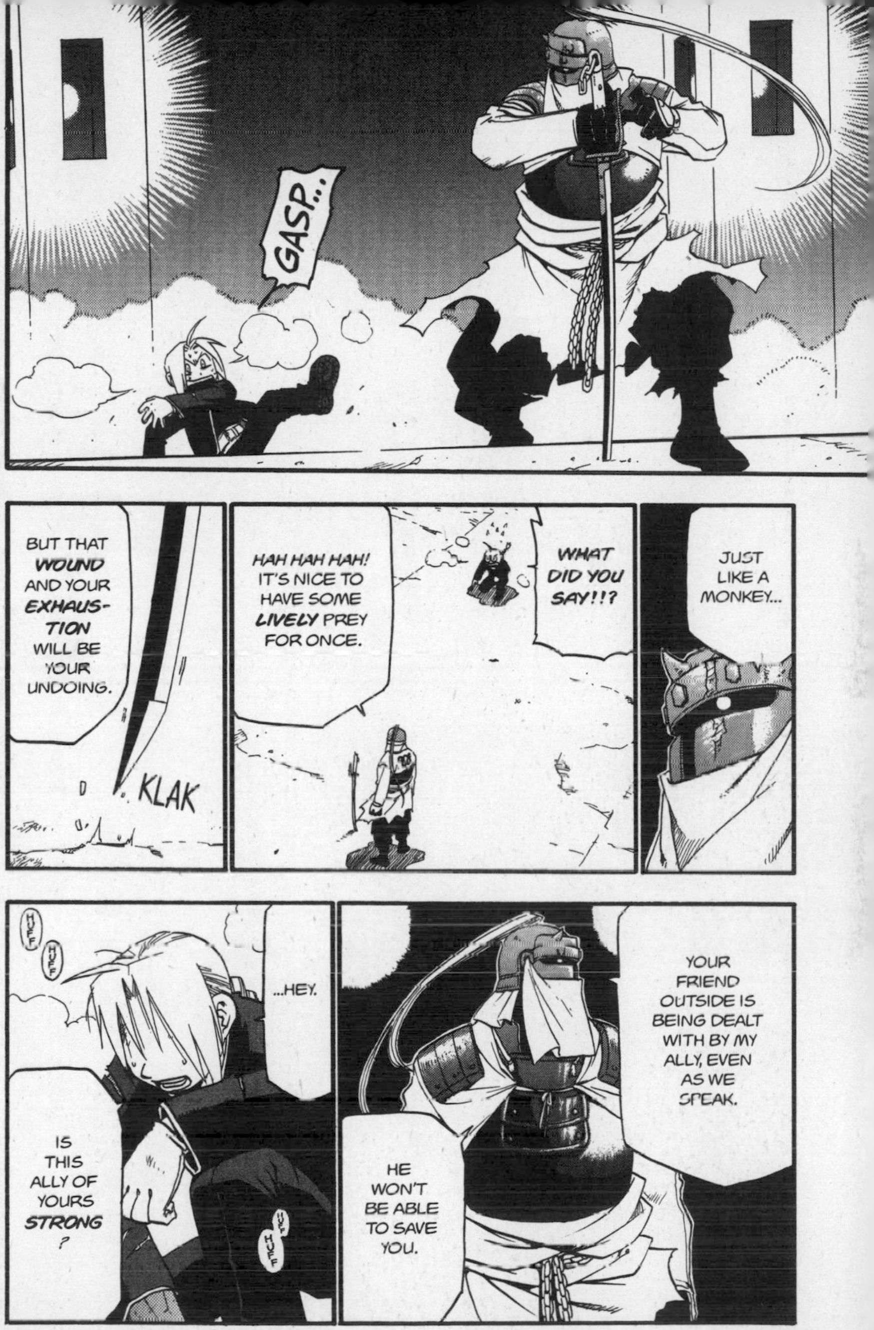
GASP...
JUST LIKE A MONKEY...
WHAT DID YOU SAY!!?
HAH HAH HAH! IT'S NICE TO HAVE SOME LIVELY PREY FOR ONCE.
BUT THAT WOUND AND YOUR EXHAUS- TION WILL BE YOUR UNDOING.
KLAK
YOUR FRIEND OUTSIDE IS BEING DEALT WITH BY MY ALLY, EVEN AS WE SPEAK.
HE WON'T BE ABLE TO SAVE YOU.
HUFF
HUFF
...HEY.
IS THIS ALLY OF YOURS STRONG?
HUFF
HUFF

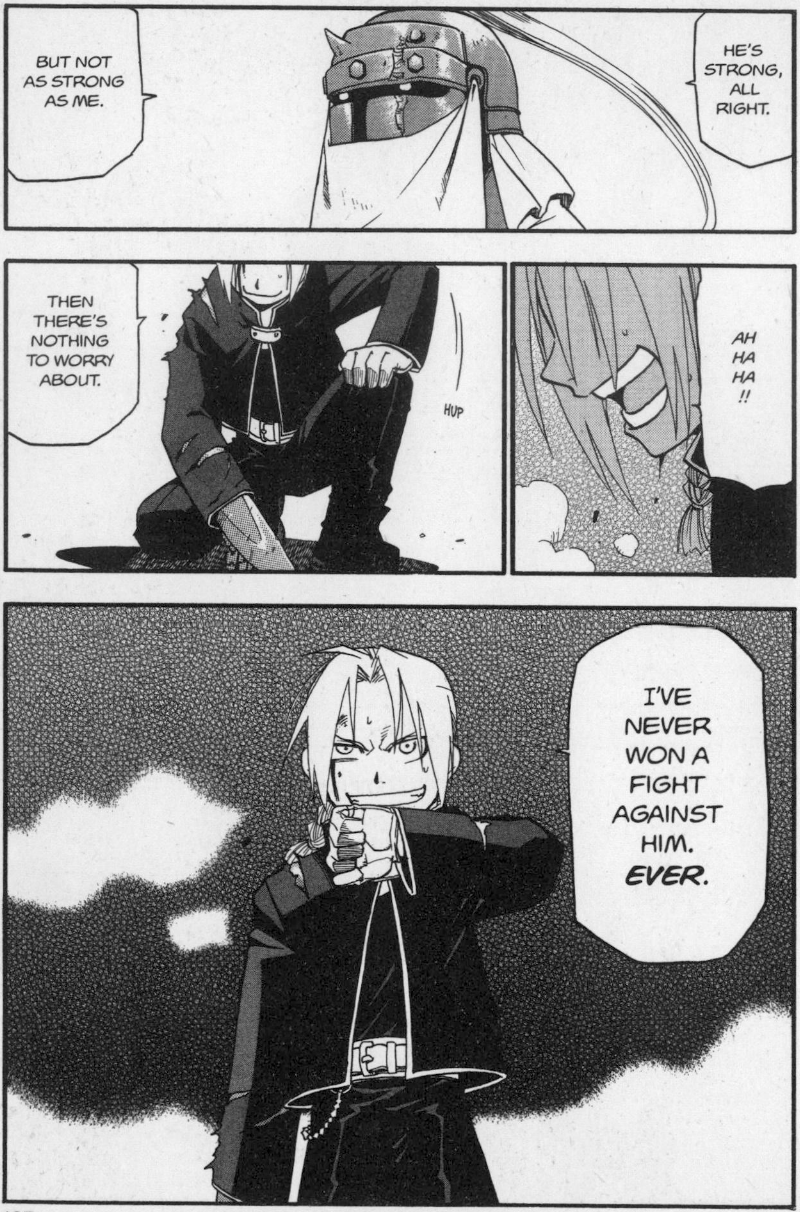
HE'S STRONG, ALL RIGHT.
BUT NOT AS STRONG AS ME.
AH HA HA !!
THEN THERE'S NOTHING TO WORRY ABOUT.
HUP
I'VE NEVER WON A FIGHT AGAINST HIM. *EVER*.

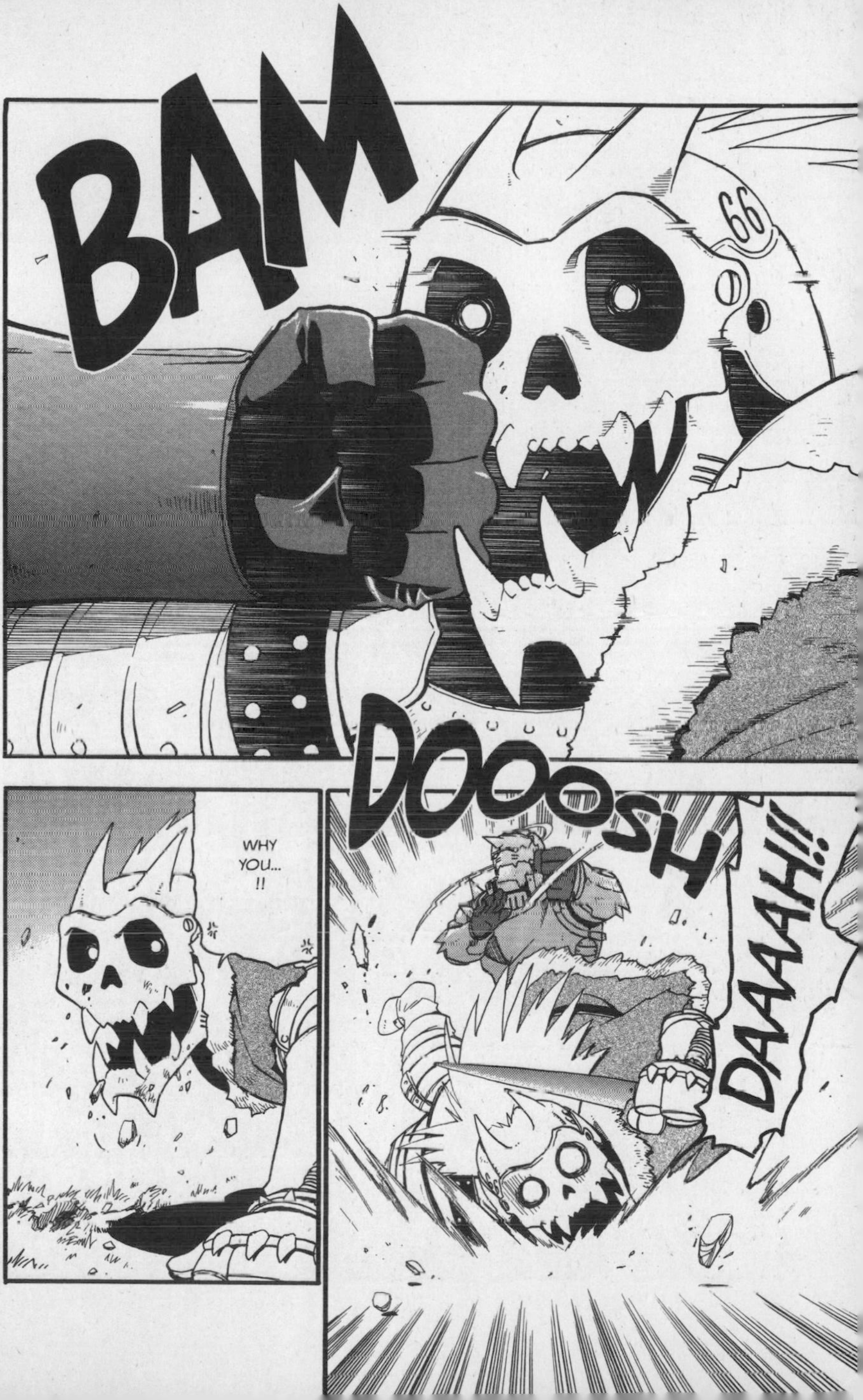
BAM
DOOOSH
DAAAH!!
WHY YOU... !!

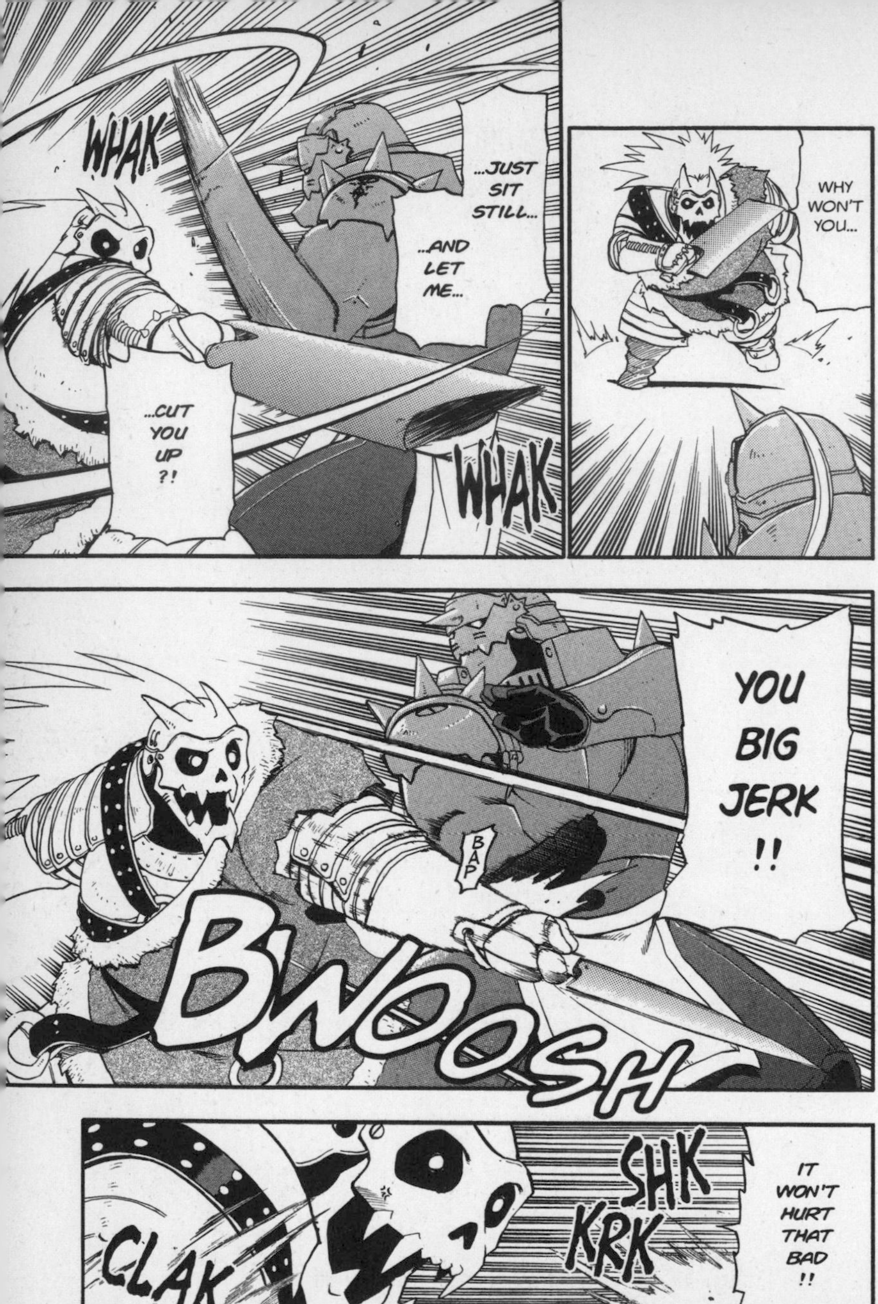
WHAK
...JUST SIT STILL...
...AND LET ME...
...CUT YOU UP ?!
WHAK
WHY WON'T YOU...
YOU BIG JERK !!
BAP
BWOOSH
SHK
KRK
CLAK
IT WON'T HURT THAT BAD !!

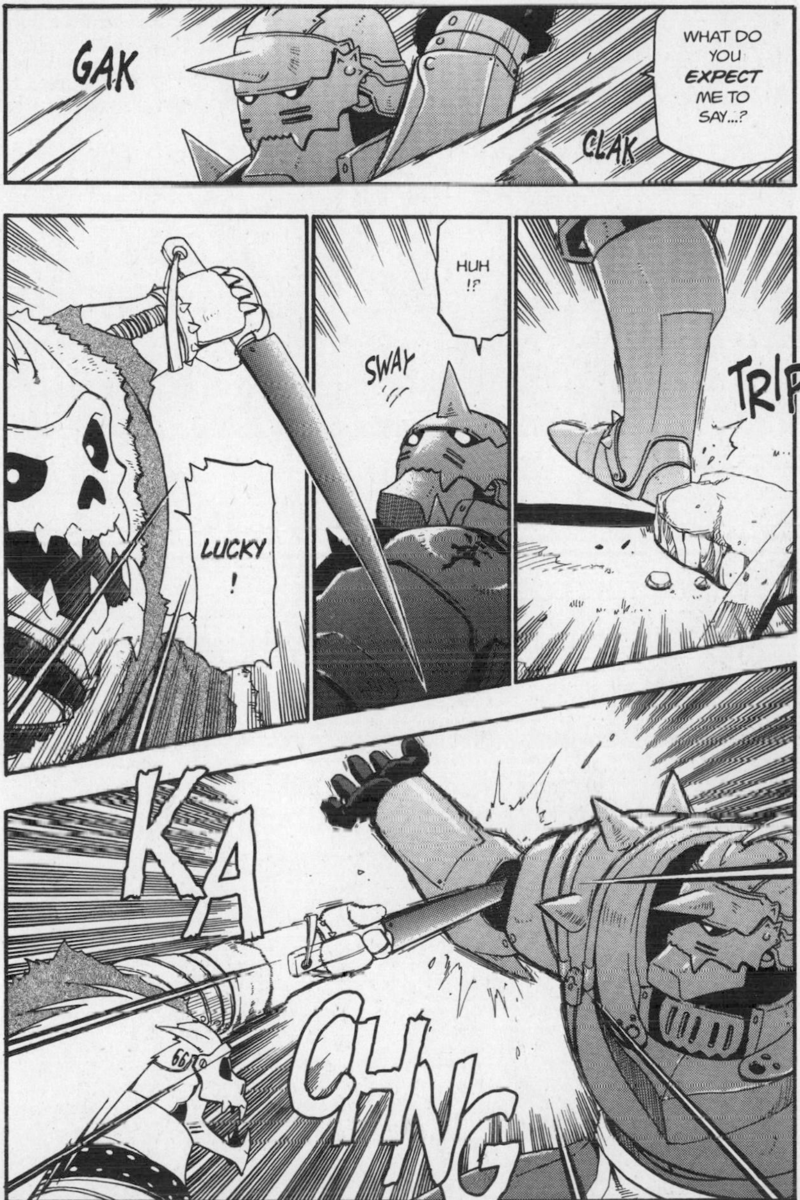
WHAT DO YOU EXPECT ME TO SAY...?
GAK
CLAK
TRIP
HUH!?
SWAY
LUCKY!
KA
CHING

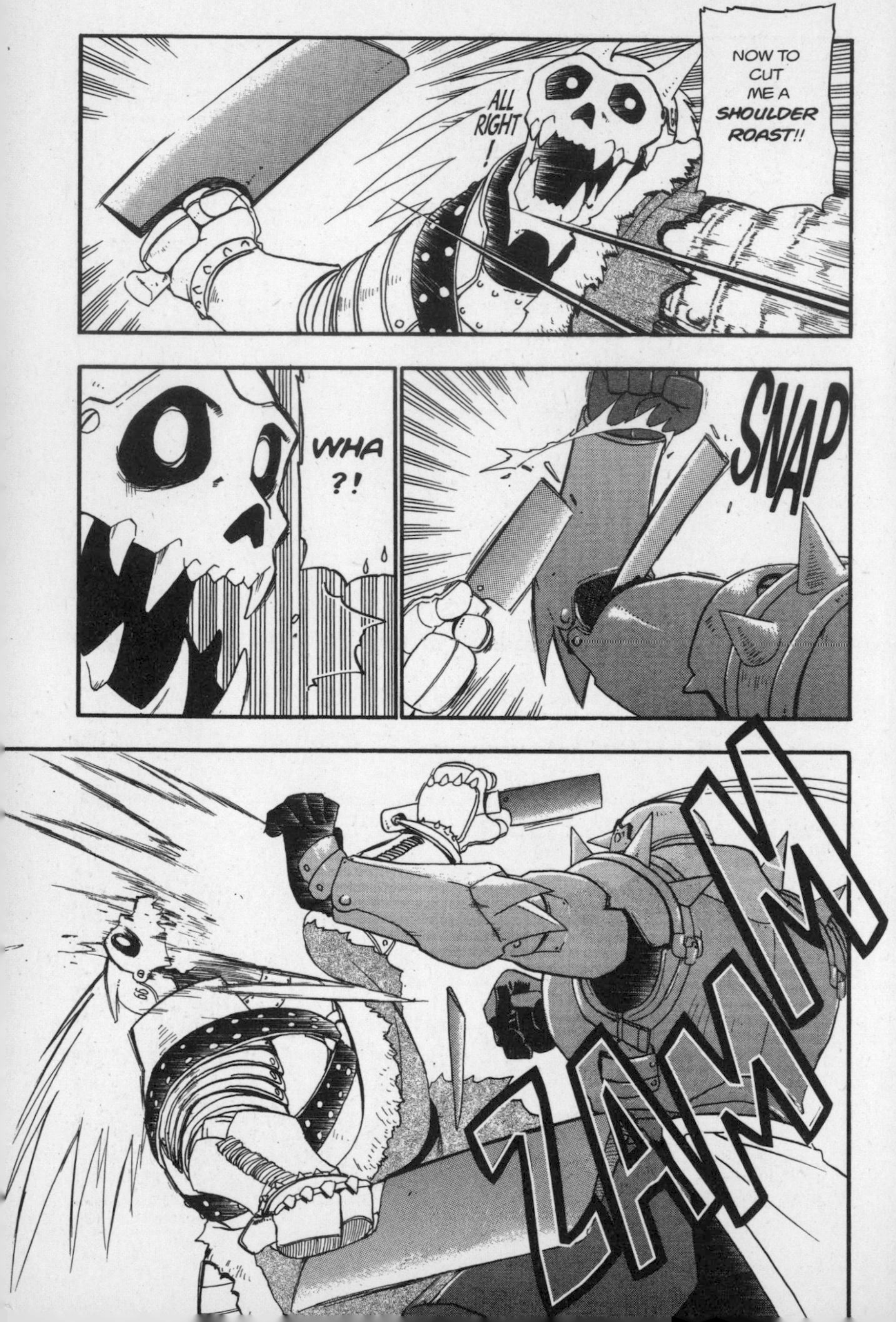
NOW TO CUT ME A SHOULDER ROAST!!
ALL RIGHT!
SNAP
WHA?!
ZAMM

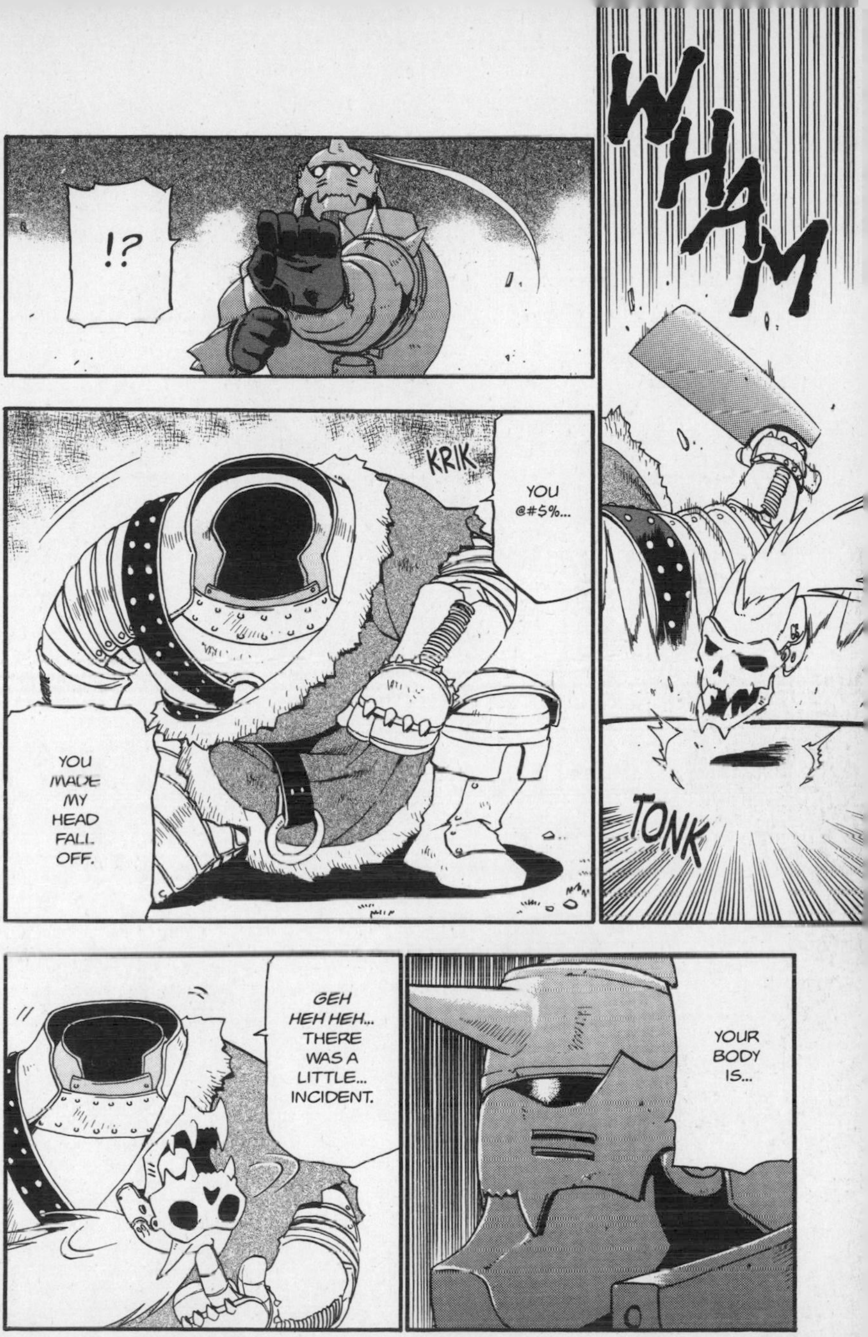
WHAM
TONK
!?
KRIK
YOU @#5%...
YOU MADE MY HEAD FALL OFF.
YOUR BODY IS...
GEH HEH HEH... THERE WAS A LITTLE... INCIDENT.

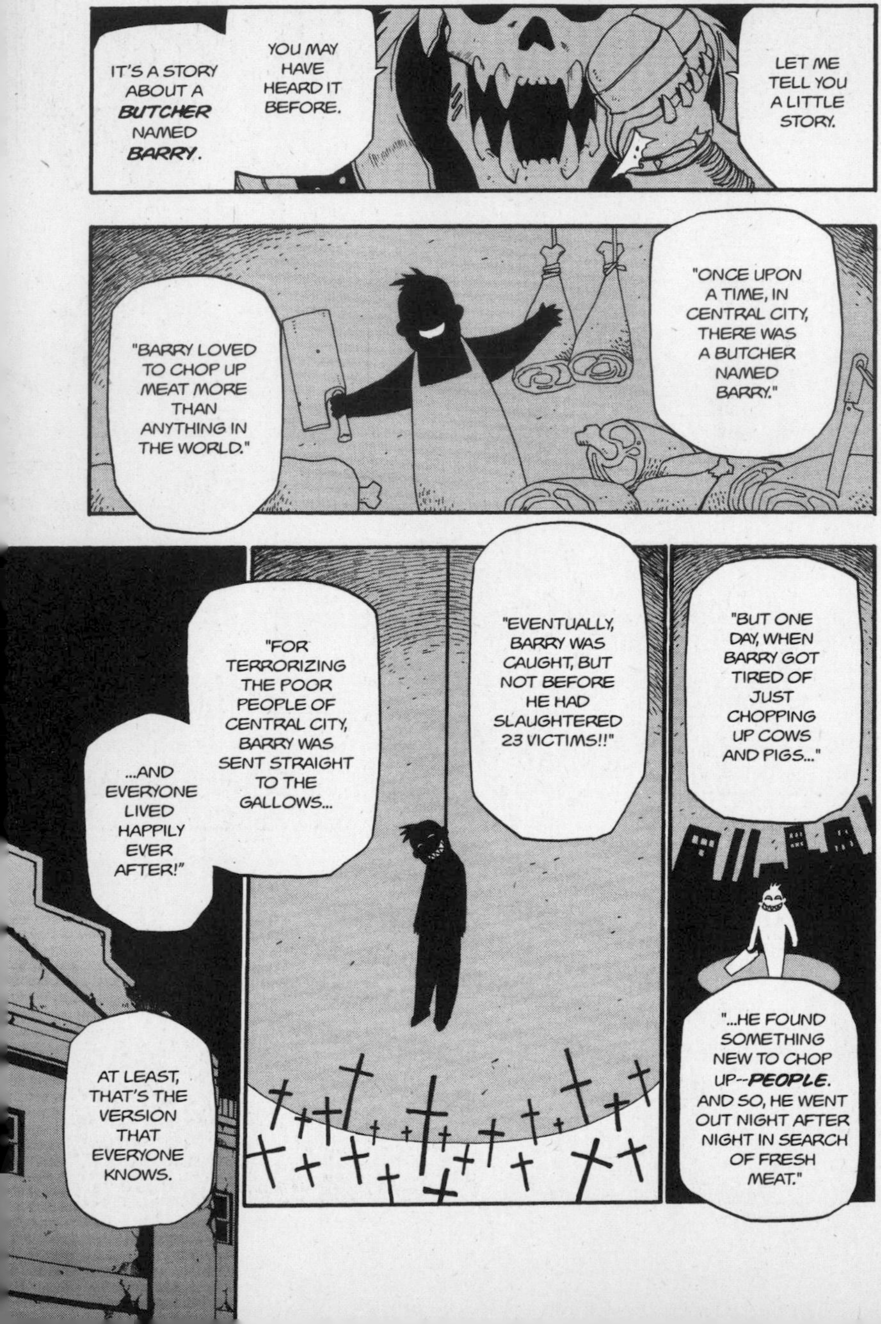
LET ME TELL YOU A LITTLE STORY.
YOU MAY HAVE HEARD IT BEFORE.
IT'S A STORY ABOUT A **BUTCHER** NAMED **BARRY**.
"ONCE UPON A TIME, IN CENTRAL CITY, THERE WAS A BUTCHER NAMED BARRY."
"BARRY LOVED TO CHOP UP MEAT MORE THAN ANYTHING IN THE WORLD."
"BUT ONE DAY, WHEN BARRY GOT TIRED OF JUST CHOPPING UP COWS AND PIGS..."
"...HE FOUND SOMETHING NEW TO CHOP UP--**PEOPLE**. AND SO, HE WENT OUT NIGHT AFTER NIGHT IN SEARCH OF FRESH MEAT."
"EVENTUALLY, BARRY WAS CAUGHT, BUT NOT BEFORE HE HAD SLAUGHTERED 23 VICTIMS!!"
"FOR TERRORIZING THE POOR PEOPLE OF CENTRAL CITY, BARRY WAS SENT STRAIGHT TO THE GALLOWS...
...AND EVERYONE LIVED HAPPILY EVER AFTER!"
AT LEAST, THAT'S THE VERSION THAT EVERYONE KNOWS.

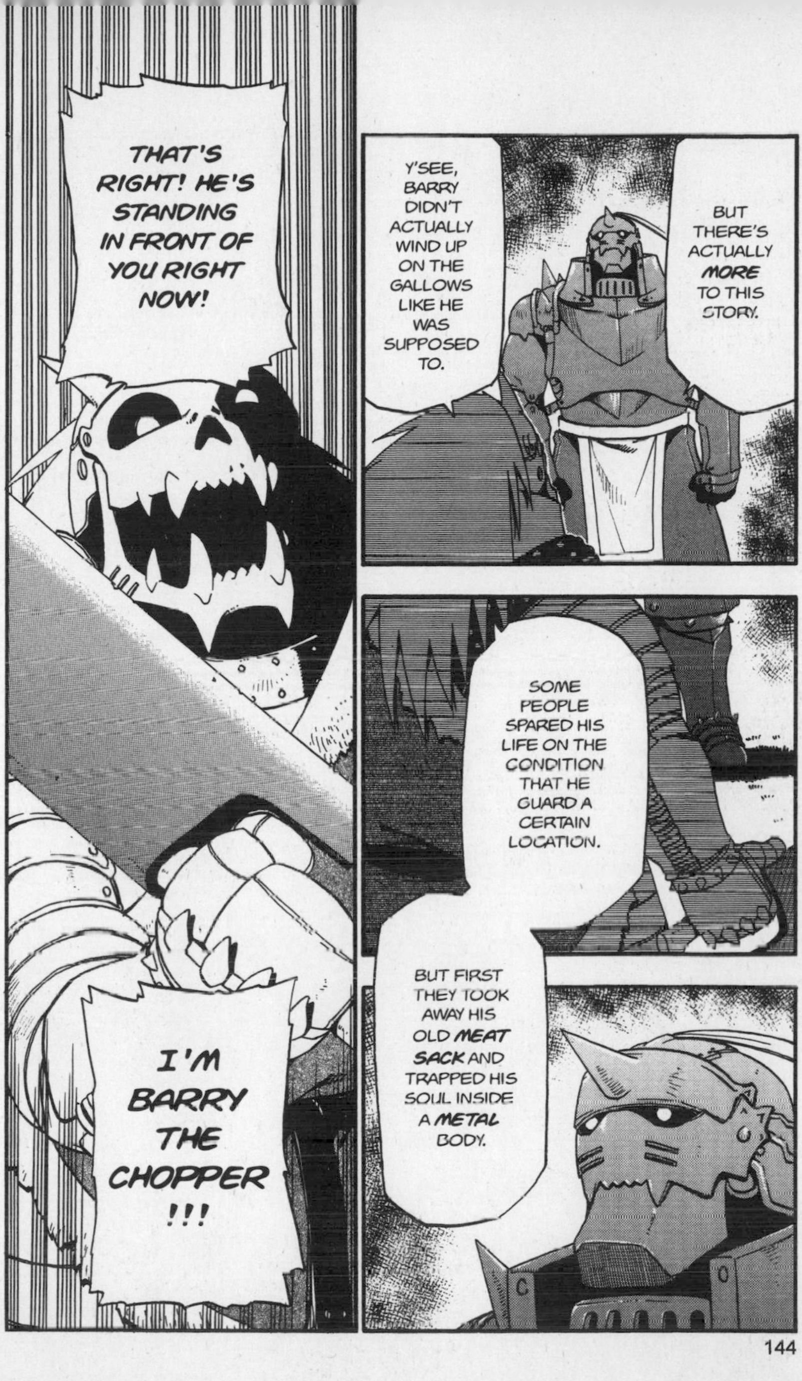
BUT THERE'S ACTUALLY MORE TO THIS STORY.
Y'SEE, BARRY DIDN'T ACTUALLY WIND UP ON THE GALLOWS LIKE HE WAS SUPPOSED TO.
SOME PEOPLE SPARED HIS LIFE ON THE CONDITION THAT HE GUARD A CERTAIN LOCATION.
BUT FIRST THEY TOOK AWAY HIS OLD MEAT SACK AND TRAPPED HIS SOUL INSIDE A METAL BODY.
THAT'S RIGHT! HE'S STANDING IN FRONT OF YOU RIGHT NOW!
I'M BARRY THE CHOPPER!!!

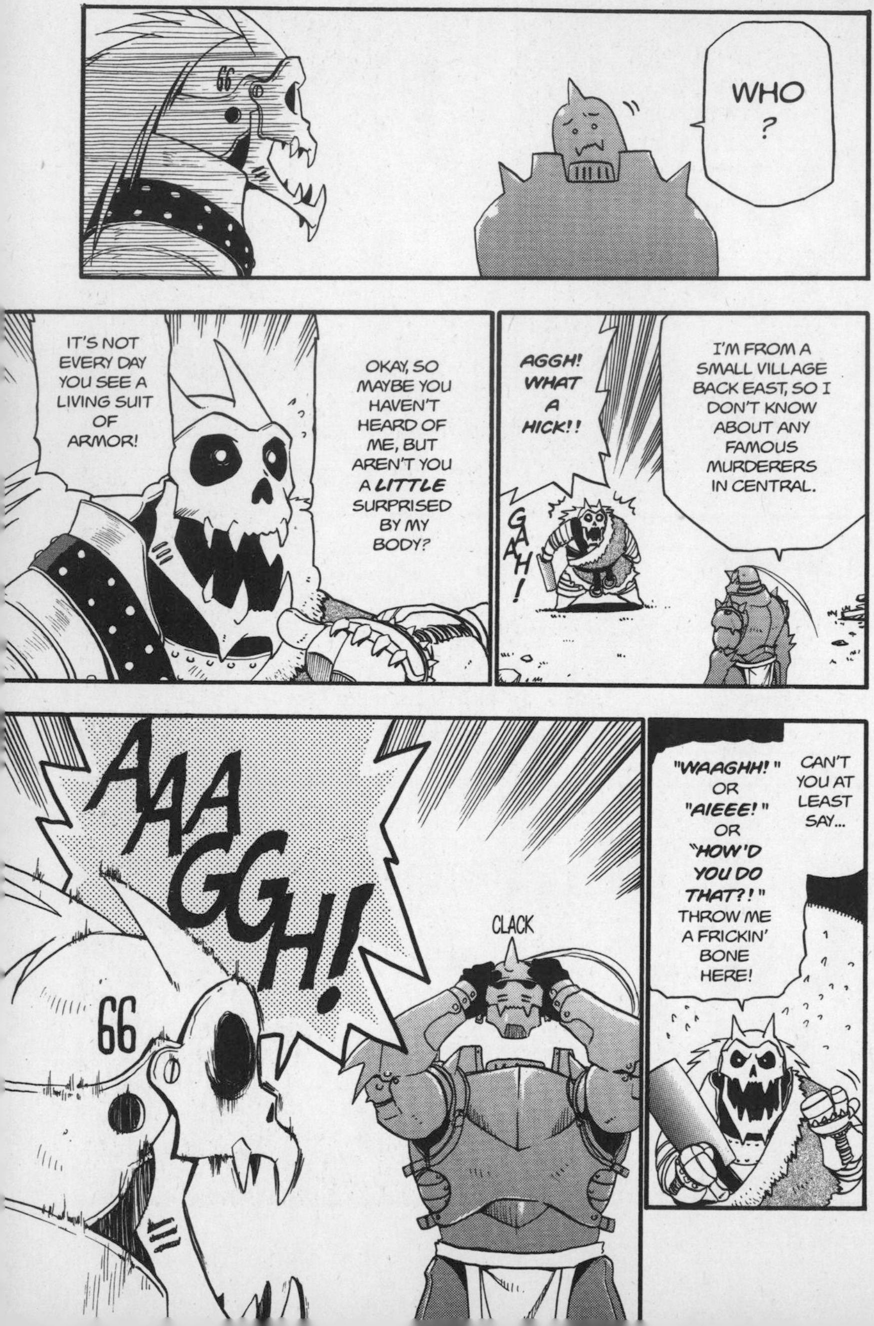
WHO ?
I'M FROM A SMALL VILLAGE BACK EAST, SO I DON'T KNOW ABOUT ANY FAMOUS MURDERERS IN CENTRAL.
AGGH! WHAT A HICK!!
GAAH!
OKAY, SO MAYBE YOU HAVEN'T HEARD OF ME, BUT AREN'T YOU A LITTLE SURPRISED BY MY BODY?
IT'S NOT EVERY DAY YOU SEE A LIVING SUIT OF ARMOR!
CAN'T YOU AT LEAST SAY...
"WAAGHH!" OR "AIEEE!" OR "HOW'D YOU DO THAT?!" THROW ME A FRICKIN' BONE HERE!
AAAGGH!
CLACK
66

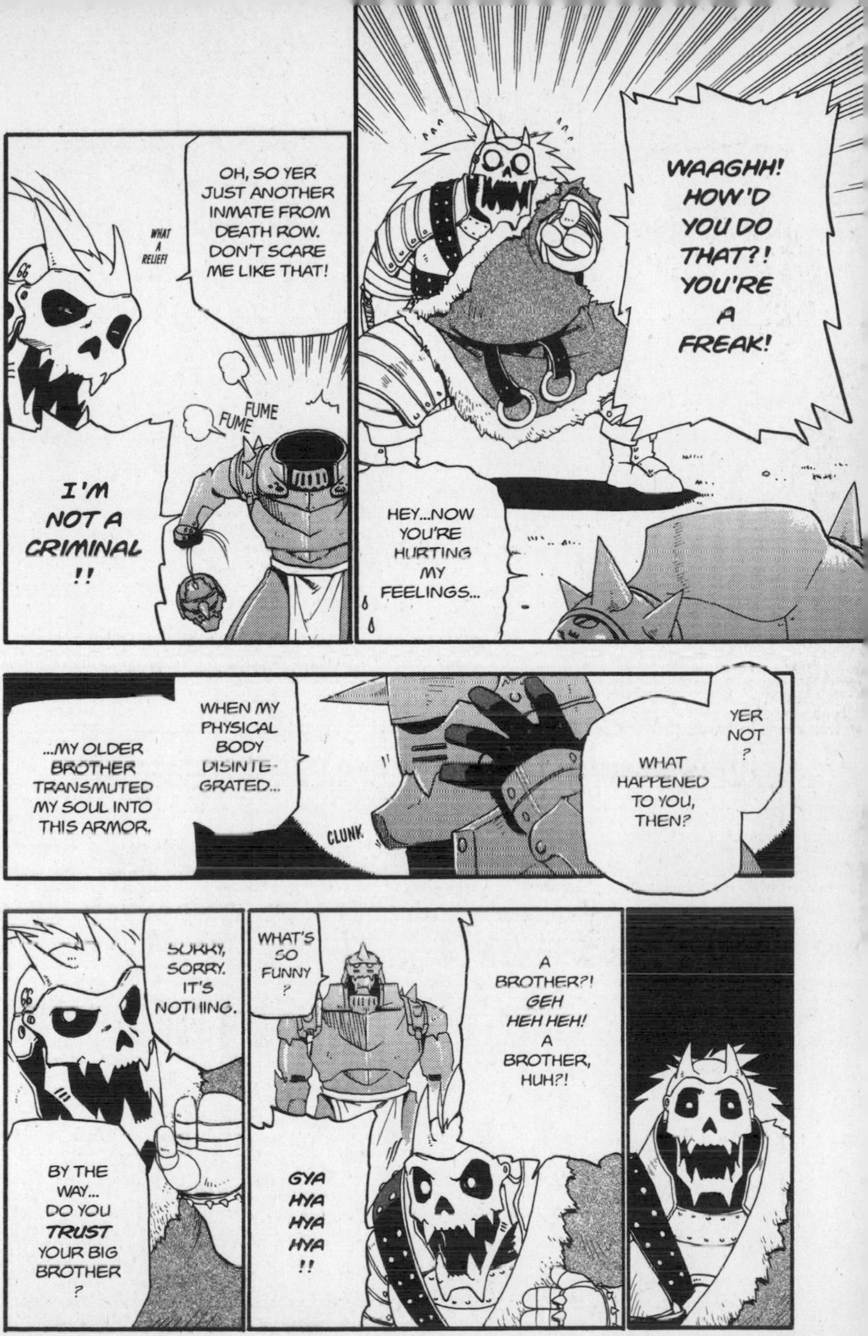
WAAGHH! HOW'D YOU DO THAT?! YOU'RE A FREAK!
HEY...NOW YOU'RE HURTING MY FEELINGS...
OH, SO YER JUST ANOTHER INMATE FROM DEATH ROW. DON'T SCARE ME LIKE THAT!
WHAT A RELIEF!
FUME
FUME
I'M NOT A CRIMINAL!!
YER NOT?
WHAT HAPPENED TO YOU, THEN?
CLUNK
WHEN MY PHYSICAL BODY DISINTEGRATED...
...MY OLDER BROTHER TRANSMUTED MY SOUL INTO THIS ARMOR.
A BROTHER?! GEH HEH HEH! A BROTHER, HUH?!
WHAT'S SO FUNNY?
GYA HYA HYA HYA!!
SORRY, SORRY. IT'S NOTHING.
BY THE WAY... DO YOU TRUST YOUR BIG BROTHER?

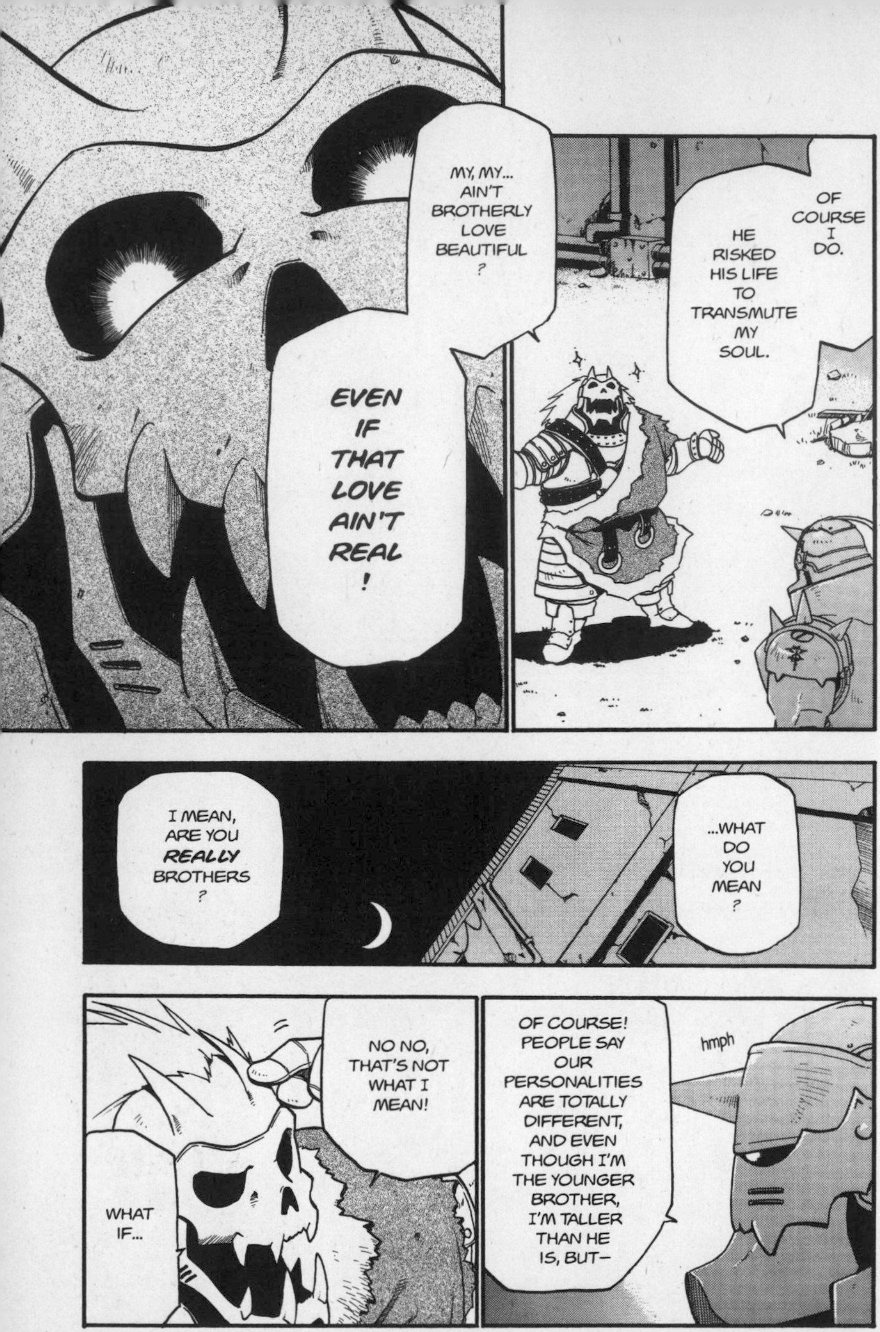
OF COURSE I DO.
HE RISKED HIS LIFE TO TRANSMUTE MY SOUL.
MY, MY... AIN'T BROTHERLY LOVE BEAUTIFUL?
EVEN IF THAT LOVE AIN'T REAL!
...WHAT DO YOU MEAN?
I MEAN, ARE YOU *REALLY* BROTHERS?
hmph
OF COURSE! PEOPLE SAY OUR PERSONALITIES ARE TOTALLY DIFFERENT, AND EVEN THOUGH I'M THE YOUNGER BROTHER, I'M TALLER THAN HE IS, BUT–
NO NO, THAT'S NOT WHAT I MEAN!
WHAT IF...

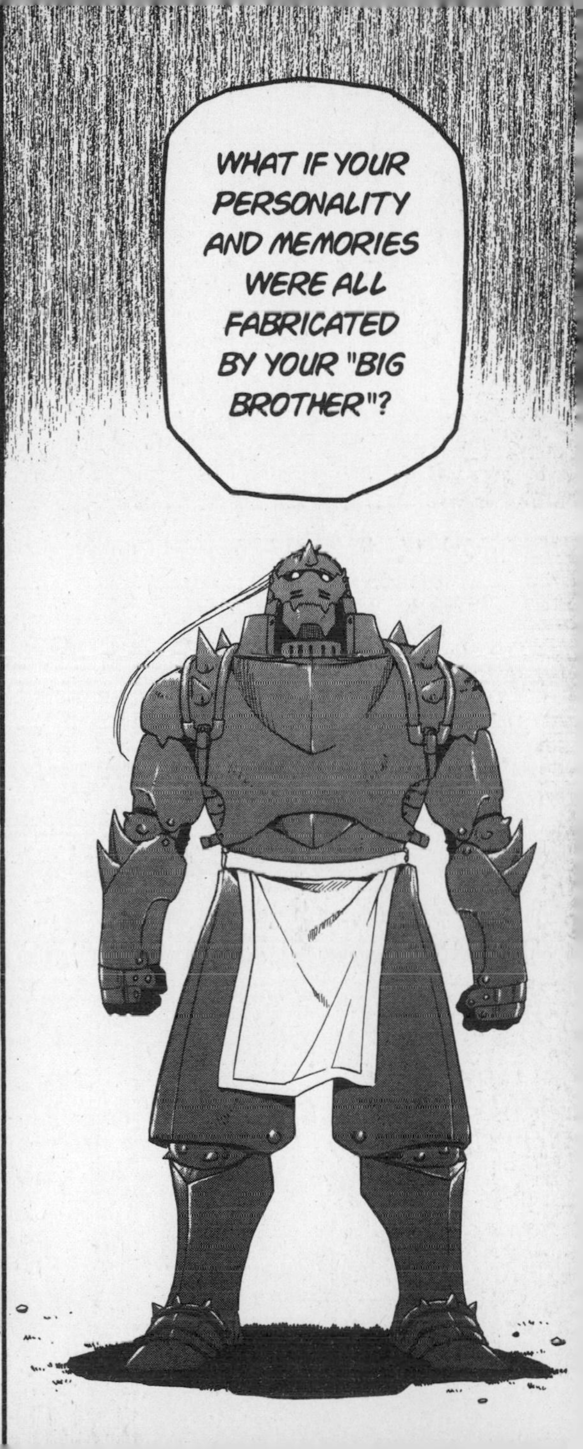
WHAT IF YOUR PERSONALITY AND MEMORIES WERE ALL FABRICATED BY YOUR "BIG BROTHER"?
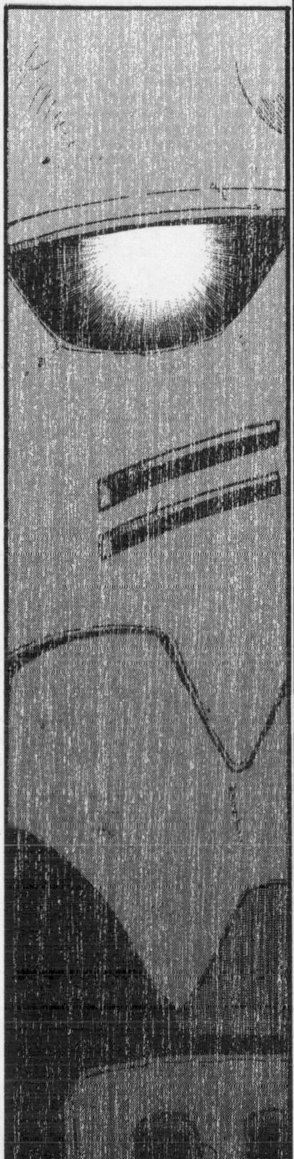

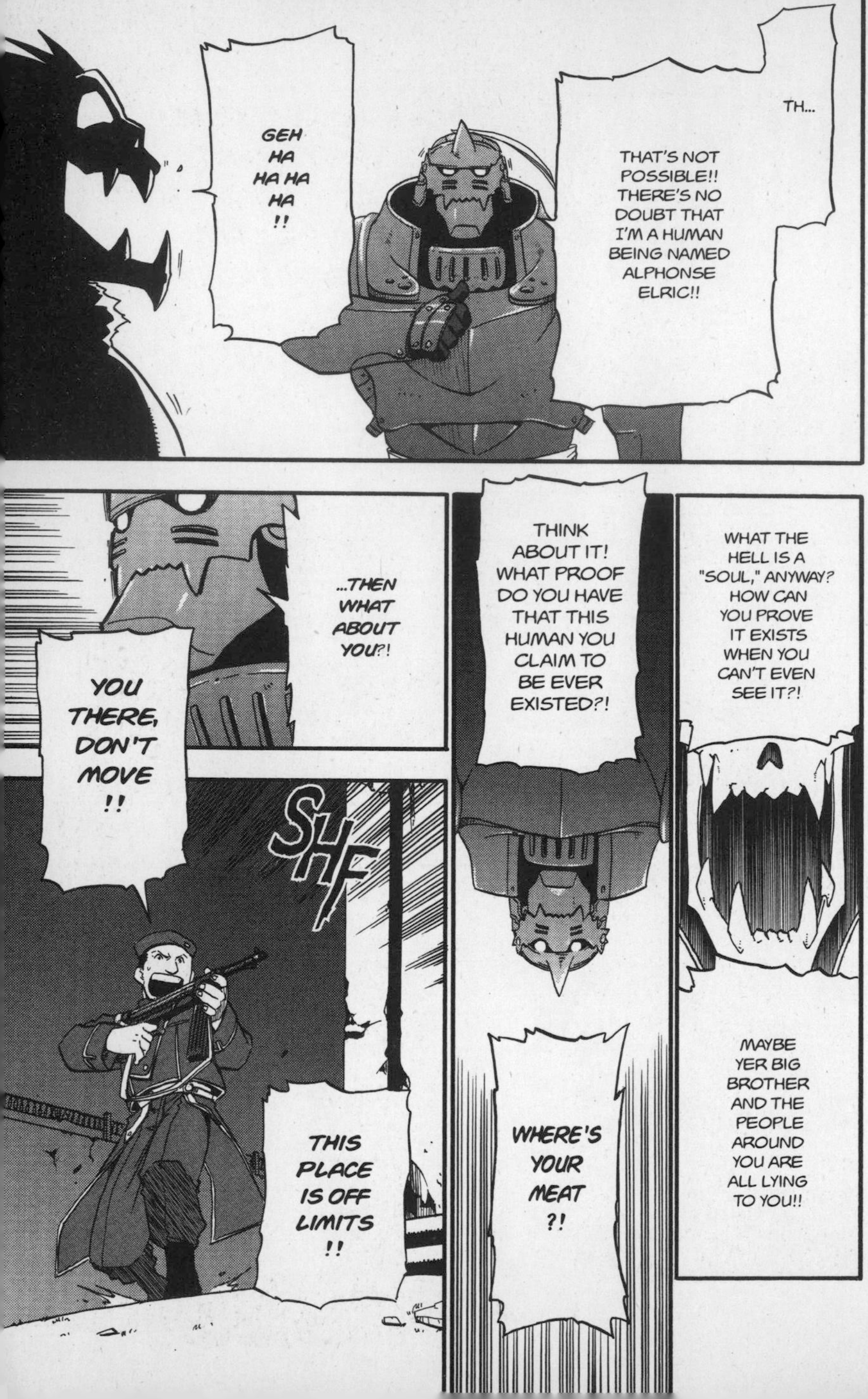
TH...
THAT'S NOT POSSIBLE!! THERE'S NO DOUBT THAT I'M A HUMAN BEING NAMED ALPHONSE ELRIC!!
GEH HA HA HA HA!!
WHAT THE HELL IS A "SOUL," ANYWAY? HOW CAN YOU PROVE IT EXISTS WHEN YOU CAN'T EVEN SEE IT?!
MAYBE YER BIG BROTHER AND THE PEOPLE AROUND YOU ARE ALL LYING TO YOU!!
THINK ABOUT IT! WHAT PROOF DO YOU HAVE THAT THIS HUMAN YOU CLAIM TO BE EVER EXISTED?!
WHERE'S YOUR MEAT?!
...THEN WHAT ABOUT YOU?!
YOU THERE, DON'T MOVE!!
SHF
THIS PLACE IS OFF LIMITS!!

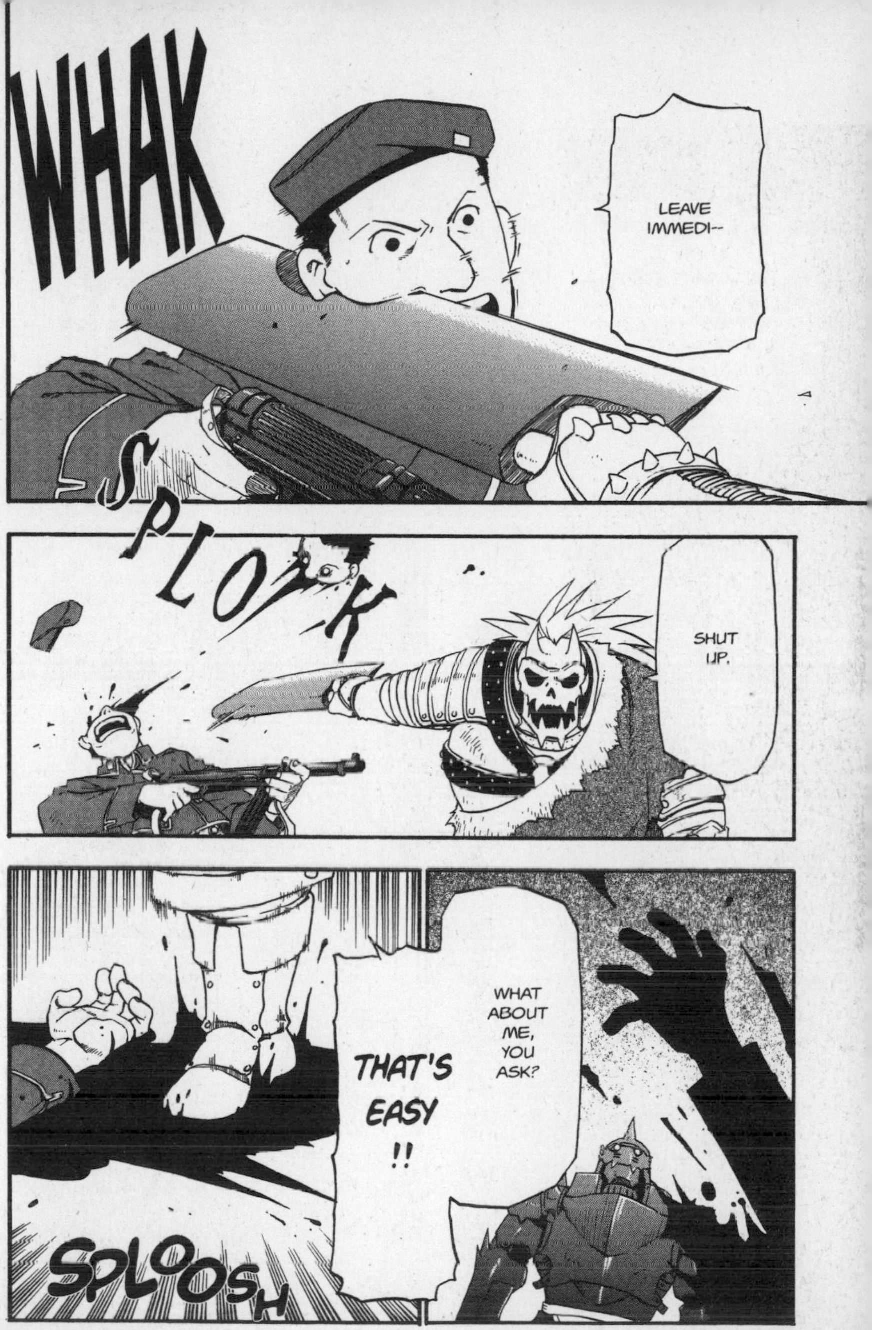
LEAVE IMMEDI--
WHAK
SHUT UP.
SPLOK
WHAT ABOUT ME, YOU ASK?
THAT'S EASY!!
SPLOOSH

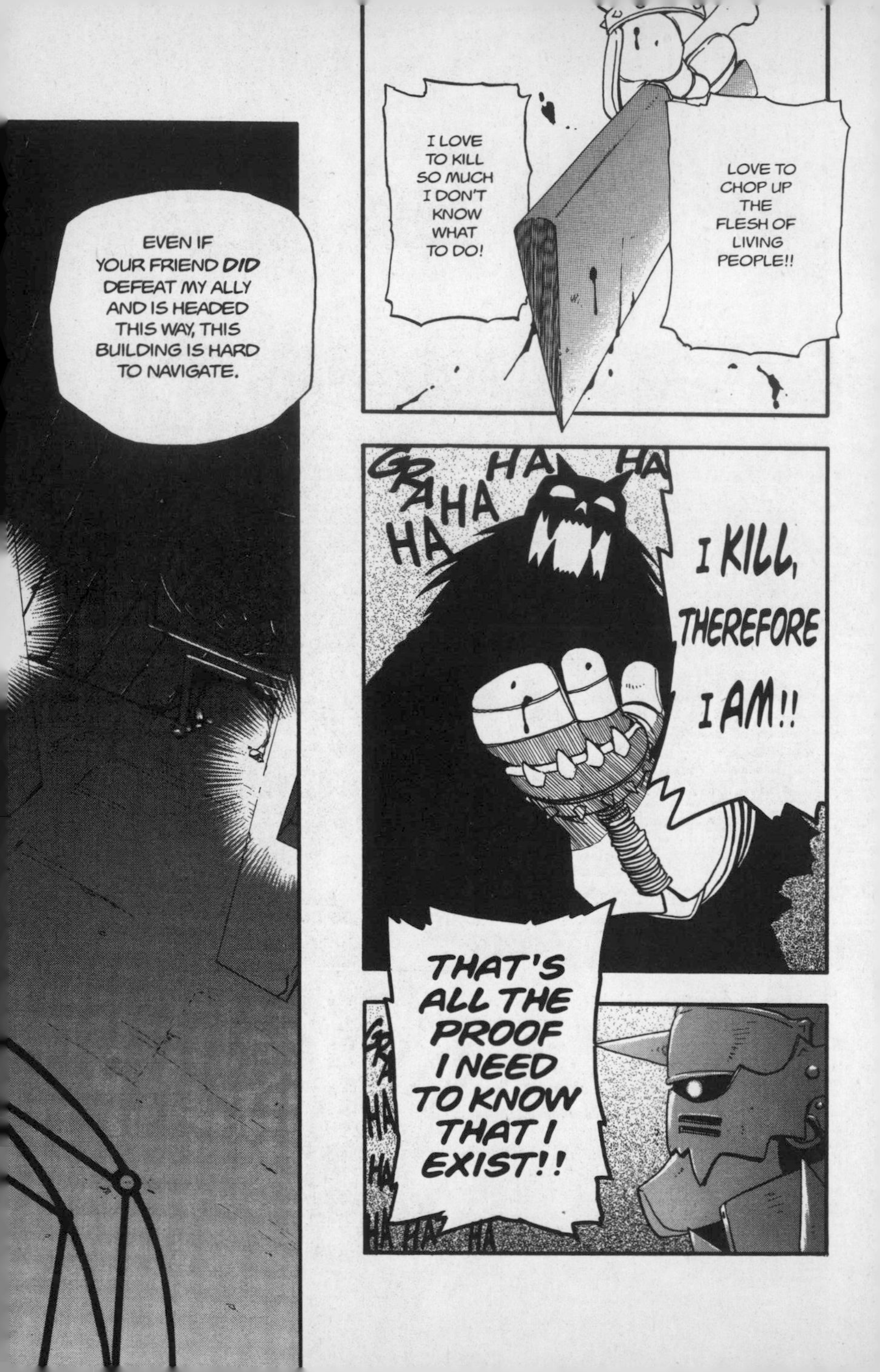
LOVE TO CHOP UP THE FLESH OF LIVING PEOPLE!!
I LOVE TO KILL SO MUCH I DON'T KNOW WHAT TO DO!
HA
HA
GRAHAHA
HA
I KILL, THEREFORE I AM!!
THAT'S ALL THE PROOF I NEED TO KNOW THAT I EXIST!!
GRAHAHAHA
HA HA HA
EVEN IF YOUR FRIEND DID DEFEAT MY ALLY AND IS HEADED THIS WAY, THIS BUILDING IS HARD TO NAVIGATE.

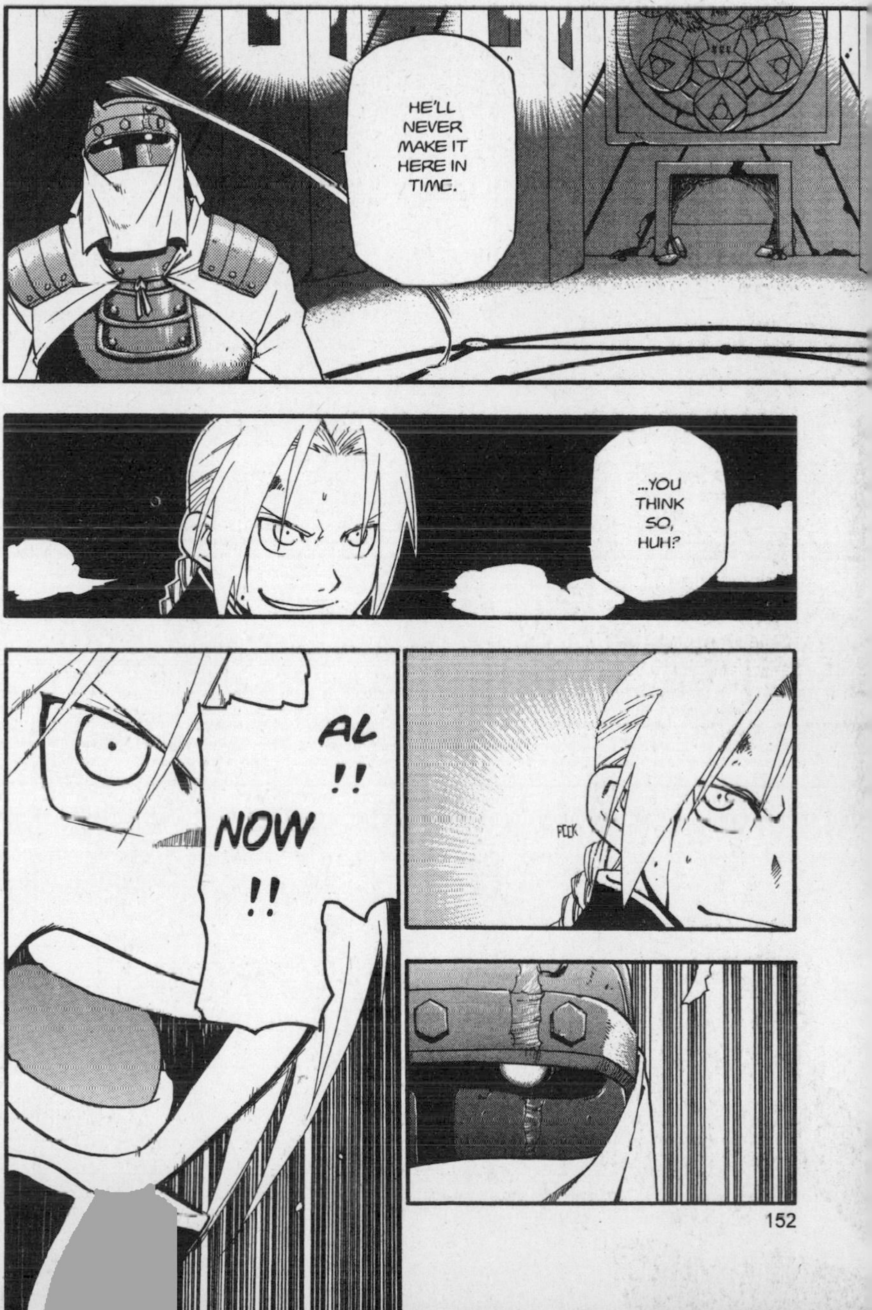
HE'LL NEVER MAKE IT HERE IN TIME.
...YOU THINK SO, HUH?
AL!! NOW!!

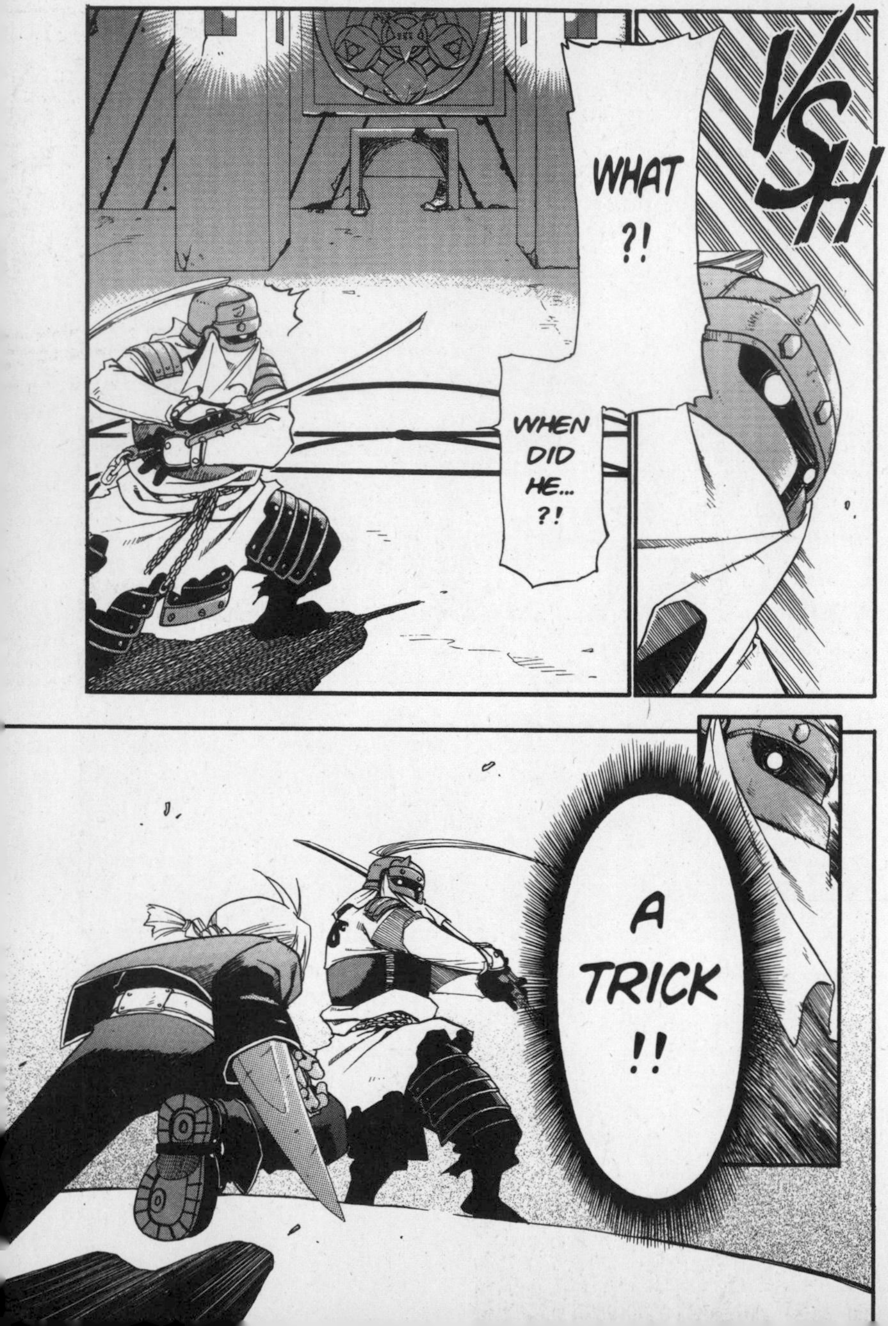
VSH
WHAT ?!
WHEN DID HE... ?!
A TRICK !!

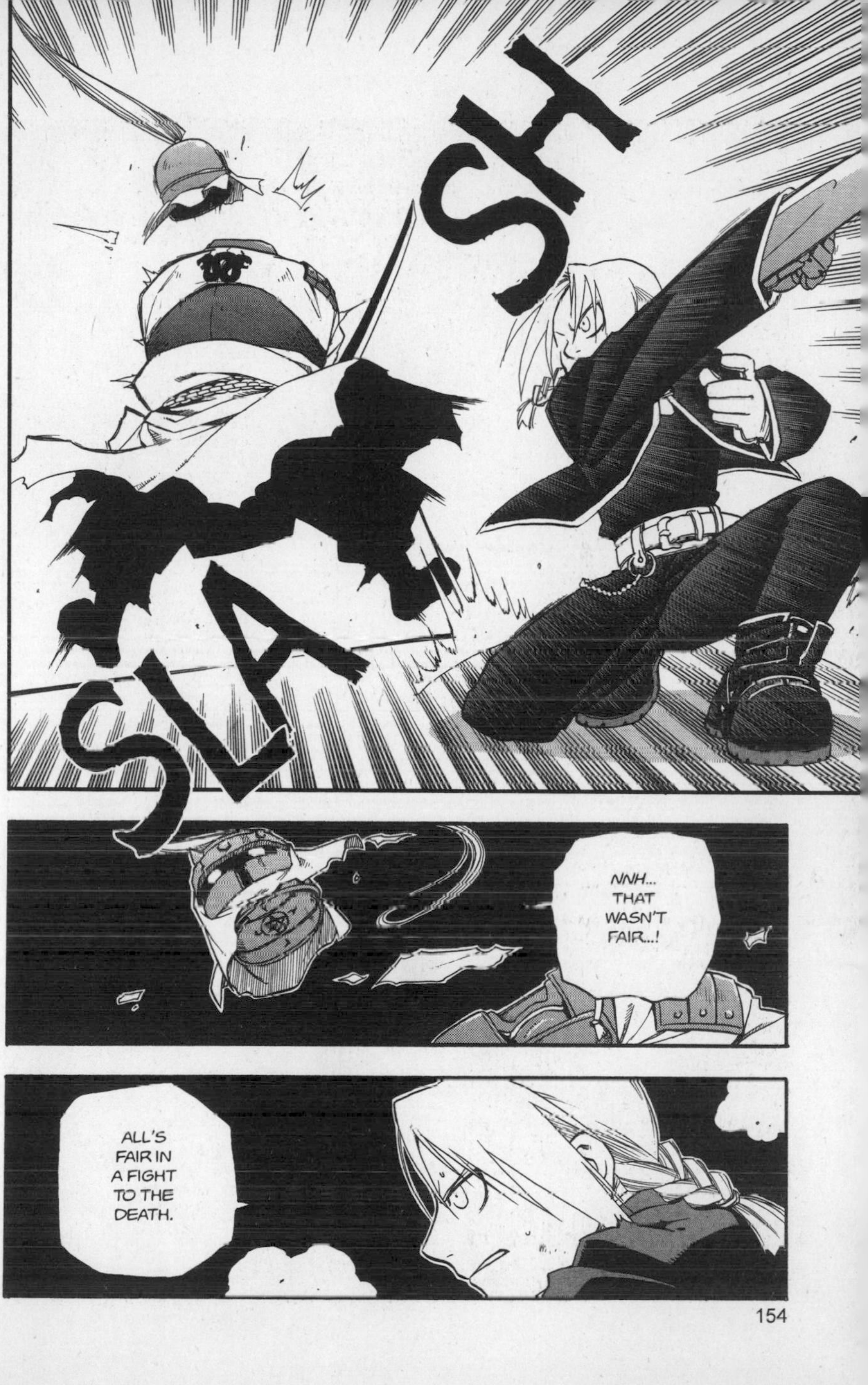
SLASH
NNH... THAT WASN'T FAIR...!
ALL'S FAIR IN A FIGHT TO THE DEATH.

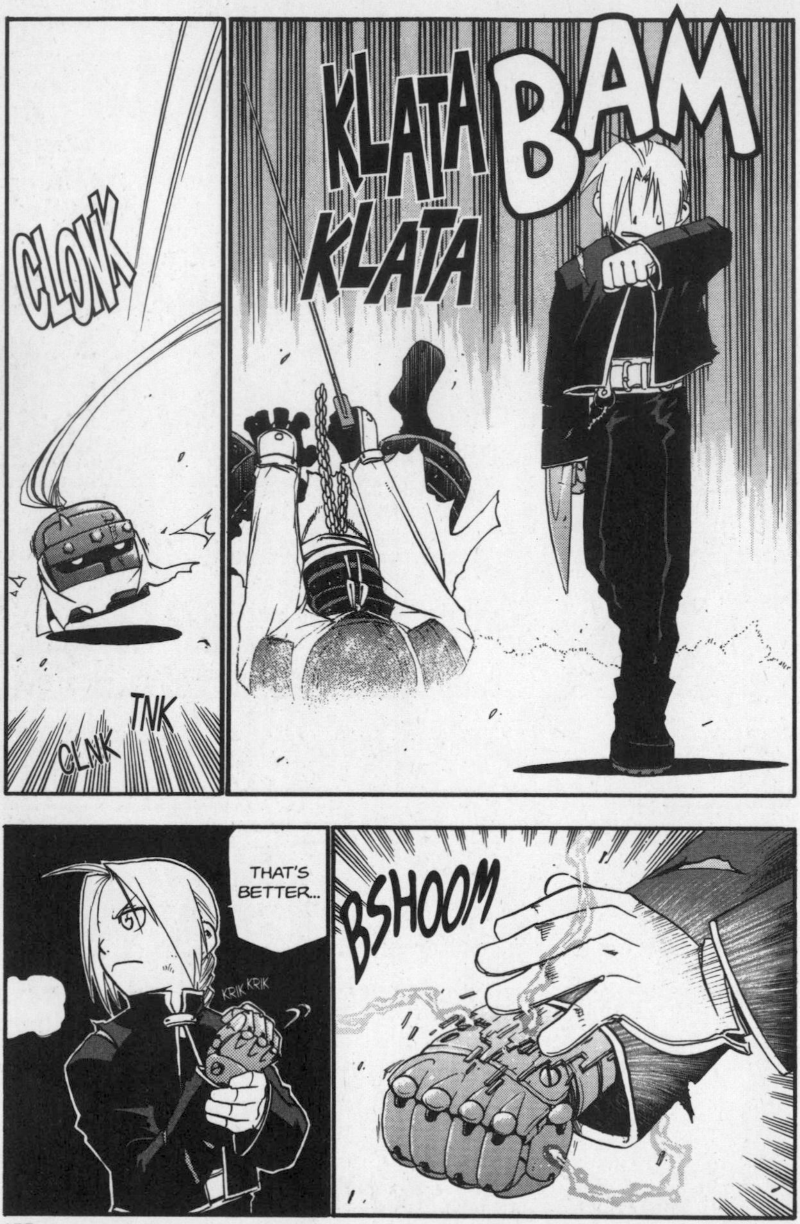
BAM
KLATA
KLATA
CLONK
TNK
CLNK
BSHOOM
THAT'S BETTER...
KRIK KRIK

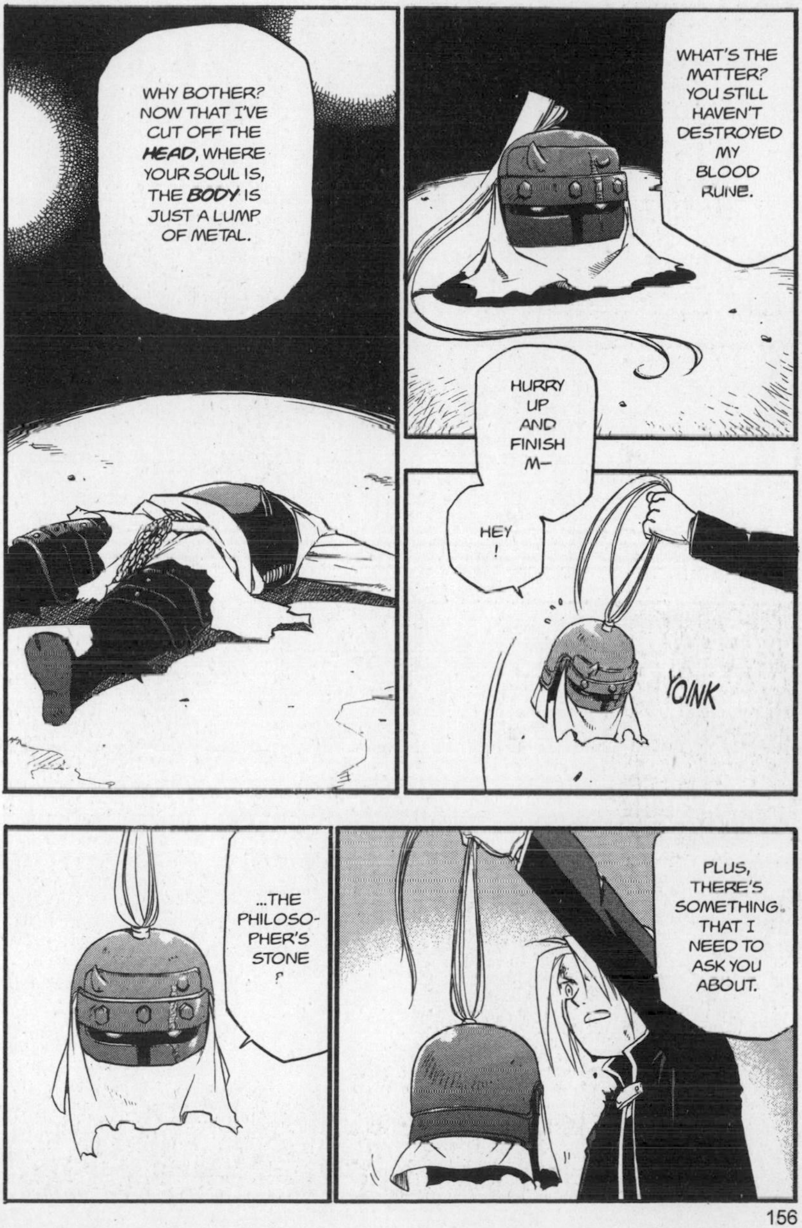
WHAT'S THE MATTER? YOU STILL HAVEN'T DESTROYED MY BLOOD RUNE.
HURRY UP AND FINISH M—
HEY!
YOINK
WHY BOTHER? NOW THAT I'VE CUT OFF THE **HEAD**, WHERE YOUR SOUL IS, THE **BODY** IS JUST A LUMP OF METAL.
PLUS, THERE'S SOMETHING THAT I NEED TO ASK YOU ABOUT.
...THE PHILOSOPHER'S STONE?

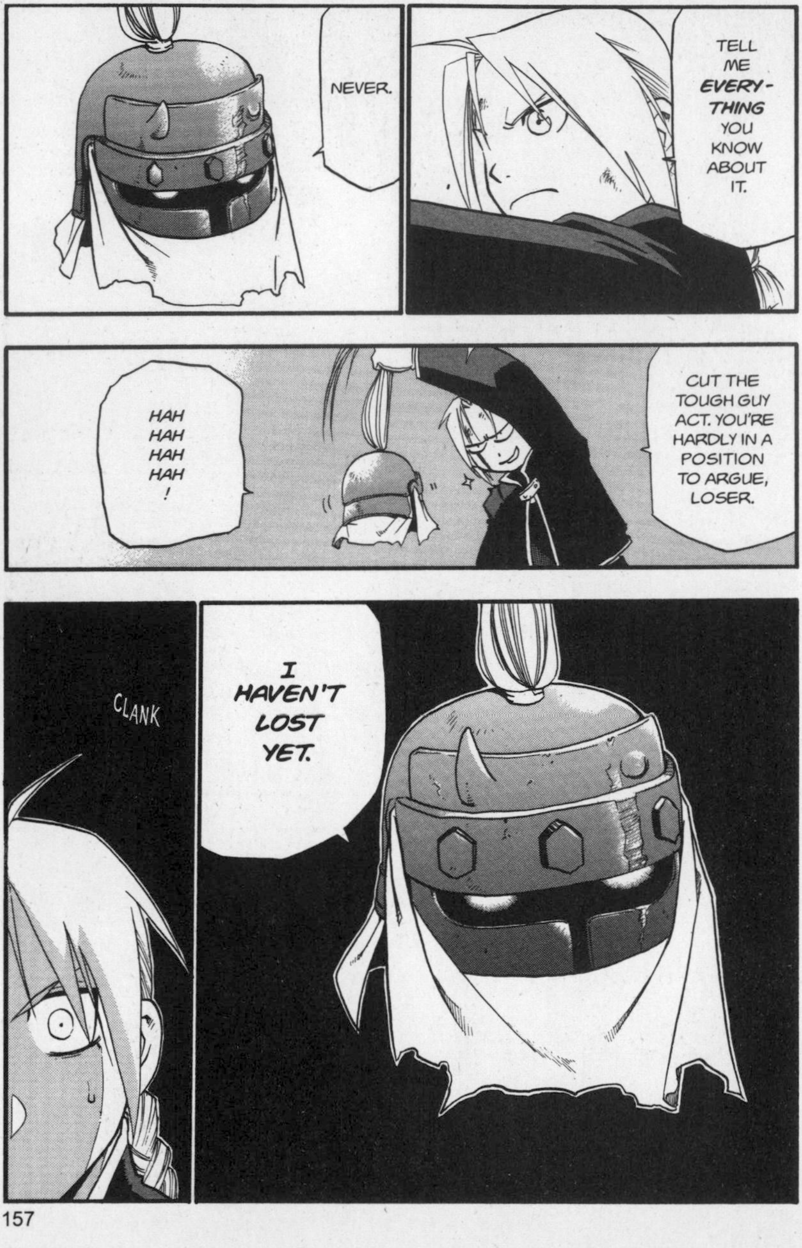
TELL ME EVERYTHING YOU KNOW ABOUT IT.
NEVER.
CUT THE TOUGH GUY ACT. YOU'RE HARDLY IN A POSITION TO ARGUE, LOSER.
HAH HAH HAH HAH!
I HAVEN'T LOST YET.
CLANK

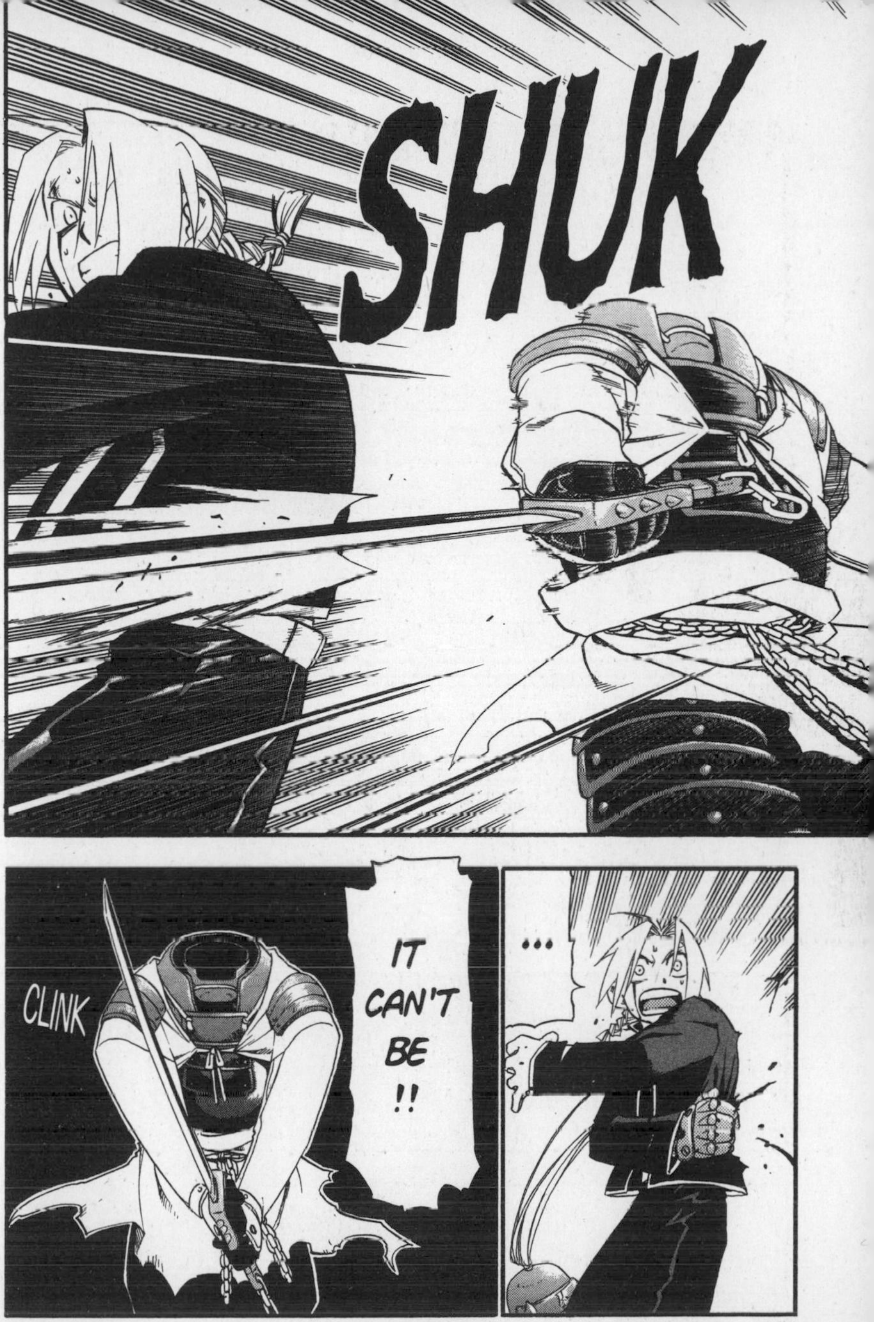
SHUK
...
IT CAN'T BE !!
CLINK

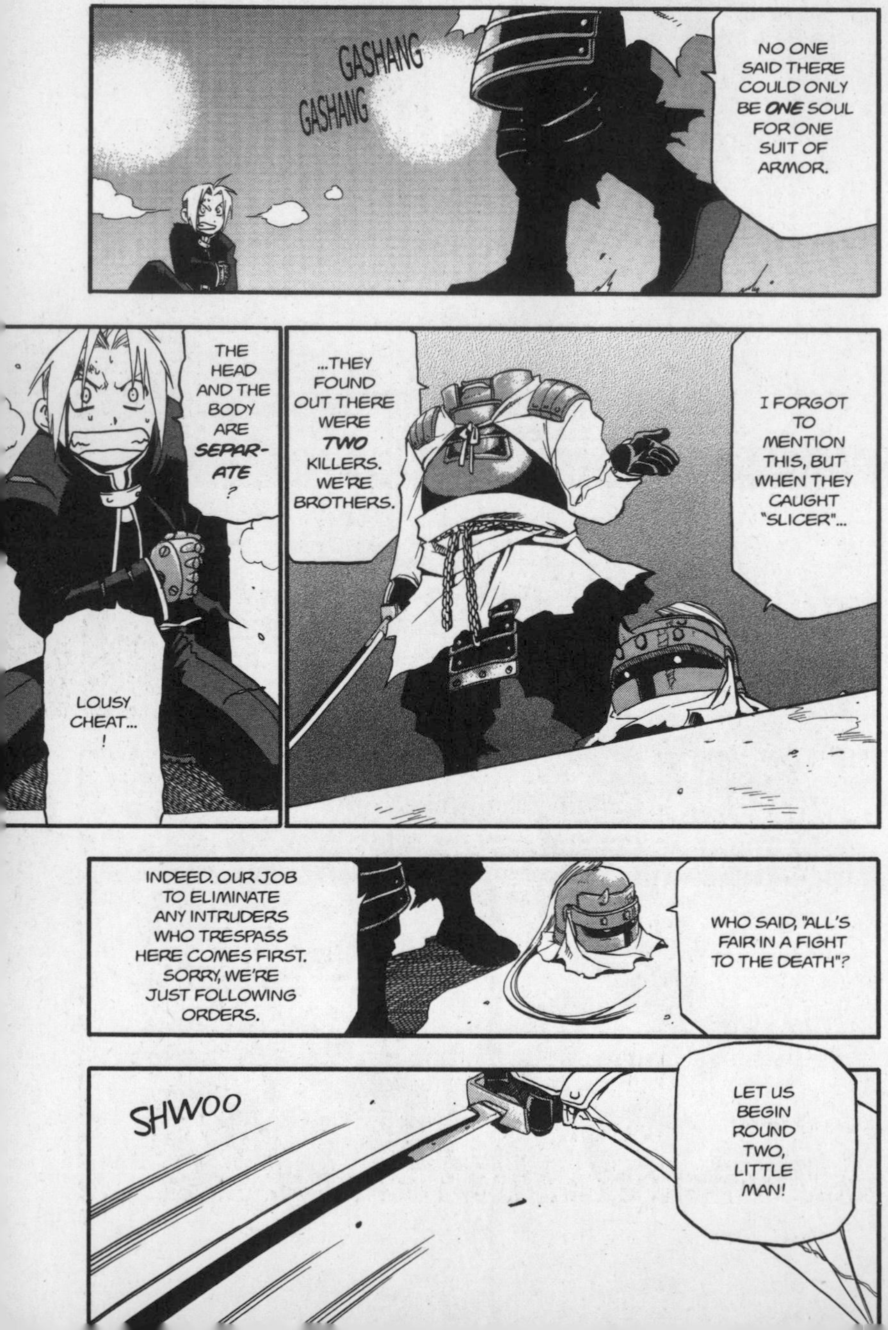
NO ONE SAID THERE COULD ONLY BE ONE SOUL FOR ONE SUIT OF ARMOR.
GASHANG
GASHANG
I FORGOT TO MENTION THIS, BUT WHEN THEY CAUGHT "SLICER"...
...THEY FOUND OUT THERE WERE TWO KILLERS. WE'RE BROTHERS.
THE HEAD AND THE BODY ARE SEPARATE?
LOUSY CHEAT...!
WHO SAID, "ALL'S FAIR IN A FIGHT TO THE DEATH"?
INDEED. OUR JOB TO ELIMINATE ANY INTRUDERS WHO TRESPASS HERE COMES FIRST. SORRY, WE'RE JUST FOLLOWING ORDERS.
LET US BEGIN ROUND TWO, LITTLE MAN!
SHWOO

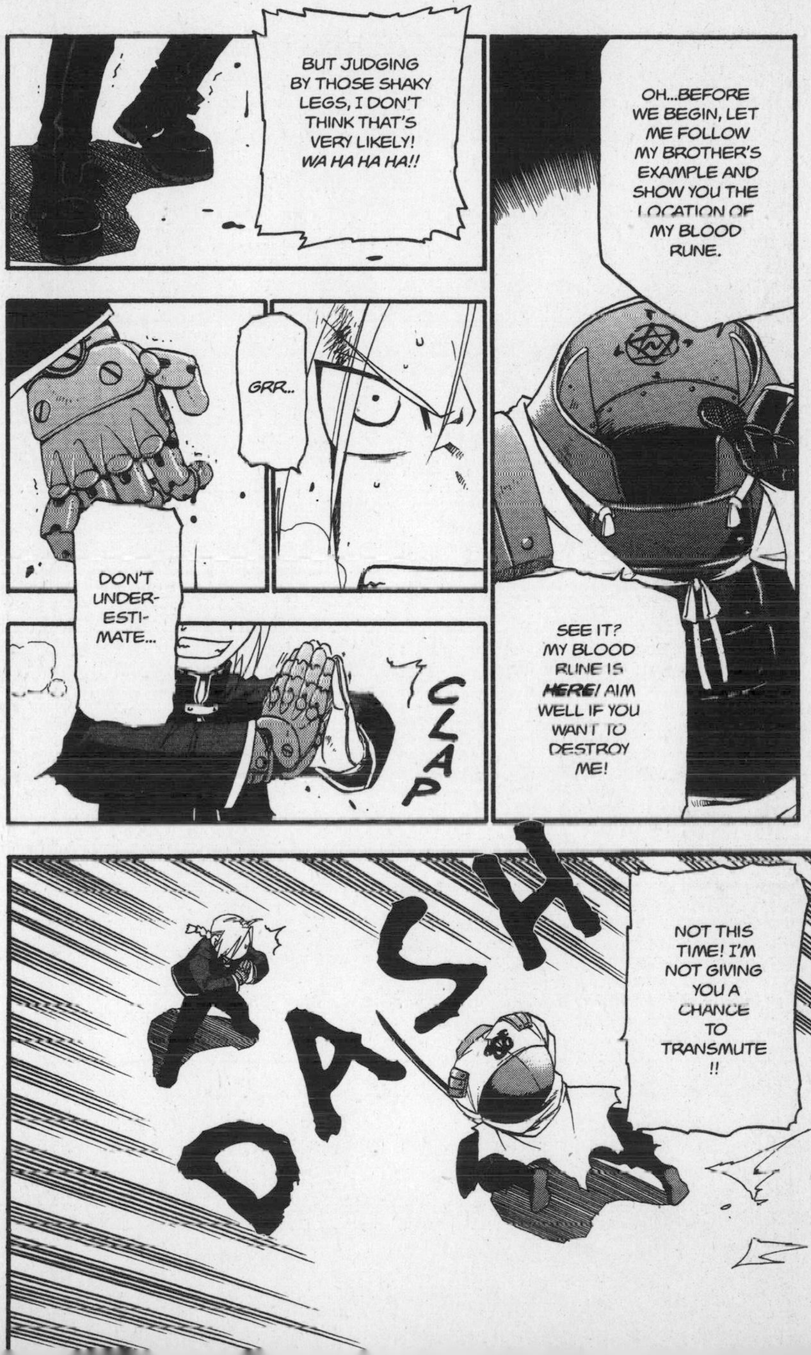
OH...BEFORE WE BEGIN, LET ME FOLLOW MY BROTHER'S EXAMPLE AND SHOW YOU THE LOCATION OF MY BLOOD RUNE.
SEE IT? MY BLOOD RUNE IS *HERE!* AIM WELL IF YOU WANT TO DESTROY ME!
BUT JUDGING BY THOSE SHAKY LEGS, I DON'T THINK THAT'S VERY LIKELY! *WA HA HA HA!!*
GRR...
DON'T UNDER-ESTI-MATE...
CLAP
NOT THIS TIME! I'M NOT GIVING YOU A CHANCE TO TRANSMUTE!!
DASH

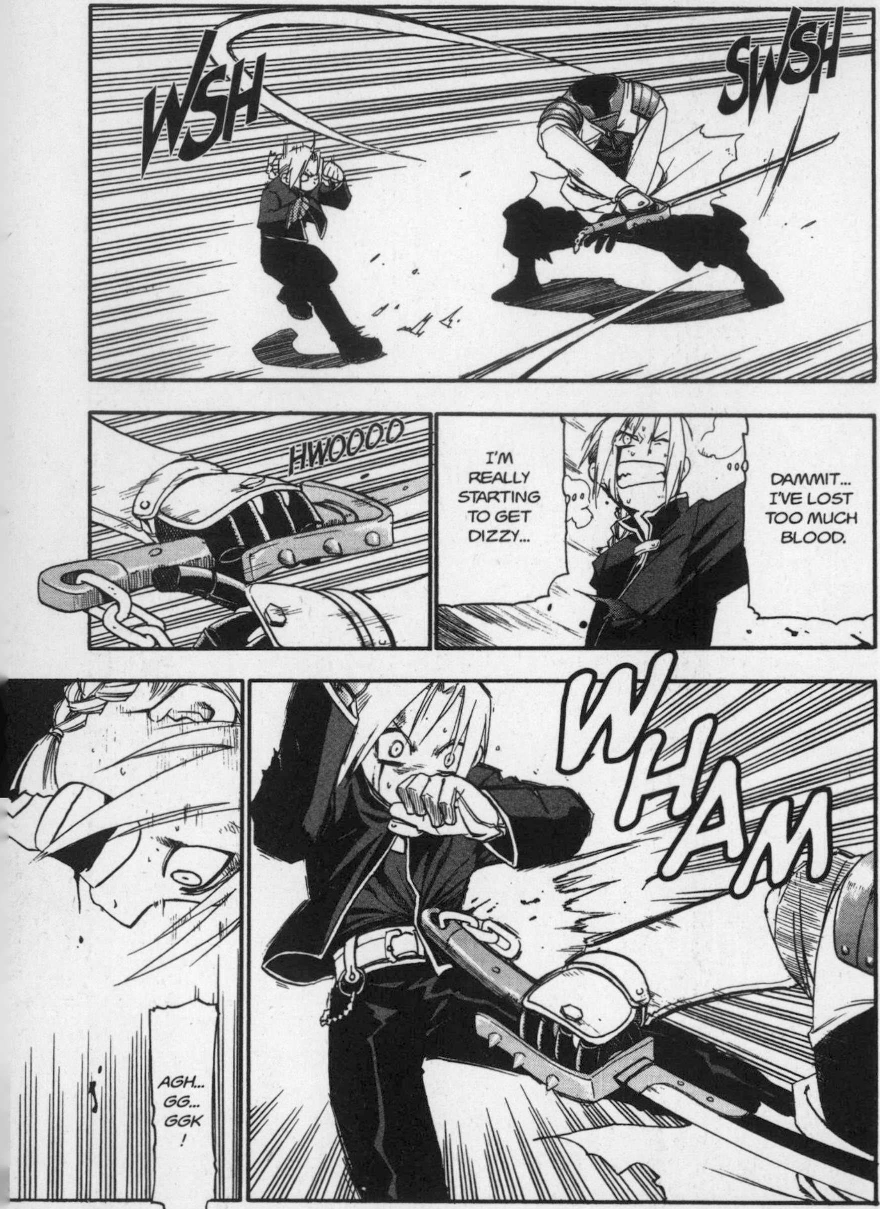
SWSH
WSH
DAMMIT... I'VE LOST TOO MUCH BLOOD.
I'M REALLY STARTING TO GET DIZZY...
HWOOOO
WHAM
AGH... GG... GGK!

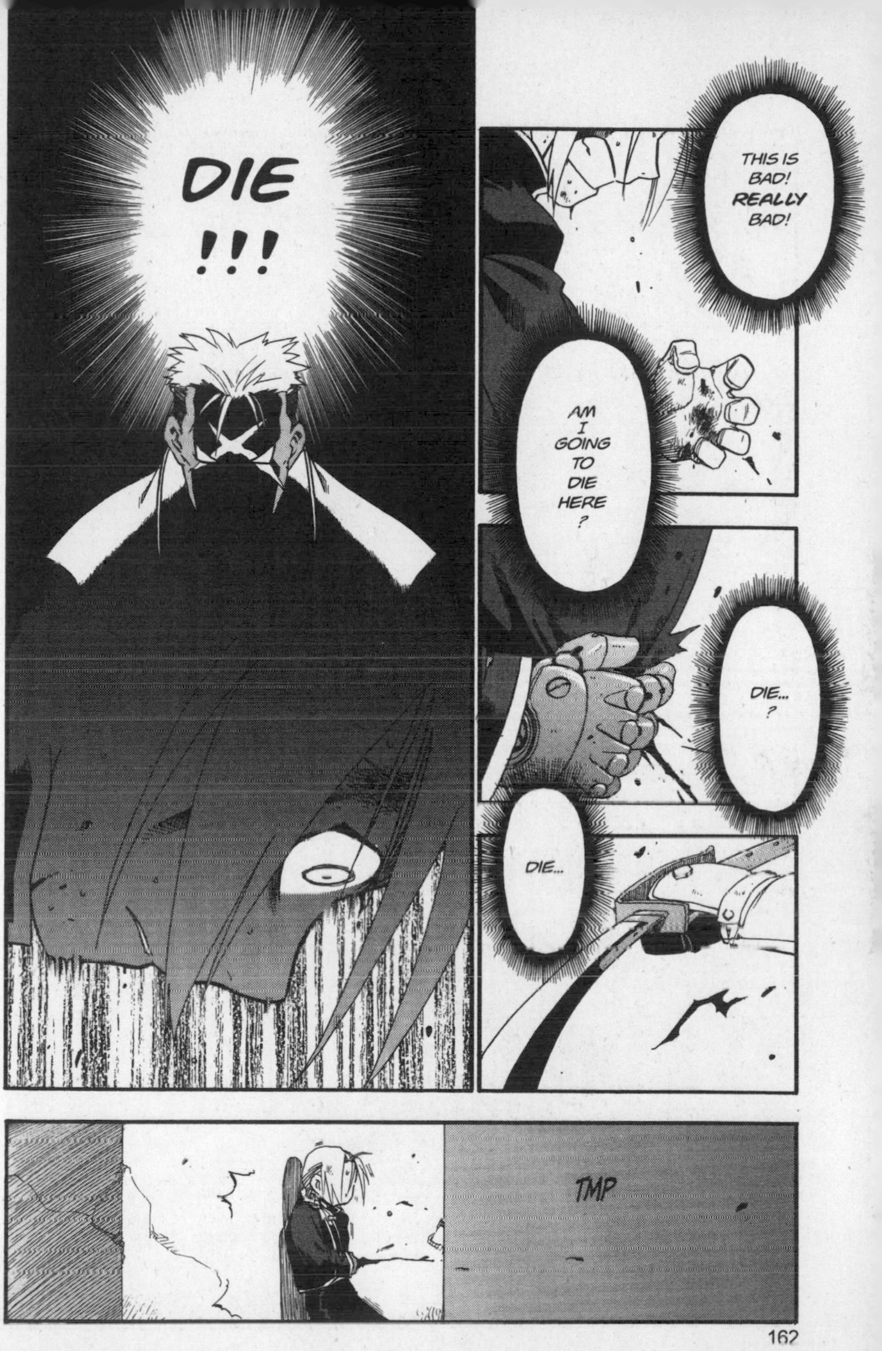
THIS IS BAD! REALLY BAD!
AM I GOING TO DIE HERE?
DIE...?
DIE...
DIE!!!
TMP

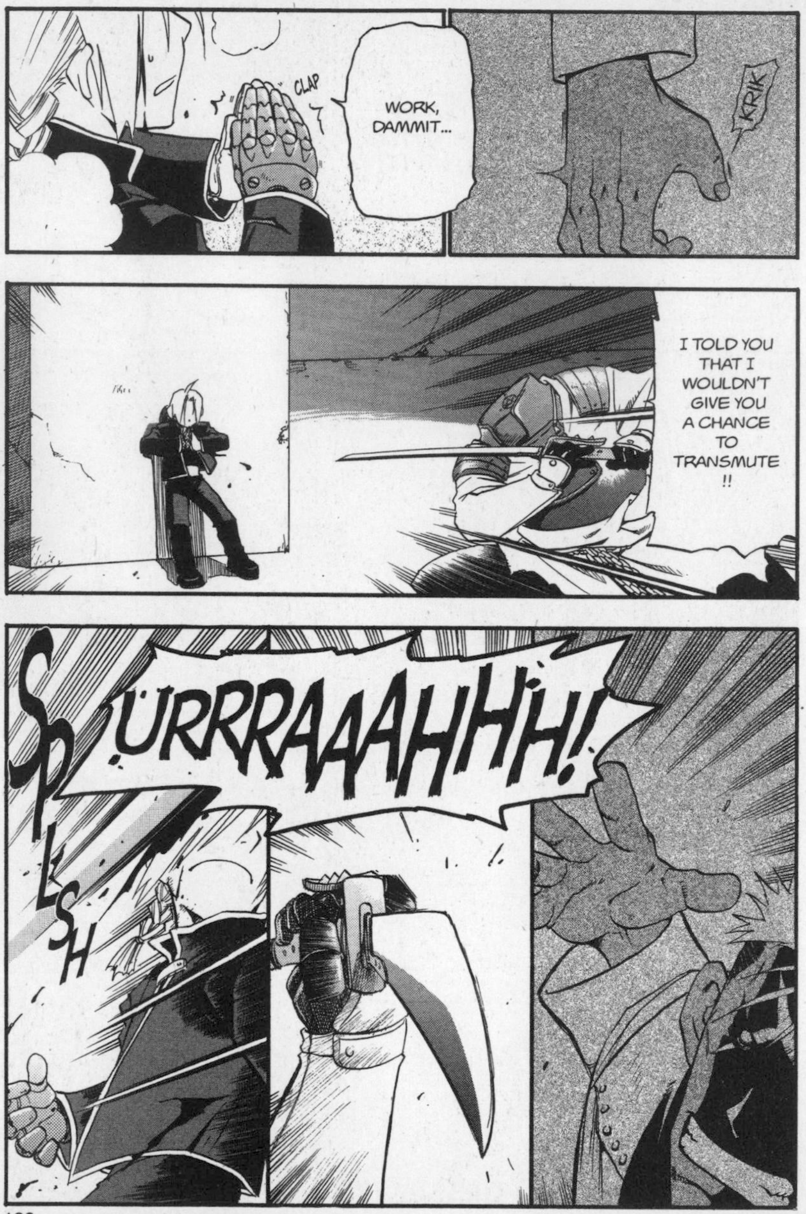
KRIK
CLAP
WORK, DAMMIT...
I TOLD YOU THAT I WOULDN'T GIVE YOU A CHANCE TO TRANSMUTE !!
URRRAAAHHH!
SPLSH

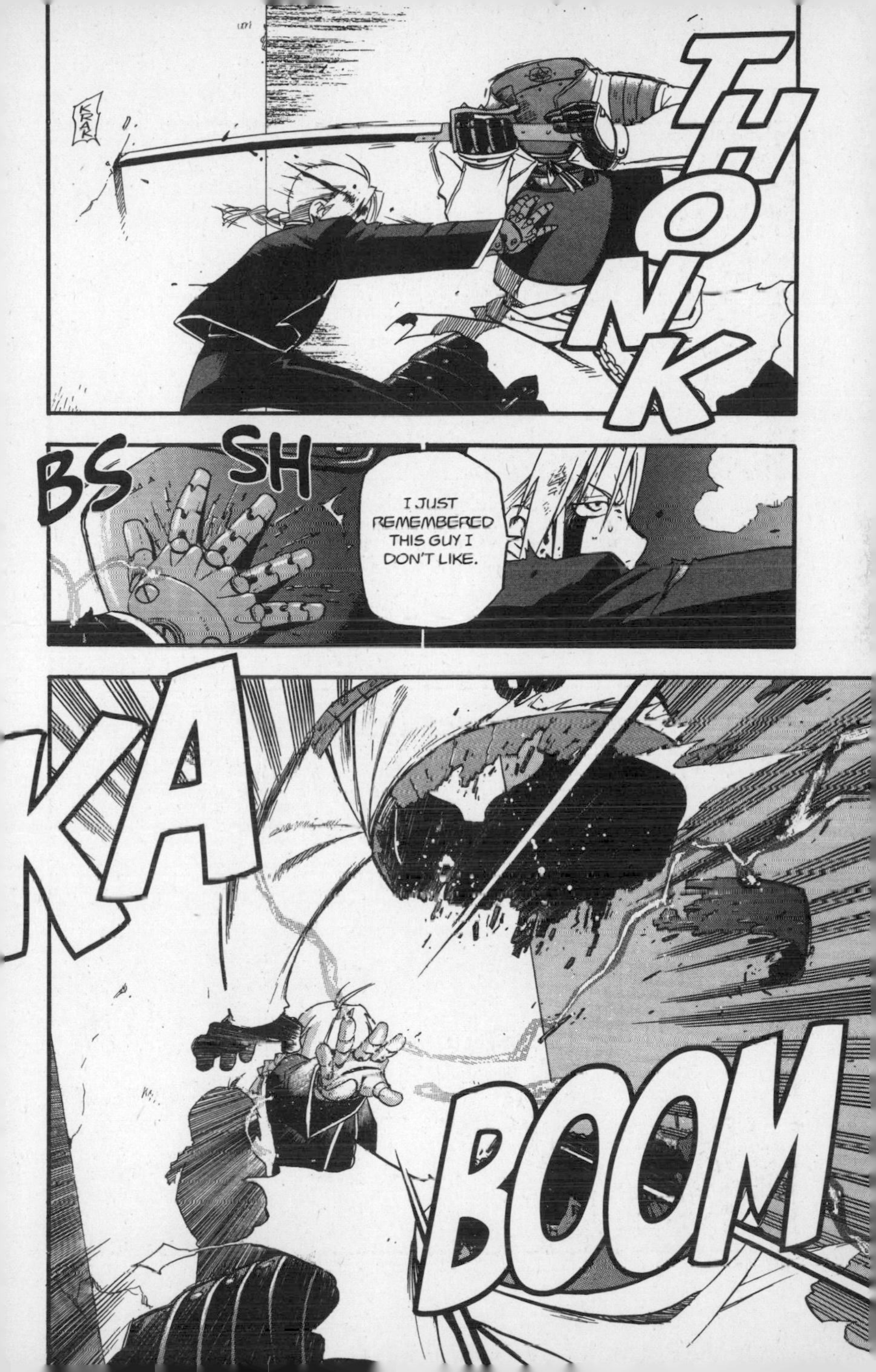
THONK
KRAK
I JUST REMEMBERED THIS GUY I DON'T LIKE.
BSSH
KA
BOOM

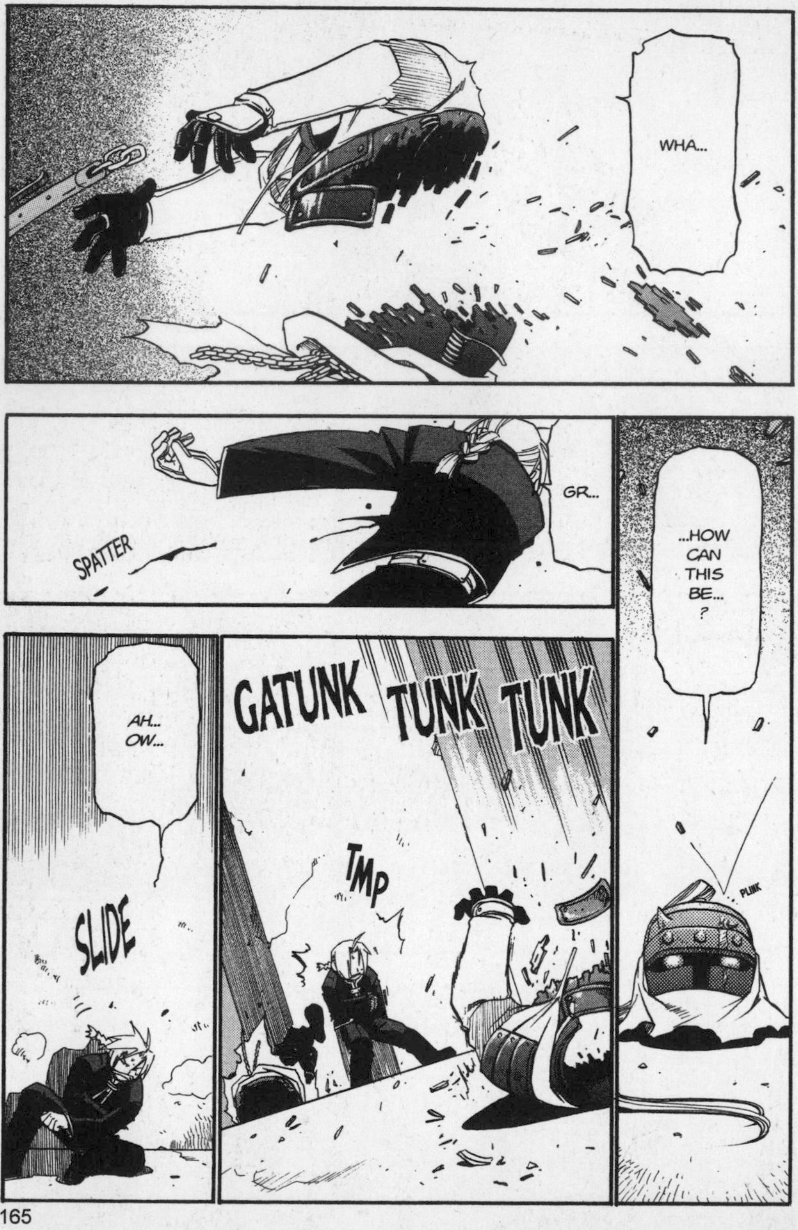
WHA...
...HOW CAN THIS BE...?
PLINK
GR...
SPATTER
GATUNK TUNK TUNK
TMP
AH... OW...
SLIDE

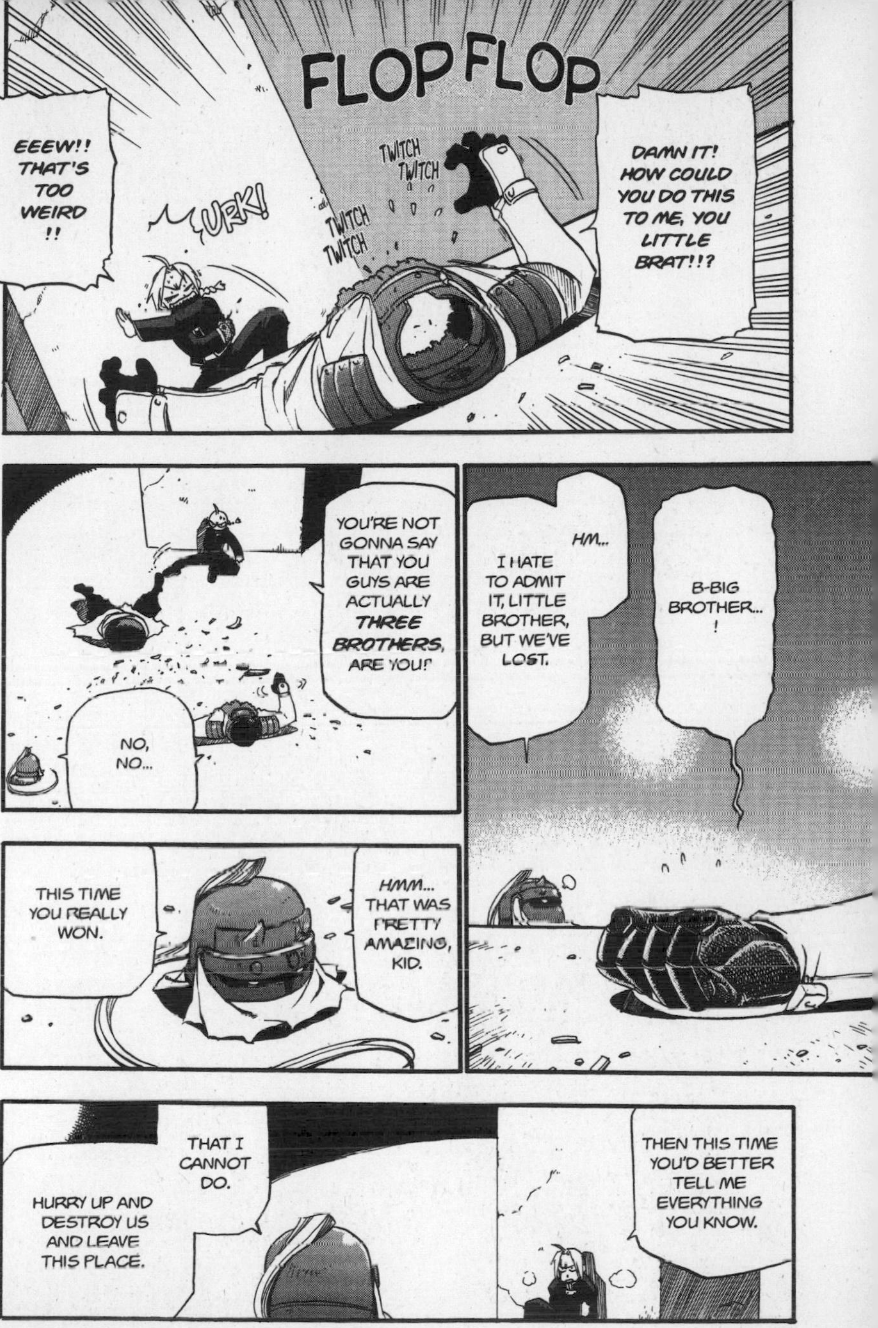
FLOP FLOP
DAMN IT! HOW COULD YOU DO THIS TO ME, YOU LITTLE BRAT!!?
TWITCH TWITCH
TWITCH TWITCH
EEEW!! THAT'S TOO WEIRD !!
URK!
B-BIG BROTHER... !
HM... I HATE TO ADMIT IT, LITTLE BROTHER, BUT WE'VE LOST.
YOU'RE NOT GONNA SAY THAT YOU GUYS ARE ACTUALLY THREE BROTHERS, ARE YOU?
NO, NO...
HMM... THAT WAS PRETTY AMAZING, KID.
THIS TIME YOU REALLY WON.
THEN THIS TIME YOU'D BETTER TELL ME EVERYTHING YOU KNOW.
THAT I CANNOT DO.
HURRY UP AND DESTROY US AND LEAVE THIS PLACE.

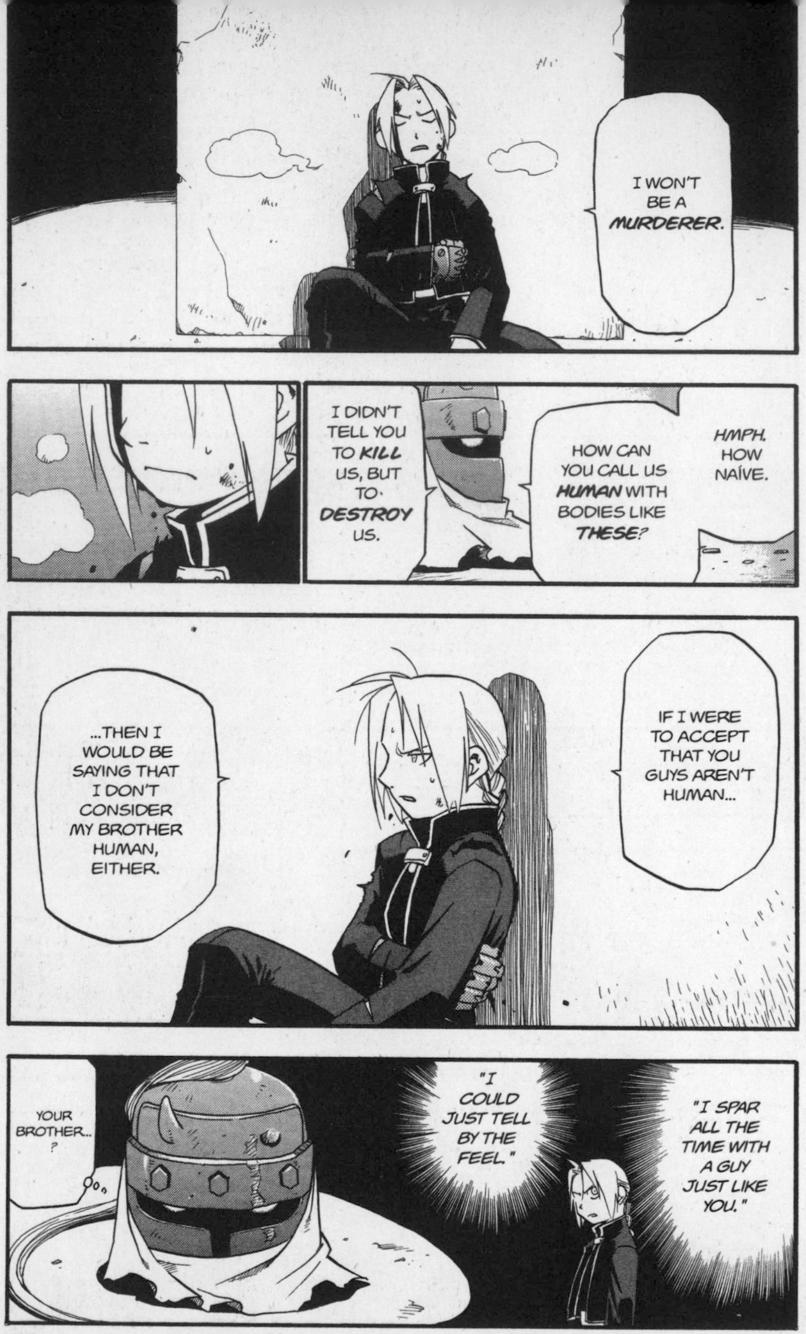
I WON'T BE A MURDERER.
HMPH. HOW NAÍVE.
HOW CAN YOU CALL US HUMAN WITH BODIES LIKE THESE?
I DIDN'T TELL YOU TO KILL US, BUT TO DESTROY US.
IF I WERE TO ACCEPT THAT YOU GUYS AREN'T HUMAN...
...THEN I WOULD BE SAYING THAT I DON'T CONSIDER MY BROTHER HUMAN, EITHER.
"I SPAR ALL THE TIME WITH A GUY JUST LIKE YOU."
"I COULD JUST TELL BY THE FEEL."
YOUR BROTHER...?

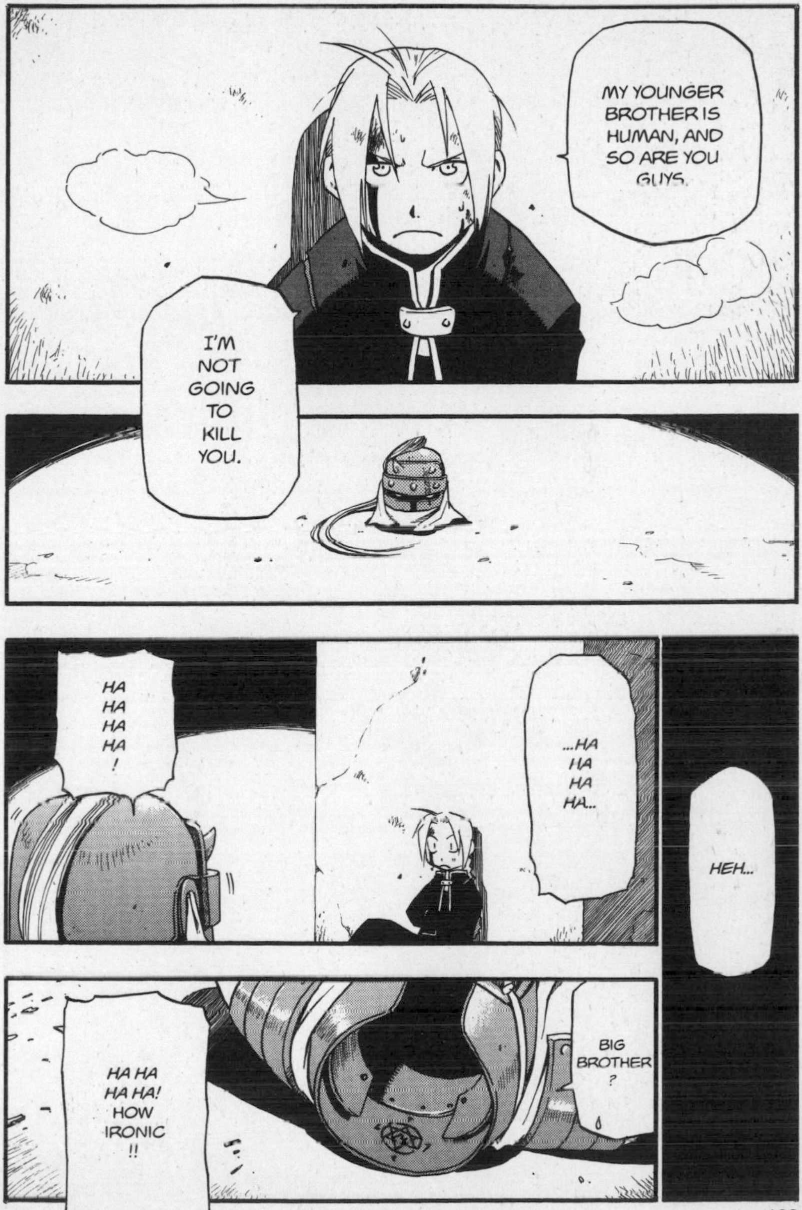
MY YOUNGER BROTHER IS HUMAN, AND SO ARE YOU GUYS.
I'M NOT GOING TO KILL YOU.
HEH...
...HA HA HA HA...
HA HA HA HA!
BIG BROTHER?
HA HA HA HA! HOW IRONIC!!

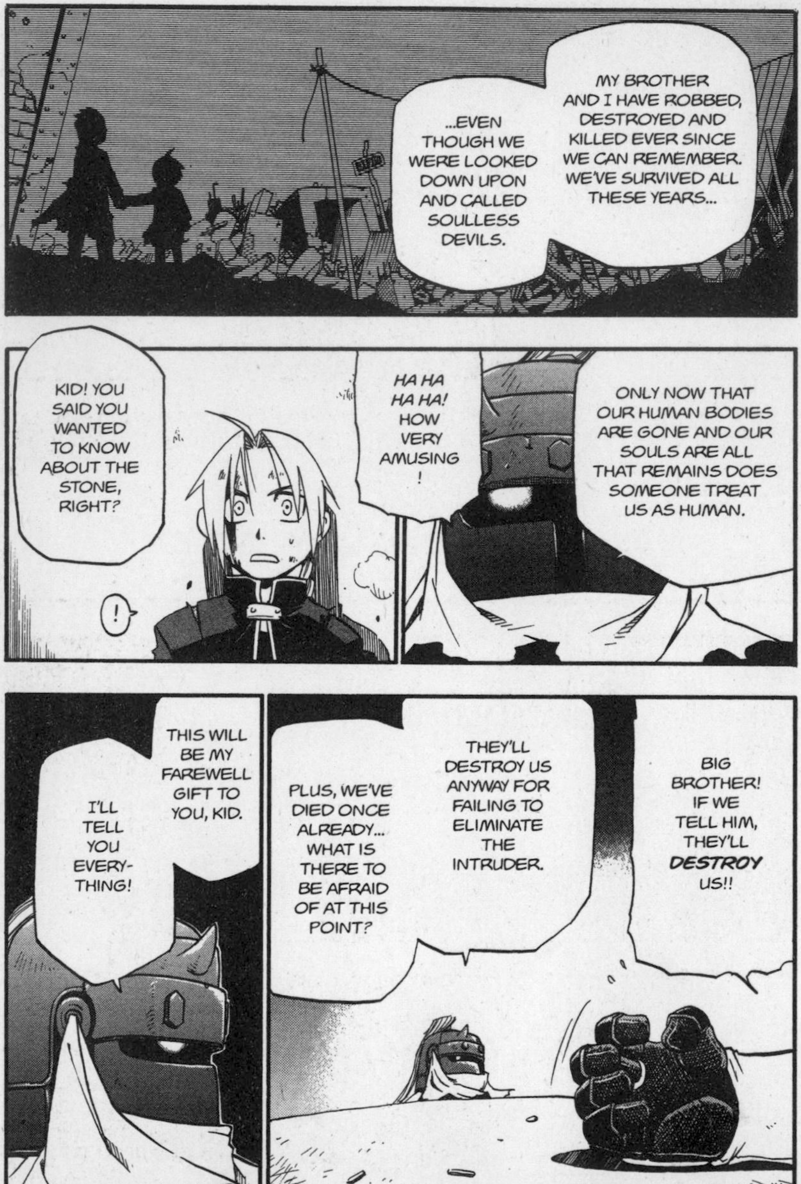
MY BROTHER AND I HAVE ROBBED, DESTROYED AND KILLED EVER SINCE WE CAN REMEMBER. WE'VE SURVIVED ALL THESE YEARS...
...EVEN THOUGH WE WERE LOOKED DOWN UPON AND CALLED SOULLESS DEVILS.
ONLY NOW THAT OUR HUMAN BODIES ARE GONE AND OUR SOULS ARE ALL THAT REMAINS DOES SOMEONE TREAT US AS HUMAN.
HA HA HA HA! HOW VERY AMUSING!
KID! YOU SAID YOU WANTED TO KNOW ABOUT THE STONE, RIGHT?
!
BIG BROTHER! IF WE TELL HIM, THEY'LL ***DESTROY*** US!!
THEY'LL DESTROY US ANYWAY FOR FAILING TO ELIMINATE THE INTRUDER.
PLUS, WE'VE DIED ONCE ALREADY... WHAT IS THERE TO BE AFRAID OF AT THIS POINT?
THIS WILL BE MY FAREWELL GIFT TO YOU, KID.
I'LL TELL YOU EVERY-THING!

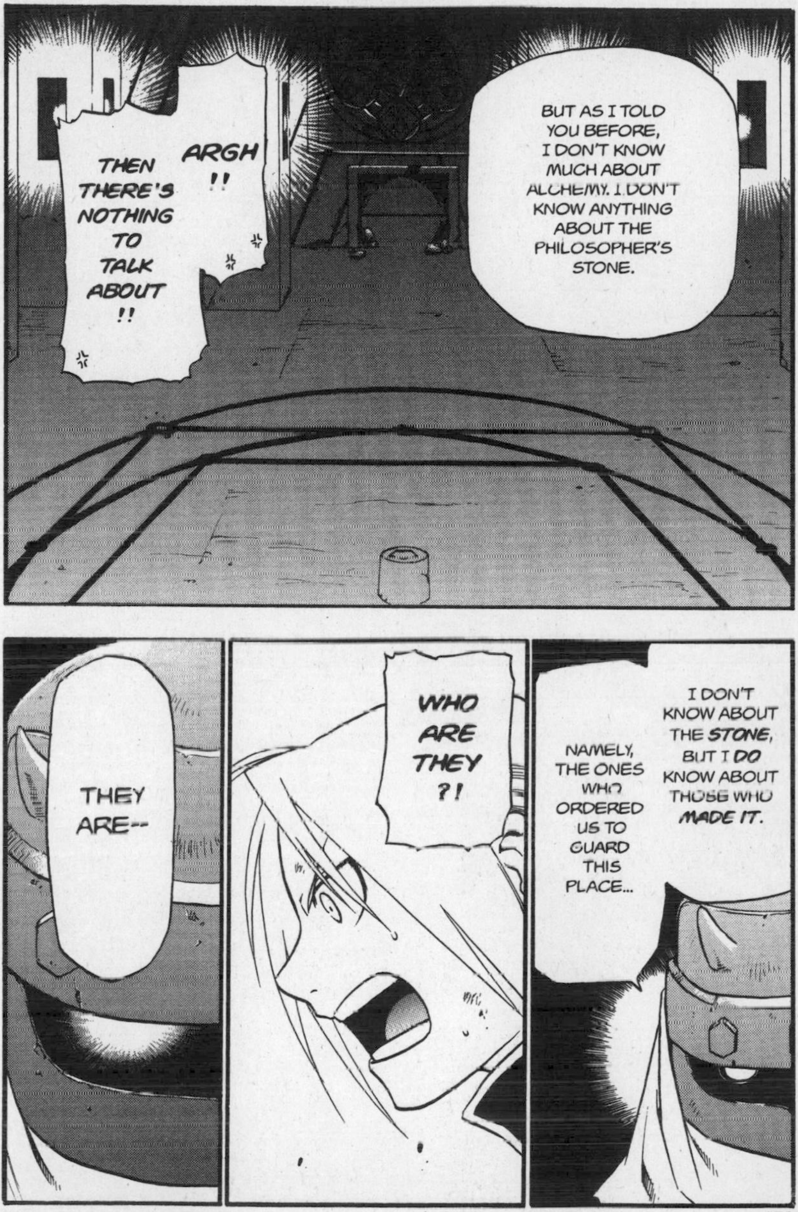
BUT AS I TOLD YOU BEFORE, I DON'T KNOW MUCH ABOUT ALCHEMY. I DON'T KNOW ANYTHING ABOUT THE PHILOSOPHER'S STONE.
ARGH!!
THEN THERE'S NOTHING TO TALK ABOUT!!
I DON'T KNOW ABOUT THE STONE, BUT I DO KNOW ABOUT THOSE WHO MADE IT.
NAMELY, THE ONES WHO ORDERED US TO GUARD THIS PLACE...
WHO ARE THEY?!
THEY ARE--

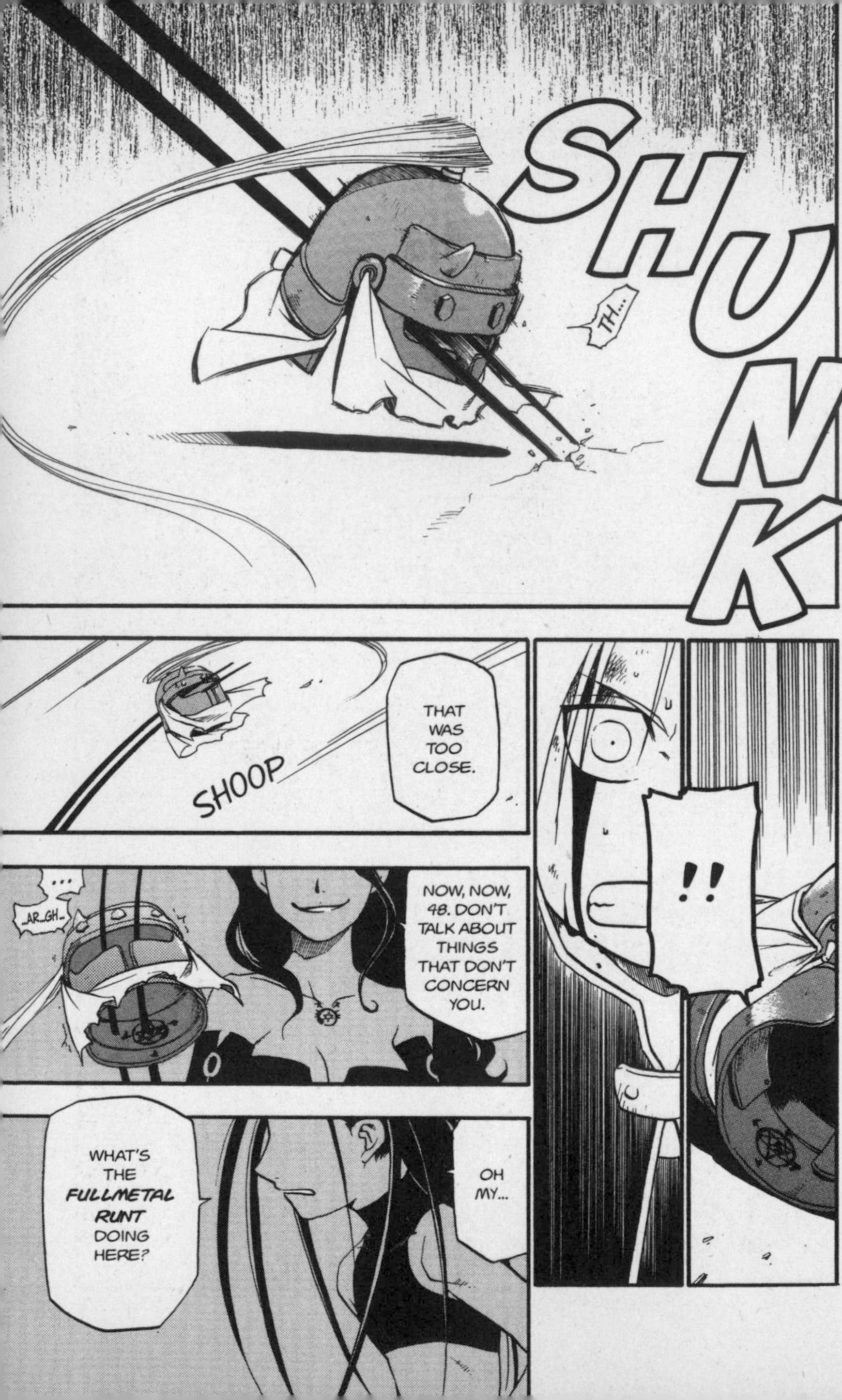
SHUNK
TH...
!!
THAT WAS TOO CLOSE.
SHOOP
NOW, NOW, 48. DON'T TALK ABOUT THINGS THAT DON'T CONCERN YOU.
...
...AR...GH...
OH MY...
WHAT'S THE ***FULLMETAL RUNT*** DOING HERE?

THIS MANGA WAS ORIGINALLY PRINTED IN MONTHLY **SHONEN GANGAN**, APRIL 2002 THROUGH JULY 2002.

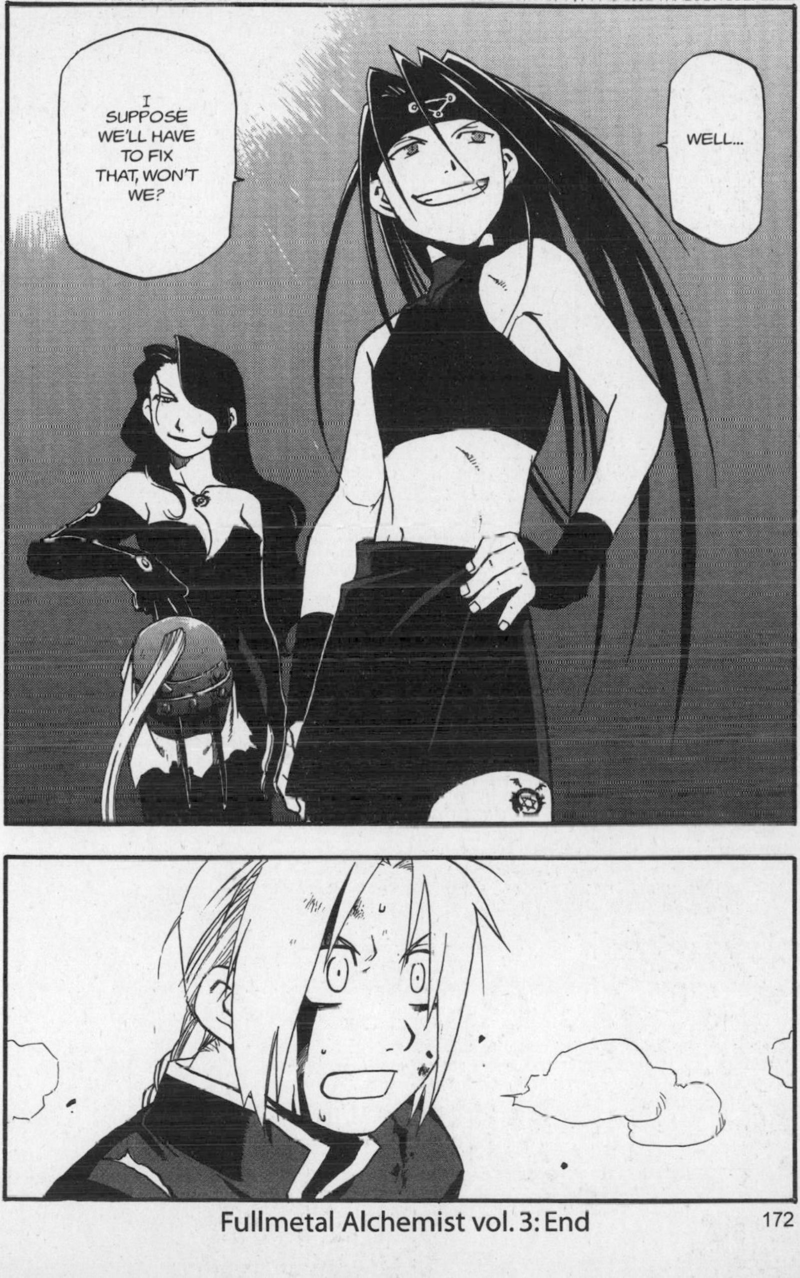
WELL...
I SUPPOSE WE'LL HAVE TO FIX THAT, WON'T WE?

Fullmetal Alchemist vol. 3: End